Malinche, Pocahontas, and Sacagawea

MALINCHE, POCAHONTAS, AND SACAGAWEA

Indian Women as Cultural Intermediaries and National Symbols

REBECCA K. JAGER

UNIVERSITY OF OKLAHOMA PRESS : NORMAN

Library of Congress Cataloging-in-Publication Data

Jager, Rebecca K., 1964–
  Malinche, Pocahontas, and Sacagawea : Indian women as cultural intermediaries
and national symbols / Rebecca K. Jager.
      pages cm.
  Includes bibliographical references and index.
  ISBN 978-0-8061-4851-9 (hardcover : alk. paper)
  1. Indian women—Biography. 2. Indian interpreters—Case studies. 3. Marina,
approximately 1505–approximately 1530—Influence. 4. Pocahontas, –1617— Influence.
5. Sacagawea—Influence. 6. Whites—Relations with Indians. 7. Indians of Mexico—Government relations. 8. National identity—United States. 9. National identity—Mexico. I. Title. II Title: Indian women as cultural intermediaries and national
symbols.
  E89J36 2015
  305.48'89700922—dc23
  [B]

                                                              2015015811

1 2 3 4 5 6 7 8 9 10

Contents

Illustrations

Figures

MAPS

Malinche, Pocahontas, and Sacagawea

INTRODUCTION

Feminizing the Story of European Expansion

When Europeans ventured into what they considered the "New World," they encountered a vast continent that was already home to culturally diverse societies with complex political coalitions and extensive trade networks. Native people had the numerical advantage and dictated the rules for interaction. Early European adventurers were vulnerable in a foreign land and forced to accommodate Indian diplomatic protocol, including a system of kinship alliances. Native women were routinely offered to and accepted by outsiders in order to initiate and maintain strategic connections. The exchange of women was an expedient to intertribal cooperation. These Indian-sanctioned unions had geopolitical consequences. Successful female intermediaries made the cultural divide navigable and collaboration possible; they bound communities together in a common future. The first Europeans accepted these female agents because they offered entrance into the Native world. This study examines indigenous female intermediaries during initial contact with Europeans, their work on multinational frontiers, and their symbolic representation over time.

Records left by European conquistadors, adventurers, entrepreneurs, and religious zealots provide only a modicum of information about the Indian women they encountered. Their observations lack Native context and detail. Incoming European men defined Native women according to their own gender ideology and typically portrayed female intermediaries as helpful and interesting, yet peripheral to the heroic events of European expansion. These masculine reports were deliberately crafted to win personal accolades and to ensure continued support from their European sponsors. An intimate relationship with, or reliance on, an Indian woman was not pertinent to the goals of their narratives.

Female intermediaries were rarely mentioned by name. Difficult translation or cultural bias led European men to substitute women's Indian names with easy generic terms, such as "squaw" or "Indian woman." Native women who participated in the most famous cultural collisions of the New World, on the other hand, were named and described: Malinche in Central Mexico, Doña Inez in the American Southwest, Pocahontas on the mid-Atlantic coast, Sacagawea in the northern Rocky Mountains, Molly Brant in the American Northeast, and Tekakwitha in eastern Canada are the most widely known. Their experiences, separated by hundreds of years and thousands of miles, suggest that Native women were intricately involved in frontier contact and mediation.

European accounts mention many other anonymous women who acted as mediators in contact zones where cultures met. Álvar Núñez Cabeza de Vaca, the Spanish conquistador who journeyed through a large section of North American from 1528 to 1536, described the ability of Indian women to serve in this role and observed that they performed this work regularly, "for women can deal as neutrals anywhere, even during war."[1] American frontiersmen mentioned several mysterious female intermediaries on the northern plains over the course of the nineteenth century. Researchers and mythmakers (including Grace Hebard, Charles Eastman, and Indian oral tradition) merged these various Indian women and credited their work to Sacagawea. If Sacagawea (recorded in fur trapper journals as the wife of Charbonneau, who accompanied Lewis and Clark) died at Fort Manuel in 1812, she could not have been the anonymous Shoshone woman who convinced her party to aid John Frémont in 1848 (mentioned in Frémont's journal) or the wise old Shoshone woman who advocated adopting the white man's way on the Wind River Reservation and later died there in 1884, according to reservation Indians and officials.[2] All three women were recognized for their intermediary work, although none was specifically identified by name. This oversight sparked controversy as to the time and place of Sacagawea's death and created the opportunity for later writers to extend her legend through time and space. Nevertheless, at least several Indian women across the northern plains facilitated interactions between Indians and non-Indians.

Anthropologist Robert S. Grumet argues that European records consistently denied the considerable influence of coastal Algonquian women during early contact in the 1600s.[3] Grumet's first example is John Smith's narrative. Smith mentions a "Queen of Appamatuck" who was present during the council that decided on his death, a decision that Pocahontas overturned, according to Smith. Both women were actively involved in determining Smith's fate, a decision of national significance for the Powhatan people. According to Grumet, female social influence was more prevalent in Native societies than European records acknowledge, and Indian naming practices further obscured Native women's participation in cross-cultural interaction. My work builds on this conception.

European men misunderstood female expertise in diplomacy. The outsiders interpreted Indian women's cooperation as proof of their attraction to European men and European culture. Their memoirs consistently presented instrumental Native women as willing and gracious Indian princesses. From a white male perspective, the Indian princess was drawn to "civilized" non-Indian culture; her help and generosity were characterized to reflect white male superiority and to justify European colonization. When the women's actions are examined within the context of their Native cultures, an alternative interpretation arises: indigenous communities deployed and respected female intermediaries. These women had feminine social obligations to act as translators, mediators, informants, and advisers in order to ease interactions and forge productive relationships with powerful newcomers. Successful female intermediaries wielded considerable influence during frontier contact, and their contemporaries (Indian and non-Indian) valued their council.

This study concentrates on three of the most famous cultural intermediaries: Malinche, Pocahontas, and Sacagawea.[4] These three women successfully negotiated cultural exchange between Indian and non-Indian people during their lives and later were represented symbolically to reinforce national creation myths in Mexico and the United States. Malinche was a young Mesoamerican woman given to Spanish conquistador Hernán Cortés, who assisted him in his conquest of Mexico from 1519 to 1521. She served as his translator, publicist, adviser, and lover. Pocahontas was a daughter of Chief Powhatan, ruler of the Powhatan Confederacy, in what is now eastern Virginia. In 1607, when English colonists arrived to make their fortunes in Jamestown, she was a vivacious young girl who befriended the foreigners and acted as a liaison between them and her people. Sacagawea was the Shoshone woman who accompanied Lewis and Clark on much of their cross-continent trek to the Pacific and back from 1804 to 1806. Sacagawea acted as a translator, cultural informant, and guide through the Columbia River Plateau. All three women provided feminine comforts and strategic advantage. Each was the medium through which communication and information flowed, linking Indian and non-Indian worlds.

Malinche, Pocahontas, and Sacagawea oriented foreigners to Native conditions and expectations, facilitated communication, and advanced cooperation by exploiting common interests. The cultural information that these women gathered, interpreted, and redistributed undoubtedly flowed in both directions. They were in a position to assess the newcomers, particularly the challenges and opportunities they introduced. At the moment of initial contact indigenous people of Central Mexico, the mid-Atlantic coast, and the northern plains were already dealing with complex ethnic and regional tensions. The women all lived in multicultural areas, during eras of profound uncertainty in which catastrophic change was anticipated. Malinche, Pocahontas, and Sacagawea looked for any advantage, tangible or spiritual, that might benefit themselves or their Native communities.

Part I of this book (chapters 1–4) examines the circumstances of each woman's life in turn. Whereas all three women have often been described from non-Indian, postcolonial perspectives, the goal here is to place their actions in the context of their Native societies and cultures. What follows is a gender analysis of initial contact, focusing specifically on the Indian women who mediated cultural exchange. Their activities are examined in relation to their Native conditions, worldviews, and gender obligations. European newcomers were not prepared to recognize these women as influential agents with diplomatic responsibilities on multicultural frontiers. Instead, they described them as smitten Indian princesses who validated the honor of European men and their mission in the New World. The men's fundamental confusion regarding the gender responsibilities of Indian women had a lasting impact on the historical representation and mythologies of Malinche, Pocahontas, and Sacagawea.

Chapter 1 examines the indigenous conditions that Malinche, Pocahontas, and Sacagawea knew prior to contact. Establishing their cultural frame of reference is important to understanding the women's motivations during that pivotal first contact with Europeans. Chapter 2 describes the initial interactions between Indians and Euro-invaders. In all three of the women's indigenous areas, experience and prophecy prepared Indian people to expect the arrival of newcomers and a dramatic transformation of their world. Malinche, Pocahontas, Sacagawea, and their Native communities were conditioned to accommodate change and to strategize in order to build a secure future in a rapidly changing multinational atmosphere. European adventurers also embraced change and worked to build a rewarding future in an environment that seemed full of resources and potential. People on neither side of the cultural collision intended to fully acculturate, but rather meant to take advantage of new opportunities.

The intermediary services that Malinche, Pocahontas, and Sacagawea provided are taken up in chapter 3. The work was grueling. They were isolated from their Native families and loved ones. Their work required highly developed communication skills in language and persuasion. They were constantly on the move, adapting to new landscapes and peoples. The women had to be quick thinking; they were always in the middle of events and always being watched. Hostility and violence could erupt in an instant. Their success and personal safety demanded an extraordinary degree of empathy, trustworthiness, and patience.

Chapter 4 deals with the intimate encounters between Malinche and the conquistadors, Pocahontas and the colonists, and Sacagawea and Lewis and Clark's Corps of Discovery. This chapter exposes a surprising degree of mutual commitment and respect between the women and their European companions. The Euro-invaders did not want to jeopardize the women's services and frequently took measures to protect them during the most perilous moments. There were also personal and cultural incentives for the men—self-designated as national heroes in the making—to display their chivalry. In the aftermath of their adventure together the Euro-conquerors attempted to provide for Malinche, Pocahontas, and Sacagawea, which may not have been a benefit to the women, but it was a gesture that extended to the women's mixed-blood sons. All three women likewise intervened to protect their male companions during tenuous encounters in Indian country. As Indian representatives, they likely felt an obligation to demonstrate their cultural ideal of appropriate feminine behavior.

Chapter 4 also exposes the colonizers' misjudgment of Native gender roles and marriage patterns, particularly regarding women's workload and sexuality. Early European characterizations of Indian women's lives implied that Malinche, Pocahontas, and Sacagawea were lucky in comparison to other young Native women because they were saved from a degrading and savage existence. According to the European men, the women's loyalty and devotion demonstrated their appreciation for this salvation. Other Indian women who fulfilled similar feminine responsibilities on behalf of Native communities (as opposed to white men) were identified as "squaw drudges" mired in uncivilized societies.

The goal of part I is to unravel the role of the female intermediary by looking to familiar sources with a specific set of questions in mind: What purpose did the female intermediary serve in Indian societies? How were Native women prepared for this role? What Native social structures were at work, particularly regarding gender and religion? What were Indian expectations for the female intermediary? In order to answer these questions we must remove Malinche, Pocahontas, and Sacagawea from the literary fantasy of the conquering nations and situate their actions within their Native frame of reference. A multidisciplinary approach (using the techniques of history, anthropology, ethnohistory, and oral tradition) reveals Native worldviews that anticipated an age of transformation, exposes Native gender responsibilities, and demonstrates how Native gender systems worked to the benefit of the invaders. A careful examination of the lives of Malinche, Pocahontas, and Sacagawea offers an opportunity to study the frontier through the lens of gender, to consider female influence in Native societies, and to acknowledge Indian women's contribution to cross-cultural cooperation during early contact. My intent is not a distant and objective gender analysis that bolsters a contemporary non-Native feminist perspective, but rather an empathetic consideration of what life was like for these three women who mediated the cultural exchange at the moment of contact.

Part II deals with the symbolic roles of Malinche, Pocahontas, and Sacagawea in the ongoing construction of a satisfying national creation story. Analysis of their myths reveals how sensitive questions regarding national origin, race, and gender have been negotiated in theory. Their pliable legends have been employed to justify or condemn European colonization, to explain Indian defeat or celebrate indigenous prehistory, and to serve as a forum for recurring discussions of race and gender.[5] Their stories have been so useful to social debates (throughout multiple centuries) that these women have been immortalized in the national consciousness, yet the authenticity of their stories has become irrelevant. Their myths have not necessarily represented the women or the time in which they lived. Instead their myths have reflected a changing national image over time. Malinche, Pocahontas, and Sacagawea are significant not because they were Indian princesses who welcomed Europeans, but rather because of the cultural explanations they provided in life and in myth.

Malinche, Pocahontas, and Sacagawea were originally mythologized to clarify how Natives and Europeans came together willingly. Nationalists in Mexico and the United States depicted a frontier experience that gave the illusion of a united citizenry; Native Americans and Euro-Americans endured the frontier together, and this shared experience became the ideological foundation for nationhood. Romantic narratives—exemplified by novels such as Ireneo Paz's *Amor y Suplicio*, John Davis's *Captain John Smith and Princess Pocahontas*, and Eva Emery Dye's *The Conquest: The True Story of Lewis and Clark*—honor Malinche, Pocahontas, and Sacagawea as gracious Indian women and nurturing mothers of new civilizations; they adopted European men and their superior culture. Throughout the histories of the United States and Mexico, such sentimental creation stories have expressed the grand theme of cross-cultural respect and admiration, established European roots in the Americas, offered membership in a shared national identity, and explained a colonial social hierarchy.

Malinche, Pocahontas, and Sacagawea have become intricate symbols in foundational creation myths. They demonstrated Indian acceptance of European men and European culture. Malinche and Pocahontas represent Indian examples of Christian salvation, thus moralizing colonization. Sacagawea's story supports one of America's most compelling national myths: that Americans had a divine mission to erect a new social order on the frontier and to extend its boundaries to the continent's natural geographical borders. Sacagawea's commitment to the American cause (later defined as Manifest Destiny) positioned her at the center of American frontier myth. The legends of all three women clarified European dominance by illustrating how loving Native women embraced the outsiders, gave birth to mixed-blood children, and symbolically offered the newcomers inheritance rights to Indian land.

As colonials in New Spain and New England pushed toward independence, they created new national identities based on a strategic blend of European and Indian elements. This hybrid cultural ideology made New World colonies distinct from the Old World and bound the colonials and Indians together in a common future completely separate from Europe. Each woman's myth became increasingly complex, as persistent revisions were needed to accommodate shifting nationalist goals. The chapters in part II trace the national narratives of Mexico and the United States to understand how both nations wove their frontier pasts into instructional histories. These national creation stories were, and are, designed to elicit respect among European nations and to present racial and gender explanations to a unified citizenry in Mexico and the United States. My work builds on Jane Tompkins's suggestion that historical literature is a forum for cultural identification. These institutionalized stories depict "a set of national, social, [and] economic interests" and have an "intended design upon their audiences": to make citizens "think and respond in a particular way."[6] My study demonstrates how national creation stories in Mexico and the United States have repeatedly been revised to address contentious social debates over time. The vague details of Malinche, Pocahontas, and Sacagawea's lives have been malleable enough to accommodate historical revisions and strategic shifts in national identity.

The troubling racial legacies of conquest have presented relentless challenges to Mexican and U.S. nationalism. Both nations claimed to be founded on Enlightenment principles of the "natural rights of man" but simultaneously denied Indian rights. Recurring epochs of social strife have provided moments of national reflection and launched periodic interrogation of national creation myths. Malinche, Pocahontas, and Sacagawea were applicable to discussions on imperialism and social inequality because they were Indian, they were women, and they were directly involved in European colonization. They became ready feminine symbols to demonstrate changing explanations of race, gender, and national origin.

Richard Slotkin has said that myths are "the language in which a society remembers its history"; they are the instructional stories that a society chooses to perpetuate.[7] The following analysis suggests that flexibility is an essential ingredient in myth making, keeping a story relevant and usable over time.[8] Typecasting and exaggeration are also important; legendary figures must be familiar and fantastic to provide an appropriate reflection of national identity. My work traces how writers have manipulated the narratives of Malinche, Pocahontas, and Sacagawea to support deliberate characterizations of women, Indians, and national formation.

Over time, the gracious Indian princess myth failed to resonate with national audiences. All three women took on more complicated roles during times of social unrest, particularly during eras that witnessed pressing demands for social justice. Malinche, Pocahontas, and Sacagawea were occasionally recast as feminine victims of masculine European conquest or as unfortunate scapegoats for Indian defeat. Even worse, Malinche and Sacagawea have been presented as traitors to their indigenous countrymen. The anonymous novel *Xicotencatl* (1826) and Octavio Paz's *The Labyrinth of Solitude* (1950) represent this guilty portrayal of Malinche. And Bonnie Butterfield's article "Sacagawea Native American Legend: Why Did She Turn Her Back on Her Own People?" (2000) expresses Sacagawea's symbolic remorse. Chapters 5, 6, and 7 of this book trace the respective developments of mythic Malinche, Pocahontas, and Sacagawea to reveal how and why these women have been designed and redesigned to convey specific messages. The myths of all three women have been used to theorize on colonization, to evaluate race and gender conditions, and to project an appropriate national image. Each woman has represented, at various times, an admirable Indian woman who welcomed an alternative to her "savage race" as well as a victim of race and gender oppression. Their fluctuating myths have always demonstrated both appropriate and inappropriate social interactions.

What follows is a postmodern analysis that accepts cultural ideologies and spiritual beliefs as significant ingredients in the telling of history. People on the frontier behaved according to their own cultural understanding, and their historical rationalization was defined by their particular worldview. I examine initial contact as a two-sided affair in which both groups operated according to their own epistemologies and their own goals for the future. I recognize that both sides of the cultural divide were forever changed by the interaction and that each has maintained a culturally relevant narrative of the contact era. I value Indian accounts from the colonial era despite contemporary academic suggestions that these sources should be dismissed because they were irrevocably contaminated by cultural domination after conquest. I also reject the current scholarly contention that primary European records are unusable fabrications. These early explanations from both sides provide context and depth; they are best understood in relation to each other.

Richard White's *The Middle Ground* (1991) describes the frontier as more than a heroic tale of Anglo conquest and Indian defeat. White demonstrates how Europeans and Indians accommodated each other's cultural differences and collaborated in creating a productive zone of interaction in the Great Lakes region (1650–1815).[9] His work does not specifically examine cultural intermediaries, but he does consider interracial marriage and focuses on early cross-cultural cooperation on a multiethnic frontier. White's balanced approach to the study of the frontier reveals Indian diplomatic complexity and sophistication. His analysis demonstrates how both groups struggled to negotiate cultural variation and to define common meaning. My study builds on White's analysis by identifying gender as a peculiar social construct that required significant accommodation.

Considerable scholarship has been devoted to Indian women who lived their lives in zones where cultures met. Sylvia Van Kirk's path-breaking study *Many Tender Ties* (1980) examines the economic work that Indian women contributed to fur-trading society in western Canada from 1670 to 1870. Van Kirk reveals how Indian women laid the foundation for the economic success of the French and credits Indian women with the creation of the métis culture. Van Kirk's work is an early and important contribution to the study of Indian women's participation on the frontier. Ultimately, Van Kirk, who was researching and writing during the 1970s, describes the Indian women as oppressed. They were overworked in both Native and Anglo fur-trading society. According to Van Kirk, their work was exploited, and their status was defined by their relationship to white men. Her analysis was pertinent to a late twentieth-century Anglo feminist debate, yet it seems alien to the eighteenth-century Indian women she examines. Native people in the upper Northwest did not consider gender a hierarchal social structure. Instead, most Indians of the Americas tended to define gender as a set of obligations to their community.[10] Both female and male duties were vital to maintaining the group, and status was bestowed according to the quality of a person's work. However, Native cultural details, including gender organization, are not a focus of Van Kirk's study. Her analysis evaluates Indian women's roles in relation to a non-Indian patriarchal system.

Clara Sue Kidwell specifically addresses the role of the female culture broker in "Indian Women as Cultural Mediators" (1992) and first poses the question of intentionality. Kidwell's brief article asks why Native female intermediaries facilitated Europeans' entrance into Indian country. These women, unfortunately, had no historical voice of their own to explain their actions. Kidwell suggests that scholars turn to ethnohistory and anthropology, in addition to European primary records, to understand the Native cultural incentives and obligations that influenced the women's decisions. Kidwell's call to reconnect these women to their indigenous cultures—to better understand their work as intermediaries—provided the initial inspiration for my work.

Other works have examined the various experiences of intermediaries during frontier encounters. Margaret Connell-Szasz's 1994 book, *Between Indian and White Worlds*, describes how culture brokers (both male and female) worked between cultures and were consequently alienated from full inclusion in either society. Her study explains the common transient experience among culture brokers. The job required significant travel and long absences from their home communities, making culture brokers susceptible to excommunication. Albert Hurtado's *Intimate Frontiers* (1999) and Ramon Gutiérrez's *When Jesus Came, the Corn Mothers Went Away* (1991) focus on the precariousness of Indian women on the California and New Mexico frontier. Both works describe Indian women's frontier experiences according to European gender constructs in order to highlight feminine subordination in non-Indian cultures. Hurtado and Gutiérrez argue that the newcomers redefined Indian women's social roles and destroyed traditional Native avenues for feminine social status. Indian women lost power and status as a result of the conquest. Paula Gunn Allen (a Pueblo Indian scholar) makes a similar point in *The Sacred Hoop: Recovering the Feminine in American Indian Tradition* (1986). However, Allen puts Indian women at the center of the tribal universe and suggests that Indian–non-Indian negotiations were doomed because outsiders failed to accept female leadership in Native societies. Allen acknowledges that Indian women were relevant before, during, and after conquest. She demonstrates how Indian women maintained influence within their Native communities despite a European standard of male dominance. Hurtado, Gutiérrez, and Van Kirk portray Indian women as victims of European masculine conquests.

This book does not gauge Malinche's, Pocahontas's, and Sacagawea's experiences according to a foreign patriarchal social structure. European gender categories and expectations were not applicable throughout much of Native America during initial contact, particularly the notions of a masculine public domain, a feminine private domain, and female respectability through chastity. What I suggest is that Malinche, Pocahontas, and Sacagawea were exchanged with the expectation that they would cultivate goodwill and facilitate cooperation; that international diplomacy was a respected feminine career; that their work was carried out in both the public and private spaces of life; and that Native gender concepts were confusing yet beneficial to early European men.

Juliana Barr's work, *Peace Came in the Form of a Woman* (2007), acknowledges the advantage Indians had as Natives and non-Natives met in precolonial Texas between 1690 and 1780. She explains that the Caddos, Apaches, Payayas, Karankawas, Wichitas, and Comanches set the course for interaction with incoming Europeans. According to Barr, the French were successful in their attempt to interact economically and politically with Indians because of their willingness to accept Native kinship standards and intermarry. She argues that the Spaniards were alienated from a rewarding alliance because of their refusal to intermarry and because of their lack of family life in presidios and missions. Wandering foreign men, without the presence of women and children, were identified as suspicious and dangerous, whereas men in the company of women and children were identified as having peaceful intentions. Barr describes the Indian wives of French men as symbols of an amicable cross-cultural relationship that allowed economic and political cooperation. I agree with Barr, but suggest further that some Indian women were active agents in establishing a mutually productive relationship. More than mere symbols, they served as translators, mediators, cultural informants, and advisers. In this way, Malinche, Pocahontas, and Sacagawea were strategic and influential participants in cross-cultural interactions.

The Native groups discussed in the following pages extended their communities through the exchange of women, and the role of female intermediary was a vital component in an entrenched system of Indian diplomacy. Yet, unlike the French fur traders that Barr discusses, intermarriage was not an immediate or acceptable strategy pursued by the Cortés entourage, the English settlers in Jamestown, or the Lewis and Clark party. These Europeans may have accepted Indian women as intermediaries, but marriage (according to European standards) was more problematic. Malinche, Pocahontas, and Sacagawea were on the front lines of initial contact. They worked as interpreters, consultants, and occasionally as negotiators and guides.

They assessed the newcomers, oriented them in Native practices, exploited areas of mutual benefit, and cultivated compatibility between groups. Their marriage to European men, although an important part of their myths, was irrelevant to their diplomatic work. In fact, Malinche and Pocahontas married European men after several years of intermediary service.

At the moment of contact both European and indigenous groups were in the process of redefining themselves in a rapidly changing world. Native people were prepared for an impending transformation because of prophecy and their previous experiences with foreigners. Europeans were involved in a global competition for wealth and empire. Each group set its own agenda and forced the other to respond during the dynamic and multilayered process of change that took place on the frontier. Female intermediaries were actively involved and were valuable to both sides; they worked as double agents. These women were adept at moving among diverse groups, negotiating multiethnic environments, and learning to respond to cultural cues appropriately. Historian William Hart calls this cultural agility "situational ethnicity."[11] Collaboration on multiethnic frontiers required "go-betweens" who were able to mute their own cultural reactions, accommodate alternative perspectives, and exhibit an amiable posture that was conducive to immediate goals. Malinche, Pocahontas, and Sacagawea were agile cultural intermediaries who offered benefits to both sides.

Malinche, Pocahontas, and Sacagawea are presented here as individuals seeking to gain a secure footing—for themselves and for others—during revolutionary eras, as well as examples of how Indian women participated in shaping frontier contact. None of them left their own words to explain their actions, therefore it is my hope to reveal the logic behind their actions by providing Indian context for their lives and choices. Their Native, gendered rearing prepared them to serve as mediators between groups. They embraced the responsibilities of an intermediary and embarked on a cultural odyssey that led to a new era. For better or worse, they introduced their Indian world to outsiders and introduced a European worldview to Native people. Malinche, Pocahontas, and Sacagawea did not live to see the power dynamic shift to the detriment of Native people; all three women died long before initial contact evolved into relentless colonization and institutionalized patriarchy. In life Malinche, Pocahontas, and Sacagawea were energetic young women who facilitated the coming of a new world. In myth their ambiguous narratives buttressed shifting national identities and provided meaningful explanations of a complicated frontier past. The pages that follow reveal Malinche, Pocahontas, and Sacagawea's contribution to national formation, both real and imagined.

PART I

Indian Women in Life

Part I examines the Native cultural incentives and obligations that drove Malinche, Pocahontas, and Sacagawea to act as intermediaries. These chapters consider the indigenous conditions that the women knew in order to understand what Native belief systems, regional tensions, and gendered expectations were at work. Long before the Europeans' arrival, Native women were routinely given to outsiders to facilitate interaction. These Indian women were active participants in building alliances in multiethnic regions. Malinche, Pocahontas, and Sacagawea approached their intermediary work according to their own Native cultural experiences. They had feminine responsibilities to assess European potential, to indoctrinate the outsiders into indigenous systems, to assist in communication, and to work toward a rewarding coexistence. Their involvement demonstrated peaceful intentions and softened the impact of colliding worlds. These women were not autonomous agents, who were free from social constraints. They had obligations to family and community that influenced their actions. In order to better understand the women and what they did, part I offers a culturally sensitive analysis of the regional indigenous conditions under which Malinche, Pocahontas, and Sacagawea operated.

CHAPTER ONE

Indigenous Social Landscapes Prior to Contact

Incoming Europeans encountered complex multinational landscapes in the Americas. Indigenous societies had unique worldviews and their own intentions for the future. European foreigners presented both challenges and opportunities to Indian groups. As cultural intermediaries Malinche, Pocahontas, and Sacagawea navigated an intricate set of Native circumstances in their respective regions, and they acted according to their own epistemologies and cultural expectations. These were flesh-and-blood women with responsibilities to their families and communities as they negotiated a revolution within their Native world.

An examination of precolonial indigenous conditions will provide a Native context for the dramatic events of initial contact. This chapter focuses on the Native worldviews that informed the decisions made by Malinche, Pocahontas, and Sacagawea. Early colonizers and nationalists portrayed the women as Indian princesses who were smitten with the newcomers and enamored with non-Indian cultures. Contemporary scholars cast them as victims, slaves to profit-seeking or lecherous European men. These portrayals emanate from non-Indian perspectives; they neglect Native context and deny the considerable influence these women wielded on both sides of the cultural divide.

Malinche, Pocahontas, and Sacagawea made critical decisions to facilitate European expansion. Analysis of their indigenous world offers insight into their reasoning and highlights their Native gender obligations. However, their experiences may not have been analogous to the experiences of other Native women in their time and place because Malinche, Pocahontas, and Sacagawea were selected as representatives during extraordinarily dangerous and transformative events. They were energetic and influential intermediaries who impacted the future of their world. The brief histories that follow reveal the cultural complexities of diverse indigenous societies, providing meaning to Indian actions and exposing gendered social organization.

Mesoamerican Cultural Legacies Inherited by Malinche

Along the Gulf of Mexico, in the forested lands of Veracruz and Tabasco, ruins of an ancient civilization date back to 500 B.C. Among artifacts that have been uncovered is evidence of ceremonial centers and artistic expression, as well as the oldest calendar inscription ever found. The material remains hint at the Olmecs' conception of time and religion. This ancient culture influenced waves of immigrants who poured into central Mexico from the northern shores of the Pacific and dispersed over the lush landscape. Migrating tribes and chiefdoms mixed with one another, exchanging ideas and technologies. Over time, dynamic interactions (intermarriages, alliances, conquests, and empires) produced a succession of civilizations that arose and collapsed in turn.

Centuries before the rise of the Aztec Empire, wandering nomads consolidated into communities and constructed the sacred cities of Tikal, Uaxactun, Copan, and Palenque in the jungles of Central America. Their most impressive urban center was Teotihuacan in the Valley of Mexico. It was the largest city in Mesoamerica during the height of its existence around A.D. 450. Scholars disagree on who created this expansive city that covered eleven square miles and was home to 100,000–150,000 people.[1] The population was most likely multiethnic and culturally complex. Teotihuacan reached its apex at about the time of the Roman Empire, in the fifth and sixth centuries, commanding resources from Guatemala to Durango. The civilization entered a period of decline in the eighth and ninth centuries as other seats of power arose.[2] Experts disagree on a specific cause for its decline, but scarce resources, internal unrest, increased warfare, ecological devastation, and a continuous influx of northern immigrants likely all led to its disintegration.

The name Teotihuacan translates from Nahuatl to mean the "place of the gods."[3] A Mexica creation story recorded in the mid-1500s by Spanish friars endows Teotihuacan with a mythological significance as the place where their world first took shape. The mysterious city was decorated with ornate palaces, sculptures, and frescos that illustrated a profound sense of time and history. Later groups elaborated on the cultural representations that decorated the ancient buildings. Their symbolic imagery appears in the codices of various Nahua groups both before and after the Spanish conquest. The abandoned pyramids and plazas of Teotihuacan were viewed with awe by generations of Mesoamericans who absorbed cultural meaning from the ancient ruins scattered across central Mexico.[4]

Central Mexico underwent a cultural renascence with the ascendance of Toltec society during the tenth century. The Toltecs adopted cultural traditions they found in the central basin and combined them with the northern traditions they carried with them as they journeyed south. Mesoamerican groups considered the Toltec civilization to be extraordinarily accomplished, yet little is archaeologically known about the Toltecs. Most of what we do know is from the sixteenth century, when Nahua peoples narrated their histories to colonizing Spaniards. In the 1400s Mexica rulers linked their heritage to Toltec ancestry in order to legitimize their own supremacy over the Valley.[5] Scholars have pieced together characteristics of Toltec lifeways from later groups (such as the Mexicas) who revered and absorbed particular aspects of a Toltec worldview.

The Toltecs migrated into the Valley of Mexico during the late ninth century and settled in the city of Tula (forty miles north of Teotihuacan). Tula would have been at its height during the tenth through twelfth centuries and grew to encompass 30,000–40,000 people.[6] It, too, was a culturally diverse environment in which factional disputes arose. According to later Nahua informants, Toltec mythology expressed a rivalry between Quetzalcoatl (the founder of Tula who had taken the name of a prominent deity) and Tezcatlipoca (the leader of a warrior faction who believed in human sacrifice).[7] Increased tensions forced Quetzalcoatl to leave; he set out across the water toward the east, and thus began Toltec decline.

The cultural and artistic remains of Toltec civilization revealed an aristocratic warrior society that sought wealth and power through the conquest of outlying towns, which were then forced to pay tribute. Archeologists have yet to determine the extent of Toltec domination. They have speculated that a sustained drought most likely initiated the downfall of the empire and the violent destruction of Tula in the 1300s. Toltec survivors dispersed and were absorbed by ethnically diverse communities throughout the central basin. The population of the Valley continued to increase during the fourteenth century, and new arrivals assimilated into an amalgamation of cultures. Competition over resources and power brought the emergence of city-states, administrative centers, and warrior cultures. The city-states were culturally related, yet completely independent from one another. These complex communities existed in reluctant cooperation, with occasional violent outbursts, until the rise of the Aztec Empire.

The Mexicas were the last of the migrating peoples to arrive from the north. They entered the Valley in the early 1300s as the Toltec Empire was dissolving. The Mexicas had difficulty assimilating into the flourishing city-states. The latecomers were considered undesirables who lacked culture, and they were violently rejected. According to surviving Mexica codices, they founded their own city of Tenochtitlán on an island in Lake Texcoco in 1325.[8] Once settled, they, too, absorbed relevant cultural antecedents from the nearby ancient ruins and established roots in central Mexico. The Toltecs' warrior culture was particularly influential in the rise of the Aztec Empire. Mexicas adopted a Toltec god of war (Huitzilopochtli), followed the Toltec warrior path, and took the Toltec ethos of conquest, tribute, and human sacrifice to remarkable new heights during the fifteenth century.

Mexica creation stories expressed their origin, their migration experience, and their eventual dominance over the Valley, often borrowing from the cultural representations illustrated in the ruins of Teotihuacan and Tula. Richard Townsend has characterized the rise of Tenochtitlán as "a renascence of the metropolitan culture that had been a legacy of the central highlands since Teotihuacan and Tula. The Mexicas cultivated a strong cultural and historical affinity with the ancient Toltecs, whom they identified with the idealized past."[9] The Mexicas justified their ascendance over the Valley by claiming descent from the admired civilization of ancient Mexico. This proved an effective strategy as they built their own sprawling empire in Mesoamerica.

Within a century this once-destitute tribe had achieved an expansive yet tenuous dominance over the Valley, reaching its zenith of power on the eve of Spanish arrival. Its island–capital city was a place of such splendor that Spanish conquistadors gasped in astonishment. Spaniards witnessed the constant bustle of more than 250,000 people participating in the various activities of Tenochtitlán. The impressive urban center was alive with fiestas, sacrifices, military training maneuvers, diplomatic negotiations, and the constant arrival and departure of warriors. Spaniards marveled at the size and productivity of the Tlatelolco market, which was visited daily by more than twenty thousand patrons. The city's magnificent palaces, temples, frescos, and botanical and zoological gardens also impressed the European invaders.

Dominican friar Diego Durán recorded Nahua histories of pre-conquest Mexico, beginning in the mid-sixteenth century. His Nahua informants claimed that their Mexica ancestors emerged from the earth at the moment of creation. In the twelfth century the tribe left from an ancestral homeland in the north and began their migration into the Valley of Mexico. They called this mysterious ancestral homeland Aztlán, which translates as "whiteness."[10] The term Aztec became the unsatisfactory name for all of the diverse groups under Mexica domination at the time of the Spanish conquest.

According to anthropologist and historian Miguel León-Portilla, Mexica wealth and supremacy emerged during the reign of Itzcoatl, who ruled between 1428 and 1440. The real power, however, came from behind the throne; Itzcoatl's nephew, Tlacael, was a royal counselor and a shrewd political strategist. Tlacael instituted a number of reforms in the tribe's political, religious, social, and economic structures to justify Mexica authority over the Valley. He reconfigured the judicial system, the army, the royal court, and the system of trade, creating an effective administrative machine that could be controlled by a small elite in Tenochtitlán. Tlacael's administrative reforms worked in conjunction with an ideological reconstruction. He expropriated Mesoamerica's ancient past for his own political agenda. Tlacael's rendition of history proclaimed that Mexica royalty descended from great Toltec leaders. To illustrate his claim, he enhanced the capital city of Tenochtitlán with impressive gardens, architecture, and public art that took inspiration from Toltec ruins.[11]

Aspects of Toltec mythology were also modified and situated within a unique Mexica worldview that was shaped by the hostility the Mexicas endured when they entered the Valley. The Mexicas identified Huitzilopochtli (a Toltec god of war) as their supreme deity, thus raising Huitzilopochtli to the level of Quetzalcoatl (the creator god of the Toltecs).[12] Because the Mexicas were dedicated to Huitzilopochtli, a mystical conception of warfare justified their conquest of all other nations, the very nations that had violently rejected them a century earlier. The rise of Huitzilopochtli coincided with the rise of the Aztec Empire. The Mexicas extended a brutal dominance over the Valley, demanding sacrificial victims to satisfy their patron god.[13] Human sacrifice had existed prior to the Aztec Empire, yet never with such vicious frequency.[14]

Acting on the royal counselor's recommendations, Mexica warriors set out to conquer the independent city-states surrounding Tenochtitlán. They quickly overtook neighboring towns. One by one, towns were forced into submission and were held to treaties that obligated them to pay exorbitant tribute (food, booty, workers, soldiers, women, and sacrificial victims) to Mexica nobility in Tenochtitlán. As the Mexicas expanded their conquest, an Aztec Empire was forged. More tribute arrived in ever-larger quantities, allowing Mexica authorities to give symbolic expression to their Toltec heritage through art and architecture in Tenochtitlán.

Jerome Offner's research has shown how the Aztec tribute system worked in the area of Texcoco.[15] Subjugated towns were allowed to remain autonomous and continue to run their own religious and social affairs. Mexicas did not necessarily impose religious or political dominance, yet they certainly imposed a new economic order. The Aztec Empire was organized into districts; each district had tribute collectors who were responsible for funneling payments to officials in Tenochtitlán. As the empire expanded, more funds and resources allowed Aztec rulers to construct impressive buildings, palaces, plazas, and temples throughout their expanding territory.

Anthropologist Frances Berdan exposed a critical strategy of Aztec economic expansion. Extracting regular tribute payments from conquered towns worked in conjunction with an elaborate long-distance trade network. It was vital to protect porters carrying tribute against pilfering enemies as resources made their way to the capital city of Tenochtitlán. To achieve the necessary security, Aztec authorities offered remote territories leniency or discounts in their requited tribute. In exchange, these communities provided safe zones and provisions for traveling Aztec warriors, porters, and traders. According to Berdan, the Aztecs created strategic buffer zones to protect the empire and the movement of its goods and people.[16]

Under Itzcoatl's reign, the Mexicas forged a coalition with the towns of Texcoco and Tlacopan to form a "triple alliance."[17] This confederation widened the staging ground for Aztec military conquests. Moctezuma I succeeded Itzcoatl in 1440. His first objective was to reassert the supremacy of Tenochtitlán and reaffirm Mexica authority over the subjected towns. He increased tribute payments, particularly in the form of resources and workers, which were needed to construct a system of hydraulic agriculture; the growing urban empire needed more agricultural land.[18] Laborers were also needed to renovate the Great Pyramids of Tenochtitlán. Large amounts of supplies and men were requisitioned for these improvements, and long processions of porters and soldiers began arriving with workers, foodstuffs, equipment, and arms. Tribute collectors organized their districts to fulfill the increased demands, yet tensions throughout the Valley were rising and punitive force was necessary.[19] Moctezuma's second goal was to expand the Aztec Empire through a new series of conquests. This renewed military focus solidified an aggressive course of expansion that dominated Aztec policy until Spanish arrival.

The number of lands paying tribute to Mexica rulers in Tenochtitlán increased dramatically by the end of the first Moctezuma's reign. In 1469 a nineteen-year-old prince named Axayacatl ascended to the throne. Young and brash, he was undaunted by the challenge of matching the military successes of his predecessor. He ruled for thirteen years and continued an Aztec pattern of conquests and reconquests.[20] Tenochtitlán's most terrifying leader was Ahuizotl, who reigned from 1486 to 1502 (he was the predecessor of Moctezuma II). Ahuizotl was revered for his murderous retribution against all enemies. After a punitive campaign to put down rebellious communities along the Gulf Coast in 1487, he staged a ritualized mass sacrifice in the newly remodeled Great Pyramid of Tenochtitlán.[21] It was a gruesome event in which prisoners were lined up along the entire length of a causeway leading into the city awaiting a hideous death. The slaughter lasted four days; blood flowed down the temple steps as invited ambassadors looked on in shock. Mexica elders conveyed a sense of horror fifty years later when Spanish friars recorded their descriptions of the monumental massacre. Ahuizotl marked a turning point in the Aztec Empire; he instilled in the rulership a mystical will to conquer. He was not an administrative warrior like his predecessors. Instead, he was the human embodiment of Huitzilopochtli. By the time of Cortés's arrival in 1519, the Aztec Empire was well along the path of ruthless expansion, an expansion that created an atmosphere of resentment among conquered groups.

The Mexicas, despite their extraordinary military successes, were never able to dominate their neighbors in the town of Tlaxcala. Tlaxcalan bandits regularly threatened Aztec tribute processions as they made their way into Tenochtitlán. The Tlaxcalans and the Mexicas were in a constant state of war, and Tlaxcala provided a steady supply of sacrificial victims for Huitzilopochtli. It is not surprising that Cortés added to his growing army of Native allies among the Tlaxcalans just prior to entering Tenochtitlán in 1520. Cortés was able to exploit Native rivalries as well as the growing animosity toward the Mexicas in Tenochtitlán. Through Malinche's counsel Cortés gained insight into Native conflicts, and through her translation he was able to persuade thousands of Indians to join the Spaniards in opposition to Aztec domination.[22]

By the time the Spaniards arrived in 1519, the Aztecs ruled over several million people of various cultures and languages. Their territory extended from the Pacific Coast to the Gulf Coast and from central Mexico to present-day Guatemala. However, this territory proved too expansive. The Aztecs had no beasts of burden, nor wheels on which to haul military supplies; they relied solely on the backs of men to carry out their conquests.[23] Within seventy-five years, the Aztec Empire had overextended itself. When Cortés landed on the coast of Vera Cruz, Moctezuma II (1502–1520) was presiding over a kingdom held together by a tenuous network of alliances, a ruthless system of tribute, brutal force, and fear. The Mexicas also had enemies whom Cortés could enlist. The Valley of Mexico was primed for war, and many were willing to support anyone who might bring change.

MALINCHE'S EARLY LIFE

Most of what we know about Malinche's life comes from a foot soldier in Cortés's army named Bernal Díaz.[24] According to his remembrance, Malinche was born in the pre-Columbian province near Coatzacoalcos around 1502. She was the daughter of a local Aztec authority and enjoyed the advantages of her privileged class as a young child.[25] In addition to material advantages, her family's social position entitled her to an elite education. All Aztec children were educated in moral and religious training, history, and rhetoric as well as ritual dancing and singing. Children of elites and exceptionally gifted children were placed in what was known as a *calmeccac*, which was akin to an academy or monastery.[26] Boys and girls were educated separately, and they began calmeccac around age seven. Religion was a pervasive force in all aspects of life, so the educational curriculum included instruction on how to address deities, make calendrical calculations, and perform rituals. Children were also trained in arithmetic, architecture, astronomy, and agriculture in order to sustain a large urban society. The art of public speaking was woven through all subjects because oral skills were necessary for negotiations throughout the empire and for reciting culturally and religiously important stories, poetry, and history. Talented speakers were critical to the Aztec Empire, which extended its authority over diverse communities with many linguistic variations. As we shall see in chapter 3, Malinche's early education was evident in her exceptional communication skills.

Malinche's young life of privilege was shattered by the death of her father when she was about ten years old. Within a few years her mother remarried another cacique and gave birth to his son. As the first child, Malinche would have inherited the honors of her noble parents,[27] but the newlyweds wanted to bequeath the family inheritance to their infant son. Díaz explains how the couple sold Malinche to Maya merchants from Xicalango under the cover of darkness, led the community to believe Malinche had died, and then staged a burial.[28]

Much like the Mesoamerican landscape, Malinche was molded by several cultures. Her early life as a child of the ruling class provided her with an Aztec education and worldview. But she reached womanhood in a Maya setting under Aztec domination. In her new Maya home in Xicalango she was no longer a member of the privileged class, she was a slave, according to Díaz. But European men routinely characterized Indian women as oppressed and enslaved by uncivilized societies, so we are unsure what her life as a "slave" entailed. Our modern interpretation conjures images that might not apply to Malinche's experience. Although she was an educated young woman of noble birth, Malinche was not a blood relative of anyone in Xicalango. Her diminished status may have made her more expendable. The Mayas traded Malinche to a Tabascan cacique, who later offered her to Cortés in 1519. Each time she was offered in an exchange, her royal heritage was likely exploited to ensure a high return. Cortés was told of her noble heritage, and Bernal Díaz recalled that it "was very evident in her appearance."[29]

The towns of Xicalango and Tabasco were part of a network consisting of sixteen regional centers with Maya roots. Both cities had access to Nahua communities in central Mexico and to Maya communities in the Yucatan, and both towns had Aztec overlords. In the early sixteenth century, Mayas were known for their elaborate system of commerce. Tabasco and Xicalango were commercial hubs for Maya trade. The area was crisscrossed with estuaries and rivers that penetrated inland and emptied into the Atlantic Ocean. It was an area of transit, with constant movement of people and goods.[30] Groups that were ordinarily hostile came to this culturally diverse environment to trade on neutral ground. Malinche honed her language skills amid diverse peoples who were involved in commerce and negotiation. In this environment she learned to speak several Maya dialects in addition to the Nahuatl of her youth, including an elite style of speaking that was reserved only for those who addressed Mexica nobility directly, known as *tecpillahtolli*.[31] It was a complicated form of communication that had to be taught. Malinche later used this lordly speech with Moctezuma II during Spanish negotiations in Tenochtitlán. She had likely developed a cultural sensitivity over the course of her life, having lived among various groups within the Aztec Empire. In order to survive in such an ethnically mixed environment, she needed to make herself useful and learn to respond appropriately to cultural cues.

This cultural agility proved valuable to Malinche, and eventually to the Spaniards. By the time she joined them, she had already learned to move from one culture to another, and to interact with diverse peoples simultaneously. We might expect that Malinche's early experiences taught her to read the signs of human interaction and to act accordingly.

NAHUA EXPECTATIONS OF WOMEN

Scholars are fortunate to have numerous Native descriptions of pre-conquest social organization. Each ethnic community (*altepetl*) maintained its own historical record, most often in the form of pictographs that were created to inform citizens and commemorate important events. These historical sources should be treated with caution because many of these Native records were translated and transcribed into alphabetic scripts during the colonial period, making them vulnerable to Spanish bias and misinformation. Yet they are important Native voices that contribute to our historical and cultural understanding of Mexico.

Fray Bernardino Sahagún was among the first Spanish chroniclers to record precolonial social organization in Mexico. He began his cultural study on the heels of the conquest in the late 1520s, and continued his work among the Indians for twenty years. The project resulted in a twelve-volume ethnographic history of Mesoamerican lifeways known as the Florentine Codex. To conduct his investigation, he selected and trained Native teenage males to act as interpreters.[32]

His work created a contemporary, albeit distorted, picture of indigenous society at the point of contact. Cultural biases are evident in
Sahagún's work because his goal was certainly to justify and facilitate
the Christianization project in Mexico. He also failed to differentiate
between Indian groups, collapsing the diverse cultures of Native
Mexico into one amalgamation. Nevertheless, Sahagún's work provided a foundation for European understanding of precolonial culture,
society, and history. With the help of his young informants, he broke
down Mesoamerican culture into component parts that he could
describe. Indigenous expectations of male and female responsibilities
are particularly relevant here.

Sahagún's early ethnology itemizes the characteristics of a good
Native mother. She demonstrated sincerity, vigilance, and diligence.
She was a watchful woman who taught and learned from others.
She was apprehensive for children's welfare. She was careful, thrifty,
and constantly at work. According to this gender standard, Malinche's
mother could not have been a "good mother." Perhaps Sahagún's
definition of a bad mother is more fitting. A bad mother was evil,
stupid, a deceiver, a fraud; she was lazy and disregarded convention.
Sahagún also defines a good daughter. She was pure, virginal, obedient, honest, intelligent, modest, well taught, well trained, and respectful.[33] Although Malinche would exhibit many of these characteristics
among the Spanish, she was far more complex than merely a good
daughter. She was also a "procuress" by Sahagún's definition. This
was a woman who hid the devil within her.[34] She was a talented
speaker who lulled others with her words. She was capable of provoking, perverting, and corrupting others. Sahagún's descriptions of
these roles reveal what was deemed appropriate behavior for Indian
women. It is clear that women were to be nurturing, hard working,
and compliant. Women were capable of persuasion, yet that skill
was to be exercised for the good of the group and not used as a
destructive force. As chapter 5 demonstrates, Sahagún's characterizations of appropriate and inappropriate feminine behavior provided
a foundation for Malinche's dichotomous myth: she was both the
selfish whore who brought down indigenous Mexico and the virtuous Catholic mother of a new mestizo race.

Fray Juan Bautista offered another indigenous record of Meso-american culture during the colonial era entitled *Huehuetlatolli* (*Discourse by Nahua Elders*). In this text elite elders described social expectations for men and women, specifically defining their obligations in marriage. Both husbands and wives had specific duties that maintained social order and pleased the gods. Feminine elders instructed prospective brides to diligently care for the home and for the family within: "If he (the husband) lives thanks to you, by our aid, you are to put him under your protection. But you are not therefore to consider yourself an eagle (warrior), you are not to consider yourself a jaguar (warrior) . . . You will tell whoever is your husband how he is to stand up, how he is to live on earth. And you will take care of what is to be drunk, what is to be eaten, or whether in your fireplace, on your hearth, something is thus to be warmed, to be heated. And you are to protect your planted furrows, your fields, and you are to take care of your workers, and you are to guard the coffers, the chests, and cover well the vessels, the bowls."[35] Women were clearly responsible for managing domestic affairs, but they were also expected to appropriately influence men's actions.

There is ample evidence indicating that precolonial Indian women were primarily associated with the domestic realm. Yet the precontact Nahua home was not understood as a private feminine domain, separate from a public masculine domain. Louise Burkhart offers a compelling argument, suggesting, "an ideology of male-female complementarity was maintained through an investment of the home with symbolism of war, not only by means of metaphor but also via direct ties to the battlefield front."[36] Nahua women were associated with home and they cared for men, yet that does not indicate female submissiveness. Mesoamerican cultures recognized and respected feminine power; they revered and feared both male and female deities. Flesh-and-blood Nahua women were vital contributors as wives, marketers, doctors, artisans, priests, and occasionally as rulers. Women and men were equally responsible for maintaining social order.[37]

There was, however, a clear expectation that women would approach their husbands with respect. This was evident in several codices, including Sahagún's *Florentine Codex*, Bautista's *Huehuetlatolli*, and *Codex Mendoza*.[38] Alonso de Zorita's study compares several Nahua colonial sources and summarizes women's domestic role and social posture. He suggests that young girls were to be trained in embroidery, sewing, weaving, and sweeping tasks early, so as to be masters by the time of marriage. They were to be discreet in speech, conduct, and appearance.[39] Women were to guard their virtue, serve their husbands, and be a proper example to others.[40]

According to the Nahua elders who informed Fray Bautista, women were instructed, "When you marry some eagle (or) jaguar (warrior), you are not to walk ahead of (or) over him. When he asks you something (or) entrusts something to you, (or) when he tells you to do something, you are to obey him properly, you are to listen pleasantly to what he says; you are not then to receive it angrily, you are not then to perturb yourself, you are not to turn your back on him. If something thus irks you, neither are you to remind him of it; your are not to belittle him there because of it, nor to act selfishly over it if he is a poor man."[41] The admonishment continues, "Softly, calmly you are to tell him what afflicts you. You are not to humiliate him before or near others, for if you humiliate him, it is as if you drag your heart, your entrails, what you cause to live, before others."[42] These Nahua gender instructions are informative to our understanding of Malinche's approach to her work as a cultural intermediary. As we shall see in chapter 3, she demonstrated appropriate feminine demeanor, according to Nahua culture, during her negotiations with male dignitaries.

Spanish colonizers valued some aspects of Mesoamerican gender standards, particularly the ones that coincided with their own. Fray Bautista suggests in the prologue of *Huehuetlatolli*, "If present-day Spanish women were to give such matters even moderate attention, their homes would be better managed, their children better taught, and their husbands better treated and less vexed by the endless, needless expense which they incur for (their wives), by which many (men) vex their souls and because of which they sometimes lose their good name and honor and leave many orphans and widows in the poor-house."[43] Bautista and Sahagún acknowledged and appreciated Indian women's service to home and family, but the Spaniards were far less willing to tackle the complexities of feminine power, social influence, sexuality, or female deities in Native Mexico.

Cultural bias distorted the gender explanations offered by conquistadors and friars. English colonists in Jamestown and American filibusters on the Northern Plains also misrepresented or neglected unfamiliar aspects of Native gender standards in their records. Foreign gender analyses that were based on non-Native paradigms (particularly patriarchy and female subordination) were insufficient in explaining indigenous gender structures. Early misrepresentations cast a long shadow over the history of Indian women. As a result, late-twentieth-century feminist scholars suggested that the oppression of women was universal, using European primary sources and their misrepresentations as a baseline for their gender comparison.

Indians groups of the Americas adapted to the arrival of Europeans according to their own circumstances, epistemologies, and designs for the future. As we turn our attention to Pocahontas, we must recognize that her Native world was also swirling with change under the increasing pressure of European intrusion. Pocahontas's people also had a long history prior to European contact, and they had their own agenda during their interactions with the English. The strategies that Pocahontas employed during her work as an intermediary were bound by Algonquian cultural standards and feminine expectations.

The Powhatan World of Pocahontas

Archaeological excavations have indicated that Powhatan civilization was the result of 1,500 years of adaptation to woodland living.[44] These Algonquians occupied the coastal plains of modern Virginia. Their homeland, which they referred to as Tsenacommacah, extended nearly one hundred miles from east to west and one hundred miles from north to south. The region encompassed nearly six thousand square miles and was home to at least fourteen thousand Native people in 1607. Their numbers had already been significantly reduced by half a century of slow but steady European encroachment and disease.

Powhatan people enjoyed a relatively mild climate with cool summers and warm winters. Four large rivers capable of supporting large European ships complemented a bountiful landscape. Numerous smaller rivers, creeks, and estuaries provided year-round marine food as well as easy communication and transportation throughout the region. Early-seventeenth-century Powhatan Indians engaged in a mixed economy: fishing, hunting, gathering, and highly successful horticulture (corn, beans, and squash). In addition to abundant marine food, productive farming, and plentiful wild game, the landscape provided a wide variety of edible plants. The harsh part of winter lasted only three months, making fresh fruits and nuts available seven months of the year. Foraging provided nourishment during periodic droughts and when the last year's provisions were exhausted before the crops were ripe. The Powhatans enjoyed a diverse diet that included nuts and berries, maize, beans, squash, fish, shellfish, and meat (raccoons, opossums, muskrats, beavers, wild turkey, brown bear, and white-tailed deer). As we will see in the next chapter, the first English colonists refused to adopt Indian subsistence methods. Instead, they relied on the Indians to provide food while describing the Powhatan people as living hand to mouth.[45]

The topography of the tidewater region and the size of its indigenous population allowed for the development of a complex political alliance between tribal villages along the major rivers. These were independent groups who came together for trade and communal defense.[46] Participating settlements were subordinate to a paramount chiefdom under Chief Powhatan, who took on the name of his people. Contemporary Indians have translated Powhatan to mean "People of the Dream Vision," and the ruler was the chief dreamer.[47] Chief Powhatan was recognized as the supreme leader who had a mystical ability to envision the path that would please the Great Spirit, *Manito*.[48] His kingly position was called *Mamanatowick*.

When Chief Powhatan became mamanatowick he inherited six tribes with 1,700 inhabitants, but his dream vision advised him to expand further. Over the course of the 1590s, through force or intimidation, he gradually brought more tribes under his reign. By the time the English arrived, he had the nominal submission, if not the full subjugation, of nearly all Algonquian-speaking groups on the coastal plain, nearly nine thousand Indians.[49] Among his Indian followers, he was seen as priest, king, and coordinator of the Powhatan alliance. He was a strong ruler whose power stemmed from his intrinsic ability to determine the correct path for the Powhatan people.[50] The Powhatan Indians, like many cultures across time and space, prophesized to explain and prepare for uncertainty and potential danger. Chief Powhatan possessed inborn gifts that allowed him to reach high levels of awareness and foresight. This highly respected type of psychic perception was viewed as an exceptional gift among various Indian peoples of the Americas. Chief Powhatan had the power to foresee events, connect with the infinite, and compel others. Because he was believed to be operating on a higher level of consciousness, the Powhatan people were inclined to trust his decisions and leadership.

In the early 1600s Powhatan prophecy warned of great change coming to Tsenacommacah.[51] According to their ways of knowing (astronomical calculations and priests' communications with the Manito), the Powhatan people were anticipating a great renewal of their world. Prior to the establishment of Jamestown, eastern Indians had already witnessed two European attempts at colonization: a Spanish excursion onto Powhatan land in 1570 and an English attempt on the Island of Roanoke in 1585. A third venture by the Virginia Company was destined to bring catastrophic change.

Chief Powhatan had an obligation to guide his people during times of anxiety and foreign threat. He contemplated his moves carefully and built up his empire in preparation for the coming challenges. Access to European trade intensified the traditional conflicts already existing between Native enemies. Depopulation and cultural disruption caused by war and epidemics heightened the need to organize for defense. More warriors were needed to face this third European intrusion and the menace that would follow. In exchange for the protection of Chief Powhatan's organized forces, Indians of coastal Virginia paid him tribute in the form of meat, corn, skins, pearls, copper ornaments, and women.

The gift of women reinforced alliances between tribes within Tsenacommacah. English observers estimated the number of Chief Powhatan's wives to be more than one hundred, though these diplomatic marriages were often temporary. As Chief Powhatan traveled through his territory, he was presented with the loveliest women. Colonial records say that it was a "great honor for a young woman to be asked by her tribe to be taken in marriage by the paramount chief."[52] The chief maintained his favorites in his household, usually twelve at a time ranked according to his favor.[53] Others he dispersed to members of his council or released to live with her people.

POCAHONTAS'S EARLY LIFE

Details of Pocahontas's childhood are scarce. She was born around 1595 and was given the name Matoaka, meaning "flower between two streams." Pocahontas was her Indian nickname, which English colonists translated to mean "mischievous or spoiled child."[54] We know nothing of Pocahontas's mother. When a wife of the great chief became pregnant, she was sent to live among her relatives. He had only one child by each wife, making all of his children half siblings. When Pocahontas reached learning age she, like all of the chief's children, was taken from her mother to be reared in Chief Powhatan's household; this ensured the child's loyalty to the Powhatan alliance. All adults in the community, including Chief Powhatan, were responsible for giving children attentive guidance. Boys were trained in hunting, fishing, and war making; girls were trained to maintain house, crops, and village. A select few (both boys and girls) were chosen for training in a spiritual discipline that served the group.

Chief Powhatan's extensive household was crowded with many children, a dozen or so wives, and servants who reduced the workload for his resident wives. The English recorded an elaborate ceremony that preceded meals in the chief's stately hut: before serving food, attendants brought Powhatan a washbasin and feathers to clean and dry his hands.[55] The English marveled at the cleanliness of Powhatan Indians, who bathed in streams daily, regardless of temperature. Even infants were bathed in cold water to ensure cleanliness and hardiness. Like Malinche, Pocahontas experienced a life of relative luxury as a child, but that lifestyle came to an end when she reached maturity. Despite being a mamanatowick's daughter, Pocahontas could not be an elite indefinitely; she was not an Indian princess.

The only legitimate queens in Powhatan society were those who were born into that role through matrilineal inheritance. Pocahontas could never have become a queen. Her influence in Powhatan society did not stem from a royal lineage. English settlers mistakenly identified her as a princess in the European sense: she was the daughter of an Indian ruler and thus an Indian princess in their minds. Pocahontas likely used the English-imposed identity to her advantage during her work as an intermediary. Some mythmakers suggested she chose to remain among the English because of their royal treatment toward her.

Powhatan Expectations of Women

Marriage in Powhatan culture was not necessarily based on love; rather, it was an institution that supported Powhatan society. Women looked for men who proved themselves to be good hunters or warriors.[56] Men sought industrious women who could provide a fine home and a good crop. To the shock of the English, considerable sexual liberty was permitted to both sexes after marriage. Men and women could have intimate or sexual relations outside of marriage.[57] Women's sexuality, however, was considered a powerful force, and it was carefully monitored during cross-cultural interaction. Native women (either married or single) were offered in cultural exchange; this diplomatic practice extended membership to the outsider and linked groups together in a cooperative future. Sexual relations with Indian women consummated an outsider's acceptance within the group.[58] From an English perspective, these sexual customs demonstrated the uncivilized nature of the Powhatan Indians.

Native marriages were more fluid than the English were accustomed to.[59] They could be dissolved at the request of either spouse. If a spouse was taken captive, which was not uncommon in Native America, the marriage was annulled. This cultural stipulation made Pocahontas available to marry John Rolfe during her captivity despite a prior marriage. Pocahontas had been married at puberty (around 1610) to Kocoum, a young warrior from a community on the fringe of the Powhatan alliance. When the English abducted her in 1613, her marriage to Kocoum ended. Thus her Indian marriage was never acknowledged in the Eurocentric construction of the Pocahontas legend. By non-Indian reckoning, Pocahontas was a beautiful and virginal Indian princess.

In Powhatan culture, men's and women's work rarely overlapped. Powhatan men and women each performed a wide variety of indispensable jobs. Women constructed homes made of bark and woven mats, collected firewood, kept fires going at all times, and made baskets, pots, and cooking utensils. They planted and harvested crops, pounded corn into flour, made bread, and prepared, served, and cleaned after meals. They were also barbers who tended to men's elaborate hairstyles. The women bore and reared children.[60] When the family was on the move, women carried all materials of home, leaving the men available to pursue game or enemies. Powhatan women also entertained important visitors and participated in diplomatic conferences.[61]

Men's jobs were few, but they were physically demanding. Men were responsible for hunting, fishing, and making war. They also produced and repaired the gear necessary for those endeavors. Hunting and war required extended periods of intense physical exertion and concentration, between which periods of recuperation were essential. When Indian men returned to the village, they rested in preparation for the next outing, held councils, maintained their equipment, and interacted with children.[62]

This was the life Pocahontas knew when the English arrived in 1607. The Powhatan people had been expanding in an atmosphere of change and uncertainty. Chief Powhatan was responsible for guiding a conglomeration of diverse trobes that shared a common language, common enemies, and a similar woodland lifestyle through the changes that lay ahead. Independent tribal villages within the Powhatan confederacy had their own religious beliefs and autonomy over their own tribal affairs. They came together to form a military alliance in defense against the anticipated transformation of their world. By the time the English landed in Jamestown, the Powhatan people had had forty years of intermittent experience with European encroachment. They had endured European explorers and slave raiders, Spanish colonists who roamed in the south, and the botched English colony in Roanoke. Powhatan people paid nominal tribute to Chief Powhatan and relied on his wisdom and spiritual insights regarding the correct course of action during this final European incursion. This time the foreigners were expected to succeed.

Pocahontas, like Malinche and Sacagawea, was on the verge of womanhood when European adventurers entered her world. All three women lived within a complex network of indigenous ethnic groups. Each of their lives played out in an era of profound transformation. The Mexicas and the Powhatans were in the process of expanding and building multiethnic warrior forces in preparation for uncertain futures. Sacagawea's people pursued a different strategy: the Shoshones of the Northern Rockies retreated into the mountains to avoid dealing with the complications brought by Europeans. But their mountainous lifestyle could not protect them from confrontations with traditional enemies who had more consistent access to European goods and technologies.

The Multicultural Plains World of Sacagawea

Sacagawea was born in the valley of the Lemhi River (in what is now Idaho) on the western side of the Rocky Mountains. She was given the name Boo-wy-ee-puh, meaning "Grass Woman," perhaps to signify the summertime in which she was born.[63] Sacagawea was the name given by her Hidatsa captors. According to linguists, Sacagawea means "Bird Woman" in Hidatsa and "Boat Paddler" in Shoshone.[64] Because her various Indian names originated with languages that had no written record, true spelling and translation remain difficult. She will be referred to here as Sacagawea.

Sacagawea's northern band of Shoshones was an isolated nomadic group with little direct experience with Europeans. When she was an infant in the late 1780s, her group was on the move after surviving a devastating smallpox outbreak; they retreated into the mountains, to the headwaters of the Missouri River, seeking protection from the scourge of European disease. Reduced in number, the Lemhi Shoshones roamed the rugged mountains, following the ripening seasons of edible plants. At the turn of the century Sacagawea's people resorted to an ancient strategy of mobility, taking advantage of available resources and avoiding encroachment on others.

Scholars disagree on a scientific explanation of Shoshone prehistory. Most believe the Shoshones were part of the "Numic expansion" that migrated into a broad stretch of land from northern California to Southern Idaho. This migration was made up of diverse peoples who were forced to spread out due to limited natural resources in an arid landscape. Anthropologists have argued about the exact time of their migration; some have suggested it took place ten thousand years ago while others insisted it was merely several thousand years ago. Sacagawea's band, the Lemhi Shoshone, is believed to have descended from the northern faction of these early migrants.

Today's Lemhi Shoshones assert that their ancestors always lived in the territory they occupied at the point of contact, including the Salmon River valley.[65] Their creation stories explain how they originated there; they did not migrate from elsewhere. The Lemhis believe they descended from Coyote, a prominent figure in Shoshone mythology. One oral tradition explains how Coyote was led to an island by a young girl. Coyote feared her because she and her mother had teeth in their vaginas, and he thought they planned to devour him. He snuck off to retrieve his tools and returned to knock out their teeth so he could have sex with them. After intercourse he was told to go out and retrieve water. In his absence many babies (Indian peoples) were born. When Coyote returned he was told to wash the last two babies with the water he brought, but he did not. Had Coyote washed them, all of the children would have been the same. The two who had been separated from the rest, became Shoshones. Coyote told his Shoshone children to be brave and not to fear other Indians, who would always be against them.[66]

Another Shoshone creation story explains that a girl told Coyote to carry a basket to her across the water and that Coyote should not look inside. Coyote could not overcome his curiosity and kept opening the basket. Every time he opened the lid, small creatures (Plains Indians) escaped, and they grew to populate a wide section of the land.[67] While both creation stories express Native inheritance to the land, they also explain diversity among Plains Indians. Plains groups were independent, yet fluid. They occasionally fought one another, but they often came together for trade, hunting, or war excursions. This intermingling created multiethnic communities, as members of one band were remarkably free to join another. There was considerable intermixing among tribes on the North American plains.[68]

The Shoshones' culture was influenced by the diversity of their region. The Lemhis adopted various strategies for food production. They combined gathering methods used in the Great Basin with the hunting methods of plateau peoples to the east. The Lemhis acquired horses from the Comanches, who lived on the southern Plains, and Lewis and Clark noted Spanish horse accessories among the Lemhis.[69] The Shoshones were accustomed to dealing with different peoples and incorporating any strategies they observed that might improve their condition.

During Sacagawea's childhood, Native life became increasingly challenging with the influx of non-Indian peoples. Disease and access to European trade intensified traditional rivalries. Shoshones enjoyed an initial advantage, being among the first mounted Plains Indians in the mid-1700s. The adaptation of the horse made a nomadic lifestyle more attractive and convenient. European trade goods, however, were more accessible to Indians who lived in settled villages, so sedentary groups had consistent interactions with the foreigners. The more aggressive Blackfeet, Crows, and the Gros Ventres (hereafter called Hidatsas) acquired guns from European fur traders working for the Hudson's Bay Company and the North West Company.[70] By the turn of the century the Shoshones were confined to the mountains and surrounded by tribes who were better armed.

The Lemhi Shoshones were forced to maintain a nomadic lifestyle in the mountains, constantly retreating from their enemies and constantly searching for food. Hunger became an increasing reality. Coming down from the mountains in search of buffalo and other game was dangerous. With only bows and arrows, hunting was more difficult and time consuming in enemy territory. The Lemhis were essentially cut off from the nourishment and trade provided by the plains buffalo. The mountainous land they occupied was unsuitable for even the most rudimentary agriculture. Fish in mountain streams, native roots and seeds, wild vegetables and fruits, small game, and occasional buffalo meat provided a difficult subsistence. At the time of Lewis and Clark's arrival, the Lemhi Shoshones consisted of four to five hundred people, a quarter of whom were warriors. The

Lemhis had dealt with ethnic and geographical pressures from their beginning, and those regional tensions intensified with the arrival of Europeans.

Just as they had in Mexico and Tsenacommacah, Europeans brought to the plains economic opportunities—new military technology and alliances—as well as worrisome changes—devastating disease, increased warfare, and incredible mortality rates. The intensity of life challenged Native leaders, social structures, traditional medical practices, and religious faith. Even the gender balance within Plains tribes was altered by the horse-and-hide economy, a competitive industry that was dramatically accelerated with European investment. Plains men and women participated in buffalo hunts and Native trade networks until the 1730s.[71] The introduction of horses made hunting and trading more aggressive and more masculine. Shoshone male status was traditionally measured according to a man's ability to hunt, his success in war, and his generosity. A capable horseman had the opportunity to enhance his status. Prior to European involvement in the horse-and-hide economy, buffalo were killed mainly for subsistence. With the influence of non-Native traders, buffalo were increasingly killed for profit and women's involvement shifted to processing the kill, rather than participating in the hunt.[72] A mounted hunter was able to bring in more animals than one wife could process. More feminine hands were needed to process the hides, and polygamy served this need. In an environment racked with increasing competition, disease, and warfare, men were declining in numbers and polygamy was a strategy for the preservation of the group. Some scholars have argued that nomadic Plains women lost prestige during this transition because they were no longer involved in the hunt, nor were they decision makers in trade because white traders preferred to barter with Indian men.[73] However, it is important to recognize that Plains women remained critical producers who were indispensable to the horse-and-hide economy.

SACAGAWEA'S EARLY LIFE

During Sacagawea's life among the Shoshones, domestic labor was in high demand.[74] She was trained to fulfill the expectations of her gender: processing the kill of a hunt, dressing skins, drying meat, carrying wood and water, gathering and preparing food, rearing children, crafting moccasins and other apparel, as well as the arduous task of packing in preparation for constant movement. Women packed, carried, and unpacked the essentials of the mobile village. The women owned and controlled the house and household goods. They cared for and carried these items, leaving men available to pursue either enemies or game in an instant. The European invaders who witnessed and recorded the heavy work done by Plains Indian women were appalled.[75] Sacagawea experienced a life filled with consistent movement, hard work, hunger, death, and uncertainty.

In accordance with Shoshone custom, Sacagawea was promised at birth to an adult male of the community. The standard transaction included payment in horses. Sacagawea was to remain with her parents until she completed her training in female tasks. When she reached maturity, she was to become a wife in accordance with the prearranged transaction. However, just prior to being delivered to her husband, when she was approximately twelve years old, Sacagawea was captured by Hidatsa warriors.[76] She had been processing the kill from a buffalo hunt when she was taken, along with several other Shoshone women and children. Indian men increased their honor within their own community by taking captives, while at the same time inflicting shame on the captive's male relatives.[77] Taking captives helped replenish population loss in an era of heightened warfare and disease.

Hidatsa warriors took Sacagawea hundreds of miles east, to their earth-lodge village along the Knife River near present day Bismarck, North Dakota. There were five Indian settlements in the area, two Hidatsa and three Mandan.[78] Both groups were involved in vibrant cross-cultural trade and had steady access to European goods from "free traders," independent European trader/trappers who sold to the large fur-trade companies. At the time of Sacagawea's captivity, the Hidatsas were recovering from an intense period of war with the Lakotas, in which they had suffered tremendous losses. Many of the surrounding Mandan village groups of the Gros Ventres had recently reorganized for mutual defense against the Lakotas. As a result, close intertribal cooperation developed. This synergism of cultures produced a more technologically advanced, sedentary agricultural lifestyle, which differed from the nomadic lifestyle Sacagawea had known among the Lemhis.

Long before the arrival of Europeans, village tribes engaged in an extensive plains trade network in which corn was the main commodity.[79] Villages along the Missouri River became of hub of indigenous commerce. Nomadic hunting groups entered the river valley in peace to pursue trade, bringing robes, meat, pelts, and eagle feathers to exchange for agricultural goods from the villages. Everyone depended on corn, a vital source of nourishment on the plains. Village women grew the corn and traded it, along with other agricultural and domestic products, while men traded in horses, guns and meat.[80] Sacagawea entered this sedentary agricultural lifestyle in an area of international commerce. Like Malinche, who came of age in a Maya trade district, Sacagawea honed her intermediary skills in a commercial hub where diverse peoples came to negotiate in a variety of languages.

The Hidatsas lived in houses made of timber, sunk partly into the ground and covered with thick roofs of earth. These houses provided better protection from the elements than the mobile skin shelters of the Lemhis. Food was more accessible and plentiful for the Hidatsas because they had a wider variety of native seeds and roots, wild vegetables and fruits, agricultural crops, and game. Sacagawea's new life, even as a captive, exposed her to a more comfortable physical existence; she was not relegated to a lifetime of slavery among the Hidatsas. After an initiation period captives could be adopted as members of family and community. Like the Shoshones, the Hidatsas practiced polygamy, and it is likely that Sacagawea became a wife of her male captor.

By European standards, Hidatsa women occupied a higher level of social status than Shoshone women. Hidatsa women participated in social and ceremonial organizations, and played a significant role in religious rites and age-grade societies.[81] Mothers negotiated the marriage of their daughters, typically for strategic purposes. A daughter could resist her mother's decision if she found the groom objectionable, but Sacagawea, as an adopted captive, may not have enjoyed such privileges.[82] She spent only a few years with her indigenous captors before she was presented to a white man. She was given to a French Canadian trader named Toussaint Charbonneau in order to facilitate future interactions. Her life experiences up to this point may have made her a logical choice to serve in this intermediary role. She was not a blood relative of anyone, yet she was experienced with cultural dislocation and had already learned to accommodate new social expectations. She would learn to tolerate Charbonneau's cultural oddities as she acclimated him to Plains trade. She was linguistically skilled and culturally pliable. She may have been simply an expendable woman, but she was also a reasonable choice to expedite interaction with Europeans and to maintain access to their trade goods. For Sacagawea, it offered an opportunity to increase her social status and influence.

HIDATSA EXPECTATIONS OF WOMEN

Sacagawea reached womanhood in a community that valued women's agricultural production and their service to others. She was taught appropriate Hidatsa feminine behavior and responsibilities. Hidatsa grandmothers instructed that a young woman should "care for the home in order to make sure the people in it would be comfortable and happy. She must be hospitable to strangers, helpful and kind to her neighbors and to the elderly and the needy, dutiful to her husband, careful of his honor and proud of his achievements, and she must let all other men alone. A woman who looked after her husband's comfort, guarded his interests, and showed hospitality to his guests would honor his name; he in turn would cherish her and they would be happy together."[83] As we shall see, European writers observed Sacagawea demonstrating many of these qualities. They recognized and appreciated Native feminine qualities that were familiar to them, but they misinterpreted unfamiliar female responsibilities.

Plains Indian women, perhaps more than any other group, were depicted in early European accounts as "beasts of burden." They were seen as overworked and degraded by uncivilized cultures.[84] By European standards, Plains Indian women were responsible for men's work: raising crops, constructing homes, producing commodities, and negotiating trade at rendezvous and trade fairs. Most appalling to European invaders was the Native practice of offering women to outsiders as a precursor to cross-cultural interaction. From a Native perspective, this practice served two functions. First, the women were given to establish kinship and trust with the foreigners. These women served as cultural intermediaries, responsible not only for wooing the outsiders but also for acclimating them to indigenous standards of behavior. Second, women's sexuality was seen as a powerful transformative force from which all things grew. According to Virginia Peters, "The concept of women as conduits of power from those who had it to those who aspired to achieve it was well established in village society, sanctioned by years of tradition and religious belief."[85] Women's sexuality was not used simply for procreation; it transferred power and established a trusted kinship alliance. The significance of Native women's sexuality was incomprehensible to incoming Europeans. They interpreted Native gender standards, particularly the functions of women's sexuality and the gendered distribution of labor, as proof of savage immorality.

The cultural excursions provided in this chapter reveal rich indigenous histories with complex cultural antecedents. Native groups made sense of European arrival according to their own epistemologies. Indigenous Americans were accustomed to ethnic and cultural diversity. Oppression and conquest existed long before the arrival of Europeans: Native groups warred with one another, they raided and took captives, they formed economic and military alliances, and formidable groups subjugated less powerful groups.

Gender, however, was not a social arena in which the powerful ran roughshod over the powerless. Both genders were capable of tremendous power that could manifest for good or evil. Men and women were responsible for an interconnected set of obligations that maintained social and spiritual order. Women's sexuality, as well as their economic and diplomatic significance to indigenous social organization, was confusing to Euro-invaders, who tended to idealize gender categories in terms of male dominance and female chastity and submissiveness. This ideological divide made gender a particular area of misunderstanding and misrepresentation. The Nahuas, Algonquians, Shoshones, and Hidatsas, like most indigenous groups, assessed the Euro-invaders to determine any tactical advantage they might offer. Malinche, Pocahontas, and Sacagawea were deployed as intermediaries to facilitate that assessment, to look for opportunities, and to defuse hostility or potential violence. Malinche, Pocahontas, and Sacagawea were exchanged to outsiders as part of a diplomatic strategy, and their status as women depended on their contributions and service to others.

CHAPTER TWO

FIRST ENCOUNTERS

When Indians and Europeans met in the Americas, both groups sought cultural exchange and engaged in cultural accommodation, but neither side was interested in complete acculturation. This chapter explores the circumstances of initial contact in Mexico, Virginia, and the American Northwest. Europeans left tangible records of their first impressions, impressions that had lasting consequences on nationalist explanations of frontier conquests. Native interpretations of initial contact are more difficult to decipher. We must respect oral and pictorial traditions as authentic and relevant sources that provide Indian voices and offer a balanced understanding. We can also examine indigenous actions for which explanations do not exist. Native interpretations of early encounters with Europeans are germane to the history and future of both nations.

In each region the cultural collision followed a unique course, yet there were some similarities that emerged: (1) Native peoples developed and revised strategies for dealing with the powerful outsiders according to their own projections for the future; (2) indigenous and European groups interpreted frontier events according to their own historical and spiritual understanding; (3) knowledge and support offered by Native peoples was critical to the newcomers' survival during the initial phase of contact; and (4) in all three locations, much of that knowledge and support flowed through female intermediaries.

CENTRAL MEXICO

On March 22, 1519, a large European invasion force landed in the Americas. Hernán Cortés and five hundred conquistadors arrived on the Yucatán Peninsula, near the Maya city of Tabasco. They were not the first Spaniards to arrive; Mesoamericans had already experienced intermittent contact with bearded white men who arrived on giant ships, and Moctezuma II had been receiving consistent reports regarding the arrival of strangers. Francisco Hernández de Cordoba made the first trip in 1517 and was violently rejected by Maya forces. The next year Juan de Grijalva anchored his ship along the jungle coast of Tabasco. This second entourage fared better among the Natives, established trade with them, and returned to Spanish Cuba with stories of great wealth. Grijalva's promise of riches inspired Cortés's mission in 1519.

Cortés was in his early thirties in 1519. He was a man on the make, eager to find wealth and glory in the New World. The governor of Cuba, Diego Valázquez authorized Cortés's mission to explore Mexico and return with a full report. Valázquez immediately began to worry about Cortés, who had earned a reputation as a flamboyant opportunist with selfish intentions. Valázquez decided to recall the expedition, but Cortés, sensing the withdrawal of his commission, quickly departed before all necessary provisions were gathered. This would not be the last time that Spanish authorities questioned Cortés's motives in Mexico.

After a rather hectic launch, Cortés's forces landed on the Mexican gulf coast in March of 1519, planning to follow Grijalva's course. Cortés immediately ordered several of the ocean vessels destroyed to prevent desertion, and then led his men to conquer Mexico in the name of Spain and Catholicism. One of Cortés's first priorities was to investigate rumors of stranded Spaniards in these lands because an earlier ship, en route to Santo Domingo, was believed to have run aground in the Yucatán in 1511. Cortés sent messengers into the countryside to find the marooned Spaniards and secure their release, but only Gerónimo de Aguilar was found. Aguilar informed Cortés that all except he and one other had perished. The other survivor, Gonzalo Guerrero, had since married an Indian woman and had a Maya family (possibly the first mestizo children in Mexico). He was considered a great cacique and did not wish to return to Spanish life. Aguilar, who was fluent in Mayan, signed on with Cortés to act as his interpreter among the Indians.[1]

It wasn't long before Tabascans approached the invaders with their weapons drawn. Cortés instructed Aguilar to explain the futility of Native resistance. A tactful negotiator, Aguilar expressed that the Spaniards had not come to inflict harm but to share goods and knowledge. Then Aguilar issued a firm warning: if the Indians chose to fight, the Spaniards would be forced to destroy them.[2] The Indians, with the numerical advantage, responded by launching an attack. Cortés rallied his troops amid a blizzard of arrows and lances. The superiority of Spanish weapons forced the Tabascans into retreat, and Cortés took possession of their city in the name of his king.

On March 25, while Cortés and one hundred of his men were exploring the countryside, a squadron of Tabascans returned to challenge the Spaniards, this time with additional support from neighboring towns. Bernal Díaz describes the assault: "Their squadrons, as they approached us, were so numerous that they covered the whole savannah. They rushed on us like mad dogs and completely surrounded us, discharging such a rain of arrows, darts and stones upon us that more than seventy of our men were wounded at the first attack. For there were three hundred Indians to every one of us, and we could not hold our own against such numbers."[3] The Spaniards resisted the attack, using muskets, crossbows, swords, and canon fire, until the tide was finally reversed by the arrival of Cortés and his mounted scouts. This was the Indians' first glimpse of warriors on horseback, and the sight caused much distraction. As the weary Spanish ground troops struggled, the Spanish cavalry rode in, and Native warriors retreated in astonishment.

After surprising the Natives with superior weapons and mounted soldiers, Cortés ordered the prisoners to be brought before him. They were fed, had their wounds dressed, and then were released with gifts and a message. Aguilar instructed the prisoners to return to their communities and inform their headmen that the Spaniards intended them no harm; they merely wanted to share Spanish goods and knowledge. They would continue to fight only if the Indians continued to resist. Cortés also instructed the Indians to invite their leaders to a parley so that the two groups could talk as brothers.[4]

Early the next morning the Tabascan caciques arrived, offering kind words and gifts of food, gold, precious stones, sandals, and twenty Indian maidens. This most precious gift, young women, was in accordance with a Mesoamerican diplomatic strategy. It was intended to ensure future relations and cement alliances with the powerful newcomers.[5] Among the Spaniards, these women immediately began their Christian training in preparation for baptism. This was crucial for legitimate acceptance among Spanish men. Cortés then allotted one woman to each of his captains.

One of these women was seventeen-year-old Malinche, whom Spaniards named "Doña Marina" after her baptism. The Spaniards were quick to recognize her Native beauty and intelligence. Bernal Díaz recalls that Malinche was immediately deemed special and was given to the Spaniard with the highest social rank, Alonso Hernández Puertocarrero. He was a rich man and a strategic friend of Cortés. Díaz stated, "One of the Indian ladies was christened Doña Marina. She was truly a great princess, the daughter of a Cacique and the mistress of vassals, as was very evident in her appearance. . . . Cortés gave one of them to each of his captains, and Doña Marina, being good-looking, intelligent, and self-assured, went to Alonso Hernández Puertocarrero, who as I have already said, was a very grand gentleman, and a cousin of the Court of Medellin."[6]

When Puertocarrero returned to Spain, Malinche became the constant and intimate companion of Cortés for the remainder of the conquest. She served as his interpreter and cultural adviser, educating Cortés on the multiethnic landscape and the far-reaching tentacles of Aztec dominance. She consistently and effectively convinced Native dignitaries to aid Cortés's army as they proceeded through Indian country toward the Aztec seat of power. She was also an effective evangelist who instructed indigenous listeners to open their hearts and minds to a loving Christian god that offered eternal salvation. For some Indians, this may have seemed a comforting message during a time of increasing warfare and uncertainty.

The conquistadors, Malinche, and growing numbers of indigenous allies marched inland across a mountainous landscape toward their target in Tenochtitlán. Negotiations were tenuous due to suspicions and language barriers that required tedious translation methods. A show of Spanish military force was occasionally necessary, and there were deadly consequences in an indigenous landscape that was already rife with hostility and discontent. Malinche informed Cortés of Native rivalries and simmering tensions over increasing Aztec tribute demands and punitive human sacrifice. The Aztec Empire was on a brutal course of expansion just prior to Spanish arrival. Through Malinche's translation, Cortés was able to persuade thousands of Indians to join the Spanish in opposition to Aztec tyranny.

Cortés and Díaz both recorded that Malinche was at Cortés's side whenever he communicated with Native dignitaries. Cortés, however, said very little about Malinche in his progress letters to the crown. As a married man who kept several Native concubines, Cortés was careful with his commentary on Malinche, but he briefly mentioned her in letter five, as he described an exchange with Indians as he neared Tenochtitlán: "She then told him that what I had said was true and spoke to him of how I had conquered Mexico and of all the other lands which I held subject and had placed beneath Your Majesty's command."[7] This was certainly a self-serving account by Cortés, in which he alone was the hero of events. Yet it proved that he trusted Malinche to give her own testimony to Indian listeners. Cortés relied on her to characterize events and persuade American Indians to join the Spanish cause.

All evidence suggests that Mesoamericans did not consider Malinche a mere slave among the Spaniards. Considerable documentation from Díaz, Cortés, and Indian pictorials indicates that she was a critical part of all negotiations. As the next chapter shows, Díaz suggested that she had extraordinary influence among the Indians. We also know that the Indians referred to her as Malintzin, her Indian name with the suffix "-tzin," which connotes honor in Nahuatl. Like the Spaniards who dignified Malinche with the title of Doña, Indians also addressed her with respect. Malinche was a woman of consequence; intelligent and persuasive, she was a woman who warranted respect on both sides of the cultural divide. Because of Cortés' association with Malinche, Natives referred to him as "Malintzin" as well. Modern readers might find it ironic that Cortés took the name of his female Indian companion during the military campaign, but the couple was seen and understood in tandem. Her oratory skills, ingrained by her Native upbringing, were instrumental to diplomatic negotiations during the Spanish conquest.

A spectacular display of Spanish resolve and military power was evident in its attack on the city of Cholula. Cholulans, allies of the Mexicas, lived just across the mountains from Tenochtitlán. The conquistadors launched a violent attack on the city in which thousands of Cholulans were slaughtered. Cortés's critics suggested that the brutal massacre was payment to the Tlaxcalans, with whom Cortés had recently negotiated an alliance. They had just emerged from a war with Cholula, and they lived in a constant state of war against the Mexicas. It was a strategic partnership for both the Tlaxcalans and the Spaniards. An alliance with the powerful newcomers provided Tlaxcala with an opportunity to defeat their traditional enemies in Cholula and Tenochtitlán. The Spaniards benefitted as well; they gained five thousand Tlaxcalan warriors as they approached Tenochtitlán.

Cortés justified the brutality against Cholula in his fifth progress letter, in which he insisted that Malinche had uncovered a Native plot to halt the Spanish advance.[8] According to Cortés, Malinche had informed him that a combined force of Mexica and Cholulan warriors were planning to attack the Spaniards as they left the city en route to Tenochtitlán. Cortés explained that an old Cholulan woman, a wife of a cacique, had approached Malinche and offered her son to her in marriage. She warned Malinche of the impending disaster and told her to gather her belongings and return to Cholula with her at once. Malinche led the elderly woman to believe that she had accepted, and then advised the woman to wait because she had much treasure to retrieve. Malinche then informed Cortés of the planned attack. Cortés used this story of Malinche's warning to justify his preemptive attack on Cholula, portraying it as an act of self-defense. Although Bernal Díaz substantiated Cortés's claim in his recollection,[9] it is difficult to determine whether the Spaniard's attack on Cholula was warranted. Malinche left no record herself. The Spanish perpetrators gave the only explanation, and they used Malinche's alleged espionage as justification for their actions. Many authorities in Spain refused to accept Cortés's account and lamented his brutality against the Indians (particularly Bartolomé de las Casas, whom chapter 5 will discuss).

In November 1519 the Spaniards finally entered Tenochtitlán. Cortés and several of his men were greeted cordially and escorted

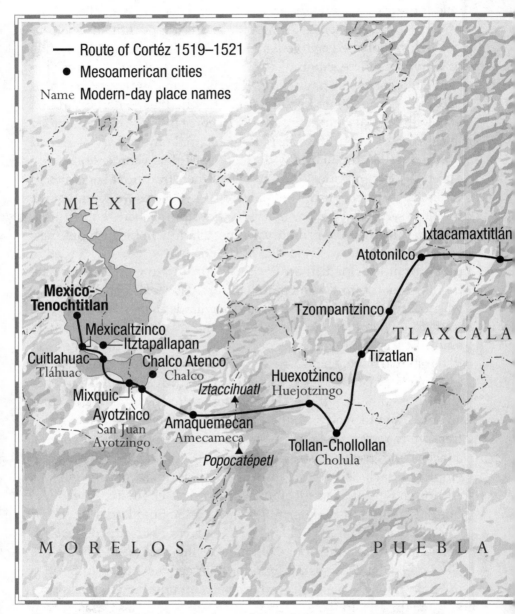

Central Mexico in the sixteenth century. Map redrawn by Carol Zuber-Mallison. Copyright © 2015 by The University of Oklahoma Press, Norman. All rights reserved.

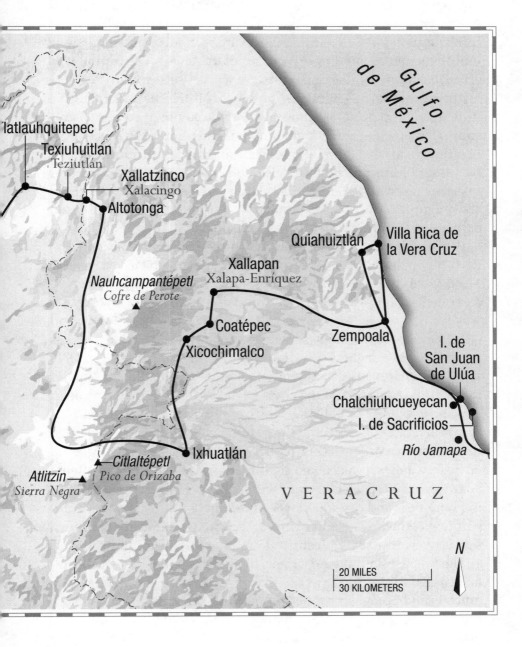

latlauhquitepec

Texiuhuitlán
Teziutlán

Xallatzinco
Xalacingo

Altotonga

Gulfo de México

Quiahuiztlán

Villa Rica de la Vera Cruz

Xallapan
Xalapa-Enríquez

Nauhcampantépetl
Cofre de Perote

Coatépec

Zempoala

Xicochimalco

I. de San Juan de Ulúa

Chalchiuhcueyecan

I. de Sacrificios

Río Jamapa

Ixhuatlán

Citlaltépetl
Pico de Orizaba

Atlitzin
Sierra Negra

VERACRUZ

N

20 MILES
30 KILOMETERS

to the top of the highest temple for a panoramic view of the capital city and the surrounding towns that fanned out over the valley. Tenochtitlán was composed of extensive botanical gardens and huge stone buildings that seemed to rise up out of the water. The capital was accessible through broad, man-made, linear causeways. Ornate architecture, impressive sculptures, and colorful frescos decorated the thriving metropolis. This grand city was the culmination of dynamic cultural interaction and adaptation, predating European social organization. The Mexicas had a long tradition of expropriating and blending cultural and religious elements from Mexico's past in order to justify a social hierarchy that placed them at the pinnacle of the Aztec Empire. The Spaniards stood in awe of the elaborate cultural expressions so artistically displayed in Tenochtitlán.

Bernal Díaz Del Castillo was among the Spanish soldiers who gazed upon the marvels of Moctezuma's imperial capital. Díaz recalls, "And when we saw all those cities and villages built in the water, and other great towns on dry land, and that straight and level causeway leading to Mexico, we were astounded. These great towns and cues [temples] and buildings rising from the water, all made of stone, seemed like an enchanted vision from the tale of Amadis. Indeed, some of our soldiers asked whether it was not all a dream."[10] Díaz includes a description of the city's incredible orchards and gardens: "I was never tired of noticing the diversity of trees and the various scents given off by each, and the paths choked with roses and other flowers, and the many local fruit-trees and rose-bushes, and the pond of fresh water." It had taken the Mexicas a century to build what Díaz described. Díaz later said with regret, "Everything was shining with lime and decorated with different kinds of stonework and paintings which were a marvel to gaze on. . . . Today all that I then saw is overthrown and destroyed; nothing is left standing."[11]

The Spanish initially experienced an atmosphere of tense hospitality in Tenochtitlán. Discussions took place in which each side (Mexica officials and Spanish conquistadors) tried to determine the other's capacity and intention. Malinche was a crucial mediator during this dialogue. Her Spanish title, "Doña," connoted a perceived royal Indian heritage, but she earned her Native suffix, "-tzin," through her work as a cultural intermediary. She advised both Native and Spanish leaders; Moctezuma II requested her council on whether he should agree to Spanish captivity. On this occasion Díaz characterized Malinche as an artful negotiator. He describes her participation in the capture of Moctezuma, saying, "and she [Doña Marina], being very quick-witted, replied: 'Lord Moctezuma, I advise you to accompany them immediately to their quarters and make no protest. I know they will treat you very honourably as the great prince you are. But if you stay here, you will be a dead man. In their quarters the truth will be discovered.'"[12]

This passage reveals Malinche's diplomatic and cultural savvy. She appeased Moctezuma's sense of honor, assured him there was "truth" and a future among the Spaniards, and informed him that he could not win against the technological power and divine favor of the Spanish. She traversed both cultures simultaneously. Malinche may have felt a tremendous sense of responsibility to ease Mexico's reemergence into the next cycle of civilization. Given her important role, it seems unlikely that she considered herself a slave. Moctezuma, like other Indian leaders she advised, thought of her as an authority during this time of difficult transition. He followed her advice. This would not be the only time Mexica authorities asked for her council.

Despite Moctezuma's willing consent to Spanish captivity and instruction (a move that ultimately sealed his doom), conditions in Tenochtitlán steadily deteriorated. Residents of the city were increasingly hostile toward the Spaniards' demands and outright greed. After several anxious weeks in the capital, Cortés was called away to the coast to greet another Spanish expedition, one under the leadership of Pánfilo Narváez. He had been sent by the Cuban governor to recall Cortés and send him home in irons to face charges of brutality against the Indians. Cortés was forced to divide his army in Tenochtitlán. He took a portion of his men back across the countryside to face Narváez in Veracruz and left the remainder of his forces under Pedro de Alvarado in the Aztec capital. Cortés would not have considered making this trek to the coast without Malinche; he needed her to obtain Indian cooperation, provisions, and accommodations along his route. The Spaniards they left in Tenochtitlán proved vulnerable without Cortés and Malinche.

Havoc erupted in the capital while the couple was away. By the time Cortés had defeated Narváez and returned, the atmosphere had turned hostile. Cortés and Malinche tried to restore peace. They first appealed to Moctezuma, pleading with him to address his citizens from a rooftop parapet. Yet Moctezuma had lost all credibility; he had broken the warrior code by appeasing the Spaniards and agreeing to captivity. His brother had assumed leadership in Tenochtitlán and was preparing an attack to rid the city of Spanish intruders. Cortés and Malinche finally persuaded Moctezuma to address Tenochtitlán one last time in an attempt to calm the attacking warriors. This would be his last act. It remains unclear who was responsible Moctezuma's death. The Indians insisted that the Spaniards killed him, and the Spaniards claimed that the Indians pummeled Moctezuma with stones during the melee. The Spaniards were trapped in Tenochtitlán and forced into a daring nighttime escape from the city. Spanish forces included approximately five hundred conquistadors (Cortés had returned from the coast with additional Spanish troops) and a few thousand Indian allies, yet they were vulnerable in a city of more than one hundred thousand angry citizens. The Spaniards later remembered their escape from Tenochtitlán as "Noche Triste"; many of their comrades did not survive. They drowned in the causeways under the weight of their stolen treasure as Indians descended over them in canoes. Cortés, Díaz, and Malinche, were among the survivors. The remaining Spanish forces retreated to Tlaxcala to regroup and tend to their wounds. They were in sorry shape.

The citizens of Tenochtitlán did not fare much better; victory celebrations were cut short when a terrible pestilence descended over the city within weeks after expelling the Spaniards. Narváez's ships had carried smallpox across the Atlantic, and the sickness brought unbearable suffering and death to Indians in and surrounding Tenochtitlán. It took nearly six weeks for the illness to run its course. The plague forced Cortés to stall his plans to reenter the capital until his indigenous allies had weathered the disease. Some Tlaxcalans undoubtedly questioned their association with the Spaniards, who had not only intensified Native warfare but also introduced a deadly sickness. The arrival of Narváez's ships, however, demonstrated that the technologically superior Europeans would likely keep coming.

Spanish ships continued to arrive, bringing more men, horses, guns, swords, and armor to Mexico. Over the next several months Aztecs and Spaniards competed for Indian alliances throughout the valley. Malinche was critical to these negotiations, and Cortés's army was soon bolstered by thousands of indigenous warriors. Cortés, leaving little to chance, sent two ships to the Caribbean to buy additional war supplies with Mexican gold. Within months Indians witnessed ten Spanish ships arrive on the coast, each loaded with men and supplies to finish the job in Tenochtitlán.

Once Spanish forces were replenished and resupplied, more Indians offered assistance. Cortés set to work constructing a string of forts along his path to retake Tenochtitlán. With the help of Indian craftsmen, the conquistadors built small boats to navigate the causeways leading into the city. Only months after Noche Triste, Cortés was ready to reenter the capital city. The battle proved difficult and lasted far longer than the Spaniards expected, given the Indians' recent experience with smallpox. Cortés reported that after ninety days of fighting, Aztec warriors asked to speak with Malinche.[13] She negotiated for hours, but the two sides were at an impasse. The Spaniards demanded complete capitulation, but the Aztec forces refused to lay down their weapons. The Indians continued fighting until there were simply not enough warriors left to fight. Moctezuma's brother finally surrendered on August 13, 1521. The Aztec Empire was finally defeated.

An obvious explanation for Spanish victory was their technological superiority. Guns, canons, steel blades, armor, crossbows, horses, and ships (to bring a steady supply of reinforcements and provisions) gave the invaders an undeniable advantage over Native peoples, despite the Indians' numerical advantage.[14] Devastating disease also proved advantageous to the conquerors. The Native death toll must have tested the Mesoamericans' faith in their ability to survive this latest foreign incursion. The conquest, however, was not a one-sided conflict. Several aspects of Mesoamerican religion and culture influenced how Natives interpreted events and the ultimate outcome.

Across cultures, divination has always been a strategy for discovering hidden knowledge through supernatural means. Nahua peoples, like many others, believed in prophecies and made confident choices when faced with difficult decisions by using prophetic understanding. As the ancient Olmec calendar inscription illustrates, a central belief among Mesoamericans involved the organization of the universe into cycles of creation, destruction, and re-creation.[15] The earthly demonstration of this natural sequence was the rise and fall of civilizations. The Aztec calendar also represented this cyclical worldview. At the time of Spanish arrival, Aztecs believed themselves to be living in the fifth world, or the "fifth sun."[16] They anticipated that the fifth sun would also be destroyed and re-created. There was rising animosity toward Aztec oppression and perhaps an eagerness to see its destruction. According to Nahua informants in the mid-sixteenth century, a complex set of beliefs surrounding the god Quetzalcoatl also influenced the outcome of the Spanish conquest.

It has been established that the Mexicas derived much of their culture from the Toltecs, whom they considered earthly fathers of all learning, and that Quetzalcoatl was a central Toltec deity. Mexica mythology explained that the decline of Toltec civilization began when Quetzalcoatl was driven from the capital city of Tula in the 1300s. After the fall of Tenochtitlán, sixteenth-century Native historians described a prophecy in which Quetzalcoatl had promised to return and reclaim his lost empire. Anthropologist Susan Gillespi persuasively argues that these Indian informants created the prophecy after the fact in an attempt to make sense of the Spanish victory.[17] While it is true that no tangible proof of Quetzalcoatl's prophesized return has surfaced in preconquest codices, Aztec peoples (as they always had) looked to Toltec mythology to explain their world.

Quetzalcoatl's prophesized return was described to Fray Bernardino Sahagún during his ethnographic investigation in the village of Tlatelolco (in Mexico City) and also to Fray Diego Durán as he worked among the Indians in Oaxtepec (south of Mexico City) in the late sixteenth century. The Nahua informants explained that Quetzalcoatl had promised to return from the east in the form of a light-skinned, bearded man, in the calendar sign equivalent to the year 1519. When Moctezuma heard of Cortés's arrival, he and his religious counselors considered whether this newcomer could be the human embodiment of the ancient deity and if the epoch of the fifth sun was destined for destruction at the whim of Quetzalcoatl.[18] According to the Mesoamerican historians who analyzed the Spanish conquest, the prophecy explained why Moctezuma had failed to take immediate decisive action to repel the Spanish invaders. If postconquest Nahua informants explained Cortés's arrival in terms of a Toltec past, it seems plausible that the Nahua people in 1519 may also have understood Cortés's arrival in terms of a Toltec past. Given that Mesoamericans viewed history in terms of cyclical events, they likely witnessed the fall of the Aztec Empire according to their own religious understanding, a preordained destiny of destruction and rebirth.

Multiple primary records (both Spanish and Native) indicate that Mesoamericans routinely referred to the invaders as *teotl* (or *teto* in plural form). Teotl is difficult to translate; Spaniards recorded its meaning as "god," "saint," and sometimes "demon." It is important to consider that Mesoamericans had a pantheon of divinities (male and female, good and evil). Each altepetl (Indian group) chose which deities to emphasize and how much reverence was due them. The term teotl was also used in connection with a human representation of a deity and to explain the mysterious or powerful.[19] According to Díaz, the initial meeting between Cortés and Moctezuma confirmed that the Indians had been expecting a great upheaval, initiated by gods, arriving from the east. Díaz recalled Moctezuma's speech: "He ended by saying that we must truly be the men about whom his ancestors had long ago prophesized, saying that they would come from the direction of the sunrise to rule over these lands."[20]

Colonizing Spaniards reveled in their identification with a Native deity. They recognized Quetzalcoatl as the supreme deity among Mesoamericans, and Huitzilopochtli (the Mexica god of war) was identified as the polar opposite, or the devil. As we will see in chapter 5, colonial Spaniards worked to synchronize adaptable pieces of Native religion with Christianity. They therefore advanced the myth that Cortés was the embodiment of Quetzalcoatl who had come back to reclaim his kingdom because it helped facilitate Spanish dominance. Teto was a nebulous Nahuatl word and an even more complex indigenous ideology. There were many Native deities capable of extreme cruelty or generosity. However, the Spanish attack on Cholula likely instilled doubts that Cortés was the reincarnation of Quetzalcoatl, particularly after he ordered the destruction of all Cholulan religious idols. During and after the conquest, there must have been Meso-americans who believed that Cortés was the reembodiment of the ancient deity, some of whom believed he came back angry, and others who believed Cortés had nothing to do with Quetzalcoatl.

Regardless of whether Mesoamericans associated Cortés's arrival with the return of Quetzalcoatl and the destruction of the fifth sun, Moctezuma had not been immobilized by this fear. Like most leaders, Moctezuma had pursued multiple (and at times conflicting) strate-gies to protect his rule. He had dispatched spies to monitor Span-iards' movement through tribute-paying towns. He had also attempted to sabotage Cortés's progress on several occasions, particularly in Cholula as the conquistadors neared his capital. Moctezuma had sent emissaries to offer Cortés gifts and to extend an invitation to visit Tenochtitlán.[21] The invitation may have been a ruse to get Span-ish forces to willingly enter the military headquarters of the Aztec Empire, where tens of thousands of warriors could be mobilized in an instant. Moctezuma had cautiously and strategically manipulated circumstances in an attempt to maintain his rule.

Toltec mythology influenced how Natives experienced the con-quest. Native pictorial manuscripts and calendrical records demon-strate several mythological and cosmological associations with Spanish arrival, evoking an undeniable parallel with Mexica ideology. Like the Mexicas, Spaniards arrived from a distant and mysterious location, both groups were intruders in a land already occupied by others, and both had a war strategy of conquest and empire building. The Spaniards came from the east, a direction associated with authority among Mesoamericans. The year 1519 held cosmological significance and was associated with the year of Quetzalcoatl's banishment from Tula. While the Aztecs were definitely in the process of expanding their empire in 1519, Cortés's arrival was likely seen in an ominous light and as the beginning of a new cycle. Just as the Mexicas had a century earlier, the Spaniards moved into the Valley of Mexico and established roots among the ruins of previous civilizations, borrow-ing and blending cultural elements to legitimize their ascendance. The Mexica had adopted and adapted Huitzilopochtli (the Toltec god of war) to explain and expand their dominance over the valley, and the Spaniards adopted and adapted Quetzalcoatl (the Toltec creator god) to advance their empire. It is important to accept Indian mythology and analysis of the conquest as an expression of indigenous cultural understanding. Native spiritual and cultural legacies remain relevant to modern Mexico. Anthropologist and cultural theorist Manuel Gamio suggests that modern Mexico was more Indian than Mexican in his famous 1916 book, *Forjando Patria* (discussed in chapter 5).

James Lockhart, the foremost expert on Nahuatl language texts, offers an analysis of the expressive modes and group consciousness demonstrated in indigenous accounts of the conquest from the colonial era. He suggests that both sides of the cultural divide had enough social and cultural similarities to allow them "to operate on an ultimately false, but in practice workable, presumption that the other side's analogous concepts were identical to their own."[22] This "Double Mistaken Identity," as Lockhart terms it, permitted the preservation of indigenous structures. He further argues that Nahua peoples continued to be self-centered in judging and explaining events according to the experiences of their local ethnic states. Meso-americans took from the Spaniards anything that was useful to their purposes, continuing a process of cultural layering that has a long tradition in Mexico. Lockhart respects indigenous autonomy of thought, and his analysis enriches the following discussions of initial contact between Algonquian groups and the English, as well as the peoples of the Northwest and the Corps of Discovery.

Tidewater Virginia

The first documented accounts of European contact with Powhatan people occurred in 1559. A Spanish exploratory party kidnapped an adolescent Indian male who was taken to Spain and christened Don Luis de Valasco.[23] He later returned with eight Jesuits to establish a mission among the Algonquian Indians in 1570, when Chief Pow-hatan was a child. Don Luis escaped after only a few nights back in his homeland and informed his countrymen of Spanish intentions in Tsenacommacah. The Jesuits, without their Native benefactor, were soon in dire straights. Don Luis implored them to flee, but the Jesuits refused and were eventually killed. It was not long before a

Spanish punitive force ended the lives of many Powhatan warriors.[24] The Indians learned from this early encounter that Europeans expected Indians to capitulate, and that they were willing to wreak vengeance when thwarted.

Thirty-six years later, in 1606, three small English ships pushed off from the mouth of the Thames River for an eight-month voyage across the Atlantic. The *Susan Constant,* the *Godspeed,* and the *Discovery* set out with just over one hundred adventurers. Their excursion was an entrepreneurial venture organized and financed by a joint stock company in London, the Virginia Company, which obtained authorization from King James. Its business plan was to acquire profits from gold, silver, or any other riches that could be extracted from the landscape. In the process, the Virginia Company was to establish an English foothold along the coastline of the Atlantic as a counterweight to Spain's colonial presence in the South. The company also hoped to locate a water route from the Atlantic Ocean to the Pacific Ocean in order to facilitate trade with Asian markets. In addition to these profit-oriented goals, the company charter stipulated that colonists attempt to convert Natives to Christianity. This benevolent goal was not necessarily a priority, but more of a strategy to deter Indians from impeding colonial commerce. The English settlers were unaware that they were fulfilling a Powhatan prophecy that foretold a catastrophic transformation to Tsenacommacah.

In the early 1600s a Powhatan prophecy had warned of great change coming to the Native world. One of the English adventurers, William Strachey, recorded the existence of the prophecy in 1612: "There be at this tyme certayne Prophesies afoote amongst the people enhabiting about vs. . . . Not long synce yt was that his Priests told him, how that from the Chesapeack Bay a Nation should arise, which should dissolue and giue end to his Empier. . . . Some of the Inhabitants againe, haue not spared to giue vs to vnderstand, how they haue a second Prophesy likewise amongsest them, that twice they should giue overthrowe and dishearten the Attempters, and such Straungers as should envade their Territoryies, or laboure to settell a plantation amongst them, but the third tyme they themselues should fall into their Subjection and vnder their Conquest."[25] Prior to the establishment of Jamestown, the Algonquian Indians had already witnessed two European attempts at colonization, the Jesuits' excursion in 1570 and an English attempt on the Island of Roanoke in 1585. The third incursion, this time by the Virginia Company in 1607, was destined to fulfill the prophecy and bring cataclysmic change.

The Powhatan people had already experienced the feats of European technology and weaponry as well as European attitudes of cultural superiority. Therefore Chief Powhatan knew he must be cautious in his approach to these strangers from across the water. The first Englishman he met was Captain John Smith. On December 29, 1607, Captain Smith, an experienced soldier and bold explorer, wandered far from the Jamestown settlement. He was captured by warriors and taken on a six-week tour of the Powhatan Confederacy. Eventually he was brought before Chief Powhatan to be either executed or adopted. This important decision was discussed at a large conference held in the great house, the most impressive ceremonial structure in Tsenacommacah. The building stretched more than two hundred feet in length and fifty feet in width. When Smith arrived, there were hundreds of Native dignitaries seated on rows of benches. The center of the congregation was dominated by a huge fire, in which fistfuls of tobacco were thrown as an offering to ensure the holy presence of the manito (the great spirit).

Smith's account of this event describes Chief Powhatan sitting atop a throne of neatly stacked mats, which raised him above his followers. He was lavishly dressed in animal skins and pearls. Women were present and involved during this important decision. Two elaborately dressed wives sat on either side of the chief. A council of men sat on mats that lined both sides of the fire. Behind them sat many young women attired differently from the rest, finely decorated with pearls over their shoulders, and their heads painted red.[26] Smith had no way of knowing why these young women, including Pocahontas, were differentiated from other female attendees.[27] Smith was initially greeted with what seemed to be pleasing comments. He was offered food while the council spoke with Chief Powhatan. Smith became concerned when two large stones were brought in and he found himself being forcibly stretched out across them as clubs were raised above his head. According to Smith, Pocahontas suddenly rushed to lay her body across his, forcing his executioners to release him. She pulled Smith to his feet as the chief gave a long speech in Algonquian. Smith did not understand the chief's words but realized

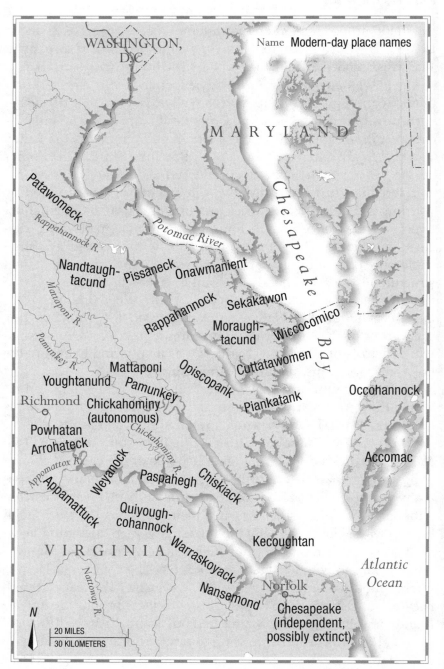

Powhatan villages in 1607. Original map from Native Voices, U.S. National Library of Medicine; redrawn by Carol Zuber-Mallison. Copyright © 2015 by The University of Oklahoma Press, Norman. All rights reserved.

from his demeanor that they would be friends and that he would be allowed to return to Jamestown.

Pueblo Indian scholar Paula Gunn Allen suggests that the ritual Smith experienced was part of a Powhatan rebirth ceremony known as *Nikomis,* in which Smith was reborn as a member of the Powhatan alliance.[28] Nikomis was not celebrated annually; it was an event signaled by a specific astrological constellation. The configuration of the stars and planets indicated that the Powhatan world was on the brink of massive change, and the ceremony was an observance to signify that the Powhatan people were ready for the transformation of their world. According to Allen, although Pocahontas was young and female, the group acknowledged her decision to save Smith. When she spared him, she made herself accountable for his membership in the Powhatan Confederacy and accepted responsibility for his indoctrination. Chief Powhatan designated Smith a *weroance* (a subchieftain over his followers in Jamestown) within the Powhatan Confederacy. Pocahontas and Chief Powhatan had assessed Smith's character and potential and decided he was a better ally than an enemy.

During the great feast of Nikomis a sacred transformation had taken place. The English and the Powhatans had become connected. The selection of Smith for adoption was not an act of love at first sight by Pocahontas, as he later rationalized. In the context of Native circumstances, Smith's rebirth initiated a new Powhatan epoch; the English had been brought into the Powhatan Confederacy. But Smith did not understand his adoption as a weroance or the significance of the Nikomis ceremony. What he did understand was that Chief Powhatan had spared his life and valued him as an English representative for future interactions. Like Pocahontas, Smith was expected to act as a go-between. Pocahontas was instrumental in the establishment of this interactive relationship between the English and the Powhatans, and she had an obligation to facilitate that bond. She did this by frequently visiting Jamestown, bringing porters carrying baskets of food, and interacting playfully with colonists.

Despite Smith's relationship with Chief Powhatan and Pocahontas, early colonists struggled to survive in the Virginia wilderness. To the English immigrants who arrived in 1607, farming was grueling peasant work, and fishing and hunting were recreational activities to be enjoyed for short periods of time. Most of the early settlers were urban-oriented Englishmen who came to seek their fortunes in the New World. They were ill prepared to toil in the fields, or to stalk and chase wildlife through the Virginia woods as a way of life. They had neither the energy nor the skills to procure their own food, and their aversion to manual labor stifled any initial progress.[29] The settlers expected Indians to provide them with food in exchange for English goods and protection against traditional enemies. The English had been aware of Cortés's conquest over the Aztecs and Pizarro's conquest over the Incas, and they expected similar success and similar rewards in Virginia. But the indigenous social landscape of Virginia was vastly different from what earlier explorers had encountered in Mexico. Algonquian Indians did not live in a strict hierarchal caste system in a sprawling urban region. They did not need protection from an oppressive empire with intolerable tribute requirements and human sacrifice. The Powhatan Indians were certainly enticed by English trade goods and were quick to realize the Englishmen's inability to provide for themselves. The Indians' early generosity had established a pattern of English dependency. Once English demands became unreasonable, Chief Powhatan instructed his weroances to deny English requests for food.[30]

The first settlers struggled to survive in the Powhatans' land of plenty. The foreigners were unwilling to venture into the countryside to procure their own food or search for profitable resources, as those efforts risked confrontation with numerically superior Indians. Jamestown was a vulnerable minority enclave within the Powhatan Confederacy. Even life inside the colonial compound was contentious due to colonists' sickness, frustration, extreme hunger, and constant bickering. The kind of wealth Spanish conquistadors had found in Tenochtitlán and Cusco was absent in Tsenacommacah. Typhoid and dysentery plagued the English community. Both maladies were uncomfortable and deadly consequences of their site selection in the marsh of the James River. Conditions in Jamestown were dire as the first winter approached. To add to their difficulties, the settlers lacked sufficient supplies from England. Virginia Company officials had sent exaggerated reports to their investors in England to ensure continued support; unfortunately such reports made desperately needed provisions seem unnecessary.

Ships bringing more colonists—but inadequate supplies—kept arriving to the impoverished colony. Chief Powhatan took advantage of the settlers' vulnerability. He instructed his weroances to exchange Indian food only for English weapons. But the colonists were unwilling to trade weapons for food, making negotiations increasingly difficult. Cross-cultural trade continued nonetheless; neither Chief Powhatan nor his weroances were able to prevent individual Indians from exchanging food for other fanciful items. Within a year of English arrival, Indian food was being stretched too thin. The Indians' supplies were inadequate to meet the demands of the English, their tributary requirements, and their own subsistence, particularly during dry seasons. Tensions in Tsenacommacah intensified as the Indians weighed the value of European trade goods against their loyalty to the Powhatan Confederacy.

To compound the English predicament, colonists stored their supply of corn carelessly. They lost all they had painstakingly accumulated to mildew and infestation. Stowaway rats, their traveling companions on the voyage from England, devoured what had not been ruined by dampness.[31] The starving English became more bellicose in their demands and resorted to theft when trade negotiations failed. The Indians responded with hostility and violence.

Chief Powhatan sent word to Smith that he was willing to provide food only in exchange for swords.[32] Smith refused the offer. Powhatan then instructed warriors to begin a systematic effort to obtain English weapons through theft, ambush, or force. Smith, who understood the Indians better than anyone in Jamestown after his six-week captivity and tour of the Confederacy, advised English officials to take firm punitive actions. The president and members of the council of the Virginia Company remained steadfast in their obedience to London officials. Their orders were clear: do not "offend or molest" the Indians.[33] So officials in Jamestown did nothing, and their passivity emboldened the Indian warriors.

When a group of Indians dared to disarm Smith, he gave them a good thrashing and took seven into custody at the fort in Jamestown. During the fracas two of Smith's men were captured. A formidable group of Indian warriors brought the two English hostages to the gates of Jamestown and demanded an exchange for the Indian warriors that Smith had taken. Smith emerged with his own force, armed and ready to fight. The Indians backed off and reported the incident to Chief Powhatan who sent Pocahontas to negotiate. She excused the warriors' behavior, asked Smith for forgiveness, and assured him that he was a friend of the Powhatan people. Smith made it clear that the prisoners would be spared and released only as a gesture to her and because of his great respect for Chief Powhatan.[34]

It was not long after this event that Smith was sworn in as president of the Virginia Company council in 1608. This marked a period of closer ties between Smith, Pocahontas, and Chief Powhatan. Smith immediately reorganized priorities at the fort. Construction that had been underway on what Smith considered an unnecessary presidential palace stopped, and construction of adequate storehouses began. He instituted military drills and twenty-four-hour, rotating guard duty. While these projects were underway, another ship from England reached the shores of Virginia. As usual, the ship brought more colonists, less-than-adequate supplies, and new instructions from London officials. One of the instructions was to persuade Chief Powhatan to become a subject of the English monarch by offering him gifts and a copper crown.[35] Powhatan accepted the English oddities with grace, but the gesture held little significance to him. It is likely that the chief left this ceremony as bewildered as Smith had left the Nikomis ceremony. Neither man was willing to be transformed. A second order from London instructed the colonists to load the returning ship with an export of possible value to show that the colony was prospering. Yet Native hostilities prevented colonists from conducting a comprehensive search for potential resources as they struggled to provide the basic necessities of life.

Smith was convinced that Chief Powhatan's strategy was to starve out the colony.[36] Chief Powhatan had forbid weroances to allow trade. Therefore Smith went up the Chickahominy River to seek trade with an enclave of Indians who remained outside the Powhatan Confederacy, and he was partially successful. In spite of Smith's leadership, the colonists were hungry, sick, and losing hope. Smith suggested attacking the Indians and seizing their supply of food, but he could not convince the council. They remained faithful to their belief in divine favor and obedient to London's instructions to not antagonize the Indians. So Smith went to Chief Powhatan, declaring his friendship and imploring him to provide food. Powhatan agreed to give corn in exchange for several of Smith's men who would remain in the Indian village to build a house in the English style of construction.[37] Smith agreed to Powhatan's terms.

The carpenters sent to Powhatan's village were Dutchmen who had been brought to Virginia as laborers. While they began making preparations for the chief's new residence, Indians loaded Smith's barge with the corn. However, the craft was unable to depart after being caught in an ebb tide, and the Englishmen were forced to spend an anxious night near the Indian village. Late that night Pocahontas slipped into Smith's camp to warn him of impending danger. With "tears streaming down her cheeks," she advised him to leave immediately, and then she vanished into the night.[38] The year was 1609, and Pocahontas was thirteen or fourteen years old. This was their last meeting in Virginia.

When Smith's barge was finally freed, he decided to continue upstream in an attempt to trade with the nearby Indian village of Opechancanough. This action was risky, considering Native hostility, but it was Smith's only plan to keep the colony fed. While Smith was away on this trading expedition, Chief Powhatan summoned the two Dutchmen. He instructed them to return to the fort and inform the "captain in charge" that Smith needed additional arms and tools. Captain Winne fell for the Dutchmen's ruse and turned over what was asked for. While Indian porters loaded weapons and supplies, the Dutchmen recruited a few more malcontents who would defect at a later time, bringing more supplies to Powhatan.[39] This was Chief Powhatan's shrewd attempt to reconfigure European alliances to his benefit.

One likely explanation for the Dutchmen's disloyalty was their second-class status among the English colonists, who considered them savages from the forests of central Europe. They had been brought to Virginia to serve as woodsmen and glassblowers.[40] Among the Indians, whose language was only slightly less understandable to them than English, they had adequate food and were treated fairly.

In fact, Jamestown had descended into such dire straits that the Dutchmen convinced a few others to defect. In the meantime, Smith ran into trouble on his trade mission and resorted to taking corn from Opechancanough without negotiating. Upon his escape Smith came across a fellow colonist, Richard Wiffin, who told him of a tragedy that had taken place in his absence. The acting president and eight other colonists had lost their lives when their boat was overturned by a storm. Wiffin then told Smith that he had come looking for him through Chief Powhatan's village, but Smith had already pressed on. According to Smith's narrative of events, Chief Powhatan had ordered Wiffin killed, but Pocahontas helped him escape by hiding him and leading the would-be assassins in the wrong direction.[41]

Throughout 1608 and 1609 the colony continued to struggle. Hungry colonists fought with each other while they faced mounting Indian hostility outside the fort. Several ships, however, brought more colonists to Jamestown during the summer of 1609. Just as Chief Powhatan was gaining confidence that the English would soon perish from starvation, their population increased to five hundred, and they needed more land. In the midst of increased tensions, Smith set out to negotiate a purchase of nearby Indian land. He managed to coerce a weroance named Parahunt into selling, and the English called the new territory Noursuch.[42] But the additional land failed to alleviate dissension among the Englishmen. Smith suffered a near-fatal injury while trying to maintain peace between English residents and their new Indian neighbors. His injuries were so severe that he was put aboard a ship en route to England, where he could receive adequate medical attention. Rumors of his death circulated in Indian country.

After Smith's departure, conditions deteriorated for both Indians and colonists. A sustained drought curtailed Indian agricultural production, and the winter of 1610 was brutal. Starvation was rampant in Jamestown; only sixty of the five hundred colonists survived. English sea captain Samuel Argall reached Jamestown with supplies just in time to prevent the colonists from abandoning the settlement altogether.[43] Had he been delayed by even a few days, it is likely that Jamestown would have followed Roanoke into oblivion. Samuel Argall had visited Jamestown the previous year and had truthfully informed London officials of conditions. It was painfully clear after the winter of 1610 that the colonists could not depend on the Indians for food. The English colonists were forced to start providing for themselves. They began dispatching regular expeditions to Bermuda for food and supplies. By 1612 the colony was revived, and the tide turned against the Indians.

Chief Powhatan watched patiently as the colonists nearly starved to death, and just when he thought he would be rid of them, more ships arrived brining more Europeans to Tsenacommacah. Not only were their numbers replenished, but the English were also circumventing the Indians and providing their own food. The Indian chief issued an order to his weroances to not allow any trade and to assault all boats and stragglers found outside the fort. The English responded by demanding the return of all weapons and tools that had been stolen since the founding of Jamestown and further threatened to bring war upon the Indians if they failed to refrain from all acts of hostility. In reply, Chief Powhatan warned the English to depart his country at once or be confined to Jamestown by force.

Hostile negotiations were often followed by violence. Indian assaults and mischief were met with harsh punitive reprisals. The colonists began a course of systematically raiding Indian storehouses, depleting their food reserves, and burning their crops. This shortsighted vengeance exacerbated the food shortage in Virginia. Winter, and the annual return of starvation, was approaching. Argall revived Smith's practice of undertaking trade voyages among remote groups, but hostilities and dwindling supplies prevented any gains.[44] The English decided that a hostage might convince Chief Powhatan to be more accommodating, and Pocahontas seemed the perfect choice.

Three years had elapsed since Smith's departure, and three years had passed since Pocahontas had visited Jamestown. During that time she had married and was living among the Potomacs, the most remote of Powhatan's tributary subjects, with whom the English had traded in the past. Yet the marriage of Pocahontas to a Potomac warrior had deepened the Potomac's commitment to the Powhatan Confederacy. The weroance in charge, Iapassus, was initially unwilling to hand her over to the English, but he relented when Argall promised English military support in the event of Powhatan's revenge. Iapassus and his wife devised a plan to trick Pocahontas into escorting a group of curious Potomacs onto an English ship.[45] As we will see in the following chapter, her subsequent captivity and marriage to John Rolfe reestablished her obligation to mediate a peaceful coexistence.

Unlike the Spaniards in Mexico, who saw immediate monetary potential and some similarity in the urban hierarchal organization of the Aztec Empire, the English were rather unimpressed with the Powhatans.[46] The stunning indigenous wealth and plumb stone architecture found in Mexico and Peru made Powhatan civilization seem primitive in comparison. Powhatan people did not live in a dynamic urban setting, but in small villages composed of huts made from forest materials.[47] Their huts were perfectly suited for the climate of Virginia, but they provided the Englishmen with a negative first impression. The English assumed that the Powhatans lacked wealth, a cultural aesthetic, and ambition. The Indians were equally unimpressed with the Englishmen's inability to provide for themselves. The colonists of Jamestown and the members of the Powhatan Confederacy ultimately saw little value in forming a lasting bond.

NORTH AMERICAN WEST

At the time of Sacagawea's birth, around 1788, Euro-Americans had only recently landed on the lower northwest coast. They knew of the Rocky Mountains but had not traversed them. The United States was still in its infancy: thirteen loosely confederated states along the Atlantic with no claim west of the Mississippi. Indians in western North America, including Sacagawea's people, had endured intermittent dealings with Europeans for more than a century before the arrival of Lewis and Clark. The British and French had been exploiting resources of the Northwest since the Hudson's Bay Company and the North West Company had begun operations in the 1670s and 1770s, respectively,[48] and the Spanish had been exploring northern Mexico since the 1540s. Euro-Americans were the last foreigners to arrive, and their entrance altered the international dynamic in the West. Once again indigenous groups assessed the newcomers, negotiated trade deals and alliances, weathered deadly epidemics, and readjusted their plans for the future.

The Lewis and Clark expedition was a realization of President Jefferson's dream of American expansion across the continent. The books in his library reveal he was an armchair explorer who read extensively on early New World excursions made by Portugal, Spain, and the English, with a particular interest in the vibrant fur trade of the Northwest. Jefferson began his elaborate plan to explore the wilderness northwest of the Missouri River well before his presidency and before the Louisiana Purchase had been officially recognized in 1803. This fifteen-million-dollar purchase had secured America's ownership of a vast tract of land (some 828,000 square miles) that extended to what is now the southwest border of Montana. The expedition was to travel beyond the limits of this newly acquired territory to search for a water route to the Pacific Ocean and to delicately inform Native people of the land's new ownership. On November 4, 1804, the path of American expansion collided with the various indigenous peoples who lived in the Mandan and Hidatsa villages.

The expedition, under the aegis of the Corps of Discovery, was a well-organized entourage armed with extensive knowledge and the latest technological instruments, although the travelers had a peculiar mission from an Indian perspective. All previous invaders had come in search of commodities, typically precious metals and furs. Jefferson's instructions to the corps emphasized maintaining intertribal peace, spreading American sovereignty, gathering topographical information, collecting ethnological data, and inventorying resources. This was puzzling to Native people, and Lewis and Clark had difficulty explaining their motives to them. As latecomers to the territory, the corps intended to avoid earning a reputation as greedy exploiters out for conquest and profit. Nevertheless, the Northwest fur trade was a primary concern because, potential financial gain aside, long-standing alliances between Indians and French and English traders were a threat to U.S. sovereignty.

While the Euro-Americans were preparing for their departure in St. Louis, Lewis and Clark engaged in conversations with experienced frontiersmen, Manuel Lisa, Antoine Soulard, the Chouteau brothers, and James Mackay, in an attempt to prepare themselves for Native customs in Northwest trade. Lewis and Clark were advised to be wary of the Teton Sioux, who had a reputation for harassing traders, pilfering merchandise, and demanding gifts from all who entered the plains.[49] They were forewarned that the Tetons exerted violent control over river trade traffic. They were accustomed to trading their highly valued beaver pelts to the North West Company (headquartered in Montreal) for European goods, and then controlling all Native access to them. After the Louisiana Purchase the goals of the expedition were to diminish French and English influence among the Indians, reorient indigenous trade, and funnel profits toward St. Louis. The captains hoped to accomplish these goals either by luring the Sioux into an American economic orbit or by organizing plains village groups in opposition to the powerful Sioux. This proved a difficult, if not unworkable, diplomatic strategy.

When the Corps of Discovery encountered a Sioux blockade on September 25, 1804, they offered the Brulés gifts as an invitation to negotiations. The Indians reciprocated with several hundred pounds of buffalo meat. Talks proceeded after the required hospitality was shown, but a communication problem hampered progress. Tensions escalated until the meeting disintegrated into an "insolent" exchange.[50] The captains set up camp along the Bad River in a misplaced hope to improve relations with the Brulés and discuss intertribal rivalries on the plains. Building intertribal relations that were productive to American interests was a cornerstone of Jefferson's Indian policy. The Plains groups, however, were baffled by Lewis and Clark's diplomatic meddling in Indian country. Thus, the captains failed in their first diplomatic effort among the Sioux. This early unsettling encounter led the captains to press on and pursue an alliance among the Mandan and Hidatsa village groups.

The expedition resumed progress up the Missouri River in late September and encountered the Arikaras, who referred to themselves as the Star-rah-he.[51] They lived in earth-lodge villages surrounded by fields of corn, beans, and squash. As in many other Indian societies, including the Powhatans, Arikara women tended to agricultural duties. The men of the expedition were not accustomed to seeing women involved in agricultural labor and frequently characterized village women as overworked "squaw drudges" who were virtual slaves to tyrannical and lazy husbands.[52] The men of the expedition enjoyed relaxed hospitality among the Arikaras, especially after their tense stay among the Sioux. Here the expedition learned to tolerate the persistent curiosity of Indian visitors.

Lewis and Clark once again tried to present themselves as diplomatic specialists who wanted to facilitate intertribal peace. Already convinced that the Tetons were violent oppressors, Lewis and Clark assumed the Arikaras were helpless victims of Sioux aggression. Yet the Arikaras didn't see it that way; they saw the nomadic Sioux tribes as a steady source of manufactured goods and a reliable market for their agricultural goods. The Arikara-Sioux relationship was a complex one in which there were occasional hostilities but also significant cooperation in trade dealings. Lewis and Clark were a potential disruption to this connection. They spoke of intertribal peace while simultaneously exacerbating tensions between village and nomadic groups on the plains. The Arikaras were gracious but cautious.[53] They provided agricultural goods and hospitality during Lewis and Clark's stay and offered information on the plains landscape and its people.

As the fall days grew colder, the expedition pushed on to establish winter quarters among the Mandan and Hidatsa villages, which were an important meeting ground for plains trade. It had long been a vibrant environment, particularly in late summer and fall when nomadic groups such as the Crows, Assiniboins, Cheyennes, Kiowas, and Arapahos arrived with their wares. White traders representing the North West Company and the Hudson's Bay Company, and (later) St. Louis increasingly entered the mix as the century turned. By 1800 the Mandan and Hidatsa villages had become the center of Plains commerce. In the fall of 1804 the expedition witnessed diverse people involved in a variety of economic endeavors. It was imperative that Lewis and Clark make a good impression and demonstrate their diplomatic expertise in this international enviornment.[54] As the Mandan and Hidatsa Indians got their first long look at the Euro-Americans, they tried to decipher their agenda on the plains. These were unlike any other white men the Indians had met; they were explorers, ethnographers, and bureaucrats who represented a great father in the East. Village Indians, who were accustomed to outsiders and adept at cultural tolerance for the purpose of trade, were accommodating.

Charbonneau had first arrived along the Knife River in 1797 as a free trader with connections to the North West Company.[55] He developed a rudimentary form of sign language and forged strategic connections (both business and intimate) with Plains groups by

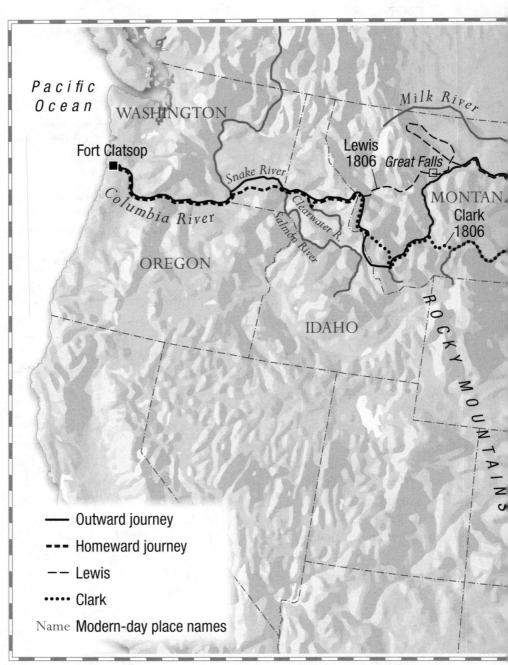

Lewis and Clark's journey. Original map from National Geographic Education; redrawn by Carol Zuber-Mallison. Copyright © 2015 by The University of Oklahoma Press, Norman. All rights reserved.

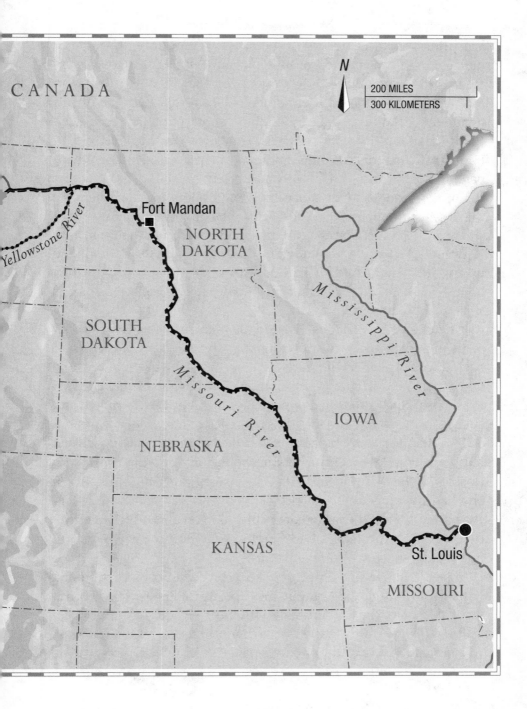

accepting Indian wives. Marital politics were routine throughout much of indigenous America, and polygamy was particularly advantageous to the horse-and-hide economy on the plains. Charbonneau took advantage of the Native tradition of kinship alliances and Native gender expectations.[56] Like his Indian counterparts, he recognized the value of multiple Native wives. They provided access to Indian trade, facilitated trusted communication, and processed hides. Indians benefited from these cross-cultural unions as well, gaining access to European goods and insider knowledge about the foreigners. By the time Charbonneau met the Corps of Discovery, he had two Shoshone wives, a fact that the captains made note of in their journals. We know that Sacagawea ended up among the Hidatsas after being taken captive as a child.[57] Charbonneau's other Shoshone wife may have had a similar experience; unfortunately almost nothing is known about her.

When Lewis and Clark arrived in the Mandan villages in October of 1804, Sacagawea was approximately sixteen years old. She had been Charbonneau's wife for two years and she was pregnant. She was experienced in cultural accommodation, having already adapted to Hidatsa expectations in a dynamic multicultural environment and later learning to tolerate the idiosyncrasies of her French husband. She was familiar with a broad stretch of the Northwest, having walked hundreds of miles east from her Shoshone homeland in the northern Rockies to the Mandan and Hidatsa villages along the Knife River. She had developed subsistence skills over a vast landscape. And she had mastered the art of communication on a multilingual frontier. Her life experiences had taught her to accept change and to tolerate diverse people and customs.

In late October, the Corps of Discovery began construction of a winter fort among the Mandan and Hidatsa villages. Throughout that cold winter the captains met with Indian leaders and European traders to gather information regarding the course of the river, the weather patterns, and the mountain passes that lay to the west. Lewis and Clark sought information regarding a possible water route to the Pacific and inquired about the Native peoples they would encounter as they made their westward journey. From these consultations the captains learned that the Lemhi Shoshones were considered the horse specialists of the northern Rockies.

On November 4, Captain Clark wrote in his journal: "A French-Canadian, Toussaint Charbonneau, visits the two explorers. He wants to hire on as an interpreter and guide. Although he has two Shoshoni Indian wives, the explorers engage Charbonneau and one of his wives who would be needed to interpret the Shoshoni language when the explorers entered that territory."[58] Evidence indicates that Sacagawea was generous and forthcoming in her dealings with strangers. Like Malinche, Sacagawea was immediately deemed special. It is likely that Sacagawea actively participated in the exchange of information that occurred between the captains, the Frenchman, and the Indians during that winter along the Missouri River. There was no further mention of Charbonneau's other wife, which leads to some interesting questions. Was she less skilled in communication? Was she distrustful of the Americans? Perhaps the other Shoshoni wife chose to appear disinterested and remained aloof. Sacagawea was extraordinary in her willingness and skill. Her potential, like Malinche's, was immediately noticed during this critical moment of initial contact.

Captain Lewis recorded the delivery of Sacagawea's son on February 11. A month later Charbonneau threatened to leave the expedition. On March 11 Captain Clark wrote, "A problem arises between the explorers and Charbonneau. Charbonneau may back out and leave the expedition, taking Sacajawea with him."[59] The discipline of traveling with an army unit such as the Corps of Discovery may have worried Charbonneau. It is also possible that Charbonneau was uncomfortable with the captains' attentiveness toward Sacagawea, particularly during childbirth. Clark, the medic on the trip, had overseen the delivery. This must have seemed strange to Sacagawea as well, but it was clearly the beginning of a lasting bond between Sacagawea's family and Clark, who later raised and educated the child after the expedition.

The captains were concerned when Charbonneau balked at the opportunity, but not necessarily because they needed him. In fact, most of their commentary on Charbonneau was unflattering. Rather, Lewis and Clark worried about losing Sacagawea's services. They knew she could be valuable when the party reached the territory of the "Snake Indians" (the Lemhi Shoshones). The Americans needed to obtain horses from the Lemhis to portage over the mountains en route to the Pacific. The captains gave Charbonneau the night to make his choice, and he quit the expedition the next day. Evidently Charbonneau was betting that the captains would give in to his demand that he be free from the corps's military regulations. As a foreign trader in Indian country, he understood the benefit of a Native woman's involvement in cross-cultural negotiations. He must have recognized that the expedition needed Sacagawea to ease interactions and interpret among the Shoshones. On March 12, 1805, Captain Clark wrote in his journal: "Charbonneau decides to quit the expedition. He does not like the prospect of having to stand guard duty. He does not want to be told which personal items he will be allowed to take. If he didn't like any man, he wanted to be free to quit. Charbonneau's demands are unreasonable, and because the agreement made was verbal, he is free to leave."[60] Two days later Charbonneau and his family moved out of the fort but remained close by, most likely waiting for the captains to reconsider. The corps continued preparations as the weather warmed and the ice on the river began to give way. Charbonneau became anxious and sent word that he would agree to obey orders if he could rejoin the expedition. Three weeks before the expedition departed, the captains reemployed Charbonneau. Sacagawea's services were part of the deal. The restoration of Charbonneau's employment demonstrated how much the captains wanted Sacagawea. Their journals consistently reveal distaste for Charbonneau, whom they characterized as an incompetent, uncivilized "squaw man" (a European degraded by his intimate relations with Indian women).

To some commentators, the decision to take Sacagawea and her infant son seemed an unlikely choice. Yet the Lewis and Clark expedition was well conceived, partly because they had studied previous New World expeditions. The captains were aware of Malinche's usefulness to Cortés through the writings of Cortés, Gómara (his biographer), and Díaz. They certainly knew of Pocahontas, and they understood Indian women's significance to the Northwest fur trade.

Lewis and Clark may have been eager to find a sympathetic Native woman who could demonstrate their peaceful intentions, communicate information, and guide the explorers through Indian country. The two captains took Sacagawea because she was a Lemhi Shoshone and she could be helpful in negotiations with that nation. She was also familiar with several Indian languages and the mountainous terrain they would be traveling through.

After Charbonneau agreed to rejoin the expedition, he and Sacagawea immediately began working as interpreters. The couple was first recognized in their official capacity on April 7, 1805, when the expedition departed the Mandan villages. On that day Clark listed the entire membership of the party, including "Shabonah and his Indian Squaw to act as interpreter and interpretess for the Snake Indians."[61] This entry offered explicit evidence of the captain's expectation for Sacagawea. However, she was not the only—or even the main—interpreter for the expedition. Lewis and Clark had left St. Louis with a Frenchman named Drouillard who was a specialist in Indian sign language. He was listed as the official interpreter of the expedition, yet his skills were often inadequate. Although Sacagawea was not paid for her services as Drouillard and Charbonneau were, Sacagawea was a valuable interpreter, guide, and cultural adviser, as the next chapter will discuss.

As the expedition approached the mountains, their journal entries reveal the captains' logic in taking Sacagawea and her infant son. Lewis and Clark knew that when they entered Lemhi territory, Sacagawea would be an asset. Success of the mission depended on penetrating the mountains, finding the Shoshone horse specialists, and then convincing the reclusive Indians to provide the necessary animals. Lewis's journal entry dated June 16, 1805, illustrates Sacagawea's importance: "About 2 P.M. I reached the camp found the Indian woman extremely ill and much reduced by her indisposition. This gave me some concern, as well as for the poor object herself, then with a yung child in her arms, as from her condition of being our only dependence for a friendly negotiation with the Snake Indians, on whom we depend for horses to assist us in our portage from the Missouri to the Columbia River."[62] Her recovery was imperative, and Clark tried a number of drastic (if not gruesome) remedies to improve her condition. For ten consecutive days (June 10–20, 1805) the status of Sacagawea's condition was recorded. Her sickness was the captains' foremost concern, and her recovery was a great relief.

After Sacagawea's illness, the expedition entered the mountainous segment of the journey in late July, and the captains increasingly recorded her usefulness. Lewis wrote on July 22, 1805, that Sacagawea recognized landmarks in her homeland: "She assures us that this is the river on which her relations live, and that the three forks are at no great distance."[63] When this information was passed on to the men of the expedition, they erupted in jubilation. They had been carrying their essentials on foot, and the soles of their shoes had been shredded by rocks and cactuses.

On Sunday, July 28, 1805, the party reached the three-forks area at the headwaters of the Missouri River. They were getting close to Sacagawea's people. On that day Lewis relayed the story of Sacagawea's capture by the Hidatsas and indicated that she showed no enthusiasm for a reunion with her lost relations.[64] The next week, Sacagawea informed the captains that they were in the area where her people camped during summer months in preparation for buffalo hunts. On August 8 she informed the captains that they could "either find her people on this river or on the river immediately west of its source; which from its present size cannot be very distant."[65] With this information Captain Lewis broke off from the main party and went in search of the Lemhis with only a few men.

Sacagawea's detractors have emphasized the fact that she did not accompany Lewis when he first approached the party of "Snake" Shoshones. Yet in an effort to entice the elusive and skeptical Indians to follow him, Lewis informed the chief, through Drouillard's sign language, that they had a woman traveling with them who was a Lemhi Shoshone. Lewis recorded his attempt to motivate the Lemhi party to accompany him to the location where Sacagawea and Clark were camped with the rest of the expedition. On August 16, 1805, he wrote, "I had mentioned to the chief [Cameahwait] several times that we had with us a woman of his nation who had been taken prisoner by the Minnetares and that by means of her I hoped to explain myself more fully than I could do by signs."[66] Lewis was clearly relying on Sacagawea to be a cultural intermediary. Drouillard, the official interpreter, was incapable of providing that level of understanding. That sensitive and vital skill went beyond the mere translation of words.

As Lewis and his Shoshone acquaintances approached the explorers' camp, Sacagawea did what she knew her people would understand. She deliberately displayed evidence that she was one of them by sucking her fingers, a sign they immediately understood.[67] It was soon discovered that her brother, Cameahwait, had risen to chief in her absence. This royal connection, by non-Indian reckoning, would later be important to the construction of her legend. But at that moment, Sacagawea was overcome by emotion. Negotiations proved too difficult and had to be postponed until after Sacagawea had been reacquainted with her people.

Diplomatic discussions were also hampered by the condition of the corps and the similar condition of the Shoshone party. Both groups had had difficulty hunting scarce game, and hunger was a pressing concern. The captains quickly realized that they had to relieve this problem before friendly negotiations could commence. Several joint hunting trips were attempted before meat was brought back for feasting. This cooperative activity was a brilliant tactic on the part of the captains. Not only had they returned the chief's long-lost sister, they shared the hardships of hunger, participated in a successful collaborative endeavor, and then joined the Lemhis in feasting. The Shoshones and the Euro-Americans embarked on an extremely productive start to a rewarding cross-cultural relationship. Once bellies were full and Sacagawea had regained her composure following an emotional reunion with the people of her youth, the captains were able to convince Cameahwait to sell horses to the expedition. This was accomplished through Sacagawea's mediation.

On this occasion, among her people, Sacagawea proved her loyalty to the Americans with whom she had been traveling. She overheard Cameahwait's plan to take the promised horses on a buffalo hunt rather than deliver the animals as planned. She immediately told Charbonneau, but he was slow to inform the captains. Captain Lewis recorded the near catastrophe on August 25, 1805:

> Charbono mentioned to me with apparent unconcern that he expected to meet all the Indians from the camp on the Columbia tomarrow on their way to the Missouri. Allarmed at this information I asked why he expected

to meet them. He then informed me that the 1st chief [Cameahwait] had dispatched some of his young men this morning to this camp requesting the Indians to meet them tomarrow and that himself and those with him would go on with them down the Missouri, and consequently leave me and my baggage on the mountain. I was out of patience with the folly of Charbono who had not sufficient sagacity to see the consequences which would inevitably flow from such a movement of Indians, and altho' he had been in possession of this information since early in the morning when it had been communicated to him by his Indian woman, yet never mentioned it until afternoon.[68]

Sacagawea was the only person in the expedition who understood Shoshone and the only one who could have informed them that the deal was in jeopardy. This act revealed Sacagawea's commitment to the expedition and to her role as an intermediary. Despite Charbonneau's lack of concern, Lewis was able to intervene and prevent his party from being stranded in the mountains without horses. Lewis did not emphasize the expedition's dire need for Shoshone horses. Instead he stressed to Cameahwait that keeping his word was vital to future trade with the United States. It is not difficult to imagine that Cameahwait envisioned a future in which the Lemhis would finally have direct access to European goods. Like Malinche's alleged espionage in Cholula and Pocahontas's warning to Smith in 1609, Sacagawea had an opportunity to abandon her intermediary mission and leave the foreigners vulnerable. All three women chose to protect the European men and ensure their survival in Indian country.

Plains Indians of the American Northwest, Algonquian peoples in Virginia, and Mesoamericans in Central Mexico tried to make the most of European arrival. They built alliances through Indian women and tried to manipulate the Europeans' entrance to benefit their own agenda. Like indigenous peoples, Europeans were also motivated by material goals and national priorities. Cultural exchanges followed a unique course according to regional conditions and left distinct legacies for the future of Mexico and the United States.

Early Europeans tried to accommodate Native customs and manipulate intertribal relations in order to benefit their cause. Conquistadors found the hierarchical social structure and religious centered life among the Mesoamericans to be surprisingly similar to their own. Nahua peoples lived in crowded urban centers that were connected to outlying communities. The Spaniards marveled at the impressive stone and wood construction that decorated the urban spaces, occasionally suggesting that the architecture in Mexico was superior to their own. Díaz noted that the religious temples he encountered in Mexico were larger and higher than any cathedral in Spain. Conquistadors were astonished by the size and productivity of the suburban market outside Tenochtitlán, which they described as more expansive and diverse than any in Europe. Cortés, Díaz, and the early friars touted the highly cultured and ordered civilization that they brought under the Spanish crown, and they celebrated their efforts to bring salvation to the Indians and end Aztec barbaric oppression in Mexico.

There were fewer similarities in North America and less cross-cultural exchange and cooperation. Algonquian groups and English colonists did not battle together to bring down an oppressive Native empire. They did not endure war and sickness together like the Spaniards and their Indian allies had. Religion was less significant to the goals of the English and Euro-Americans. The Spanish had launched their quest for empire on the heels of a hard-won Catholic victory over Muslim Moors, and advancing Catholicism was an instrumental part of the Spanish agenda in Mexico. Fray Sahagún and Fray Durán were among the first wave of Spanish religious authorities to study indigenous religion. They looked for ways to make Catholicism applicable to the religious lives of Mesoamericans. There was no such synchronization of religious ideologies in North America. English colonists in Jamestown and the Corps of Discovery were less interested in learning or sharing religious doctrine (with the exception of Pocahontas, who was converted during her captivity).

Unlike the Spanish in Mexico, the English and Americans did not pursue long-term strategies to indoctrinate Indians into a new colonial society. Miscegenation was not considered an acceptable colonial strategy among the English or the Euro-Americans in the New

World. Algonquian peoples (with the exception Pocahontas) were never envisioned or portrayed as potential English citizens. Neither were Indians of the Northwest imagined as relevant actors in an American future. Early English and American filibusters in Indian country tended to view Native groups as obstacles, not as a potential laboring class. Compared to the extensive urban civilization in indigenous Mexico, Indian communities in the north had low population densities and fewer permanent villages, allowing more separation between the races. Indians and non-Indians in North America were more likely to maintain physical and ideological separation during initial contact and its immediate aftermath.

CHAPTER THREE

Malinche, Pocahontas, and Sacagawea as Cultural Intermediaries

When Indians and Europeans met in the Americas, forging and maintaining a productive relationship required cross-cultural communication and understanding. Indian women were routinely extended to
outsiders to facilitate interaction. Frontier men and women navigated
language barriers and cultural peculiarities in order to establish some
common ground. Successful female intermediaries exploited mutual
opportunities and maintained trusted relationships. European men
(conquistadors, adventurers, and explorers) were puzzled by women's
roles in Native societies, but they accepted these female agents because
they offered entrance into Native worlds.

Europeans left considerable evidence of the intermediary work
that Malinche, Pocahontas, and Sacagawea provided during initial
contact. Unfortunately, these sources tell us little about the women's
obligations to their Native communities and even less about the
women's personal goals. European accounts instead reveal the invaders'
cultural judgments; their biases have instilled lasting confusion and
misinformation about Indian women. Despite this frustrating reality,
we can look to these flawed records to itemize the work Malinche,
Pocahontas, and Sacagawea provided on multicultural frontiers. The
goal is to examine the European conquerors' descriptions of the women,
subtract European prejudice, and place the women's activities in a
Native context. What drove these women to behave as they did?

This chapter seeks to answer this question, exploring why these
women embraced foreigners and advanced their goals in Indian country. Malinche, Pocahontas, and Sacagawea were not smitten young

girls, enamored with non-Indian men and cultures. And they were not hapless feminine victims caught in a whirlwind of masculine aggression and adventure. They were a vital component of Indian diplomatic strategy, and they had an obligation to perform as intermediaries. These women were actively engaged in mediating a cultural exchange and softening the impact of colliding worlds. The previous chapters have shed light on the women's personal circumstances and their cultural worldviews: All three women were conditioned to expect the advent of a new world. Their status and value as Indian women depended on fulfilling culturally specific gender expectations. These women were deployed with an expectation that they would indoctrinate foreign men into indigenous social and economic systems.

The work Indian woman provided in Native societies was often characterized by incoming European men as onerous and barbaric. Yet when Malinche, Pocahontas, and Sacagawea provided similar service on behalf of European men, the three women were described as gracious, exceptional, and separate from their degraded "squaw" sisters. European men benefited from the women's obligation to engage and care for the outsiders. Their feminine responsibility to provide nourishment and comfort was familiar to the invaders, although the foreigners were culturally unprepared to understand the women's diplomatic role on a competitive multicultural frontier.

Incoming European men recognized a distinction between a masculine public sphere and a feminine private sphere. These dichotomous gender domains were irrelevant in Native societies that tended to define gender categories as a set of interactive and complimentary obligations. A second difference separating Native and non-Native gender ideology was that precontact Native gender structures were not hierarchal. Both the masculine and the feminine were capable of immense power in the natural world, the spiritual world, and in social organization. Both genders could exercise considerable influence and had intricate responsibilities in maintaining social order and spiritual balance. European men were unaccustomed to the power of the feminine in Native religions, societies, and sexual intercourse. Incoming non-Natives recognized the masculine as the dominant force in religion, society, and sex. These vast ideological gender differences had profound effects on initial contact and on European characterizations of indigenous peoples.

Malinche in the Middle

The previous chapter established that Spanish colonizers capitalized on Mesoamerican mythologies and furthered their ascendance over Mexico by endorsing the prophesized return of Quetzalcoatl. According to mid-sixteenth-century Nahua informants, the ancient Toltec deity had been expected to reappear and reclaim his kingdom by deposing the Toltec god of war, Huitzilopochtli (a patron god of the Mexicas). Native people associated Cortés with the return of the ancient deity in their prophecy for the downfall of the Aztec Empire, an explanation that the Spaniards endorsed. The anticipation of Quetzalcoatl's return was explained to three different Spaniards (Sahagún, Durán, and Díaz) at three different times in three different locations. Díaz describes Moctezuma's speech at their initial meeting in Tenochtitlán: "you must truly be the men about whom his ancestors had long ago prophesized, saying that they would come from the direction of the sunrise to rule over these lands."[1] It took Moctezuma time to decide on a course of action. He turned to Malinche for council and ultimately followed her advice as many other Native leaders had. But why would Moctezuma, who had his own cabinet of religious and military experts, consult with a young woman who lived among the Spanish?

There is record of a Mexica creation myth that might provide insight into Malinche's influence over indigenous dignitaries, including Moctezuma II. According to the Native histories recorded by Fray Diego Durán in the late sixteenth century, Moctezuma I (1440–1469) had dispatched an expedition to find the ancestral homeland of the Mexicas (Aztlán). The explorers returned with a mythical tale in which they had been turned into birds and flown to meet Huitzilopochtli's mother, who was still living in the mysterious land. She was angry that her son never returned to Aztlán. She was also irritated that Huitzilopochtli's descendants lived in such decadence in Tenochtitlán. She warned the emissaries that invaders would eventually expel Huitzilopochtli and conquer the Mexicas, just as they had relentlessly conquered others.[2]

This creation myth identified an ancient goddess named Malinalxóchitl, who was Huitzilopochtli's sister. She was described as a beautiful and cunning sorcerer. Malinalxóchitl had traveled with her brother during the Mexica migration from Aztlán in the 1300s until dissention split the group. The migrants had grown to distrust Malinalxóchitl's magic and convinced Huitzilpochtli to abandon his sister and her wizard followers. Half of the tribe left with Huitzilopochtli. Malinalxóchitl and her followers founded their own city and named it Malinalco (a city later conquered by the Mexicas under Moctezuma I in the fifteenth century that still stands). Hostilities between brother and sister continued, culminating in a series of battles between Huitzilopochtli and Malinalxóchitl's son, Copil. Copil was eventually defeated when Huitzilopochtli ripped out his nephew's beating heart and threw it into a great lake. As Copil's heart descended to the bottom, an island arose. Huitzilpochtli and his followers settled on the island and built their grand city of Tenochtitlán; thus began the Aztec Empire.[3]

Unlike Quetzalcoatl, who was studied extensively and celebrated by Spaniards, we know almost nothing of Malinalxóchitl. According to linguist Anna Lanyon, Franciscan evangelists ignored this central female deity because they were culturally unprepared to understand such a complicated and powerful female.[4] Yet the Nahua peoples would have known of the mythical goddess. Could Malinche have been understood in association with Malinalxóchitl's return to avenge her son's death and finally defeat Huitzilpochtli? Malinche's American Indian name was Malinalli, which is strikingly similar to Malinalxóchitl. Perhaps Indians associated Malinche with the return of Malinalxóchitl, as some associated Cortés with the return of Quetzalcoatl. Could this explain Malinche's influence with Moctezuma II and her remarkable success in persuading other Native leaders to join the Spanish in opposition to Aztec domination and human sacrifice?

The mythical story of Malinalxóchitl illustrates the power and influence of the feminine, and it also demonstrates the belief that male and female gods (including Quetzalcoatl and Malinalxóchitl) moved between the mystical and mundane worlds.[5] Both females,

Malinalxóchitl and Malinche, were instrumental in the creation of new societies. They led the departure from what had been and introduced what was to come. Could Malinche have felt a mystical connection to Malinalxóchitl? On whose authority was Malinche acting? The Spaniards or indigenous mythology? Could it be that Malinche (Malinalli) was named and trained for her life's work by a mystical force that that we do not understand but that she respected? Malinalxóchitl and Malinche were both feminine agents of change, and Mesoamericans may have recognized the similarities of these two influential females. Malinalxóchitl and Malinche were both significant to the rise and fall of Mexican civilizations, and each of their myths possessed themes of destruction, rebirth, exile, and disinheritance.[6]

Malinche inherited Mexico's dynamic cultural legacy and Nahua mythologies. Her Native worldview certainly influenced her choices. Her actions may have also been prompted by conditions in the Valley of Mexico: increasing Aztec tribute demands, punitive human sacrifice, and rising Native resentment. Malinche could have been driven by a spiritual connection to Malinalxóchitl or a personal sense of obligation to bring change. We can piece together only a few facts of Malinche's life, but it is clear that even her personal circumstances drove her to embrace change. Her lifetime coincided with dark times for Mesoamerican peoples. At the turn of the sixteenth century, the Aztec Empire was on a brutal path of military and economic expansion. The arrival of the Spaniards in 1519 intensified Native rivalries and introduced more deadly weapons. To compound the devastation and uncertainty, Nahua peoples dealt with unimaginable mortality rates from strange and deadly diseases that wiped out thousands of people in a matter of weeks. These harsh realities were taking place within an atmosphere of anticipated doom. The fifth sun was on the verge of collapse, which would pave the way for the emergence of a new cycle.

Malinche carved out a position of influence for herself when Tabascan officials offered her to Cortés. We know nothing about the other nineteen young women who were also given to the Spaniards. Did they offer minimal or ineffective intermediary skills? Were they suspicious of Spanish intentions? Did they decide to remain silent and irrelevant to a Spanish future in Mexico? Malinche made herself immediately noticeable and ultimately indispensable to negotiations during the conquest. Her personal life prepared her for this monumental moment. She was born the daughter of privileged parents within the Aztec Empire and received an elite education. She learned a painful lesson in humility after her mother and stepfather traded her to a Maya cacique from Xicalango. She was exchanged a second time to Tabascan merchants, who later offered her to the Spanish in 1519. Malinche reached womanhood in a vibrant multicultural atmosphere of negotiation and commerce. She was intelligent, highly educated, linguistically talented, acquainted with multiple indigenous perspectives, and aware of the rising hostility toward the Aztecs. She lived intimately with the Spaniards, learning their language, their religion, and their vision of the future. As the conquerors continued toward the Aztec seat of power in Tenochtitlán, she advised Cortés on diplomatic intricacies within the diverse and contentious empire. Malinche was well prepared to take an active role in mediation, and her actions demonstrated a consistent effort to minimize the violence and hardship that came with regime change.

Malinche's elite lineage, physical beauty, education, and language skills awarded her respect and status that other Indian women did not enjoy. She immediately took an active role in cross-cultural communication and proved her value as an indispensable intermediary. Malinche spent all of her time in the company of the most important conquistadors. Other indigenous women, who were perhaps less talented or less vital to the mission, were undoubtedly shared among the lower ranks of the Spanish military.[7] But from the beginning Malinche established herself as a valuable member of the Spanish expedition. Both Díaz and Cortés recorded that she always accompanied Cortés. The conquistadors must have been extraordinarily careful not to treat her harshly and jeopardize her continued loyalty and expertise.

Malinche may have felt a tremendous sense of responsibility and obligation, perhaps thinking of herself as the one chosen (by implicit forces) to facilitate the next cycle of civilization. It seems unlikely that she considered herself a slave (either Maya or Spanish). Moctezuma clearly considered her an authority during this time of difficult transition; he sought and ultimately followed her advice. Díaz describes her, saying, "Doña Marina was a person of the greatest importance who was capable of enormous influence among the Indians."[8] As we will see in chapter 5, Native historians also depicted Malinche as an instrumental dignitary in their pictorial explanations of the conquest in the mid-sixteenth century. She was typically portrayed in the center of the frame, giving a speech and commanding the attention of others. Díaz and Native historians portrayed Malinche as a woman of consequence and influence.

The Natives demonstrated respect for Malinche during the conquest as well. As previously noted, Indians referred to her as Malintzin, which was her Indian name, Malinalli, with the added suffix of "-tzin" to connote respect. Indians also referred to Cortés as Malintzin because his message came through her. As Díaz put it, "The reason why he received this name was that Doña Marina was always with him, especially when he was visited by ambassadors or caciques and she always spoke to them."[9] Regardless of how Cortés and Malinche were perceived by Mesoamericans—whether or not their arrival was associated with the earthly return of Quetzalcoatl and Malinal-xóchitl and the end of an epoch—together, the couple brought changes to the political and spiritual landscape of Mexico. Malinche was not merely a translator for Cortés; she was influential and persuasive. She was a strategic diplomat and a passionate evangelist. She served as a tactful negotiator, a cultural consultant, and a spiritual adviser. Spanish and Indian leaders alike relied on her input.

Cortés's trust in Malinche's skill is evident in his repeated reliance on her diplomatic and communication skills. Following a grueling battle in the city of Tlaxcala Cortés had the prisoners assembled to hear his speech, which came through Malinche. His post-battle speeches always contained two essential messages: that the Spanish could release them from Aztec oppression and that the Spanish could lead them toward divine favor and eternal salvation. He then released the prisoners to carry his message to their caciques. A few days later Tlaxcalan caciques approached the Spaniards for clarification. On this occasion Díaz characterized Malinche's evangelical skills: "Doña Marina and Aguilar were so practiced that they could explain it very clearly."[10] Malinche had perfected Cortés's message as they trekked inland toward Tenochtitlán. She explained and shaped Catholicism so that it was understandable and applicable to Indian lives. She and Aguilar likely capitalized on the Spaniards' reputation as teto. The Tlaxcalans were cautiously willing to consider religious instruction in exchange for a Spanish alliance in opposition to their traditional enemies in Cholula and Tenochtitlán. The conquistadors left Tlaxcala with a thousand warriors and then pressed on toward Cholula. Cholulan caciques sought out Malinche as the entourage approached to ask why the Spaniards, who claimed to come in peace, approached their city with Tlaxcalan warriors. Malinche immediately informed Cortes, who asked the Tlaxcalan warriors to halt and wait on the outskirts of Cholula until his return. According to Díaz, Malinche's skilled translation often derailed violence and saved the Spaniards and Indians from further injury.[11] Negotiations ultimately failed in Cholula, however, and it was Malinche's warning that supposedly instigated the Spanish attack on the city. Malinche was deeply involved in diplomacy and also in strategizing when diplomacy proved unsuccessful.

During the final battle for Tenochtitlán, Aztec officials asked for Malinche. She tried desperately to convince Aztec authorities that the Spaniards could not be defeated a second time in Tenochtitlán. She had witnessed a convoy of Spanish ships delivering military supplies and men to the conquistadors as they recuperated in Tlaxcala after La Noche Triste. She had also witnessed the impact of the Spanish supply line on surrounding indigenous leaders. Thousands of Native warriors provided aid to Cortés's reconquest of the Aztec capital in April 1521. Spanish and Native records indicate that Malinche routinely summarized events for Indian listeners, offering her own testimony on Spanish military power as well as their religious and political intentions in Mexico.

Her role as an intermediary was a diplomatic position, and she was seen as a sensitive and trustworthy authority on both sides of the conflict. It is unknowable how much her religious conversion influenced her decisions, but she was certainly among the first indigenous evangelists in Mexico. The Spaniards relied on her and Aguilar to explain the Christian faith to potential Indian allies. As a skilled and persuasive orator, Malinche convinced thousands of apprehensive Natives to believe in Spanish promises of liberation and salvation. Malinche was a double agent; her cultural explanations informed opposing factions as each decided on a course of action. She explained, for example, why Aztec tribute collectors were greeted with fear and animosity in the communities that hosted Spanish forces. Cortés was able to take advantage of long-standing Native rivalries through her astute cultural insights. Her savvy diplomacy allowed Cortés to enlarge his army as he inched his way across Mexico toward his target in Tenochtitlán. She, perhaps more than anyone, understood both sides of the divide. She understood Native hostilities and mythologies as well as Spanish capacity and intentions. It is difficult to imagine the stress of her job as an intermediary, trying to mitigate violence and ease the coming of a new order.

Malinche's loyalty to the Spaniards was later interpreted as a rejection of her Indianness. There is consistent evidence, however, that Malinche acted with concern for her indigenous countrymen. The most persuasive example came years after the Spanish victory in Tenochtitlán, when Malinche had the opportunity to address her Indian family who had rejected her as a child. By 1524 Cortés was ready to expand Spanish domain, and his entourage set out to conquer Honduras. Along the way, the party stayed in Coatzacoalcos, the town of Malinche's birth and the place she was forced to leave as a child when her mother sold her to Maya merchants. In accordance with Cortés's proven campaign strategy, he summoned the caciques of the province to hear his speech. Among the assembled caciques were Malinche's mother and half brother. Both wept in fear of her revenge. Díaz describes Malinche's reunion with her relatives: "When Doña Marina saw her mother and half brother in tears, she comforted them, saying that they need have no fear. She told her mother that when they had handed her over to the men from Xicalango, they had not known what they were doing. She pardoned the old woman, and gave them many golden jewels and some clothes. She sent them back to their town, saying that God had been very gracious to her in freeing her from the worship of idols and making her a Christian, and giving her a son by her lord and master Cortés, also in marrying her to such a gentleman as her husband Juan Jaramillo. . . . She would rather serve her husband and Cortés than anything else in the world."[12]

Díaz's description of the event was certainly a reflection of his Christian Spanish perspective, and it is unclear how much Nahuatl Díaz understood. Yet he witnessed tension, tears, and the calming effect of Malinche's words on her family. He also may have asked Malinche about the dramatic scene later, as the Spaniards continued on their southern course. If this passage accurately represents the event, even partially, it reveals Malinche's commitment to both sides. She treated those who had sold her as a child with compassion and explained her satisfaction among the Spanish. The scene describes Malinche as graciously forgiving her mother and brother, while assuring them that her fate with the Spaniards had been rewarding. She offered herself as proof of the contentment gained through accepting Christianity and a Spanish future. It is interesting to ponder the fear that her relations felt. Were they fearful because Malinche was now a powerful woman of significance, no longer the defenseless child they had discarded?

Díaz's eyewitness account suggests that Malinche remained committed to her role as an intermediary. She attempted to engage her mother and half brother (both Indian officials) in a discussion of Catholicism and the coming civilization. Once again, she translated Cortés's message, shaping the information to make it applicable to Indian understanding. She embraced changes the Spaniards brought (Catholicism, the expulsion of human sacrifice, and the end of Aztec oppression), yet she attempted to soften the blow to Indian peoples. Her loyalty to the Spaniards was not a vindictive rejection of her people but a commitment to their future. Had Malinche lived to see the legacy of her work, perhaps she would have felt regret or remorse, but during the conquest she was young, passionate, and driven in her mission to facilitate a new civilization in Mexico.

In less than one and a half years the small Spanish force had traversed unfamiliar rugged terrain occupied by Native hostility, and ultimately captured the Aztec capital of Tenochtitlán. The early battles in the area of Tabasco provided Cortés with two advantages that influenced the outcome of his conquest. The first was a successful campaign strategy that engaged Indian allies as he marched inland. Once the Indians were convinced of Spanish military supremacy, he released prisoners with gifts and a message of peace and salvation. The second advantage was Malinche. She gave voice and meaning to the conqueror's grand plan. Through Malinche, Cortés was able to communicate two essential messages to the Indians: that the Spaniards could release them from the harsh rule of the Aztecs and that Spanish supremacy was inevitable because of their divine favor.

POCAHONTAS IN THE MIDDLE

Pocahontas reached womanhood during a pivotal moment for the Powhatan people. The Nikomis ceremony in the winter of 1607 indicated that the Powhatan people were ready to embark on a sacred transformation of their world. From a Powhatan perspective, Smith's rebirth as a weroance signified the group's acceptance of a new reality that included the English. Smith was unaware that his arrival was interpreted according to a prophecy that foretold a third, and ultimately successful, foreign invasion. He did not understand his adoption or the significance of the Nikomis ceremony. He did appreciate his release, and he understood that Chief Powhatan valued him as an English representative in future interactions. Like Pocahontas, Smith was expected to act as a go-between to facilitate a cooperative future. Pocahontas was instrumental in establishing this new relationship. When she rushed forward to spare Smith from execution, she made herself responsible for his adoption into Tsenacommacah.

Why did Pocahontas rush forward to claim Smith? She left no account of the rescue scene, and Smith's egocentric explanation seems unlikely. He was oblivious to Powhatan women's capacity to decide on a captive's fate, and this time the decision was extraordinarily important. The prophecy, the arrival of the English, Smith's captivity, and the astrological event of the Nikomis all indicated that dramatic change was coming. The verdict on Smith would impact the new direction of the Powhatan people. Pocahontas and Chief Powhatan ultimately decided not to begin their new future with an act of violence.

Native scholar Paula Gunn Allen enters the nebulous world of Powhatan mythology and oral tradition to provide a mystical explanation of the Powhatan worldview. She begins by describing a creation story in which Sky Woman fell to Turtle Island (earth) and formed the Powhatan world. Thus Powhatan life descended from the feminine, according to Allen.[13] She describes Smith's rescue during the feast of Nikomis as part of a Powhatan renewal ceremony to recognize that the prophecy had commenced and the group was ready for the rebirth of the Powhatan world.[14]

She describes Pocahontas as a Beloved Woman, a feminine spiritual order in the tradition of Sky Woman.[15] According to Allen, Pocahontas was identified as exceptional from an early age (six or seven years old) and chosen to begin training for the spiritual responsibilities of a Beloved Woman.[16] She had to have been a particularly gifted child to be selected for this religious instruction. Only after she completed significant training could she have become a member of this elite category of Powhatan women. Her distinction as a gifted and skilled Beloved Woman was evident in her significant role during the Nikomis ceremony. Smith's description of his rescue includes mention of two rows of young women, "all their heads and shoulders painted red; many of their heads bedecked with the white downe of Birds . . . and a great chayne of white beads about their necks."[17] Allen's ethnographic research indicates that these young women, including Pocahontas, were Beloved Women.

As a Beloved Woman Pocahontas was believed to have the capacity to read the signs of the natural world: wind, clouds, geological formations, ocean tides, streams, storms, stars, forests, birds' flight pattern. Her honed talents also endowed her with the ability to interpret the currents of spiritual forces and human interaction. She had a unique gift (both natural and refined) that enabled her to listen on a level others were incapable of.[18] Allen describes a Pocahontas that had extraordinary insight into the forces of nature, the mystical world, and human interaction. She could access and process information from multiple worlds. This gave Pocahontas a broad understanding that her community respected.

Early European observers were ill prepared to understand the power of the feminine in the Powhatan spiritual world. Pocahontas and her people, however, respected the talents of a Beloved Woman. When she saved Smith, the Powhatan people acknowledged Pocahontas's spiritual gifts and her training as a Beloved Woman. They considered her capable of making this important assessment and trusted her decision to adopt Smith as part of the Powhatan Confederacy.[19]

From Pocahontas's perspective, she had assumed the responsibility of facilitating the bond between her people and the newcomers. Pocahontas's commitment was not limited to Smith but extended to the rest of the colonists, just as Malinche's commitment extended beyond Cortés. These women were working on behalf of a mutually productive international relationship. Smith notes, "Now once in foure or fiue dayes, Pocahontas with her attendants, brought him so much provision, that saved many of their lives, that els for all this had starved with hunger."[20] Pocahontas brought the colonists food when they were starving, she negotiated disputes to spare bloodshed, and she offered warnings before violence erupted. It is, however, plausible that Pocahontas genuinely liked Smith. He reported being cheerful with Indian children during trade, always offering them trinkets of delight, and she was a prepubescent girl when she met Smith.

Smith (like Cortés) was an experienced frontiersman and soldier of fortune. His globe-trotting experiences taught him to deal delicately with strangers in foreign lands, according to the particulars of the situation. Over the course of his stay in Virginia, Smith interacted with the Powhatan Indians as a captive, as a trader, and as an enforcer; each situation called for a different demeanor. He reportedly used intimidation and force selectively, preferring to charm Indians into trade. He was known to conduct trade pleasantly and fairly, unless someone tried to cheat him. Smith was the only Jamestown resident who consistently returned from trading missions with supplies.[21] During his negotiations in Indian villages, he likely exhibited frustration over the slothfulness of his fellow countrymen; he repeatedly expressed this irritation in his memoirs. Cultural intermediaries have the ability to recognize foibles within their own cultures, to read the signs of human interaction, and to demonstrate the appropriate posture in a racially diverse environment. The behavior of Smith and Pocahontas demonstrated this cultural sensitivity, and the two often approached each other with a posture of accommodation and friendship.

Pocahontas interjected with peace and friendship during another tense moment of potential brutality, according to Smith. When the Indians insisted that English weapons were the only acceptable payment for Indian food, both sides increasingly resorted to theft and violence to obtain goods that were being withheld. In May of 1608, Smith and his men had a hostile exchange with a formidable band of warriors intent on disarming the Englishmen, resulting in a melee in which both sides took captives. Chief Powhatan sent "his messengers and his dearest daughter Pocahontas to excuse him of the injuries done by his subjects; desiring their liberties, with the assurance of his love."[22] Smith made it clear that the prisoners would be spared and released as a gesture to her and because of his great respect for her father.

The following year Pocahontas again interrupted hostility and bloodshed during Smith's trading mission in the chief's village. Smith and Chief Powhatan negotiated a deal that exchanged Indian food for carpenters, but this was part of the Chiefs elaborate ruse to trick the colonists into delivering weapons and tools to the Indian village. Smith recorded in his account, "For Pocahontas his dearest jewel and daughter, in that darke night came through the irksome woods, and told our captaine great cheare would be sent us by and by: but Powhatan and all the power he could make, would after come kill us all, if they that brought it could not kill us with our owne weapons when we were at supper. Therefore if we would live, shee wished us presently bee gone. Such things as shee delighted in, he would have given her: but with tears running downe her cheeks, she said shee durst not be seene to have any: for if Powhatan should know it, shee were but dead, and so shee ranne away by her selfe as she came."[23] It is intriguing to consider Pocahontas's tears. Had she become emotionally invested in Smith and feared for his safety? Did she consider herself a failed intermediary, a disappointment to her community and to her training as a Beloved Woman? Perhaps her sadness was a manifestation of multilayered disappointments and self-doubt.

After Smith's injury and his presumed death, Pocahontas's attention turned toward her marriage to a Potomac warrior. The Potomacs were the most remote of Powhatan's tributary subjects. Members of the community had traded with the English in the past, even after Chief Powhatan instructed an end to all trade with the insolent colonists. Yet Pocahontas's marriage deepened the alliance between the Potomacs and the Powhatans. When Captain Argall appeared seeking trade in 1612, and proposed taking Pocahontas as a strategic captive to force Chief Powhatan into a more accommodating position, the weroance agreed only after Argall promised that Pocahontas would not be harmed and offered an assurance of English support in the event of Powhatan's revenge.[24]

By 1612 the English had begun to turn the tide and were finally in a position to offer military defense to indigenous groups. Some scholars argue that Pocahontas was betrayed by her own people, cast off to foreigners much as Malinche and Sacagawea had been. Whether it was a betrayal or not, these women were likely offered to outsiders because they had specific skills or experience in cultural mediation. They were part of a diplomatic strategy to calm tensions, facilitate interactions, and build strategic alliances during a time of uncertainty.

After her capture, Argall informed Pocahontas that she was being held as ransom for eight Englishmen and the return of stolen goods. He also assured her that she was his noble guest and that she would be treated as a princess, not as a prisoner. The English then sent a message to Chief Powhatan explaining that Pocahontas was safe and being treated with kindness. They indicated that she would continue to receive this kind treatment as long as Powhatan dealt fairly with the English.[25] The chief did not reply for three months, but ultimately returned seven prisoners and some disabled muskets. He also promised five hundred bushels of corn and his eternal friendship upon Pocahontas's return. But Argall considered Powhatan's gesture to be partial payment and refused to release Pocahontas.

Pocahontas's imprisonment lasted nearly twelve months. Among the English she resumed her work as a cultural intermediary; older and wiser, she was in a better position to study the colonists and rebuild goodwill between the Powhatans and the English. She was held in the care of Reverend Alexander Whitaker, who instructed her in Christianity and baptized her as Rebecca. Her renewed responsibility as an intermediary, her isolation and vulnerability inside Jamestown, and her desire for continued fair treatment led her to be receptive. She may have intended to study Christianity to understand how it served the colonists, and more importantly, whether it might be adaptable to the lives of the Powhatan people as they made their way through the great transformation. Pocahontas was immersed in English life, learning the language, customs, culture, religion, economic goals, social organization, and gender expectations. She absorbed it all; she was baptized as a Christian, became an English "lady," married an Englishman, and gave birth to his son. Ultimately, Pocahontas traveled to England as a representative of both the Powhatan people and the Jamestown colony. At the time of her death (at age twenty-two) she was a successful and respected double agent, facilitating cooperation and pursuing the interests of both sides.

According to English observations, Pocahontas was not an unwilling captive in Jamestown.[26] There is no way of knowing whether her compliant behavior was genuine, whether it was contrived in order to gather information, or whether she was merely trying to survive her captivity. The English described a great love between John Rolfe and Pocahontas which led to their wedding in 1614, approximately a year after her abduction. Their marriage may or may not have been a romantic one, but it was certainly a strategic union; through it Rolfe gained a wife and access to Powhatan land. Chief Powhatan gave the couple a generous stretch of land as a wedding gift. Rolfe also gained access to Pocahontas's agricultural expertise. With the success of Rolfe's tobacco plantation, the English finally discovered a profitable export. Pocahontas was crucial to her husband's entrepreneurial success, and his status in the Virginia Company steadily increased. He had married an "Indian princess," eased Indian hostilities (at least for the moment), and produced a profitable Virginia commodity at long last. Pocahontas also benefited from the union: she was no longer a captive. She was a mature and respected intermediary who was privy to insider information about the English. She had a second chance to build intercultural peace and cooperation. Her marriage to Rolfe, and the birth of their son, Thomas, provided a more stable connection that bound the English and the Powhatans in a common future. Both sides of the cultural divide sanctioned their marriage, which established a period of relative peace.[27]

Many of today's Powhatan Indians do not believe that the union between Pocahontas and Rolfe was based on love. In the late 1990s Chief Roy Crazy Horse of the Powhatan Renape Nation addressed the romanticized English interpretation of Pocahontas's captivity, saying, "In 1612, at the age of 17, Pocahontas was treacherously taken prisoner by the English while she was on a social visit, and was held hostage at Jamestown for over a year. During her captivity, a 28-year-old widower named John Rolfe took a 'special interest' in the attractive young prisoner. As a condition of her release, she agreed to marry Rolfe."[28] Whether readers choose to believe the English tale of a great love that united Pocahontas and Rolfe or Chief Roy Crazy Horse's description of their marriage as a condition of Pocahontas's release, one fact is undeniable: their union de-escalated hostilities.

While Pocahontas and Rolfe were setting up their plantation estate and refining their crop of tobacco, financiers and publicists in London were scrambling to come up with a new angle to keep the Virginia project afloat. After Smith's return to England in 1609, the terrible winter of 1610, and the more realistic reports offered by Captain Smith, Captain Argall, and Secretary Strachey, investors in London turned skeptical and money began to dry up. The Virginia Company was, after all, a commercial endeavor, and stockholders expected a return on their investment. By 1611 the company was seen as a shaky New World venture, one that had yet to produce a profit and had failed in its mission to establish a successful English colony that could rival Spanish Florida.

When word made its way across the ocean that the English had achieved their first Indian convert to Christianity, the Virginia Company decided to capitalize on a marketing opportunity. Catholic Spain touted exaggerated success in Christianizing American Indians in an attempt to deflect the condemnation that the Black Legend had created. Pocahontas's religious conversion was England's chance to appear holy in its colonizing mission. This colonial success story was even more tantalizing because England's convert was the daughter of an Indian chief. She was characterized as an "Indian princess," she loved and married an Englishman, gave birth to his son, spoke English, and appeared poised and gracious as she toured London.

Virginia Company officials arranged to bring Lady Rebecca to London in 1616 to illustrate England's noble pursuit in the New World. She was the toast of the town and was entertained by the city's most influential citizens. On these occasions she was elaborately dressed in fine European fashion and seen at the swankiest affairs in the city. The Virginia Company also arranged for Lady Rebecca to be received by the Queen and to sit for a formal portrait to commemorate the Indian princess.[29] Pocahontas's quiet dignity complemented her European costume as she mingled among London's elite. Pocahontas must have realized that the princess-like impression she made on the English worked to her benefit. She had her own agenda in London as she consorted with England's most powerful and wealthy citizens: royalty, clergy, and aristocracy. She traveled to England as a diplomatic, economic, and spiritual agent, representing both Virginia colonists and Powhatan people.

The English ship en route to London in 1616 carried valuable Virginia tobacco, a promising colonial entrepreneur, his Indian princess wife, and their infant son. Their arrival in London was intended to demonstrate the potential of Jamestown. As Pocahontas rode the wind and sea aboard the *Treasurer,* she no doubt participated in the discussions on how to best represent the colony and showcase the opportunities in Virginia. She likely understood the importance of making a good impression in the English capital. Since Pocahontas was characterized as an important royal ambassador of a great indigenous nation, she required a group of twenty Indian attendants. Her Indian entourage consisted of priests and priestesses who were also on a fact-seeking mission. Pocahontas and her Indian compatriots acknowledged that their world was undergoing transformation, and they sought any information that might help Tsenacommacah. The entertainment (plays, orchestras, and galas), religious services, and great feasts that Pocahontas attended in London must have seemed like ceremonies of great significance.

Whatever information Pocahontas gained in England, she did not take home to Tsenacommacah. She was unable to complete her mission because she died at the start of their return voyage in 1616. The following year Chief Powhatan died. His brother, Opechanca-nough, replaced him and Powhatan-English relations rapidly deterio-rated.[30] Tsenacommacah was left without the guidance of Pocahontas, Chief Powhatan, or John Smith, the three figures who were bound together in 1607. Chief Opechancanough proved less tolerant of the English. Tensions continued to rise, particularly when the colonists hit hard times, made demands, and violated agreements. The Pow-hatans responded with violence, but by 1620 their numbers had been greatly reduced by European disease.

According to Chief Roy Crazy Horse, compulsory education man-dated by the English finally brought about a major violent confron-tation in the 1620s.[31] The "Powhatan Uprising" began when Indians attacked the English on March 22, 1622; they burned schools and unleashed full-scale war. A truce was not reached until 1632. In 1644, under Opechancanough's leadership, the Indians rose up again in retaliation against the rapid dispossession of their land as colonists expanded tobacco plantations upriver. In 1646 several Powhatan groups signed a series of treaties that established them as autono-mous tributary tribes. Distrust and suspicion erupted in war again in 1654. Through the remaining decades of the century, disease, dis-possession, and warfare decimated the Powhatan people, forcing them to disperse and move inland as a tactic of survival. Yet they sur-vived; in 1983 Powhatan descendants gained official recognition as the Powhatan Renape Nation.[32]

Sacagawea in the Middle

Late in the eighteenth century, Hidatsa warriors captured an adoles-cent Lemhi Shoshone girl. This traumatic experience set in motion a chain of events that would take the young girl on an arduous physical and cultural journey that lasted the duration of her short life. She lived with her captors for several years before she was offered as a wife to Toussaint Charbonneau. Sacagawea's marriage to Charbonneau was a strategic decision for both her Hidatsa family and Charbonneau. The cross-cultural union cultivated diplomatic, intimate, and economic bonds on an increasingly competitive frontier. The couple acted as intermediaries, facilitating communication, trust, and trade. The job required extraordinary tolerance and extended travel away from home. It was grueling work, but successful intermediaries were rewarded. Charbonneau increased his inventory and established himself as an expert in Indian country with those he worked for: the North West Company, Manuel Lisa, and the U.S. government. Sacagawea also benefited; her marriage and intermediary work offered her the chance to exercise her feminine influence and to garner respect. She was no longer a captive child, but an adult woman working in service to her community. Like Malinche and Pocahontas, Sacagawea excelled in an international environment that was swirling with change.

By the time Lewis and Clark arrived at the Mandan villages in 1804, Charbonneau had already established himself as a familiar and trusted visitor among the Indians. He had been in the area for seven years and had acquired two Indian wives, Sacagawea and one mysterious other. We don't know if Sacagawea had an opportunity to refuse Charbonneau as a husband or whether she willingly embarked on a life among foreigners. Eyewitness accounts suggest she was gracious in her approach to strangers. According to Captain Lewis, Sacagawea was a contented soul. On Sunday, July 28, 1805, the Corps of Discovery reached the headwaters of the Missouri River and was getting close to Sacagawea's Shoshone tribe. After knowing Sacagawea for nearly nine months, Lewis described her: "Our present camp is precisely on the spot that the Snake Indians were encamped at the time the Minnetares of the Knife River first came in sight of them 5 years since. From hence they retreated about 3 miles up the Jefferson River and concealed themselves in the woods, the minnetares pursued, attacked them, killed 4 men a number of boys and made prisoners of all the females and 4 boys. Sah-cah-gar-we-ah or Indian woman was one of the female prisoners taken at that time;

tho' I cannot discover that she shews any immotion of sorrow in recollecting this event, or of joy in being again restored to her native country; if she has enough to eat and a few trinkets to wear I believe she would be perfectly content anywhere."[33] This character description suggests that she harbored no resentment, although weeks later she was overcome by emotion during the reunion with her Shoshone relations. Her experience as an adopted captive sculpted her public demeanor and her intermediary work. She had learned to accept change, to accommodate new cultural expectations, and to make herself useful to those around her. This was a strategy that ensured survival and social acceptance among the Hidatsas, and it proved a productive strategy among non-Indians, too.

The Corps of Discovery left St. Louis with an official Indian interpreter. George Drouillard was a specialist in sign language, but like Aguilar, there was a limit to his skill. He was no cultural intermediary; he was a specialist in Indian sign language. Drouillard and Aguilar were male foreigners in the company of an invasion force. They could not signify peaceful intentions in the way Malinche and Sacagawea could. Malinche and Sacagawea were offered as symbols of peace to initiate cultural exchange. They had an obligation to indoctrinate the foreigners in indigenous systems and to ease future interactions. The role of cultural intermediary was a difficult feminine career that carried with it responsibilities, a rigorous workload, extensive travel, and potential risk in a tumultuous environment. Young, able-bodied women who were capable of a substantial workload were the most likely to be given in a cultural exchange.

Some young women were uniquely qualified for this delicate international work. Specific character traits or personal experiences were likely considered. Malinche and Sacagawea shared common characteristics: they were both described as intelligent, compassionate, multicultural, and multilingual. Each was culturally agile, with intimate knowledge of multiple Indian groups. They were accustomed to indigenous diplomatic customs and understood the tensions within multiethnic areas of transit and commerce. Malinche came of age within a Maya trade network, and Sacagawea reached womanhood in the mix of plains trade. Both women were experienced in cultural accommodation and communication. As intermediaries they were expected to acclimate the outsiders to Native customs in diplomacy and trade, and to mediate the needs of both foreigners and Indians. Pocahontas's experience was different. She was a spiritually gifted child, in training as a Beloved Woman when she claimed Smith. Her success as an intermediary was limited until she reached maturity and married Rolfe. All three women had personal characteristics and experiences that were conducive to their work as intermediaries.

Sacagawea's life among the nomadic Lemhis and the village Hidatsas provided valuable skills that she and the men of the expedition relied on during the arduous journey to the Pacific and back. Her experience with moving constantly across the landscape, subsisting on nature, and adapting to new cultures and environments, as well as her communication skills, proved beneficial to the Corps of Discovery. She was familiar with the routes that they would take through the mountains. She had traversed them while on buffalo hunts as a Lemhi child before she walked 750 miles east to the Mandan and Hidatsa villages when she was taken captive. With the exception of her newborn son, Baptiste, Sacagawea was the youngest member of the expedition, yet she may have been the most prepared for the undertaking.

While planning the expedition, Lewis described to his cocaptain the desired attributes of recruits: "When descending the Ohio it shall be my duty to enquire to find out and engage some good hunters, stout, healthy, unmarried men, accustomed to the woods, and capable of bearing bodily fatigue in pretty considerable degree."[34] The captains commissioned only individuals with superior stamina and unquestioned loyalty. More than one hundred potential recruits failed to measure up to these standards, but Sacagawea exceeded most of the qualifications.

On November 4, 1804, Captain Clark recorded Charbonneau's initial visit to the Euro-American camp. Clark mentioned Charbonneau's two Indian wives and immediately expressed interest in Sacagawea, who "would be needed to interpret the Shoshoni language when the explorers entered that territiory."[35] Charbonneau certainly recognized Sacagawea's value to the expedition and attempted to leverage her skills to improve his status and relieve himself of any military drudgery. The group departed the Mandan villages on April 7, 1805, with thirty-one men, one woman, and a two-month-old infant. On that day, "Shabonah and his Indian Squaw" were listed on the official roster as "interpreter and interpretess for the Snake Indians."[36] Despite this clear expectation, the captains rarely mentioned either of them in this capacity.

Lewis recorded his initial encounter with the Lemhis on August 16, 1805: "Cameahwait is assured that he will soon see that Captain Clark has a woman with him who is from the Lemhi Shoshone Nation. She had been captured by the Minnetares. This woman can speak Shoshoni and would help explain the purpose of the expedition."[37] According to Lewis, Sacagawea was needed to explain the expedition's purpose and to express their desire for horses and a Shoshone guide to help them through the mountains to the Pacific. Lewis wanted her to convey his offer: protection against Shoshone enemies, rifles for hunting, and "all the wonderful things trade with the United States will bring."[38] Sacagawea accomplished her mission among the Lemhis. She established a peaceful environment to pursue cross-cultural understanding and cooperation. Lewis and Clark spent several days hunting and feasting with Sacagawea's people. Lewis described Cameahwait's delight in the "finest food he has ever tasted." Sacagawea was instrumental to providing a mutually productive atmosphere at Camp Fortunate (in what is now Montana). Cameahwait ultimately agreed to provide the expedition with horses and a guide in exchange for future access to American goods.

Despite goodwill and hospitality at Camp Fortunate, there were tense moments. On August 19, 1805, Captain Lewis recorded a "custom" that threatened Sacagawea's continued service to the expedition. He wrote, "The Shoshonis have a custom that a young girl's father promises his daughter in marriage when she is still an infant. The man who will receive a girl pays for her, usually with horses or mules. At about fourteen years of age the girl is given to her purchaser. Sacajawea had been sold as an infant. The man who purchased her is present when she returns with the expedition. He is twice Sacajawea's age and already has two wives. Since Sacajawea had a child by Charbonneau, the Shoshoni is no longer interested in her."[39] Lewis was culturally unprepared to understand the complexities of Shoshone gender customs. Lewis's characterization of Sacagawea being "sold" at birth was a simplification. At the time of her birth, the Shoshones had recently retreated to the mountains to recover from a devastating epidemic and increasingly violent Native warfare. Men were declining in numbers, and polygamy was a strategy of survival. This man would have been in his late teens when he agreed to provide for the infant girl. He offered a horse to Sacagawea's family who agreed to raise her until age fourteen, training her for the role of an adult female. Shoshone circumstances and expectations for marriage were irrelevant to Lewis's cultural judgment. Arranged marriages were not uncommon across cultures, and they typically involved a dowry or bride price. Charbonneau was twenty-one years older than Sacagawea. Their age difference was never mentioned, and not that uncommon across cultures as the nineteenth century opened. Lewis, like many later commentators, characterized Native marriage and gender customs as proof of uncivilized societies that degraded Indian women.

Cameahwait's deal with the captains was compromised when he decided to take the horses on a hunt along the Missouri River prior to delivering the animals to the expedition. This unexpected movement of the Indians could have left the Euro-American party stranded. Sacagawea was the only member of the Corps of Discovery who understood the Shoshone language; she also understood the repercussions of Cameahwait's decision. She immediately informed Charbonneau, who was slow to relay the message to the captains. The catastrophe was narrowly avoided thanks to Sacagawea's astute awareness and loyalty. Sacagawea may have seen value in a Lemhi-American alliance that would make trade goods more accessible to Lemhi people. She may have been working to preserve a Shoshone relationship with the United States.

There must have been opportunity for Sacagawea to sneak off and rejoin the people of her youth. Yet she remained loyal to her role as an intermediary, working to negotiate satisfaction on all sides. The Euro-Americans wanted horses and the Lemhis wanted direct access to European goods. Sacagawea participated in brokering the deal and then prevented hostilities when the deal was in jeopardy. Commentators have suggested that this incident proved that Sacagawea chose a life among Euro-Americans. Rather than choosing one side over the other, however, perhaps Sacagawea was acting according to what she believed was in the best interest of a peaceful and mutually productive future.

On October 13, 1805, the Euro-American troop was approaching Nez Perce country, and here Captain Clark specifically addresses Sacagawea's worth as an intermediary: "The presence of Sacajawea with the expedition convinces all Indian people of the peaceful intentions of their party. Having a woman with the expedition is a sure sign the expedition is not a war party."[40] A few days later he again mentions her calming influence: "The instant Captain Lewis appears with Sacajawea, the people come out of the lodges and seem completely at ease. This made trade possible between the two groups."[41] From this journal entry (and several others), it is clear that her posture was not one of trepidation or hostility, but one of contentment. She never exuded fear or danger; there is no record of her displaying any desire for rescue or escape. She was not simply a symbol of peace; she was actively engaged in cross-cultural interactions. She helped establish a nonthreatening atmosphere in which she could facilitate an exchange of information and goods. Beginning with her first meetings with the captains in the winter of 1804, she shared relevant information about various Indian groups. She was acquainted with the Nez Perces (the Shoshones' neighbors to the west), she was familiar with various nomadic mountain groups in addition to her own Lemhi Shoshone relations, and she was accustomed to Gros Ventre groups in the diverse environment of the Mandan and Hidatsa villages. Her vast knowledge of Plains Indians was advantageous to Lewis and Clark's mission.

When the expedition came upon abandoned Indian camps, Sacagawea was called upon to investigate and determine which tribes had occupied them. On May 29, 1805, Lewis and Clark made a joint entry that recognized Sacagawea's knowledge of the various Native cultures in the region. They reported, "The Indian woman examined the mockersons and told us they were the Indians which resided below the Rocky Mountains and to the north of this river—her nation make their mockersons differently."[42] On July 19, 1805, Captain Lewis recorded another instance: "[Clark] saw early in the day the remains of several Indian camps formed of willow brush which appeared to have been inhabited some time this season. This the Indian woman with us informs that they do this to obtain the sap and soft part of wood and bark for food."[43] Her cultural knowledge of shelters, food-gathering practices, and clothing was helpful to the explorers, and it is clear that the captains often relied on her input. The journal entries for the spring and summer of 1805 frequently mention her cultural and geographical knowledge. As the trip wore on, she was mentioned less. Perhaps her skills were, by then, taken for granted.

Like Pocahontas, Sacagawea was specifically recognized for her generous efforts to supply food for the foreigners. Her knowledge of edible plants, roots, seeds and bulbs was a tremendous advantage to the men of the expedition. These outsiders would never have known the forest's delicacies or where to find them. The journals mention many occasions on which Sacagawea provided nourishment. Lewis wrote on April 9, 1805, "When we haulted for dinner the sqaw busied herself in searching for wild artichokes which the mice collect and deposit in large hoards. This operation she performed by penetrating the earth with a sharp stick about some small collections of driftwood. Her labour soon proved successful, and she procured a good quantity of these roots."[44] On April 30, 1805, Clark recorded, "Squar found and brought me a bush something like the current, which she said bore a delicious froot and that great quantities grew on the Rocky mountains [cherries]."[45] On May 8, 1805, Clark mentioned another treat of the wilderness: "Squar gathered on the sides of the hills wild lickerish and the white apple as called by the angegies [engages] and gave me to eat."[46] On the return trip during the winter of 1805–1806, meat was scarce, and Captain Clark was impressed with Sacagawea's frugalness. On December 3 he described how Sacagawea boiled two shank bones from a less-than-adequate elk to gain a pint of grease. During the spring of 1806 she continued to gather nourishment from the forest, treating the men to an abundance of wild onions and fennel roots from the area of Kamiah, Idaho. She also gathered, dried, and stored what food she could for their journey back through the mountains. Without her additions to the men's diet, discomfort and sickness would certainly have been a more severe obstacle to the corps.

Scholars have bickered over Sacagawea's significance to the expedition. As we will see in chapter 7, some historians and writers rebelled against her heroine status and suggested that her contributions were exaggerated, particularly in regard to her role as a guide. The journals recorded several occasions on which she reassured the men that they were on the path to her people and to the "great falls" described by the Mandan Indians. On July 22, 1805, Lewis wrote, "The Indian woman recognizes the country and assures us that this is the river on which her relations live and that the three forkes are at no great distance. This piece of information has cheered the spirits of the party."[47] On August 8, 1805, Sacagawea was again recognized for her geographical knowledge. Lewis wrote, "Indian woman recognized the point of high plain to our right, which she informed us was not very distant from the summer retreat of her nation. . . . She assures us that we shall either find her people on this river or on the river immediately west of its source. . . . It is all important with us to meet with those people as soon as possible."[48] Sacagawea's geographical information was consistent and reliable as the group journeyed through the mountains.

Clark provided the most compelling evidence of her service as a guide on July 14, 1806, when the group was on its return trip. He wrote, "The Indian woman, who has been of great service to me as a pilot thru this country, recommends a gap in the mountains more south which I shall cross."[49] This southern pass through the Rockies, which Sacagawea had traversed as a child with the Lemhis, later became the Bozeman Pass. The expedition relied on her recognition of landmarks as they searched for the cached dugouts they had buried the previous August. These journal entries prove that Sacagawea reassured the captains along their course, made recommendations, and was relied upon for her geographical knowledge.

At various junctures the expedition did employ temporary Native guides; there was a Shoshone guide named Old Toby and a few Nez Perce men who served in this short-term capacity. Sacagawea was never listed as an official guide of the expedition. Skeptics of Sacagawea's service as a guide insisted that the Corps of Discovery traversed an uncharted, rugged wilderness. Yet Sacagawea had trekked across these same mountains when she was taken captive with the other Shoshone women and children. We know that Sacagawea's childhood friend escaped the Hidatsas and returned to the Lemhi Valley on her own. Indians were experienced in this landscape, having routinely crisscrossed the mountains and traveled through the hostile territory of their enemies. The expedition had the benefit of Indian topographical information in addition to the knowledge of the Hudson's Bay Company and the North West Company as well as Spanish maps. The expedition's success depended heavily on the willingness of Indian peoples to share their knowledge. The legend of the Lewis and Clark expedition has often neglected the reality of Indian expertise, participation, and generosity.

It would be difficult to suggest that the expedition would have failed if not for Sacagawea. It is reasonable, however, to suggest that the captains anticipated her potential value to the success of their quest. They knew she was a member of the "Snake" Shoshones from the Rocky Mountains, from whom the expedition intended to buy horses. They knew she could be helpful as an interpreter, and they hoped she could recognize landmarks as they approached the land of her childhood. But she exceeded these expectations. Captain Lewis noted that Sacagawea signified peace as the corps approached Indian groups with whom they wanted to interact; her presence and demeanor created a hospitable environment for acquiring necessities and information. She translated words and intentions as she displayed good will to all sides. She diligently gathered, stored, and prepared the fruits, roots, and vegetables that the men enjoyed. The captains came to trust and rely upon Sacagawea's information regarding mountain trails and landmarks. They consulted her knowledge of indigenous cultures when the expedition came upon abandoned Indian camps. The captains also came to appreciate and admire her resourcefulness, as well as her courage and calmness in the face of danger. As we will see in the next chapter, Sacagawea's personal characteristics also impressed the captains.

Like Malinche and Pocahontas, Sacagawea was endowed with specific talents in perception and communication that made her dealings with people memorable. All three women had an eye to the future; they accepted and steered the changes that came to their world. Sacagawea may not have had much choice in joining the expedition, yet she made the decision to aid the group along its journey. She demonstrated her commitment to her intermediary role through her actions. She did all that was in her power to provide comfort, defuse tensions, and facilitate cross-cultural understanding and exchange.

All three women were uniquely qualified for the role of cultural intermediary. Malinche was highly educated, multicultural, and multilingual. She had had experiences among diverse indigenous groups before she was exposed to Spanish intentions, culture, and religion. Pocahontas was trained in an elite spiritual discipline, that of a Beloved Woman. Despite her protection of Smith and her willingness to provide food and goodwill, her early intermediary efforts were constrained by her youth. At age eleven she struggled to exert influence over the forces of cultural conflict, but her skills matured with age and experience. Pocahontas's efforts as an adult intermediary had more impact. Sacagawea had significant experience and knowledge of diverse groups in the Northwest prior to her work with the Corps of Discovery. She, too, was multilingual and multicultural as well as experienced in an area of commerce. She had already served as an intermediary, facilitating interactions between her Hidatsa family and her French-Canadian husband.

As we will see in the next chapter, European men often described Indian women as mistreated slaves or drudges. European invaders considered indigenous civilizations barbaric and savage compared to their own. Male foreigners misunderstood indigenous gender structures and disapproved of the workload and treatment that Indian women endured in Native communities. Their descriptions of other Indian women helped to justify the cultural genocide that occurred during the colonial era. Yet the European conquerors valued, even admired, the skills and character that Malinche, Pocahontas, and Sacagawea exhibited. Their work benefited the invaders and was considered gracious and helpful rather than demeaning and exploitive. The white men considered themselves chivalrous rescuers.

The long-accepted portrayal of these women as slaves to men (either Indian or white) is misleading, particularly within Native cultural context. These women were not slaves. They had obligations to their tribes as Indian women, and meeting those obligations brought them security and respect. They may have had unwanted sexual experiences among the white men, or they may not have. European invaders rarely discussed such matters, leaving ample room for x-rated academic theories. We know that sexual violence against Native women was and is a reality of conquest—across time, space, and cultures. But evidence in the case of these three particular women suggests that their sexuality was protected during their time among the invaders. There was a concerted effort to maintain the loyalty of Malinche, Pocahontas, and Sacagawea. Had they been treaty harshly, their vital skills would have been jeopardized. The women worked with leaders, not rabble: Malinche spent most of her time in the company of Cortés, Pocahontas spent her captivity with Reverend Alexander Whitaker, and Sacagawea spent her time with Captains Lewis and Clark. Not all conquerors were rapists and not all Indian women were helpless victims. The functions of sex were complex across indigenous societies, and European men did not understand the sexual or marriage customs of Indians. As we will see in the next chapter, each of the women had sex with white men, each woman gave birth to a mixed-race child, and each of those children was claimed and reared by whites. Malinche and Jaramillo (her eventual husband), Pocahontas and Rolfe, and Sacagawea and Charbonneau were rewarded with land grants and in all three cases their children inherited a portion of that land. Malinche, Pocahontas, and Sacagawea were skilled and dignified women who earned the respect of those around them.

CHAPTER FOUR

INTIMATE FRONTIERS

The historical record leaves us unsatisfied when it comes to the intimate lives of Malinche, Pocahontas, and Sacagawea. We know the women had sex with white men and gave birth to mixed-race children, but we don't know if it was consensual or forced. Contemporary academic interpretations have insisted that it was forced. In her 1994 book Frances Karttunen describes Malinche's sexuality: "Nor is it likely she had any choice about sexual activity or bearing children."[1] Scholars have had difficulty imagining that Malinche, Pocahontas, or Sacagawea willingly aided or had sex with the newcomers. The women had to have been coerced or duped, or they sought revenge for their treatment in Native societies. These accepted explanations deny the women's intelligence, skill, agency, and cultural obligations. What if they were shrewd women with diplomatic responsibilities and an eye toward the future? What if, as the invaders suggested, the women saw value in the invaders' path? None of these women lived to see the eventual devastation that Indian people endured during colonization. Our sympathetic, scholarly hindsight distorts the realities that Malinche, Pocahontas, and Sacagawea lived.

European men did not understand the practice of giving Native women to outsiders, but they accepted the women and relied on their expertise. Malinche, Pocahontas, and Sacagawea acclimated the newcomers to their surroundings, bridged the cultural divide, advised both sides, and worked toward cooperation. Close examination of primary documents suggests that these three particular women were, more often than not, treated with respect while among the invaders. The previous chapter demonstrated that all three women were extraordinarily committed to their intermediary roles. The women's competence and devotion earned the reserved admiration of their white male companions. We can never know if the women enjoyed a mutual affection with these men, though there is ample evidence of mutual trust and respect.

This chapter will examine the relationships between the male invaders and the Indian women in their company. A second focus will highlight how Indian women were perceived and described by the foreigners. Anglo frontiersmen considered themselves to be saviors who relieved Malinche, Pocahontas, and Sacagawea from the harsh existence of their Native world. They consistently portrayed other indigenous women as drudges, mired in uncivilized cultures. The conquerors' misconception had lasting repercussions on how Indian women were depicted in the historical record and laid the foundation for the mythology that engulfed each woman. Women's roles in Native societies were incomprehensible to European men; Indian women worked and managed agricultural fields, processed commodities, built and controlled their homes, and were intimately involved in diplomacy and trade. They were vital to subsistence, commerce, international relations, and the spiritual and social organization of their communities. European men misjudged their workload and described Native women as exploited and oppressed, not as relevant contributors. While Indian women were portrayed as beasts of burden, Malinche, Pocahontas, and Sacagawea were deemed exceptional and admirable for providing similar feminine work on behalf of the newcomers.

The function of women's sexuality was varied and complex across precontact Native America. Some groups believed women had the capacity to transfer power through sex, and many Native communities exchanged women to outsiders to cement alliances. It is unlikely that these women were given as either sexual or domestic slaves. For Mesoamerican, Algonquian, and North American Plains groups, women were extended as part of a diplomatic strategy to initiate trusted interaction, establish economic or political alliances, and form lasting kinship bonds. Able-bodied, able-minded, and amiable young women were selected for this important work. Specific character traits or life experiences were likely considered, particularly if women demonstrated a capacity to thrive in a multifarious environment. Being a cultural intermediary was a prestigious and influential position; daughters of indigenous leaders were often chosen to initiate and legitimize strategic cross-cultural relationships.

We don't really know if the women had any choice in their fate. In their time and place, arranged marriages were often based on strategy and ambition. Arranged marriage was not an unfamiliar custom to the European newcomers, but the foreigners were surprised that these women served as informants and mediators during international negotiations. In addition to assessing and wooing the outsiders, they looked for mutual benefits and acclimated outsiders to indigenous conditions and expectations. We know that Malinche, Pocahontas, and Sacagawea spent countless hours at the side of the conquerors. They endured tremendous hardships together; they overcame adversity and hostility to establish a modicum of cross-cultural peace and understanding at the moment of contact. Malinche, Pocahontas, Sacagawea and the men in their care were involved in passionate work, and their mission had dramatic consequences for the future.

Historical records indicate that none of the women ever displayed resentment or a desire to escape. Each of them had opportunities to abandon the foreigners (Malinche in Cholula, Pocahontas when she warned Smith of danger in 1609, and Sacagawea among the Lemhis in the Rocky Mountains), but instead intervened and protected the newcomers during their most vulnerable moments. This was proof to the colonizing men that Malinche, Pocahontas, and Sacagawea preferred a life among them. The men valued the women's commitment and reciprocated with respect, protection, and kindness. Malinche and her fellow intermediary Doña Luisa were entrusted to high-ranking conquistadors and given armor during their perilous escape from Tenochtitlán on La Noche Triste. Pocahontas was treated as a princess and placed in the care of Reverend Whitaker during her captivity in Jamestown. Captain Clark saved Sacagawea from rushing floodwaters, tended to her medical needs, and gave her a horse to portage over the mountains. These particular men and these three Indian women felt obligations toward one another.

MALINCHE AND THE SPANISH

When the Maya entourage approached the Spaniards in peace, days after their initial battle in 1519, they came bearing gifts to initiate negotiations. Díaz describes the items they brought, and then says, "These gifts were nothing, however, compared to the twenty women whom they gave us."[2] He remembers that Cortés received the Maya overture with pleasure as he instructed Aguilar to explain Christianity and the young women's need to be baptized prior to being dispersed among his captains. Díaz continues, "One of the Indian ladies was christened Doña Marina. She was a truly great princess, the daughter of Caciques and the mistress of vassals, as was very evident in her appearance. . . . I do not clearly remember the names of all the other women, there is no reason for naming any of them. But they were the first women in New Spain to become Christians."[3] Díaz's remarks demonstrate the Spanish intent to re-create their own religious and social organization in Mexico. They were willing to accept these young women and establish kinship connections with the Mayas of Tabasco, yet the women had to be baptized to legitimize their intimacy with the Christian men. Cortés recommended that if the caciques sincerely wanted to be "brothers," they, too, should stop worshiping idols and commit themselves to the one true Christian Lord. Díaz also indicates that the other nineteen women proved less significant to the outcome of the conquest. We know that the Spanish military force continued to acquire Native women as they made their way to Tenochtitlán, but clearly not all of the women were instrumental intermediaries.

The invading Spaniards grew accustomed to the Indian diplomatic protocol of exchanging women to reinforce alliances. In the town of Cempoala, after a Spanish show of force, the Cempoalan caciques came forward and offered women. Díaz explains, "as we were now their friends they would like to have us for brothers and to give us their daughters to bear us children. So, to cement our friendship, they brought eight Indian girls, all the daughters of the chiefs, and gave one of them, who is the niece of the fat Cacique, to Cortés. All eight of them were dressed in the rich shirts that they wear, and finely adorned as is their custom . . . and with them came other girls to be their maids."[4] The "fat cacique" clarified that seven of the women were to be given to the captains but that his niece was specifically for Cortés, indicating, "She is the mistress of towns and vassals." Like the Mayas in Tabasco, the leaders of Cempoala decided that an alliance with the Spaniards was prudent, and they, too, wanted to strengthen their alliance by offering elite women. Immediately after this exchange, the caciques began to voice grievous complaints against Moctezuma. According to Díaz, Cortés accepted the Cempoalan women with a "gracious smile" and said, "before we could accept the ladies and become their brothers, they would have to abandon their idols which they mistakenly believed in and worshipped, and sacrifice no more souls to them; and that when he saw those cursed things thrown down and the sacrifices at an end, our bonds of brotherhood would be very much fimer."[5] Aguilar and Malinche relayed Cortés's message and began instructing the young women in Christianity so that Spanish men could receive them.

The Cempoalan caciques replied that they could not give up their idols or their sacrifices to them because their health, harvest, and all that was dear to them depended on the favor of their gods. They did promise to take immediate steps to curtail sodomy.[6] Cortés responded by ordering his men to storm the temple, overthrow the idols within, and fight the Indians if they resisted. The fat cacique pleaded with Cortés as conquistadors ascended the temple steps, insisting that his people would surely perish without their idols. Cortés's army persisted and sent the idols crashing down the stairs. But the fat cacique called off his warriors, fearing Spanish reprisal or abandonment because the Cempoalans did not want to face Moctezuma's wrath without Spanish support. Cortés and Díaz both noted significant indigenous anxiety within the communities that offered aid to the Spanish.

The Spaniards continued to the towns of Jalapa and Socochima, and Díaz again mentions Malinche's skill in explaining the Spaniards' intention to "end human sacrifices and robbery." Both towns offered food and assistance to the conquistadors. In the town of Xocotlan the Spaniards were given gifts and more women, this time with a stated purpose: "given four women to grind maize for our bread, also a load of cloth."[7] Díaz specifically distinguishes these women as servants, not as elite daughters of caciques. As the conquistadors progressed inland toward Tenochtitlán, Malinche and Aguilar perfected their message to increase the likelihood of Indian support.

The conquistadors traveled with scouts far in advance, on the lookout for potential danger. They were followed by musketeers, crossbowmen, and a growing army of indigenous warriors. Spanish horsemen flanked both sides of the traveling troop. Each man carried his own weapons, always alert for the battle cry. In September, as the group approached the town of Tlaxcala, scouts sent word to Cortés that he must prepare his forces for a difficult fight. Tlaxcalan warriors were particularly fierce, having lived in a constant state of warfare against the Mexicas in Tenochtitlán. Tlaxcalans adopted a hostile posture immediately after their sentries noticed that the Spanish forces included indigenous warriors from within the Aztec Empire. At the conclusion of an intense battle on the outskirts of Tlaxcala, Cortés ordered the prisoners be nursed, fed, and then brought before him to hear his speech. Malinche and Aguilar told them "not to be foolish but to make peace with us for we wished to help them and treat them as brothers."[8] The Spanish finally entered the town of Tlaxcala in peace after twenty-four days of intermittent skirmishes.

Tlaxcalan caciques provided the conquistadors with lodging and provisions. To demonstrate and strengthen their commitment to the Spanish, they offered five "young virginal women," according to Díaz, "the most beautiful of their daughters and nieces who were ready for marriage." The eldest cacique, Xicotenga, reserved his daughter specifically for Cortés. Cortés responded with gratefulness and respect but recommended the young women stay in the care of their fathers until the Spaniards accomplished the tasks for which they had been sent: to end idol worship, human sacrifice, feasting on human beings, and "other abominations which they practiced." Malinche and Aguilar set to work translating, describing Spanish intentions, and explaining Christianity. The Tlaxcalans received Cortés's message but respectfully asked the Spaniards not to make such demands. Cortés decided not to allow his men to raid the temples as they had in Cempoala. The plan in Tlaxcala was to illustrate Spanish goodness by accepting the women without violence. Only the exchanged women needed immediate religious instruction and baptism. Díaz describes them as "handsome for Indian women." Xicotenga's daughter was baptized Doña Luisa and given to Pedro de Alvarado, Cortés's second in command. Díaz remembers, "When Xicotenga's daughter Doña Luisa was given to Pedro de Alvarado, the greater part of Tlaxcala paid her reverence, gave her presents and looked on her as their mistress."[9] Spanish acceptance of Xicotenga's daughter was important to a trustworthy relationship and a new, mutually productive future.

The exchanged Tlaxcalan women were given the title of Doña after baptism. Díaz offers details of only a few of these women, but he clarifies that Luisa and Pedro had a long marriage that produced several "splendid" heirs. It is difficult to know if their marriage was a loving union, but Díaz assures readers that Doña Luisa and Doña Marina were respected on both sides of the cultural divide. He also assures readers that both women were given Spanish armor and protection as they fled Tenochtitlán on La Noche Triste. After the conquest colonial Spaniards continued to address Malinche and Luisa with the honorific title of Doña.

Díaz provides nearly all of Malinche's personal information (and slight details on other Indian women). He describes Malinche's appearance, her royal heritage, her Native upbringing, her intelligence, and her loving forgiveness when she reunited with the indigenous family who had cast her off as a child. Díaz provides an intimate look at Malinche as a woman and a contributor to the creation of New Spain. He was a young man himself, just twenty-five years old when he met nineteen-year-old Malinche, and witnessed her tremendous influence on those around her. Díaz describes Malinche as a dignified Native beauty who was given to the Spaniard with the highest social rank: "Doña Marina, being good-looking, intelligent, and self assured, went to Alonso Hernandez Puertocarrero, who as I have already said, was a very grand gentleman, and a cousin of the Court of Medellin."[10] He also notes her uncommon strength, resourcefulness, and "manly valour." He describes her during the Tlaxcalan campaign, saying, "But let me say that Doña Marina, although a native woman, possessed such manly valour that though she heard every day that the Indians were going to kill us and eat our flesh with chillies, and though she had seen us surrounded in recent battles and knew that we were all wounded and sick, yet she betrayed no weakness but a courage greater than that of a woman. She and Jeronimo de Aguilar spoke to the messengers we were now sending, telling them that the Tlascalans must make peace at once, and that if they did not come to us within two days we would go and kill them in their own city and destroy their country. With these brave words the prisoners were dispatched."[11] According to Díaz, Malinche was impressive during battle and negotiations in Tlaxcala. Malinche was the beautiful indigenous heroine of Díaz's tale.

Cortés was nearly silent regarding his Indian mistress/interpreter. He had reasons for his vagueness in the letters he wrote to King Charles; his critics regarded him a renegade who ran amok in Mexico, and he was also a philanderer who had trouble with monogamy. He had many mistresses and at least nine children, including a son by Malinche and a daughter by Moctezuma's daughter Tecuichpotzin (named Doña Isabel after her baptism). Unlike other Spaniards who committed to indigenous women and began families in Mexico (Gonzalo Guerrero, Pedro de Alvarado, Aguilar, and Díaz, who ultimately settled with his common-law Maya wife in Guatemala), Cortés had no intention of committing to Malinche or Tecuichpotzin. He was a man of tremendous social ambition; both of his Spanish wives were his social betters. He had married his first wife, Catalina Suarez de Marcaida, in Cuba in 1515 and brought her to Mexico after the fall of Tenochtitlán. It must have been awkward to have his Spanish wife living in close proximity to Malinche, who was pregnant with his child at the time.

Cortés set up a household in Coyoacan (a suburb of Tenochtitlán), and it was full of women. Malinche lived there with several of Moctezuma's female relatives, and then Catalina arrived from Cuba in 1522. Díaz escorted her to the house in Coyoacan, and he recalls that Cortés was not happy to see her. Catalina was also displeased, particularly by the harem-like situation she found.[12] She died shortly after her arrival, under mysterious circumstances; several of the witnesses summoned at the time of her death noticed bruises on her neck. Cortés was forced to answer questions about her death for the remainder of his life. Malinche gave birth to Cortés's son, Martín (named after Cortés's father), in 1523. He was taken from Malinche almost immediately. Cortés sent him to Spain to be raised by his relatives, educated, and legitimized by papal decree. Martín was worth keeping; Malinche was not. The boy did not grow up knowing his mother.[13]

In October 1524 Cortés assembled his conquistadors one last time for an expedition to Honduras. This was Malinche, Cortés, and Díaz's last trip together. It was an eventful two-year campaign for Malinche. She encountered and forgave her indigenous mother and half brother, as they wept in fear of her revenge. She married Juan Jaramillo (one of Cortés's officers) and gave birth to his child, Maria, who would not grow up knowing her mother, either. Malinche is believed to have died in 1528, but there are no records regarding the specifics of her death. And there is no way of knowing whether her brief marriage to Jaramillo was based on love, duty, ambition, or convenience.

The Honduras expedition was a colossal failure, and the group endured a disastrous return voyage after their ship was overtaken by a violent storm. Malinche's knack for survival carried her through the two-year ordeal. She delivered Jaramillo's daughter during the tumult, and the couple and their infant daughter returned to Mexico after the expedition. By 1528 the family was settled on a land grant that was given in recognition of their service to New Spain. Malinche's few remaining years are a mystery.

Malinche's name lived on, however, appearing in court proceedings after her death. In 1529 Cortés came under official scrutiny when the Spanish Crown ordered a *residencia*, a judicial inquiry, to investigate his behavior during the conquest. It was an exhausting and grueling affair for Cortés. A legion of witnesses was called to testify before the court. They were questioned under oath about every aspect of Cortés's conduct in Mexico, including his relations with Indian women and the death of his Spanish wife. According to linguist Anna Lanyon, who examined these court records, witnesses were specifically asked whether he lived in carnal sin with the daughter of Moctezuma or with Malinche.[14] The answer was obviously yes. He had had children by both women and then negotiated their marriages to other Spaniards. During Cortés's hearing Aguilar came forward with damning testimony against his commander. He claimed Cortés had had sex with all of the women inside the Coyoacan home. Cortés defended himself by claiming he had merely been providing for the Indian women in accordance with a promise he had made to Mocte-zuma, who had implored him to care for his daughters and nieces. No one corroborated Cortés's promise to Moctezuma, nor would it have helped deflect charges of sexual impropriety. By 1529 Cortés had many enemies like Aguilar, who felt slighted in their share of postconquest booty and prestige.

Jaramillo also appeared in colonial court records after the conquest. After Malinche's death, he remarried to a Spanish woman. The couple had no children together, but they raised Malinche's daughter, Maria. Family problems were aired in the Spanish court after Maria initiated proceedings concerning her inheritance to the Spanish land grant. The case lasted twenty years. There were doubts about Jaramillo and Malinche, and conflicting stories regarding the circumstances of their marriage. Cortés's biographer, Gómara, who was not in Mexico but recorded Cortés's recollections, claimed that Jaramillo was drunk during their wedding ceremony, suggesting that the marriage was a sham. Díaz was not at the wedding, either, but he told the court that Jaramillo was not intoxicated, according to his informants who had attended. Jaramillo's second wife also testified, claiming that her husband's marriage to Malinche was nothing but a disaster to his reputation.

Maria, Malinche's grown daughter, had married the viceroy's nephew, Luis de Quesada, in 1542. That same year the couple brought a legal suit against Jaramillo, who by then was among the wealthiest men in New Spain. Maria and Luis discovered that Jaramillo intended to leave his second wife the entire land grant that had been given to him and Malinche after the conquest.[15] Doña Maria had to prove that her mother's marriage to Jaramillo was legitimate and sanctioned by the church in order to validate her claim to the land. Witnesses swore under oath that Malinche and Jaramillo had been married in accordance with the Holy Church. They attested to Malinche's service, honor, and loyalty during the conquest as well as her intelligence and courage.

Does the contentious court case between father and daughter suggest that Jaramillo's feelings toward Malinche were disingen-uous, or was his Spanish wife intent on depriving Maria, his mestizo daughter, of her inheritance? Unfortunately, we don't know the nature of Malinche and Jaramillo's relationship. We do know that Malinche spent her last years recognized as Doña Marina; she was characterized in court as a significant woman of the conquest and the legitimate wife of a Spaniard. In her last years Malinche also witnessed unfathomable mortality rates among Mesoamericans due to European disease, disease that likely took her life in 1528.

Whenever Malinche enters into the Spanish or indigenous historical record, she is consistently portrayed as a critical force in the outcome of the conquest. She was addressed with an honorific title in both Indian and Spanish vernacular (with the suffix of -tzin among Indians and the title of Doña among the Spanish). She maintained her Spanish title after the conquest and passed it on to her daughter. Maria married the viceroy's nephew and petitioned the courts using her mother's prestige. There is considerable evidence indicating that Malinche was admired for her skills, her character, and her devotion to establishing a New World. Cortés arranged her marriage to Jaramillo and rewarded the couple with land. He claimed the son he had with Malinche, named him after his father, made sure he was legitimized by the pope, educated him in Spain, and left him a substantial inheritance. Díaz certainly admired Malinche, as did the witnesses who were summoned to testify in Maria's case against her father.

Other elite Native women are occasionally characterized as admirable in historical records as well. The first generation of friars sent to indoctrinate the indigenous population indicates an appreciation for Nahuas' expectations of the feminine. Friar Bautista's *Huehuetlatolli* (*Discourse by Nahua Elders,* discussed in chapter 1) highlights elite women's fidelity to husband and family, their skillful handling of domestic affairs, and the expectation that they be discreet and respectful in speech, appearance, and conduct. Fray Sahagún also acknowledges Nahua women's social expectations in the *Florentine Codex.* Yet Sahagún and Bautista (as well as other colonizing Spaniards) were culturally unprepared to understand all facets of feminine power in Native societies and religion. They focus only on familiar feminine standards: service to husband and home, as well as obedience and purity.

Malinche was Cortés's interpreter, diplomat, cultural adviser, and intimate companion. She was not his slave; she did not behave as a slave, and she was not interpreted as a slave by the Native dignitaries she addressed. By the end of the conquest Malinche and Cortés had traveled thousands of miles together, they had convinced thousands of Indians that Spanish political and religious changes were advantageous, and they had brought forth a mixed-blood son. Together the couple changed the course of Mexican civilization, and their son, Martín, took the symbolic mantle of being the first mestizo child. Malinche and Cortés are entangled with one another in the historical moment of the conquest and in the foundational narrative of modern Mexico.

POCAHONTAS AND THE ENGLISHMEN

In 1609 Smith returned to England, put down his musket and compass, and took up his pen. He wrote several of accounts of his New-World exploits over the course of his life, which often overlapped one another, and offered various renditions of events. His works include *True Relation of Such Occurrences and Accidents of Note as Happened in Virginia* (1608), *Map of Virginia* (1612), *The Proceeding of the English Colony in Virginia* (1612), *Description of New England* (1616), and *The Generall Historie* (1624), the last of which modifies and merges all of the others. Like Cortés, Smith had self-serving goals in mind as he recorded his commitment to England's colonial enterprise. In addition, he had a template to follow. As a young man, Smith's restless mind had devoured histories of the Spanish conquest in Mexico. He had read Gómara's *Historia de la Conquista de Mexico* and a later work by Peter Martyr entitled *Decades of the New World;* Smith likely considered Cortés to be a role model.[16] As an adventurous male growing up in the Age of Exploration, Smith absorbed a pervasive view of the New World as a pristine environment for Europe's bravest men to conquer in order to build an improved civilization. He was twenty-six years old when he embarked upon his own American adventure. He left the Thames in 1606, confident that English adventurers would be more honorable than the dubious

Spaniards. Smith knew of Malinche's usefulness to Cortés, and his writings often characterized Native women as resources for sympathetic assistance and advocates for European men.

The famous rescue scene Smith describes, in which Pocahontas rushes forward to protect him from certain death, is a familiar scenario in many of his adventure tales. According to Smith, Native women routinely came to his rescue. In 1624 he acknowledges the strange coincidence in a letter he wrote announcing the completion of *The Generall Historie* to Lady Frances, Duchess of Richmond and Lennox:

> Yet my comfort is, that heretofore honorable and virtuous Ladies, and comparable but amongs themselues, haue offred me rescue and protection in my greatest dangers: even in forraine parts, I haue felt reliefe from that sex. The beauteous Lady Tragabigzanda, when I was a slaue to the Turks, did all she could to secure me. When I overcame the Bashaw of Nalbrits in Tataria, the charitable Lady Callamata supplied my necessities. In the vpmost of many extremities, that blessed Pokahontas, the great Kings daughter of Virginia, oft saved my life. When I escaped the cureltie of Pirates and most furious stormes, a long time alone in a small Boat at Sea, and driven ashore in France, the good Lady Madam Chanoyes, bountifully assisted me.[17]

Smith's memoirs frequently describe his dire straights in foreign lands and the feminine compassion that came to his aid. Smith's boastful narratives warrant scrutiny, and persistent scholarly skepticism will be taken up in the chapter 6. Smith was, however, an experienced frontiersman. He likely understood the best posture to exhibit as a captive and may have learned to cultivate and capitalize on any sympathy during hostile encounters.

Smith assumed that his gracious feminine rescuers were compelled by his masculine English charm. He describes Pocahontas's attentive protection (speaking in third person): "hee had the Salvages in such subjection, hee would have made himself a king, by marrying Pocahontas, Powhatans daughter. It is true she was the very nomparell of his kingdome, and at most not past 13 or 14 yeares of age. Very oft shee came to ure fort, with what shee could get for Captaine

Smith, that ever loved and used all the countrie well, but her especially he ever much respected: and she so well requited it, that when her father intended to have surprised him, shee by stealth in the darke night came through the wild woods and told him of it. . . . If he would he might have married her, or have done what him listed. For there was none that could have hindered his determination."[18] Smith tries to quell allegations that he inflamed Native hostilities in Virginia by assuring readers in 1624 that he had earned respect and influence among the Indians. This passage describes a loving and willing Pocahontas. According to Smith, she would have married him; it was his discretion that prevented their union.

Smith, like Cortés, was forced to defend himself against persistent accusations of impropriety. He, too, had enemies among his fellow colonists, some of whom sent word to London officials that Smith intended to enrich himself by wooing Pocahontas. He answered their charges, saying, "But her marriage could no way have entitled him by any right to the kingdome, nor was it ever suspected hee had ever such a thought, or more regarded her, or any of them, then in honest reason and discretion he might."[19] Smith recorded her age at their first meeting to have been approximately eleven years old, making her thirteen or fourteen by the time Smith left Virginia in 1609. According to Smith, he watched with respectable admiration as Pocahontas matured into womanhood. By the time of his departure, she was an appropriate age for marriage on either side of the cultural divide. In fact, Pocahontas married a Native warrior a short time later.

For the most part Smith avoids discussing Pocahontas's sexuality, preferring to present her as a smitten young girl. He does relay one peculiar ritual during his visit to the town of Werowocomocao. He and four fellow colonists were sent as representatives of King James to offer Chief Powhatan a copper crown. While waiting for the chief's arrival, Smith and his compatriots were befuddled by the feminine entertainment:

> Then presently they were presented with this anticke; thirtie young women came naked out of the woods, onely covered behind and before with a few greene leaves, their bodies all painted, some of one colour, some of

another, but all differing, their leader (Pocahontas) had a fayre payre of Bucks hornes on her head, and an Otters skinne at her girdle, and another at her arme, a quiver of arrows at her backe, a bow and arrowes in her hand; the next had in her hand a sword, another a club, another a pot-sticke; all horned alike: the rest every one with their severall devises. These fiends with most hellish shouts and cryes, rushing from among the trees, cast themselves in a ring about the fire, singing and daunces; having spent neare an houre in this Mascarado, as they entered in like manner they departed. Having reaccommodated themselves, they solemnly invited him to their lodgings, where he was no sooner within the house, but all these Nymphes more tormented him then ever, with crowding, pressing, and hanging about him, most tediously crying, Love you not me? Love you not me? This salutation ended, the feast was set consisting of all the Salvage dainties they could devise: some attending, others singing and dauncing about them; which mirth being ended, with fire-brands in stead of Torches they conducted him to his lodging.[20]

Smith neglects to mention how he or his fellow Englishmen responded to the young women's invitation to "love you not me." Smith describes the event without further commentary. His report hints at European disapproval of Indian disregard for female chastity. Among all of Smith's claims, this one proves difficult for mythmakers to assimilate into a nationalist creation story of a virginal Indian princess who graciously welcomed honorable European males. This passage is avoided in early historical narratives of early Jamestown, although Smith retells the event a few times. He may have been trying to demonstrate his honor as a gentleman, never tempted by the nymphs who "tormented" him. As we will see in chapter 6, nationalist histories prefer Smith's portrayal of Pocahontas as a sensitive and attractive young girl who prevented her people from savagely killing him.

Colonist William Strachey, who lived in Jamestown for more than a year between 1610 and 1611, offers a less known account of Jamestown and Pocahontas. The difference in his presentation of the story may reflect his life experience and his position in the Virginia Company. Although he was an educated gentleman from a landed family, he had had a difficult career as a struggling author after being fired as secretary to the English ambassador in Constantinople. He signed on to a Virginia Company expedition to Jamestown, turning to the New World for a fresh start like so many others, despite the fact that he was older than most, in his early sixties. The fleet of seven ships, carrying a new company president, new colonists, and much-needed supplies, was hit by a disastrous storm that ran his ship, the *Sea Venture,* aground on Bermuda, where the passengers stayed for eleven months before finally making it to Virginia. He arrived at the colony in the midst of what colonists refers to as the "starving time." Only sixty of the five hundred colonists survived the disastrous winter of 1609–1610. Strachey was secretary of the treasury in Jamestown and had been instructed to faithfully compile information for company officials in London. There were to be no more exaggerated reports. He conducted interviews among the original colonists and Indians regarding the earliest days of the settlement. He later organized his records for publication of his own book entitled *The Historie of Travell into Virginia Britania, 1612.* For this work he corresponded with Smith and consulted his writings, often copying them word for word.

Strachey corroborates much of Smith's account, although he offers a different interpretation of Pocahontas. He describes her physically: "Their younger women goe not shadowed amongst their owne company until they be nigh eleven or twelve returnes of the Leafe old, nor are they much ashamed thereof and therefore would the before remembered Pochohuntas a well featured but wanton (mischievious) young girle Powhatans daughter, sometymes resorting to our Fort, of the age then of 11 or 12 years, gett the boyes forth with her into the market place and make them wheele, falling on their handes turning their heeles upwards, whome she would follow and wheele so her self naked as she was all the Fort over."[21]

Like Smith, Strachey was confused by Powhatan sexual customs: "They are people most voluptious, yet the women very Carefull, not to be suspected of dishonesty without the leave of their husbands, but he giving his consent, they are like Virgills Scrantice and may embrace the acquaintance of any Stranger."[22] He goes on to suggest that their sexual appetites caused their own "country-disease" (syphilis). Even worse, Strachey disillusions tenderhearted readers by informing them that Smith's loving savior (who later became Rolfe's young bride) had an Indian husband: "Pocohuntas, vsing sometyme to our Fort in tymes past, now marryed to a private Captayne called Kocoum some 2 yeares synce."[23] Much has been made of Strachey's reference to Kocoum being a lowly private captain, stressing that Pocahontas was not married to an important Indian chief. Yet virtually nothing is known about Kocoum, the circumstances of their marriage, or the bride price that was paid. If he was indeed a private captain, not a great Indian chief, perhaps that was due to his age. Young warriors were not chiefs; that was a leadership position bestowed after a proven record of wisdom gained through experience. Kocoum may have attracted Pocahontas by proving himself to be an excellent hunter and warrior.[24] Except for Strachey, English colonists and mythmakers denied the existence of Kocoum and consistently portrayed Pocahontas as a virginal Indian princess. From an English perspective, Rolfe was a much better catch for Pocahontas anyway.

Smith (and the mythmakers who studied his works) praises Pocahontas for possessing the foresight to appreciate and accept Englishmen, Christianity, and the new world order. The reality that she was kidnapped and held for ransom in Jamestown for more than a year needs careful explanation. According to English descriptions of her captivity in 1613, she displayed an inner desire to learn Christianity and fell in love with an attentive colonist who aided in her spiritual salvation. John Rolfe was in the throes of sorrow when he first met Pocahontas. He had been aboard the *Sea Venture* with Strachey in July 1609 when the ship was struck by a hurricane and ran aground in Bermuda. Rolfe's English wife and child did not survive the ordeal. In 1610 he arrived in Jamestown a grieving twenty-eight-year-old man. He sought solace in the company of Reverend Alexander Whitaker, who was Pocahontas's sympathetic jailer and religious instructor. Rolfe began assisting Pocahontas in her linguistic and religious studies. Over time, and despite his better judgment, he fell in love with his eager student.

Rolfe attempts to explain his conflicted feelings in a letter to Governor Sir Thomas Dale. He insists that although he could have attracted a more appropriate mate, he was drawn to Pocahontas. Yet he was haunted by the "passions of [his] troubled soul," wondering if his attraction to Pocahontas was the work of the devil. Lovesick and tormented, he vows, "I make betweene God and my owne Conscience be a sufficient wyttnes, at the dreadful day of Judgment (when the secrets of all mens harts shalbe opened) to condemn me herin yf my chiefe intent and purpose be not to stryve with all my power of boddy and mynde in the undertaking of soe weighty a matter (no waye leade soe farr foorth as mans weakness may pmytt, with thevenbridled desire of Carnall affection) for the good of the Planacon, the honor of Countrye, for the glorye of God."[25] Rolfe assures the governor of Pocahontas's "greate apparance of love to me, her desyre to be taught and instructed in the knowledg of God." He avoids mentioning the possibility that marriage to Pocahontas might entitle him to Virginia land (which it did). Instead he professes that his only motivation is to facilitate her spiritual conversion. He characterizes her as a noble savage burdened by her uncivilized nature; she was "blynde," "hungry," and "naked."

Rolfe describes his overwhelming Christian duty to save Pocahontas. His words, however, demonstrate a concern for potential criticism: "Nowe if the vulgar sorte, whoe square all mens actions by the bare rule of theire owne filthiness, shall taxe or taunt me in this my godly labor, Lett them knowe tis not my hungrye appetite to gorge my selfe with incontinencye, Sure (if I woulde and were soe sensually inclined) I might satisfie suce desire, though not without a seared Conscience, yet with Christians more pleasing to the eye and less fearefull in the offence unlawfully Comytted."[26] Rolfe stresses his godly inspiration; he was not physically attracted to Pocahontas.

Governor Dale sanctioned the marriage and sent word to Chief Powhatan, who also consented to the union. Chief Powhatan did not attend the ceremony in 1614, although he sent Pocahontas's relatives in his place and offered the couple land as a wedding gift. It is difficult to determine whether Pocahontas or Rolfe married for love; marriages in Powhatan culture and in English culture were often based on ambition, not necessarily love. According to English colonial interpretations, Pocahontas and Rolfe experienced a genuine and pure love that transcended racial boundaries and initiated a period of peace. Colonists referred to the years 1614–1616 as "Pocahontas's

Peace." Smith characterizes their union, saying, "I have read the substance of this relation, in a letter written by Sir Thomas Dale, another by Master Whitaker [the revernd], and a third by Master John Rolfe; how carefull they were to instruct her in Christianity, and how capable and desirous shee was thereof, after she had beene some time thus tutored, shee never had desire to goe to her father, nor could well endure the society of her owne nation: the true affection she constantly bare her husband was for her love, as he deeply protested, was wonderfull and she openly renounced her countries idolatry, confessed the faith of Christe and was baptized."[27] Pocahontas may have been kidnapped, but according to Smith and Rolfe, she was grateful.

The English attempted to strengthen the kinship bond that was rekindled by Pocahontas's marriage to John Rolfe in 1614. The expanding English population and potential profits from tobacco exports required additional Indian land. Tobacco became an exciting Virginia commodity after Rolfe's first successful crop. Colonists exported twenty thousand pounds of tobacco in 1617, and forty thousand pounds in 1618.[28] According to historian Frances Mossiker, early colonial tobacco plantations averaged five thousand acres; by 1704 tobacco plantations averaged thirty-seven thousand acres. To facilitate English territorial expansion, a messenger was sent to Chief Powhatan requesting another daughter to wed Jamestown governor Sir Thomas Dale. The messenger was Ralph Hamor, Strachey's replacement as official secretary of the colony, who served in that role from 1611 to 1614. He later reconciled his reports and published *A True Discourse of the Present Estate of Virginia* in 1615. Most of his work deals with how the colony secured an adequate food supply after the devastating winter of 1610. He also describes Pocahontas's capture at the hands of Captain Argall, her spiritual conversion, her marriage to John Rolfe, and the peace that resulted from their union.

In May of 1614 Hamor approached Powhatan with Thomas Salvage as interpreter. Powhatan immediately recognized Salvage as an English boy who had participated in a cultural exchange with the Powhatans, run away, and never returned. Chief Powhatan immediately asked what had become of the Powhatan boy that was sent across the waters to meet King James in exchange for Salvage. Discussion further degenerated when Powhatan turned to Hamor and asked why he was not wearing the necklace of pearls he had given to Governor Dale, which the chief had insisted all official messengers wear. The chief then asked about his daughter and her new life. Salvage relayed Hamor's reply: "his daughter was so well contented that she would not change her life to returne and live with him, wherat he laughed heartily and said he was glad of it."[29] Considering Powhatan's previous interrogation of Salvage and Hamor, his laughter may not have been genuine pleasure.

After an uncomfortable start, Hamor finally turned to the matter at hand. He began by professing Governor Dale's brotherly friendship and explained that the English had heard of another "exquisite perfection" young daughter who was just twelve years old. Chief Powhatan immediately grasped where the conversation was going and interrupted, but Hamor persisted, informing Powhatan that the honorable Governor Dale was willing to accept the child as a "wife and bedfellow" now that the two groups were already "united together." According to Hamor, Powhatan's reply was respectful and firm: "But to your purpose, my daughter whom my brother desireth, should within these few daies to be wife to a great Woroance for two bushels of Roanoake (a small kind of beads made from oyster shells that were used as currency) and it is true she has already gone with him three daies jorney from me."[30] Hamor then suggested Powhatan call her back because the child was not old enough for marriage. Hamor stressed the importance of peace and assured the chief that Dale would offer far more in payment, but Powhatan was adamant: "he loved his daughter as deere as his owne life, and though he had many children, he delighted in none of them as much as in her, whom if he should not often beholde, he could not possibly live." He also reminded Hamor that he had already given one daughter and instructed the Englishmen not to "bereave" him of a second. Pocahontas was already married to Rolfe, and her father had never seen her again.

Smith retells the story of Hamor's meeting with Powhatan in his *Generall Historie of Virginia*, with a slight variation. He suggests that the Chief already "sold" his daughter to a nearby "werowance."[31] Yet the word "sold" is his translation. Smith did not understand

Powhatan gender customs; the bride price recognized a wife's value and indicated the potential husband's skill as a provider. Powhatan did not sell his daughters to enrich himself. In fact, he refused Governor Dale's higher offer and clarified that he loved his daughter dearly and could not bear to go without seeing her. Chief Powhatan's response to Hamor is telling. He was unwilling to give another daughter to the Englishmen, regardless of the price, and ended the discussion instructing Hamor to urge him no further. Unlike Smith, who considered twelve-year-old Pocahontas too young to consider as a potential mate, Governor Dale was eager to accept a twelve-year-old Indian princess. He likely wanted to secure another large tract of Powhatan land to establish his own successful tobacco enterprise. Governor Dale recognized the value of Native diplomatic and economic kinship ties, but by 1616 Chief Powhatan was unwilling to continue the intimate connection.[32]

Rolfe's love for Pocahontas may or may not have been genuine. He suggests that he was willing to accept the savage bride regardless of her looks or the social liabilities a union with her might bring, but he neglects to mention the significant advantages she brought him. Rolfe came to Virginia with a plan for economic success. His disastrous voyage on the *Sea Venture*, nine stranded months in Bermuda, and the loss of his English wife and daughter did not deter his ambition. Through all of his hardships, he managed to arrive in Virginia with Spanish tobacco seeds that he had smuggled from Trinidad. His plan was to blend the Spanish variety with local Virginia tobacco. Pocahontas provided him with invaluable information about the best time to plant and harvest tobacco and the best locations for such a crop as well as the vast acreage that Chief Powhatan gave as a wedding gift. While Rolfe was providing religious instruction, Pocahontas provided agricultural instruction. Virginia's first successful harvest was sent to England in March of 1614, the same year Rolfe and Pocahontas were married. The following year their baby, Thomas, was born. He was named for Governor Sir Thomas Dale, who had sanctioned their union and then attempted to marry his own Indian princess.

We do not know much about Pocahontas and Rolfe's brief marriage and virtually nothing about Pocahontas's relationship with the other colonists. We do not know to whom she turned during childbirth. Powhatan custom was for the mother to isolate herself, with a female relative to serve as midwife. There is no official record regarding Thomas's birth, but it seems likely that Pocahontas snuck off to the forest in the company of another Powhatan female. We do know that Pocahontas insisted that her sister, Matachanna, travel to England to help care for Thomas in 1616. We also know that during the final moments of her life she was surrounded by the Powhatan attendants who had accompanied her across the Atlantic, including Matachanna and her priest husband. This is compelling evidence that she did not reject her Powhatan family or culture as Smith, Hamor, and Strachey imply.

The trip to London must have been an astonishing experience, although not a happy one for Pocahontas. It was a seven-week voyage aboard the *Treasure*, the very ship she had been captured on three years prior. This time Captain Argall took her on a much longer journey. There were over a hundred passengers and crew on board the cramped and dingy ship. It carried Pocahontas (Rebecca) and one-year-old Thomas, John Rolfe and a shipment of his Virginia tobacco, a dozen Native representatives (including Matachanna and her husband, Uttamatomakkin), and Sir Thomas Dale (whose term as governor was completed). The Indian contingent was horrified that the ship, with no facilities for excretory purposes, traveled day and night. They were accustomed to docking at night to sleep and perform bodily functions. Like most transatlantic ships in the early seventeenth century, the *Treasure* was damp, cold, crowded, filthy, and infested with vermin.

Their arrival in London provided an opportunity for the Virginia Company to celebrate the economic opportunity in Virginia and revive financial interest in the colonial endeavor. Religious authorities and the English court reveled in the conversion of an indigenous soul. As the Virginia entourage was paraded around London, Pocahontas grew weaker. A respiratory illness led organizers to relocate Pocahontas and her family to the countryside. They took refuge in Brantford, yet Pocahontas's condition continued to deteriorate. As her health declined her mood soured, particularly after a surprise meeting with John Smith.

Pocahontas's encounter with Smith, whom she had thought dead, suggests that she felt betrayed. By 1616 Chief Powhatan (in Virginia) and Pocahontas (in England) were both showing signs of distrust. Smith relates his uncomfortable exchange with Mrs. Rolfe in *The Generall Historie*: "Being about this time preparing to set saile for New England, I could not stay to doe her that service I desired, and she well deserved; but hearing shee was at Branford with divers of my friends, I went to see her: After a modest salutation, without any word, she turned about, obscured her face, as not seeming well contented."[33] According to Smith, Pocahontas needed time to gather her composure. When she rejoined the group, she informed Smith,

> You did promise Powhatan what was yours should bee his, and he the like to you; you called him father being in his land a stranger and by the same reason so must I doe you: which though I would have excused, I durst not allow of that title, because she was a King's daughter; with a well set countenance she said, Were you not afraid to come into my fathers Countrie, and caused feare in him and all his people (but mee) and feare you heare I should call you father; I tell you then I will, and you shall call mee childe, and so I will bee for ever and ever your Counriemen. They did tell us always you were dead, and I knew no other till I came to Plimoth; yet Powhatan did command Uttamatomakkin to seeke you, and know the truth, because your Countriemen lie much.[34]

Pocahontas was gravely ill when she had this encounter with Smith. Yet her frustration with him is palpable. Was she frustrated that Smith had abandoned her? According to Smith, she would have married him if not for his honor and discretion. Had she envisioned a life as Smith's wife? She indicates that her father doubted the stories of his death and instructed Uttamatomakkin to look for Smith in the far-off land. Did she lose faith in her mission to build a common future with the Englishmen who "lie much"?

She died shortly after this exchange with Smith. Just after the Virginians started back across the Atlantic, she was carried ashore on a litter, too weak to walk, in Gravesend on the southwest bank of the Thames. Her husband, child, sister, and brother-in-law continued on to Virginia after her death. Matachanna, young Thomas's care-taker, was also desperately ill. When the child showed signs of ill-ness, the party stopped to leave Thomas in the care of others. He was left in England to be reared by his paternal uncle, Henry Rolfe. Thomas never saw his father again; John Rolfe died in Virginia a few years later at the age of thirty-seven. Thomas did not grow up knowing either of his parents.

Thomas remained with his uncle until he was twenty years old. He married in 1632, but like his father, he lost his young wife after the birth of their daughter in 1633. In 1635 he ventured to Virginia, perhaps in an attempt to discover his heritage. Thomas claimed a portion of his father's estate (John Rolfe had remarried and had another heir in Virginia) and began a new life as a colonial planta-tion owner. He married the daughter of a prominent colonist, gained access to more land, and had a baby girl. Little is historically known about Thomas's life in Virginia. Colonial records indicate that in 1641 Thomas petitioned the governor of Jamestown for permission to visit his mother's relatives, who were by then enemies of the colony. After a devastating Indian attack in 1644, he was commissioned a lieutenant in charge of Fort James. In exchange for defending the English against his indigenous relatives, he was awarded an exten-sive stretch of property that was adjacent to the fort. Thomas died in obscurity around 1680.

The historical record is flattering to Pocahontas, yet other Pow-hatan women are described as downtrodden by an onerous lifestyle. John Smith and William Strachey both acknowledge Powhatan women as industrious, maintaining crops and home, but Powhatan men are characterized as slothful. The English, who considered hunting and fishing leisure activities, could not understand Indian gender roles. To them, constructing homes and tending to crops were men's work. From a seventeenth-century English perspective, Indian women were overworked and degraded while Indian men came and went as they pleased. Strachey observes, "The men bestowe their tymes in fish-ing, hunting, wars, and such man-like exercises without the doores, scorning to be seen in any effeminate labour, which is the Cause that the women be very paynefull, and the men often idle."[35] The seemingly inappropriate treatment of Indian women in Powhatan

Simon Van De Passe, *Pocahontas*, engraving, 1616.

society—the laborious and sexually exploitive existence they suffered—became further justification for the English to displace Indian civilization.

From an English perspective, Powhatan gender and sexual customs exemplified the uncivil nature of their society. Important English visitors enjoyed feasts of incredible proportions, extravagant entertainment, and comfortable lodging, which occasionally included a female companion. There were undoubtedly Englishmen who accepted Indian women as bedfellows. These intimate connections were a strategic part of Indian hospitality. In 1612 Strachey observes, "After this verbal Entertaynement, they cause such victual as they haue or can provide to be brought forth with which they feast him fully and freely, and at night they bring him to the lodging appointed for him, whither vpon their departure, they send a young woman fresh paynted redd with Pochoe and oyle to be his bedfellow."[36] In the morning, influential guests were again lavishly fed and sent on their way with provisions of meat and bread. This pattern of generosity and intimacy was an Indian invitation to peaceful relations and a common future. Indian men and women enjoyed more sexual freedom than the English were accustomed to, leading the English to disapprove of Indian gender customs and to disrespect Indian marriages. For instance, Pocahontas's marriage to Kocoum was mentioned only briefly by Strachey and otherwise avoided. Her marriage to an Indian man was insignificant; her marriage to Rolfe was paramount.

Jamestown colonists consistently interpreted Pocahontas as an Indian princess who rejected her royal title and Indian lifeways to live among the English. She repeatedly aided the English colony, converted to Christianity, married an Englishman, lived in his world, produced a mixed-blood son, and traveled to England where her likeness was captured in an engraving by Simon van de Passe.[37] Like the engraving that presents her in the latest European garb, the Virginia Company presented Pocahontas from an English perspective and flaunted the fact that she chose the superior race, thereby legitimizing the conquest as a benevolent endeavor. Her marriage to Rolfe solidified European rights to the indigenous landscape. English colonials portrayed Pocahontas (as Díaz had portrayed Malinche) as a welcoming Indian woman and a perfect indigenous mother of a new biracial era.

SACAGAWEA AND THE CORPS OF DISCOVERY

The twenty months that Sacagawea spent with the Lewis and Clark expedition provided the only tangible record of her life. Their journals reveal appreciation for her work ethic, fortitude, compassion, and for her approach to humanity. The expedition arrived in the Mandan and Hidatsa villages in late October 1804, and Charbonneau appeared with two young Indian wives a short time later asking to hire on as an interpreter/guide. Captain Clark recorded engaging the French-Canadian and one of his Shoshone wives as interpreters on November 4. Charbonneau and Sacagawea immediately moved into the fort, and she delivered a baby, Baptiste, on February 11. Captain Lewis describes a "tedious labor, marked with violent pain."[38] Lewis called for Rene Jessaume, a free trader living among the Mandan, to assist Clark with the delivery. Hidatsa custom was for a woman to give birth in her mother's lodge, in the care of female clanswomen, and for the grandmother to bury the placenta and tend to mother and child postdelivery.[39] It must have been strange for Sacagawea to have her baby in an army camp full of foreign men, and even more awkward to have Clark and Jessaume serve as her midwives. After many hours of labor, Jessaume emerged and requested two rings of a rattlesnake tail, which locals believed would hasten the baby's delivery. Lewis provided the rattle, which was ground up, diluted with water, and given to Sacagawea to drink. The baby boy was born ten minutes later. From that day forward, Lewis and Clark were extraordinarily devoted to the young Indian mother and her child.

Because Charbonneau provided a more-than -adequate tent, the two captains bunked with the family. Lewis describes the shelter as being "made of tanned buffalo hides sewn together with sinew to fit around the cone-shaped lodge."[40] Their cohabitation assured Sacagawea's protection from the sexual interests of the other men in the expedition; she was the only woman in the company of between forty-five and fifty men who were a long way from home and loved ones. Sacagawea was a valuable member of the expedition and spent almost all of her time in the company of the captains. This physical closeness provided an opportunity for a close emotional relationship to form, and the captains' journal entries express a clear yet reserved admiration for Sacagawea.

Baptiste was an infant when the group departed Fort Mandan and a nineteen-month-old toddler at the end of the journey. The captains refer to the youngster as Pompy, a term of endearment, although some have suggested a racist one. The boy provided laughter, warmth, and worry as Lewis and Clark endured the trials of parenthood (teething, cholera, and the mumps), which on occasion kept the captains "walking the floor all night." When the baby was sick, the captains recorded his condition and the medical care he received every day (May 22–28, 1806) until his health was restored. Clark worried about the child's survival during Sacagawea's near-death illness (June 10–20, 1805). On June 16 Lewis wrote, "Sacajawea is near death. Four-month-old Jean Baptiste is held in the arms of his ailing mother. Lewis is extremely concerned not only for both of them but also for the expedition's need for an interpreter who can speak with the Shoshoni people."[41] This quote indicates a sincere concern for the well-being of Sacagawea and her young son and also acknowledges her strategic value to the expedition.

In addition to the entries regarding the nourishment and intermediary services Sacagawea consistently provided (discussed in the previous chapter) and the medical attention mother and child occasionally needed, the captains also offer an assessment of her character during a few critical instances. In May 1805, just before Sacagawea became ill, Charbonneau lost control of a "pirogue" when a burst of violent wind tore the rudder from his hands. This was the second time in as many months that he could have cost the expedition dearly. Lewis records his frustration with the Frenchman:

> Toward evening Charbono, probably one of the most timid Waterman in the world, is at the helm of the white pirogue. . . . A sudon squal of wind stuck her obliquely, and turned her considerably, the steersmen alarmed, instead of putting her before the wind, lofted her up into it,

the wind so violent that it drew the brace of the sail out of the hand of the man who was attending it and instantly upset the pirogue. . . . The boat filled while Charbono still crying to his god for mercy, had not yet recollected the rudder. . . . Lewis almost dove in and swam 300 yards fighting the waves to save the precious articles [papers, instruments, books, medicine, all indispensable to the enterprise]. . . . The articles which floated out were nearly all caught by the squar who was in the rear. This accident had like to have cost us deerly.[42]

Charbonneau needed rescue by the five-man crew as he "cr[ied] to his god for mercy," but Sacagawea remained calm and clear-headed as she recovered the indispensable items that washed overboard: "During this life and death struggle, Sacajawea remains in the back of the sinking vessel [with her baby in one arm] grabbing valuable articles as they float from the boat." Two days later Lewis had not forgiven Charbonneau, but said this of his young wife: "Sacajawea demonstrated fortitude and resolution equal to that of any man on board the stricken craft."[43]

The captains and the Charbonneau family spent a year and a half in each other's company, night and day. They often walked along the shore together. In late June 1805 Clark, Sacagawea, Baptiste, and Charbonneau hiked to the Great Falls of the Missouri River and were surprised by a sudden storm. Clark led them into a deep ravine to take refuge under a rock ledge. The rain quickly turned into a torrential downpour, with hail, thunder, and lightening. With little warning, the raging water, carrying rocks and debris, thundered toward the group. They began frantically climbing up the steep bank to get out of the ravine. Charbonneau scampered to the top first but was overcome by panic. Sacagawea climbed with only one free hand, as she clung to Baptiste with the other, and with Clark pushing her upward from behind: "Without his [Charbonneau's] help Clark and Sacajawea scramble to safety above the water."[44] Once again Charbonneau is described as inept in the face of danger, and Sacagawea as steadfast. Charbonneau's reputation was further tarnished when he struck Sacagawea during an evening meal and was reprimanded by Clark.[45] Charbonneau is consistently portrayed as an awful boatman and dreadful husband, as well as unreliable in an emergency.

Sacagawea is consistently described as resourceful, dependable, and calm in a crisis. The journals also indicate her compassion and generosity. She gave the last lump of sugar to her brother to taste, and Chief Cameahwait was delighted. When Captain Clark was recovering from an illness, she gave him a precious piece of bread made from the last of the flour, even though she had been saving the flour for her baby's first solid food. On another occasion, when the captains were pursuing trade with Pacific Northwest Indians, Sacagawea offered her prized blue beaded belt in exchange for a coveted otter pelt that had not been available no matter what the captains offered. The men of the corps inadvertently recognized the attributes that reinforced the practical qualities of diligence, reserved emotion in times of crisis, steadfastness through adversity, and generosity, which had been instilled in Sacagawea by a Shoshone childhood education.[46] Sacagawea illustrated all of these characteristics during the expedition, and the Euro-Americans benefited and made note of them.

Clark, a more outgoing and personable character than Lewis, forged a tighter bond with the Charbonneau family. His affection for the young boy was demonstrated by his willingness to bunk with the child during times of sickness and health and to administer medical care when needed, as well as by his affectionate nickname for the child. Clark also made a couple of grand gestures at the end of their journey together. In late July 1806 Captain Clark named a remarkable rock formation "Pompy's Tower" and a nearby creek "Baptiste's Creek" after his young travel companion.[47] In one of Clark's last entries (August 17, 1806), he offers this assessment of Charbonneau and Sacagawea: "This man has been very serviceable to us, and his wife was particularly useful among the Shoshones. Indeed, she has borne with a patience truly admirable the fatigues of so long a route, encumbered with the charge of an infant, who is now only 19 months old. We therefore paid Chaboneau his wages amounting to $500.33, including the price of a horse and a lodge purchased from him."[48] Sacagawea was paid nothing, officially.

Clark's most enduring act of friendship was his offer to raise and educate the boy as his own: "I offered to take his little son a butiful promising Child who is 19 months old to which both himself and his wife were willing provided the child had been weened. They observed that in one year the boy would be Sufficiently old to leave his mother and he would then take him to me if I would be so friendly as to raise the Child for him in Such a manner as I thought proper, to which I agreed."[49] We know that young Baptiste made it to St. Louis and that Clark fulfilled his promise. There are records of Clark paying for the boy's education. He graduated from St. Louis Academy in 1823 at eighteen years old, and then spent six years traveling Europe. He returned to St. Louis alone in 1829. By then he spoke French, German, Spanish, and Shoshone. Deciding to begin his own career in the West, he signed on with the American Fur Company and the Rocky Mountain Fur Company, led hunting expeditions for wealthy clients, worked as a scout for Stephen Kearny, and hauled military supplies in preparation for the Mexican-American War. After the war he became an alcalde (mayor) at Mission San Luis Rey de Francia in California and fathered a daughter by a local Hispanic woman. Like his father, however, he did not commit to his children or their mothers. Baptiste resigned as alcalde in the midst of some questionable land deals and was lured to the California Gold Rush, where he prospected for a short time. He later worked as the manager of a hotel. He fell from the historical record and died in Oregon in 1866 at the age of sixty-one.

Sacagawea's life after the expedition is garbled, and two widely separated dates have been said to mark her demise. The uncertainty stems from the habit of European men referring to Indian women as "squaw" or "wife of . . ." in primary records. Charbonneau's polygamous lifestyle also contributed to the confusion surrounding Sacagawea's later life. We know that Charbonneau and an Indian wife delivered Baptiste to St. Louis, but do not know for certain whether that wife was Sacagawea. In 1807 the government awarded each male member of the expedition a land grant of 320 acres. Land records confirm that Charbonneau bought additional land on the Missouri River near St. Louis from Clark in 1810, but he then sold it back to him several months later. Sacagawea's name was on none of these records, of course, yet there is written evidence that Clark specifically invited her and Charbonneau to St. Louis, and it seems likely that she accompanied Baptiste and Charbonneau there.

Charbonneau apparently missed his life in the mountains and headed back up the Missouri River, signing on with the Manuel Lisa Fur Trade Company in 1811. Company records verify his employment, and other fur trappers mention him in their journals. Henry Brackenridge recorded that Charbonneau and an Indian wife were with his party as it departed St. Louis for the West in 1811.[50] Another trader, John Luttig, recorded in his journal on December 20, 1812, that "the wife of Charbonneau" died of "a putrid fever."[51] The lack of a name for Charbonneau's wife leaves room for doubt about the wife being Sacagawea, which chapter 7 will discuss. Luttig also mentions that the woman left a "fine daughter." The following year Charbonneau officially signed over formal custody of a son (Jean Baptiste) and a daughter (Lisette) to Clark. There is no further record of Lisette in Clark's papers, and it is believed she died in childhood. Charbonneau continued a relationship with Clark, working occasionally as a trader/trapper and occasionally as a translator for the government at the Upper Missouri Agency. It is likely that Clark, the territorial governor of Missouri, helped Charbonneau secure this government job. Soon after Clark's death in 1838, Charbonneau lost his government employment. He spent the last years of his life around Fort Mandan, where he died in the 1840s.

Most scholars accept that Sacagawea died in 1812 at Fort Manuel. During the early stages of Indian-white contact, more than cultural information and trade goods were exchanged; Euro-Americans introduced alien sicknesses that devastated Native peoples. The more contact Indians had with the newcomers, the greater their risk of infection. Sacagawea's time living in St. Louis—where she was exposed to diseases that her body had no immunity to—may have contributed to the "putrid fever."[52] Death by sickness was a fate shared by Malinche and Pocahontas as well. All three women lost their lives as a result of close contact with outsiders (perhaps it was an occupational hazard).

Wyoming historian Grace Hebard offers an alternative end to Sacagawea's story. Hebard suggests that Sacagawea lived a long life in the West that included living among the Comanches for twenty-seven years as a wife and mother, where she was known as Wadze-wipe; aiding John C. Frémont's expedition in 1848 as the anonymous "woman of the Snake Nation"; and returning to the Shoshone people on the Wind River Reservation as the wise old woman known as Porivo who advocated for the white man's way until her death in 1884.[53] As chapter 7 will discuss, her evidence is twofold: first Frémont's journal, reservation officials, and the Indians interviewed by Hebard describe each of these Indian women much the same as Lewis and Clark described Sacagawea. Second, she claims that Sacagawea would never have left Baptiste alone among strangers in a strange land.

Although Hebard believed that Baptiste's transition to white society would have been exceedingly difficult, the adjustment may not have seemed so awkward to Baptiste or Sacagawea. Baptiste had known Clark since birth, having spent nineteen months sharing a tent with him and being in his care during times of sicknesses. Baptiste was familiar with white ways; his father was French and he had been raised among Americans during the expedition. He had not lived within a stable and secure environment among Indian relatives, but rather spent his life on the move, mixing with diverse peoples. Sacagawea lived through several cultural transitions herself: when she joined the Hidatsa, when she was given to Charbonneau, and then again when she joined the Americans. While these transitions must have been traumatic, they were also part of a Native existence that was swirling with change. Nevertheless Hebard's theory clouded the circumstances of Sacagawea's death and launched further investigation despite the fact that academics insisted the biographer had operated on the margins of acceptable scholarship.

Like Malinche and Pocahontas, Sacagawea most likely died as a young woman in her twenties. She escorted and introduced the newcomers to Natives, yet she did not live to witness the repercussions of her work. From a non-Indian perspective, she was a feminine noble savage who understood and appreciated the superiority of the coming order. The men of the expedition found her to be surprisingly knowledgeable, nurturing, and compassionate despite being an Indian woman. Other Native women mentioned in the journals are described as miserably overworked, unattractive, and lacking dignity and virtue. Lewis observes, "They treat their women but with little respect, and compel them to perform every species of drudgery."[54]

Later in the same entry he suggests, "The chastity of their women is not held in high estimation, and the husband will for a trifle barter the companion of his bed for a night or longer if he conceives the reward adequate."[55] Sacagawea was deemed special and is portrayed as nurturing and helpful, not exploited and overworked.

Both captains acknowledge her consistent, diligent efforts to obtain food for the group, as well as her expertise on topography, routes, and abandoned Indian camps. When the corps finally encountered the Shoshone people (from whom the Americans needed horses to portage over the mountains), Clark wrote, "Sacajawea would once again prove her value as an interpreter."[56] The captain's recognition of Sacagawea's skills, generosity, and motherhood justified her inclusion in America's frontier fable of taming the wilderness. She was separated from other Indian women and imagined as a sympathetic Native woman and a feminine complement to the masculine heroics of the expedition. The distinction between Sacagawea (a nurturing mother who demonstrated resilience and devotion) and other unfortunate Indian women (degraded and overworked) provided a historical foundation that fueled her legend.

A scarcity of facts prevents any absolute understanding of Sacagawea's life. The details of her Native experience were of little concern to her literate Euro-American companions. Their interest in her was one-dimensional: she was viewed as a feminine asset that eased their transcontinental journey. As the journals progress, it is clear that she earned the explorers' admiration. They describe her according to their own Euro-American expectation of femininity. She was taken out of her Native cultural context, but never considered a legitimate female member of Anglo culture. Instead she occupied an abstract space. Like Pocahontas, Sacagawea was neither completely "savage" nor completely "civilized."[57] Over time Sacagawea evolved from her modest beginning in the original journal entries, which describe her as a steadfast and knowledgeable Indian woman and an interesting side note to the main events, into America's symbolic "Indian princess" who welcomed and aided the newcomers.

Lewis and Clark make numerous references in their journals regarding the degradation of other Indian women. On August 19, 1805, Lewis describes Shoshone gender roles: "They [women] collect the wild fruits and roots, attend to the horses or assist in that duty, cook, dress the skins and make all their apparel, collect wood and make their fires, arrange and form their lodges, and when they travel pack the horses and take charge of all the baggage; in short the man dose little else except attend his horses hunt and fish. The man considers himself degraded if he is compelled to walk any distance, and if he is so unfortunately poor as only to possess two horses he rides the best himself and leaves the woman or women if he has more than one, to transport their baggage and children on the other, and to walk if the horse is unable to carry the additional weight of their persons."[58] The explorers were appalled by the work assigned to Native women. Five days later, on August 24,1805, Lewis writes, "Charbonneau is given trade goods to use to purchase a horse for Sacajawea."[59] As a woman in the company of Euro-Americans, Sacagawea would not suffer such indignity.

Euro-American observers misunderstood and misrepresented Native gender roles. Their distorted impressions have colored subsequent interpretations of Indian women and Native American societies. For instance, cultural comparisons of Native and non-Native gender ideologies have remained problematic over time. The gender hierarchy, gender domains, and gender expectations that incoming Europeans recognized were absent in Native societies.[60] In the days of Lewis and Clark, Euro-Americans defined wives and children as dependents; family and home were legally the property of men. A woman's sexual purity was essential for respectability in American society. But these Euro-American gender standards had little relevance in Native America.[61] Throughout Native America, Indian women were not defined as dependents or property; they were contributing members of society, whose work was critical to the maintenance of the group. Plains Indian women provided shelter and nourishment for their people. They processed commodities (hides and furs), participated in trade dealings, and mediated cross-cultural discussions. Status for Shoshone men and women was determined by the quality of their work and their commitment to the group. Their work was complementary or "bi-turnal," and each task was necessary to their group's preservation.[62] Women's sexuality was not a measure of their virtue; rather, it was understood as a powerful force with profound repercussions, and it was certainly monitored in cross-cultural relationships.[63]

Malinche, Pocahontas, and Sacagawea were double agents actively involved in designing a new multinational future. They mediated between colliding worlds, softened the changes brought by Europeans, and tried to perpetuate Native lifeways. All three women lived and worked intimately among the newcomers. Unlike most of their Native contemporaries, these women had firsthand knowledge of the foreigners, including their capabilities, their intentions, and their foibles. Malinche, Pocahontas, and Sacagawea offered relevant cultural information to both sides and worked to limit hostility and hardship. These women and their white male companions developed a mutual respect, and they were surprisingly committed to each other. They trusted and protected each other on dynamic and competitive multinational frontiers.

PART II

INDIAN WOMEN IN MYTH

The lives of Malinche, Pocahontas, and Sacagawea were obscured by centuries of deliberate mythic abstraction. The remaining chapters of this book consider specific historical and cultural interpretations that introduced strategic elements to each woman's story and redirected the national narrative. Analysis of each woman's mythic alterations reveals an interesting pattern in the development and maintenance of national identity in Mexico and the United States.

The women's mythic evolution begins in the vague records left by European conquerors. These self-centered masculine tales identify the women as Indian princesses drawn to superior men and cultures. Later writers elaborated on and expanded their stories to legitimize colonization. All three women were idealized as loving Indian women who offered inheritance rights to the land; they mothered mixed-blood children and gave birth to new nations. As Indians and as women, Malinche, Pocahontas, and Sacagawea symbolized a hospitable and fertile landscape brimming with potential. Mexican and U.S. mythmakers have simplified the frontier past by suggesting that the women's activities were inspired by a heterosexual love that transcended race and brought the best of the Old World together with the best of the New World.

Over time both nations have struggled to historicize the complexities of European conquest, particularly festering racial tensions. Romanticized portrayals of national formation began to face relentless cynicism under the stress of colonial social hierarchies. The foundational fiction of interracial love was repeatedly challenged during epochs of social strife and discontent. Historical revisions have occasionally assigned new meanings to the women to accommodate shifting national moods and project an alternative national image. These women have been symbolized as beautiful, feminine compliments to Euro-masculine heroics, noble savages eager for instruction, slaves to the men around them, victims of colonization, and scapegoats for Indian defeat.

CHAPTER FIVE

MALINCHE

Over the course of nearly five hundred years Mexicans have created and re-created contradictory versions of mythic Malinche. Interpretations have been deliberately crafted to support contemporary social agendas and shifting goals for the future. Indians told their story of the Spanish conquest in Native pictorial codices beginning in the mid-sixteenth century. Several Indian records depict the Spanish invasion as a single event in a long historical narrative, and often not the most significant episode. Indians who lived with the memory of the conquest typically portrayed Malinche as instrumental to negotiations between Spanish conquistadors and indigenous caciques. She appears at the center of events, finely dressed, with speech scrolls emanating from her mouth.[1] Indians who lived through the conquest and recorded it for posterity recognized Malinche as a central figure who explained Spanish intentions for a new future.

Sixteenth-century Indian historians often worked under the direction of Spanish colonial authorities. Spanish friars began arriving in Mexico during the late 1520s, less than a decade after Cortés's victory in Tenochtitlán. Franciscans recorded the first information on the indigenous cultures of Mexico, and they frequently included Indian historical renderings. The goal of these cultural investigations was to learn about the Natives in order to facilitate their spiritual conversion. Recent scholars have been skeptical of these Indian codices, suggesting that Spanish religious and linguistic instruction contaminated a pure indigenous perspective. This is an unfortunate reality, but not reason enough to disqualify Indian history and deny autonomous Native thought. Indigenous historians were capable of incorporating Spanish information without abandoning their pre-contact worldview. After all, Mesoamericans had a long tradition, predating Spanish arrival, of adopting and blending diverse cultural and religious elements to explain their interconnected multicultural reality in Mexico.

Central Mexico experienced successive waves of immigration prior to Spanish entrance, and Mexicans had practiced cultural accommodation long before 1521. In the generations following the conquest, a majority of Indians went about their lives, taking advantage of Spanish information when it was beneficial, interpreting the newcomers' actions in terms of similar aspects of their own culture, and reconstructing Christianity to suit their needs.[2] Indian worldviews were not contaminated by Spanish influence; rather, Spanish influence added yet another layer of cultural and religious input. Indians told a historical tale of the conquest from their own unique perspective, one that included the Spanish information they deemed relevant to their experience. Colonial Indian portrayals of Malinche (in the *Lienso de Tlaxcala* painting and the *Florentine*, *Tlzatlan*, and *Tepetlan* codices) illustrate a significant female intermediary who negotiated between cultures during a diplomatic reorganization in Mexico and a rulership change in Tenochtitlán.

Colonizing Spaniards, on the other hand, presented an alternative Malinche. They portrayed her as a minor character that illustrated a willing acceptance of Spanish instruction. Cortés described Malinche as an interesting feminine side-story that validated the conquistadors' heroics. Others highlighted her Christian salvation in order to moralize Spain's colonization project in Mexico and repudiate the Black Legend. Spaniards in the colonial era (Cortés, Gómara, Díaz, Sahagún) provided a foundation for mythic Malinche, illustrating how Indians welcomed a Spanish Christian alternative in Mexico. Indians and Spaniards created strategic histories of the conquest, and Malinche is a relevant character in nearly all of them.

As Spanish rule was increasingly rejected during the push for Mexican independence, mythic Malinche changed radically. Within a few hundred years of the conquest, Malinche began to emerge as a more haunting figure. Embittered nationalists reimagined her as a scapegoat to be blamed for indigenous defeat; she became a feminine traitor who assisted the Spanish colonizers. After independence, Malinche was presented as a Mexican Eve, a sexual figure who gives into temptation to satisfy her own feminine desire for male attention, a polar opposite to the Virgin of Guadalupe, the ultimate Mexican female. Mexicans have struggled to accommodate dichotomous images of Malinche: Did she nurture the coming of a new Christian world and mother a new race that blended the best of indigenous and Spanish heritage? Or was she a whore who slept with the enemy and opened Native Mexico to Spanish domination? Mythic Malinche has never recovered from this bipolar legacy.

Malinche's role in the conquest has been difficult to reconcile with the ongoing discourse concerning Mexican history. This chapter will follow Malinche's ideological journey through Mexican nationalism; it will analyze generational and cultural issues that have shaped each mythic portrayal. It is a long journey that begins in the colonial period and extends into the present, as commentators in our own time have also strategically manipulated her legend to address contemporary social concerns. Mythic Malinche exists outside the confines of reality and offers little information about her lifetime. Analysis of mythic Malinche reveals insight into the myth's creators and their nationalist agendas over time. As collective sentiments in Mexico have changed, mythic Malinche has also changed.

COLONIAL PERIOD

Sixteenth-century Native codices offer a compelling portrait of the indigenous perspective on Malinche.[3] Malinche is featured prominently in the Native pictorials that Fray Bernardino de Sahagún included in his ethnographic study of preconquest Mexico. Sahagún arrived in New Spain in 1529 as a member of the first contingent of religious men sent to begin the work of saving Indian souls. Sahagún took a keen interest in indigenous lifeways and was the first to chronicle Native society, culture, and religion in his *Florentine Codex*.[4] His goal was to gain insight into the Native perspective for the purpose of translating Christianity and making it applicable to Indian

Malinche shown with speech scrolls conveying Cortés's message, from *Floren-tine Codex.*

lives. His ethnographic study is divided into twelve books and contains more than two thousand Native historical images. Many pictorials in book twelve, which specifically covers the conquest, focus on Malinche. Native historian/artists depicted her in the center of events, speaking to dignitaries, with attention focused on her. Her clothing often suggests high social status; some sixteenth-century codices show her wearing shoes, which is a clear indication of status.

In an Indian historical painting known as *Lienso de Tlaxcala* Malinche is portrayed as a poised woman, directing events. The Tlaxcala municipal government commissioned the wall hanging to highlight the city's commitment to the Spaniards.[5] The original eighty-seven scenes recount the arrival of the Spaniards, their alliance with the Tlaxcalans, and their cooperative effort to defeat the Aztec seat of power in Tenochtitlán. The commemorative artwork was created three decades after the establishment of Spanish colonial rule when it would have been counterproductive for the Tlaxcalans to express regret or resentment toward their Spanish overlords in such a public

Malinche translating from a palace rooftop, from *Florentine Codex.*

display. In several of the surviving scenes, Malinche is featured prominently, negotiating in the center. In the *Tizatlan Codex* she appears
as a dignified orator, instructing Natives as she leads Cortés along
the path to Tenochtitlán. Malinche appears a larger figure than Cortés,
receiving more tribute than the Spanish captain in the *Tepetlan Codex.*
These tangible Indian records suggest that Malinche was considered a central figure in the transformation of the indigenous world.

Indians who lived with the memory of the conquest consistently
portrayed Malinche as a woman of high social status, commanding
the attention of those around her. She frequently appears as the largest
figure in the center of the frame as she directs others. Indigenous

Malinche translating along the route to Tenochtitlán, from *Florentine Codex*.

peoples during and after the conquest interpreted Malinche as an authority during the critical moment of the conquest. Her indigenous contemporaries addressed her with respect by adding the suffix "-tzin" to her Indian name, and Indians referred to Cortés in relation to her. These fragmentary pieces of Indian evidence indicate that

Malinche shown poised and larger than Cortés as she negotiates in Tlaxcala, from *Lienso de Tlaxcala.*

Malinche did not behave as a slave, nor was she regarded as one by her Indian contemporaries. Rather, Malinche was an indigenous woman of consequence and respect, who was intricately involved in the coming of a new social order.

Records left by the conquistadors are more vague in regard to Malinche. Cortés mentions her sparingly in his progress letters to the king. His description of the conquest is carefully crafted, intended to highlight his contribution to the crown and minimize questions regarding his behavior. Bringing attention to Malinche would not have benefited Cortés. He was a married man who had already earned a scandalous reputation for taking concubines. His Spanish wife died under mysterious circumstances shortly after arriving in Mexico to live in his Coyoacan household, which was also home to

Malinche depicted as a dignified orator under Cortés, from *Tizatlan Codex*. Her shoes indicate status.

several young Native women, including Malinche who was pregnant with his child. Cortés was a man of dubious distinction.

Cortés, the Spanish crown, and religious authorities all had reason to be cautious in their characterization of events in Mexico. During and after the conquest, Spain was caught in the uncomfortable grip of international condemnation. A community of nations had questioned the legitimacy of Spain's empire and the behavior of Spanish

Malinche and Cortés receiving tribute in Tepetlan, from *Tepetlan Codex.*

conquistadors. Members of the Spanish court and theologians debated charges of excessive violence and Indian exploitation in the colonies. Bartolomé de las Casas loudly criticized Cortés's brutality in Mexico, particularly the horrific massacre in Cholua.[6] Las Casas's most famous work, *A Short Account of the Destruction of the Indies* (1552) is an exposé on the atrocities committed by the conquistadors in the Americas; he was a renowned defender of the Indians and tireless in his criticism of Cortés.

Justifiable rumors regarding Cortés's behavior among the Indians haunted his prowess in Mexico. From the moment of his departure from Cuba in 1519, he faced relentless inquiry. Cortés's narration of events was certainly deliberate, and he was forced to defend his actions for the rest of his life. In his official progress letters, written between 1519 and 1526, consolidated and translated as *Hernán Cortés: Letters from Mexico,* he rarely mentions Malinche. In letter two he describes her as an Indian woman from Tabasco who is acting as his translator. In letter five (discussed in chapter 2) he elaborates, "I replied that I was the captain of whom the people of Tabasco had spoken, and that if he wished to learn the truth he had only to ask the interpreter with whom he was speaking, Marina, who traveled always in my company after she had been given me as a present with twenty other women. She then told him that what I had said was true and spoke to him of how I had conquered Mexico and of all the other lands which I held subject and had placed beneath Your Majesty's command."[7] Malinche's significance seems irrelevant in this self-serving account. She is presented as a reflection of Cortés to verify his heroic deeds. He stresses that Indians were talking of his greatness throughout the region, that caciques bestowed women upon him, and that all of his efforts were on behalf of his king and country. Yet Cortés inadvertently mentions that Malinche provided more than mere translation; he relied on her to convince American Indians to join his march against the Mexicas.

Cortés did not hesitate to use Malinche as a witness to his valor, particularly when his reputation needed validation. As critics questioned his violence in Cholula, Cortés justified the brutal massacre in letter five. He insists that Malinche had uncovered a Native plot to halt the Spanish advance, forcing his preemptive assault. It is a claim that Bernal Díaz supports in his rendition of events.[8] Bartolomé de las Casas refused to accept their explanations; however, Las Casas and Díaz were involved in their own ideological feud. Díaz, who was awarded an encomienda in Chiapas after the conquest, was an outspoken critic of the policies and outrageous claims made by Las Casas, the bishop of that city. Díaz accused him of misrepresenting the facts and exaggerating the violence of the conquest in order to deny encomenderos their right to indigenous labor.

Unfortunately Malinche left no record of her own to settle the questions surrounding the Cholula massacre.

The events in Cholula tainted Malinche's image as well. Hundreds of years later when the Spanish were ousted from independent Mexico, her alleged actions in Cholula became the metaphoric act that established her as a traitor to her race. Her rejection of a Cholulan husband and her decision to side with the Spaniards symbolized her repudiation of an Indian heritage and Indian men. The fact that she did not consider Cholulans to be her countrymen was irrelevant to this mythic interpretation of Malinche as traitor/whore. Her negative feminine image was further substantiated by her sexual relationship with Cortés (which produced a child) and her subsequent marriage to another conquistador (with whom she also had a child). Long after European disease killed Malinche's body, after Spanish promises went unfulfilled in Mexico and Spain was rejected, she reemerged as a Mexican Eve. During the independence era, she became the feminine perpetrator of Mexico's original sin because she chose her own sexual gratification over Indian welfare. Spanish explanations for their attack on Cholula became the foundation for Malinche's mythic representation as the Mexican Eve.

Early Spanish histories of the conquest present Malinche in contradicting roles in relation to Cortés. Francisco López de Gómara, who was Cortés's faithful secretary after his return to Spain but was not directly involved in the Mexican expedition, published a biography of Cortés translated as *Cortés: The Life and the Conqueror*. According to Gómara, who used Cortés himself as his source, victory in Mexico was attributed to Spain's divine favor and the actions of heroic Spaniards. An indigenous female had no significant role in this portrayal of the conquest. Unlike the Indian perspective of Malinche as a respected intermediary who explained the coming changes, Gómara refers to Malinche as an Indian female slave/interpreter. A participating conquistador who gave Malinche significant attention was Bernal Díaz, who wrote *Historia verdadera de la conquista de la Nueva España* thirty years after his experience as a foot soldier in Cortés's army (it was published in 1632). Although some consideration must be given to the fact that Díaz finished his tale as an elderly man in his seventies, his account provides the most detailed information about Malinche's life and her role in the conquest. His introduction suggests that he was unsatisfied with the representation put forth by Cortés and Gómara. Díaz claims his motivation was to provide the real truth, which involved more than the heroics of Cortés.[9]

Students and scholars of the conquest gravitate toward Díaz's work. It is unique for several reasons. First, he directly participated in the events he described. Second, he wrote with little to lose and little to gain. He lived as a poor man, and he died a poor man not long after his book was completed; Díaz was not protecting his wealth or prestige. He writes of the participants (Indians and Spaniards) as people with complex motivations, and he records both their admirable and less-than-admirable qualities. He never attempts to obscure the savagery or violence of the conflict, yet his words certainly reveal a sincere belief that he and his fellow conquistadors were valiant soldiers of the cross. They endured extreme hardship and risked everything to bring light to the Indians who they believed had been living in darkness.

Díaz provides an intimate look at Malinche, both as a woman and as a contributor to the creation of New Spain. He testifies as to her royal heritage, her intelligence, and her attractiveness. As an old man, Bernal Díaz relishes his memory of her: "One of the Indian ladies was christened Doña Marina. She was truly a great princess, the daughter of a Cacique and the mistress of vassals, as was very evident in her appearance." And he describes her: "good-looking, intelligent, and self assured."[10] Díaz characterizes Malinche as an elite Native beauty, whom Cortés awarded to the Spaniard with the highest social rank. Díaz also notes her strength, resourcefulness, and courage. Remembering the Tlaxcalan campaign, he writes, "though she heard every day that the Indians were going to kill us and eat our flesh with chillies, and though she had seen us surrounded in recent battles and knew that we were all wounded and sick, yet she betrayed no weakness but a courage greater than that of a woman."[11] Díaz credits her skilled diplomacy for preventing further bloodshed, convincing Tlaxcalan caciques to lay down their weapons and make peace with the Spaniards.[12]

Like the Tlaxcalan artisan/historians, Díaz portrays Malinche as a major figure in the conquest. On several occasions he highlights her skill as an orator and her influence among Indians. He was particularly impressed by her strategic negotiation during the capture of Moctezuma. Díaz recalls that she was careful not to offend Moctezuma, assuring him that the Spaniards would show him the honor that "a great Mexica prince" deserved. She also assured him that among the Spaniards he would learn "truth" (the Christian path, according to Díaz). He recognizes Malinche's careful and simultaneous accommodation of multiple cultures, and he respects her efforts to curtail bloodshed. From his vantage point, Malinche was instrumental in the outcome of the Spanish mission. She was an Indian princess who adopted and nurtured Christianity in an indigenous world. Díaz's interpretation establishes Malinche as an appropriate symbolic mother of New Spain, one who cared for and protected both Indians and Spaniards. He describes a Malinche who deserved commemoration.

Díaz celebrates Malinche's compassion in his description of her return to her home village of Coatzacoalcos in 1524, which she was forced to leave as child. He describes Malinche's mother and half brother weeping in fear of her revenge because she was no longer the defenseless child they had discarded but an adult woman in the company of an invading force. On this occasion, according to Díaz, she lovingly forgave her mother and brother for their betrayal. She assured them (as well as the Spaniards who were reading his tale) that her life with the Spaniards was beneficial because she had found truth and happiness in the Christian Spanish path and wanted the people of her home village to benefit from a life "free from the worship of idols."[13] There is no way of knowing whether Díaz's account is an accurate portrayal of events in Coatzacoalcos. His knowledge of Nahuatl was questionable, although he had known Malinche for nearly five years and she was competent in his language. Díaz's portrayal verifies Malinche's love for her kinsmen and her commitment to a Spanish future in Mexico.

Díaz acknowledges that Malinche's indigenous childhood was a force that shaped her character and contributed to her usefulness to the conquest. He affirms both her noble heritage and her honorable characteristics. Díaz's Malinche is an Indian princess, a daughter of a cacique, and he tells readers that this status clearly showed. For some later writers his description legitimized her as a perfect mother of the new mestizo race: compassionate, intelligent, and beautiful, she was a royal Indian princess who adopted Christianity and spread the word of God. Díaz launched an admirable, mythic Malinche, an appropriate Native mother who advanced Christianity and gave birth to New Spain. Her children (a son fathered by Cortés and a daughter fathered by her legitimate Spanish husband) mythologically brought together the best of both worlds.

Díaz's work is the only colonial account that highlights Malinche's contribution or devotes attention to her background and personal character. His narrative describes an American Indian woman's rapid transformation into a Spanish lady. He is also the only early writer to address her as "Doña Marina"; Cortés and Gómara consistently refer to her as "Indian woman" or "slave." From Díaz's perspective Malinche was a positive figure, an intercessor between Spanish and Indian peoples, and she was concerned for the well-being of both. Some nationalist writers (discussed below) embraced Díaz's characterization because it honored both Spanish and Indian contributions to Mexican nationalism. Díaz's Malinche emerged as the symbolic mother of a new mestizo race, a race that benefited from a harmonious union of Spanish and indigenous heritage. This exaggerated copasetic narrative helped mute the more violent realities of the conquest.

Mythic Malinche was developed further by Fray Sahagún's ethnographic study of Mesoamerican culture and society. He began his cultural study in the late 1520s and continued his work among the Indians for twenty years. Sahagún does not mention Malinche specifically, yet his gender observations (discussed in chapter 1) shaped her legend from the onset. Sahagún itemizes the characteristics of a "good Native mother" and a "bad Native mother," a "good daughter" and a "bad daughter,"[14] and Malinche exhibited all of Sahagún's feminine characteristics, both good and bad. Malinche was a complex historical and cultural figure. She could also be identified as an example of Sahagún's "procuress," a woman who hid the devil within her. She was dangerous because she was a talented speaker and capable of provoking others.[15] Sahagún's descriptions of appropriate and inappropriate feminine behavior sentenced mythic Malinche to eternal bipolar abstraction.

Cultural perspective determines where Malinche fell on the scale of appropriate feminine behavior. From the Spanish perspective, she was a fine example of the feminine ideal. She was hardworking, honest, intelligent, obedient, well taught, and well trained. She used her gift of persuasion to bring Christianity to American Indians. Her participation in the conquest, however, ultimately brought the destruction of Native Mexico. She disregarded convention when she accepted Christianity and devoted her life to bringing change. Her words lulled Natives into believing that the Spaniards' Christianity would be their salvation.

Throughout the course of Mexican nationalism, Malinche has fluctuated between Sahagún's representations of good and bad female. The interpretation of Malinche's character was revised as Spanish colonial authority began to fracture under the pressure of rising Mexican nationalism. Within a few hundred years of the conquest Native Mexicans and descendants of the conquistadors (who came to think of themselves as Mexicans) were increasingly irritated with the arbitrary control of a far-off monarchy. Like the Aztec Empire, the Spanish Empire overextended itself. Once Spanish domination replaced Aztec domination, Malinche was reinterpreted as the bad woman who had opened Native Mexico to harsh authoritarian Spanish rule. Even worse, she had betrayed Native Mexico through her immoral sexual behavior; she had slept with the Spanish enemy. She became the example of Sahagún's bad woman, a whore/traitor who sold out Native people. She emerged as the scapegoat for the American Indian failure to overcome the Spaniards; her words duped Indians into accepting the new order. Her own sexual gratification took precedence over her commitment to Native Mexico.

We must pause to acknowledge that prior to the Spanish definition of "Indian" as a racial category, Natives did not see themselves as one people. Malinche could not have been disloyal to the Indian race because a single Indian race did not exist. Yet mythologically, (and using a sexual metaphor) she opened Native Mexico to unnatural, foreign domination.

INDEPENDENCE ERA

There was a void in the discussion of Malinche throughout the seventeenth and eighteenth centuries. The story of the conquest, and of Malinche's role in it, lay dormant as descendants of the conquistadors deemphasized the conflict. Creoles (Spaniards born in Mexico) responded to the European criticism of their ancestors by deflecting attention away from the conquest and highlighting an impressive and autonomous Mexican identity. They accomplished this by promoting the Virgin Mary's appearance in Mexico. The legend of the Virgin Mary, as the dark-skinned Virgin of Guadalupe, revealing herself to an Indian was useful to Creole attempts to bond with the Indian majority while alienating Spanish religious authorities. Ancient indigenous cultures were suddenly described as extraordinary civilizations with rich histories and cultures, with art that celebrated a unique and admirable Mexican prehistory. Creole patriots did not characterize Mesoamericans as barbarians in need of guidance and salvation, as the conquistadors had. Instead Creoles celebrated them as creators of spectacular societies and intelligent people who were receptive to Christianity. According to Creoles in the Independence era, the Virgin Mary chose Mexico, a pristine environment with advanced civilizations, as the site for a renewed Christian paradise. Just as conquistadors had expropriated the legend of Quetzalcoatl for their own uses, their Creole descendants expropriated the Indian legend of Guadalupe.

During the push for independence (from the last decades of the 1700s through the 1820s) Spanish colonial culture was ridiculed, and nationalists began calling for the restoration of Native Mexico. Writers were virtually silent in regard to Malinche during this process, yet a brief examination of rising nationalist sentiment and the expanding devotion to the Virgin of Guadalupe is relevant to how Malinche emerged as the Mexican Eve in the postindependence era. Malinche came to symbolize feminine betrayal, the opposite extreme to the Virgin of Guadalupe.

The experience of the conquest began a difficult marriage of Spanish and Mesoamerican cultures. This uncomfortable union is at the center of Mexican national identity. Much of Mexico's nationalist production illustrates a persistent struggle to merge the Spanish and indigenous past. The shared experience of the conquest proved a difficult theme in the creation of Mexico's national narrative. Should Mexico's frontier and colonial past be celebrated as a heroic victory of Spanish Christianity, or should the loss of an undisturbed Native Mexico be mourned?

By the mid-eighteenth century, Mexican patriots experienced difficulty in their attempt to indoctrinate Spanish and Indian peoples into a single national character. The problem was complex: how to celebrate the conquerors, the conquered, and the by-product of their union, the mestizo. A concept of national identity clearly needed to engage a diverse population, yet a strict social hierarchy based on race hampered efforts to build an all-inclusive nationalism. The colonial caste system placed pure-blood Spaniards (Spanish from the mother country) as the ruling class, Creoles and mestizos (Spanish and mixed-blood Spanish born in Mexico) significantly below them, and Indians at the bottom rung of the social order. Beyond relegating Indians to the bottom of the social hierarchy, establishing a social structure proved increasingly difficult as descendants of the conquistadors were joined by a large influx of Spanish immigrants. These incoming Spaniards came with a preconceived notion of the New World colony: they considered it inferior because of its remoteness from the centers of Western culture.[16] The savagery of the conquest demonstrated their assessment.

Throughout the colonial era, there was a tense atmosphere of competition between Creoles (Spaniards born in New Spain) and Gachupines (Spaniards who immigrated to New Spain). The conquest figured prominently in their contest for wealth and power. The conflict centered on whether Creoles should benefit from their ancestors' victory, or whether they should be punished for the brutality of the conquest and their miscegenation with the "uncivilized." Creoles answered this question by denying the atrocities committed by their ancestors and celebrating ancient Mexican civilizations.[17] They insisted that the conquest brought a unique opportunity for a new and improved civilization. New Spain was a fresh start for European Catholicism, where elitism and excess could be eliminated. Creoles described Indians as admirable people who were eligible for Christianity and miscegenation. The Gachupines, on the other hand, who had come to Mexico after the conquest to exploit opportunities in a burgeoning export economy, were unconvinced. They condemned

Creoles as a degenerate class that had been adversely affected by the savage culture and climate of Mexico.[18] Gachupines were unimpressed with Indians, Creoles, and the conquest, and they were appalled by interracial sex.

The viceroy and the expanding population of Gachupines deemed Creoles unfit to engage in colonial administration or lucrative export. Descendants of the conquistadors fought against their devalued status by creating a unique Mexican identity, an identity that only those born in Mexico could claim. Creoles thus looked to Native cultures for their own nationalist purpose.[19] They celebrated Mexico's ancient indigenous past by presenting its elaborate cultures as equal to ancient Greek and Roman civilizations.[20] Creoles attached themselves to Mexico's impressive prehistory by professing the splendor of pre-Colombian civilizations and celebrating their success in bringing Christian enlightenment to honorable Indians.[21] Many Creole intellectuals, because they were barred from the highest levels of religious and colonial administration, entered the priesthood. As parish priests they were able to guide a distinct Mexican consciousness through their sermons, writings, and lectures and as they converted Indians to Christianity.[22] Creole intellectuals of the independence era cleansed their historical record by avoiding the sensitive issue of the conquest, glorifying ancient indigenous cultures, and celebrating a purified Mexican Catholicism that was sanctioned by the mother of God.

The Mexican legend of the Virgin Mary steadily gained momentum during the seventeenth century. According to the indigenous religious story, the Mother of God revealed herself to Juan Diego while he was on a pilgrimage to a pre-Columbian sacred site devoted to Tonantzin (an indigenous mother goddess) in the area of Tepeyac Hill. Creole clerics embraced the Mexican apparition because, from a nationalist perspective, her appearance provided an autonomous foundation for Mexican Christianity, which Spanish religious authorities from Europe could not control. The Virgin Mary's earthly return as the Virgin of Guadalupe advanced Catholicism in Mexico because it showed that the Mother of God had adopted the Indians. Creole clerics thus bonded with Indians and adopted the Virgin of Guadalupe both as Mexico's patron saint and as a nationalist symbol during the push for independence.[23]

For two hundred years after the Virgin Mother revealed herself to Diego in 1531, Mexican devotion to her continued to expand. The cult of Guadalupe first spread to Mexico City, the seat of Spanish authority, and eventually to rural areas in the countryside.[24] Creole clerics encouraged mestizos and Indians to pray for her divine intervention to relieve the hardships of colonial Mexico (epidemics, oppression, and rising flood waters). Spanish colonial authorities were ambiguous of, if not concerned by, the rising cult, because Guadalupe undercut Franciscan explanations of Catholicism and fostered a distinct Mexican religious consciousness. Many in the clergy, including Fray Sahagún, believed that the Virgin Mary was soiled by her association with the goddess Tonantzin and worried that Guadalupe was merely a disguise for Indians to continue their pagan reverence.[25] To the chagrin of Spanish religious authorities, Mexicans (Indians, Creoles, and mestizos) modified Christianity and created a religious hybrid specifically suited to their needs.

It is significant that Indians responded to a female Christian representative and claimed Guadalupe as their own intercessor in order to soften the harshness of Spanish Catholicism. Creoles capitalized on the growing devotion to the Virgin of Guadalupe and celebrated ancient Mesoamerican cultures in an attempt to unite their cause with the Indians in a struggle against Spanish oppression. Together, Indians and Creoles forged a syncretism in which Spanish religion and culture commingled with Mesoamerican religion and culture.[26] Creoles fueled the legend of Guadalupe and cultivated a distinct Mexican nationalism in order to further separate themselves from Spanish colonial authorities and resident elitist Gachupines.[27]

Díaz's mythic Malinche did not fit into this emerging nationalist construction: she had helped the Spaniards infiltrate Mesoamerica and brought massive destruction to Mexico's ancient world. During the push for independence Creoles distanced themselves from the violence perpetrated by the conquistadors and distinguished themselves from the oppressive Gachupines. Creoles no longer saw themselves as Spaniards. They saw themselves as Mexicans and Gachupines as foreigners. The glorification of Mexico's indigenous past and the veneration of Guadalupe were part of a Creole strategy to build an alliance with the Indian majority. This tenuous partnership rallied under the banner of the Virgin of Guadalupe.

Creole patriotism was illustrated in the work of clergy throughout the next century. A preacher named Miguel Sánchez (1594–1674), a diocesan priest who served in the chapel dedicated to Guadalupe at Tepeyac, published the story of the apparition in the mid-seventeenth century. Sánchez later served as the chaplain to the nunnery of San Jerónimo in Mexico City where Sister Juana Ines de la Cruz (1648–1695) studied.[28] She, too, was passionate in her praise for the Virgin of Guadalupe and the uniqueness of Mexican Catholicism. Mexican nationalism and the growing rejection of Spanish colonial authority percolated for generations until dissatisfaction reached a crescendo as the turn of the century approached. In 1794, Dominican Fray Servando Teresa de Mier gave a famous open-air nationalist sermon that praised Mexico's ancient civilizations and the purity of a distinct Mexican Catholicism. He used the Aztec calendar stone to demonstrate that Christianity had roots in Mexico prior to the arrival of Spaniards in the 1500s. Mier suggested that the apostle St. Thomas, whom he said the Indians knew as Quetzalcoatl, taught the doctrine of Christianity 1,750 years before Spanish arrival.[29] According to Mier, the apparition of the Virgin of Guadalupe to Juan Diego in 1531 was a reappearance of Catholicism designed to restore their ancient Christian faith.[30] Mier was eventually expelled from Mexico for such blasphemy but continued to advocate for Mexican independence from exile. The work of Sanchez, La Cruz, and Mier illustrates Creole religious explanations of an autonomous Mexican Catholicism and early Mexican nationalism.

Mexico has a long tradition of religious and cultural layering as a strategy for self-determination. Mayas incorporated cultural aspects of the ancient Olmecs, Mexicas adapted the culture and religion of the Toltecs, conquistadors constructed their churches directly over Indian sacred sites, and Creoles borrowed and blended cultural antecedents from indigenous and Spanish ideologies to explain the birth of modern Mexico. In the same way, Creoles, mestizos, and Indians (making up the vast majority of the citizenry) made adjustments to

Spanish Christianity and accommodated aspects of Mesoamerican religion and culture in order to build support for a broad independence movement.

By the mid-seventeenth century, the Virgin of Guadalupe was the benevolent mother of Mexico. Malinche was no longer useful as an idealized Indian woman who was committed to facilitating Spanish Christianity, as Díaz had portrayed her in the colonial era. The Virgin of Guadalupe had become the ultimate feminine symbol. Instead Malinche came to be interpreted as the Mexican Eve who had given into temptation, slept with the conquering Spaniards, and led Native Mexico into ruin.

Both the Virgin of Guadalupe and Malinche influenced Indian decisions to accept Christianity (along with other contributing factors). However, the Virgin of Guadalupe was the protective feminine intercessor who eased the harshness of the Christian God and Spanish colonial rule, whereas Malinche was the opening through which Spanish authority and religion had come. The Virgin of Guadalupe was (and is) a religious symbol not confined by the realities of the mundane world. She could be prayed to, to ease pain and suffering, to bring rain, to halt floodwaters, and to relieve the devastation of raging epidemics. And unlike Malinche, she was a virgin.

After Mexican independence in 1821 Malinche's loyalty to the Spaniards came to be reinterpreted as a betrayal of Indian people. Signaling a rejection of all things Spanish, the change reincarnated Malinche as a seductive traitor/whore whose lust for Cortés had led to the destruction of her people. Malinche was singled out to carry the burden of responsibility for American Indian defeat. She worked to increase Cortés's Indian allies, helped the conquistadors exploit traditional rivalries, turned Indian against Indian, and eventually brought devastation to indigenous Mexico. Malinche represented the dark side of the feminine condition. She became Sahagún's "bad woman."

In the era of political turmoil following independence, the lessons of the conquest demonstrated the vulnerability of a divided nation: the Indians had been divided, defeated, and overrun by a foreign power. The infant nation faced the challenge of building consensus and an inclusive nationalism, one that would garner respect in the community of nations. *Xicotencatl*, the first historical novel to use the theme of the conquest to address these national concerns, was published anonymously in Philadelphia in 1826.[31] Although the author used the conquest as the historical stage, his or her motivation was clearly manifested in this time of political uncertainty. In order to provide meaning for the sociopolitical problems of a newly independent Mexico, the narrative focuses on one embellished event of the conquest: the story centers on the alliance of Tlaxcala with the Spaniards to illustrate how internal rivalries made Mexico susceptible to foreign domination. The author demonizes Spanish influences and conduct, glorifies Mexico's pre-Columbian past, and supports a republican ideology for Mexico's future.

Xicotencatl contrasts a fallen Malinche against Tetuila, a fictitious good woman who remains loyal to Native people.[32] While Tetuila fights the sexual advances of conquistadors, Malinche is a seductress who trifles with men's attention. She is the symbol of the evil brought on by accepting European ways. The rejection of Malinche is mirrored by a similar attitude toward Cortés. *Xicotencatl* condemns Cortés for his depraved behavior that ultimately contaminates Native Mexico. By impregnating Malinche, Cortés deposited a toxic foreign influence that resulted in a morally deficient Spanish tyrannical rule. *Xicotencatl* denounces Malinche, Cortés, authoritarian rule inherited from Spain, and interracial sex during the conquest.

Just as *Xicotencatl* consistently characterizes Malinche and Cortés as sexual deviants, Octavio Paz's *Labyrinth of Solitude* repeated this portrayal of their depraved union in the 1950s.[33] Paz identifies Malinche as La Chingada, which literally translates as "the fucked." He likewise refers to Cortés as El Chingón, or "the fucker." Mexico's national origin, as *Xicotencatl* and *Labyrinth of Solitude* explain it, mythologizes Malinche and Cortés negatively. The conquering Spaniard and the female Indian are condemned for the immorality of the conquest. But their progeny, the mestizo who ultimately inherits Mexico, is innocent.

Interest in Malinche waned after the foundation of an independent, republican Mexico. Just as Spanish intellectuals avoided the subject of the conquest after the establishment of colonial New Spain, and as Creoles deflected attention away from the conquest during the independence era, Mexican intellectuals in the mid-1800s also neglected

the conquest as a topic of study.[34] Outsiders, however, were capti-
vated by the tale. By the mid-nineteenth century scholarly attention
on Malinche was again confined to an interesting sidenote. In these
foreign academic works she occupies a paragraph or a page at most.

William Prescott's three-volume study, *History of the Conquest of
Mexico* (1843), is considered the most comprehensive text on the
conquest, and it provides a limited description of Malinche's historical significance. Relying on the work of Díaz, Prescott summarizes Malinche's childhood experiences and how she came to be in
the possession of Cortés. He acknowledges her intelligence, her
skillful translation, and her selective interpretive style that ensured
Cortés's desired results. Prescott provides a few sentences to illustrate her character: "That remarkable woman had attracted general
admiration by the constancy and cheerfulness with which she endured
all the privations of the camp. Far from betraying the natural weakness and timidity of her sex, she had shrunk from no hardship herself,
and had done much to fortify the drooping spirits of the soldier;
while her sympathies, whenever occasion offered, had been actively
exerted in mitigating the calamities of her Indian countrymen."[35]
Despite this positive portrayal, within his three-volume text that
totals 1,243 pages, Malinche is briefly mentioned on 14.[36]

While Mexican intellectual attention on Malinche dwindled, popular culture and oral tradition sought to explain her role in the birth
of modern Mexico. Malinche came to be associated with the legend
of La Llorona.[37] In the 1850s there were frequent reports of a ghostly
woman wearing a flowing white dress, with a veil covering her face.
The feminine ghost floated through the streets, mourning the loss
of her children. This ghost was identified as La Llorona (translated
as "weeping woman"). Much like the legend of Malinche, the legend
of La Llorona has various renditions that demonstrate both positive
and negative feminine characteristics. Both of their legends illustrate
appropriate and inappropriate sexual behavior, and both display
elements of feminine betrayal and selfishness. Some tales of La Llorona characterize her as a victim while others identify her as the
perpetrator who killed her own children. The weeping feminine ghost
came to be interpreted as Malinche, who had come back to mourn
what she had destroyed. The legend of La Llorona expresses the

remorse that Malinche might have felt had she lived to see the consequences of her participation in the conquest.

Mexican literature began a fascination with Malinche in the latter half of the 1800s, when nationalist writers were inspired by Mexico's victory over Napoleon's army in 1867. After the French-imposed monarchy was kicked out of Mexico, ending six years of foreign occupation, the republican victory revived Mexico's national spirit. The work of Octavio Paz's grandfather, Ireneo Paz (1836–1924), illustrates this renewed commitment to nationalist themes. Ireneo Paz wrote two historical novels on the conquest, Amor y Suplicio, translated as *Love and Torment* (1873), and *Doña Marina* (1883). Compared to the author of *Xicotencatl*, Paz offers a more sympathetic interpretation of the conquest by softening the image of Malinche and the Spanish. Whereas *Xicotencatl* was written soon after independence, during an era of animosity toward Spain, Paz wrote at a time of reconciliation between Spain and her former colony. Paz's nationalist goals were different as well; instead of demonizing the Spaniards as an unwanted European interference that introduced corruption and immorality to Mexico, he celebrates Spain's contribution to Mexico and characterizes Spain as the best of European civilizations.

Ireneo Paz adopted a deterministic mode of analysis to explain the conquest. He built on the work of Eligio Ancona (1835–1893), whose acclaimed novel, *Los Martires del Anahuac*, presents the conquest as inevitable, predestined by the American Indian gods and by the Christian God. Ancona suggests that both Mesoamericans and Christians believed that the conquest was their destiny and that their gods were testing them. For Paz, Cortés and Malinche were motivated by their belief in predestination and by the power of love. Paz establishes a Cortés/Malinche romantic paradigm that symbolizes a harmonious encounter between the Spanish and the Indians. He characterizes their union as an intense love that crossed racial boundaries. This suggests that modern Mexicans were born from a loving and beneficial union, not from a deviant sexual act. He portrays Malinche as a noble Indian woman whose actions were dictated by love and destiny, not moral weakness. Paz reinvents the story of the conquest to offer a positive interpretation of the origin of the mestizo, providing readers with a positive self-image.

Unlike the author of *Xicotencatl*, Paz's intent was to consolidate and celebrate Spanish and Indian elements in Mexican heritage. He acknowledges American Indians' contributions to Mexico, while tempering the atrocities committed by Spanish conquistadors. For Paz the union of Spanish and Indian people produced the greatest good, the mestizo. Both of his narratives present several women who choose Spanish males over Indian counterparts. He emphasizes the attractiveness of European civilization and validates Malinche's choice. *Amor y Suplicio* and *Doña Marina* represent a national impetus to resolve Mexico's complicated past and create a consolidated heritage that Mexico could build on. By the end of the century elite mestizos controlled Mexico's future, and it was their turn to shape Mexican history and nationalism to legitimize their authority.

After Paz established love as the overriding force that bound Cortés and Malinche together, the romantic theme was available to later writers. Gustavo Rodriguez's *Doña Marina* (1935), Jesus Figueroa Torres's *Doña Marina: Una India Ejemplar* (1957), and Hammon Innes's *The Conquistadors* (1970) all illustrate this romantic literary tradition that celebrates Mexico's union of cultures. Innes's historical text employs the romantic pattern and confirms Malinche's significance to the conquest as a testament to the emerging women's movement: "She was almost certainly in love with him—at any rate, she gave herself to him and eventually bore him a son. But what ever the nature of their personal relations, the fact is that, without the proud and dominant character of this Indian princess to convey his thoughts, it is doubtful whether Cortés would ever have reached Mexico other than as a captive."[38] These romantic portrayals sanctified the union of cultures, justified the conquest, and alleviated Spanish guilt. Each work was published when Mexico's Indian heritage was deemed a noble characteristic of *mexicanidad* (Mexican nationalism). They honor Malinche as an Indian and as a woman; she is again portrayed as an Indian princess and as the perfect mother of a modern mestizo Mexico.

The allegorical nature of the romance genre is perfectly suited for the project of nationalism. These novels are patriotic histories that have been institutionalized by schools as required reading. The protagonists are typically idealized lovers separated by class, race, or regional ties, coincidently the same obstacles that challenge national unity. Romantic passions provided the rhetoric for nationalist projects, muted antagonisms, and focused on mutual benefits. Early patriotic romance novels were designed by a mestizo bourgeois to construct a cultural tradition that explained their conjugal connection to Mexico, ensuring their paternity rights to the landscape. The metaphor of love offered national unity, bringing together diverse regions, economic interests, and races. These fabled emotional bonds deflected social tensions that threatened national development and solidified a collective identity.

Institutionalized romance novels offered "foundational fictions" and illustrated how national identities were imagined into existence within gendered parameters and legitimized nationalist ideals through heterosexual love.[39] The familiar experience of a man and a woman falling in love and creating a new family (and a new era) is perfectly suited for explaining the birth of a new nation. It is an organic experience that need not be questioned. The romance genre has enjoyed a long tradition, yet it exists alongside a more contentious narrative that occasionally challenges the celebrationist tone and the happy endings presented in these romantic stories of national formation.

Twentieth Century

The difficulty in unifying the conquerors (Spanish), the conquered (Indian), and the mestizo (mixed race) into an all-inclusive national identity continued to inspire Mexico's cultural production in the twentieth century. In the social climate of the Mexican Revolution (1910–1920) the national dialogue intensified. The ideological alliance between Creoles and Indians professed during the independence era never evolved into a unified nationalism, nor was racial equality established in Mexico. Male elites who claimed Spanish ancestry continued to determine the national agenda after independence. Indians and dark-skinned mestizos were relegated to the margins of modernization and prosperity in an ambience of positivist thought. As the twentieth century approached, *científicos* (national leaders with tremendous faith in modernity and science) controlled the government and national policies. They believed economic progress resulted from unrestricted individual interest and foreign investment. Native elements in Mexican culture and society were consistently suppressed, while Mexican officials favored positivist ambitions to bring order and progress to Mexico through science, technology, and implementation of foreign doctrines.

By the turn of the twentieth century discontent was rampant. Positivist policies benefited few, while repression and the police force controlled many. Alienated mestizos and Indians resented economic and political disparity, the concentration of land ownership, and a government that extended opportunities only to foreign investors and a tiny segment of Mexican elites. Within one hundred years after independence most Mexicans were excluded from liberal policies that had been intended to bring prosperity to modern Mexico. This harsh reality prevented large numbers of citizens from feeling a sense of belonging to greater Mexico. Instead their loyalties were to their local communities, which existed in isolation.[40] The large, dissatisfied majority began to rally under the banner of the Virgin of Guadalupe as the Mexican Revolution gained momentum. She was a compassionate and effective ally in times of rebellion and crisis, and she again became the unifying symbol for the disenfranchised majority. The Virgin of Guadalupe was available to all Mexicans, and she emerged as their protector again, just as she had during the push for independence.

The Mexican Revolution brought about ten excruciating years of fighting and refocused attention on the need to unify the nation. It was clear that any legitimate government would have to address the needs of all Mexicans. National harmony demanded the inclusion of Indians and mestizos into a national consciousness. After the militant phase of the revolution, its ideals were continued through impassioned cultural production during the Mexican Renaissance (1920s–1960s). During that time cultural disseminators attempted to calm the social antagonisms that had torn the nation apart during the revolution.

The nineteenth-century ideology of indigenismo (celebration of the Indian) was revived during the renaissance, but modifications were needed to address twentieth-century social conditions. The indigenismo of the independence era presented ancient Indians who had built Mexico's impressive temples and pyramids as advanced peoples who had lived in advanced societies. Yet during the first hundred years after independence, living Indians were judged as backward, a hindrance to the modernization of Mexico. Living Indians were consistently denied any role in the national agenda; their alienation had been a significant factor in the revolt of 1910. After the revolution, intellectuals developed new strategies to celebrate Indian contributions and build an inclusive national consensus.[41] The theme of the conquest, and Malinche's role in it, was reimagined to ground the discussion in Mexico's history. An updated version of mestizaje (the celebration of Mexico's racial mixing) was also needed in order to finally indoctrinate Indians and mestizos in a productive and shared national identity.

The foremost advocate of twentieth-century mestizaje was José Vasconcelos.[42] His conceptualization of miscegenation evolved out of a contemporary fascination with genetics. He based his theory on a quasi-scientific notion: "If we observe human nature closely we find that hybridism in man, as well as in plants, tends to rejuvenate those types that have become static."[43] By this logic the Mexican was a superior hybrid stock. He extended his theory to encompass all Latin Americans, who had been degraded by European eugenicists in the 1920s.[44] This hypothesis relieved an inferiority complex that had been imposed on Latin America by foreign social scientists.

Vasconcelos outlined a superior Mexican identity in comparison to other groups; Mexicans were different from "whites" in North America.[45] According to his analysis "whites in the North" suffered from excessive materialism and social injustice caused by a segregated society. Mexicans had avoided these social maladies because of their tradition of miscegenation and their biracial heritage.[46] Vasconcelos borrows from Mesoamerican cyclical mythology and employs the ancient notion of the fifth and final sun (the belief that the Aztec Empire was predestined to fall) to describe how the indigenous world had ended and reemerged as something new. He describes twentieth-century Latin Americans as the fifth and final race, the ultimate "cosmic race" of the future.[47] He argues in his book La Raza Cósmica (1926) that the mestizos stood at the forefront of the coming multiracial age, and he prophesizes that "whites" will eventually turn to their southern brothers for help in their quest for real freedom.[48]

In Vasconcelos's view, the mestizo was uniquely qualified to create a more open and universal civilization. The mestizo had learned to accommodate the most contradictory human types. He says, "We are not addicted to local tradition or to European, but desire to know and to try all—East and the West, the North and the South."[49] He explains that the political instability in Mexico was due to the fact that the mestizo was a relatively new species, and not due to Mexican inferiority (as foreign commentators implied). The first step toward reaching maturity in the community of nations was to dedicate Mexico to a high ideal. He identifies the high ideal of the United States as a celebrated faith in democracy and equal opportunity. According to Vasconcelos, Latin America should thus define its purpose: "Broadness, universality of sentiment and thought, in order to fulfill the mission of bringing together all races of the earth and with the purpose of creating a new type of civilization, is I believe, the ideal that would give us in Latin America strength and vision."[50]

Vasconcelos draws a distinction between the colonization in Latin America and its counterpart in North America. The Spaniards mixed with indigenous populations in the south because of their admirable level of civilization and because the Spaniards held less prejudice than other colonizers. Spain made the conscious decision to pursue a mixed-race standard in contrast to the North American strategy of segregated races. He characterizes the North American structure as an imperial system of domination, in which two races remained alienated. He describes the Spanish preference for a mixed race by celebrating the union of Cortés and Malinche: "On the other hand we have in the south, a civilization that from the beginning accepts a mixed race standard of social arrangement not only as a matter of fact but through law, since the Indian after being baptized became the equal of the Spaniard and was able to intermarry with the conqueror. The wedding of Cortés—who is accused of having murdered his Spanish wife in order to marry, or at least to live undisturbed with, his Indian love La Malinche—is symbolic of the new state of affairs and of the whole of the race situation in our country. The

example of Cortés in taking an Indian woman for his wife was followed by many others, it went on then and has been going on since."[51]

There were problems with Vasconcelos's version of Mexico's past;
the most significant was his claim of Indian-Spanish equality. Racial
equality was not a reality in Mexico. The relationship between Spanish and Indian peoples was not based solely on love; it was also based
on a power structure intended to benefit the Spaniards. The Conquistadors did not bring or offer Spanish women as items of cultural
exchange. But Indian women were made available to Spanish men,
and some were taken against their will. And Cortés neither married
nor committed himself to Malinche. After the conquest he returned
to Spain without his Native "wife," taking only their young son.
These harsh facts were insignificant to Vasconcelos's nationalist agenda.
His goal was to celebrate Mexican uniqueness and define a national
purpose that would bring Mexico respect in the community of nations.
His high ideal of a multiracial society based on openness, love, and
respect was intended to alleviate the inferiority complex that had
been imposed on Latin Americans by European social Darwinists.
Vasconcelos tweaked the scientific understanding of natural selection to define an ideal Mexican race; according to his theory, the
process of natural selection in Mexico was based on romantic love
and mutual respect.

Vasconcelos presented an idealized union between Spanish and
Native peoples, celebrated mestizaje, and validated the origin of the
mestizo. His notion of mestizaje, however, was purely biological. He
expressed no interest in reviving precolonial indigenous cultures.
The Indian contribution to Mexico was limited to their mixed-blood
progeny. His work did, however, reflect Mexico's long tradition of
selective cultural accommodation. He blended a contemporary understanding of genetics with an Indian belief in *el quinto sol* (the fifth
and final sun). Cortés and Malinche had launched Mexico's new
beginning and initiated the cosmic race; they set the example for
how interracial love could bring forth a new and improved human
species. Vasconcelos's Mexican creation story and his vision of the
future put the mestizo in the vanguard; the mestizo could lead
humanity to a new age in which human consciousness would expand
beyond the limits of science, logic, materialism, and politics. His hope

was that integration and synthesis would become the basis for human development as peoples and nations mixed according to the natural selection of love.

It is a beautiful idea, and if you read *La Raza Cósmica* and Díaz's memoir of the conquest concurrently, you can imagine that there were at least some Spanish conquistadors who admired Mexico's indigenous civilizations. Unfortunately for Vasconcelos, his analysis of the conquest did not reflect the social reality in Mexico. His claim of a respectful and copacetic union between Spanish and Indian peoples begged the question, Why, then, were Indian peoples isolated from national consciousness? In the prologue of his 1948 edition of *La Raza Cósmica* (published after his failed presidential bid) Vasconcelos is forced to admit that the underdevelopment in Mexico, particularly where Indian elements were prominent, is difficult to explain. He suggests that the reality of the Indians' condition was due to their lack of a "civilized culture to unite them," except for the Spanish influences that had permeated their souls. For instance, they had no common Indian language and relied on Spanish. And whenever they came together, Indians rallied under the Spanish Christian symbol of the Virgin Mother. Vasconcelos does not attribute the Indians with any agency in creating the symbolism of the Virgin of Guadalupe or with participation in the development of a modern Mexican cultural consciousness.

Vasconcelos's ideal of an advanced mixed race did not succeed in bringing universal understanding, nor did it establish crosscultural love and respect in Mexico. He never recovered from his disillusionment and was dismissed by Mexicans until the Chicano movement in the United States (discussed below) revived his thesis in the 1970s. Vasconcelos's belief that the natural selection of love could or should displace unions based on systems of power (whether they be political, economic, racial, or gender systems) was applicable to the social discontent of the 1970s. Vasconcelos's prediction that North Americans would eventually turn to their southern brothers for inspiration ultimately proved correct.

Mexicans had an alternative to Vasconcelos's affirmative interpretation of the conquest and miscegenation. Manuel Gamio was an anthropologist/archeologist who characterized crossbreeding in

Mexico as counterproductive to both the Spaniard and the Indian.[52] Unlike Vasconcelos, Gamio recognized tremendous value in Mexico's precolonial Indian heritage. He believed the artistic splendor of ancient Mexico should be unearthed, revived, and incorporated into Mexican nationalism.[53] Gamio reinvigorated the cultural ideology of indigenismo for the twentieth century. Despite earlier (1790s–1820) Creole appreciation for indigenous cultures, after independence government officials deemed Indian peoples barbarian and a hindrance to modernity.[54] Reversing a century of liberal scorn, Gamio resurrected the artistic glory of indigenous Mexico and reenlisted ancient Indians (although not necessarily living Indians) in the project of Mexican nationalism.

Gamio did not limit his study to the past. As he unearthed the ancient Maya ruins of Teotihuacan in central Mexico, he conducted an ethnographic study of people in the surrounding area. The information he collected convinced him that modern Mexico was essentially an Indian nation. He explained that the contemporary condition of Indian people was due to poor diet, lack of education, and isolation. Their reality was the result of relentless exploitation and neglect after the conquest. Gamio, a secular liberal, criticized the spiritual conquest and the Catholic Church for instituting a folk Catholicism in Mexico and then abandoning the Indians.[55] Like the liberals of the nineteenth century, Gamio's goal was to transform what he believed to be a backward population into a modern nation that commanded international respect. Unlike earlier liberals, however, he argued that Mexican identity should be based on its historical qualities and not on foreign doctrines. His solution was to celebrate Mexico's unique prehistory. The artistic remains of ancient indigenous cultures that he unearthed proved that Mexico was an elegant and cultured nation. According to Gamio, contemporary Indians should also be studied in order to facilitate their inclusion in Mexican nationalism. Gamio's objective was to make living Indians loyal to Mexico rather than to their local villages. He believed that the study of Native cultures (past and present) would bring Indians into a unified national society.[56]

Gamio characterized modern Mexico as essentially an Indian nation and suggested that the colonial experience was merely the bridge that connected the indigenous past to the present. The Spaniards were gone; they had abandoned Mexico, and all they had bequeathed to the nation was a conquered and degraded population. This is the thesis of his 1916 book, *Forjando Patria* (*Forging Homeland*). His book is not a study of Mexico's indigenous roots, but rather a study of the physical decay of Native Mexico. It reveals his enthusiasm for the opportunities that the Mexican Revolution would bring: finally the minority elite would be divested of their monopoly over Mexican progress and culture. Finally the obstacles to an inclusive nationalism would be eliminated.

In the opening pages of *Forjando Patria* Gamio suggests that Mexico could not become a unified nation, as other nations were unified, until it had a common language, character, and history. Because of Mexico's many languages, rural isolation, poverty, and illiteracy, Indian communities were *pequenas patrias* (small home villages) whose inhabitants did not participate in national life. Indians were foreigners in their own country. Gamio's aim was to create a strong unified Mexico by forging a nation based on a common language, universal access to education, and economic equilibrium. Ultimately, his goals were to de-Indianize the population and to instill an inclusive national consciousness.

Gamio's thesis focuses on Indian people. Yet it is important to recognize that he describes contemporary Mexico as an Indian nation, claiming that the mestizo was more Indian than European. He regarded the mixing of Spaniards and Indians as "inharmonious" and counterproductive. He does not refer to Cortés and Malinche specifically, but he describes miscegenation during the conquest: "The white man possessed the native woman wherever and whenever he saw fit. Therefore the offspring of these inharmonious and forced unions had none of the advantages of a normal origin. Moreover, the Mestizo, or half-breed, born under these circumstances was educated by the mother, since the father abandoned the woman sooner or later and he in turn increased in body and spirit the indigenous masse-passive enemies of the white colonists."[57] Malinche is absent from this narrative, yet the Native woman is characterized as a victim of sexual conquest. She is abandoned with her "half-breed" child, the result of the "inharmonious and forced" union. The Spaniard, after quenching his lust, is gone. Gamio describes the Indian woman as the vehicle through which a demoralized Indian culture continued; she alone brought up her children to become "enemies of the white colonists." Gamio merged the Indian and the mestizo because both were raised by Indian mothers. Native cultural traditions were preserved through her, although in an eroded state. Gamio insists that these orphaned citizens be indoctrinated into Mexican nationalism, a nationalism that highlighted ancient Indigenous artistic splendor.

The opposing theories of Gamio and Vasconcelos were debated in many forums (books, articles, lectures, and even in the muralist movement, which will be discussed shortly) from the 1920s through the 1960s. Gamio promoted cultural mestizaje, in contrast to Vasconcelos's focus on genetic mestizaje. Yet Gamio did not intend to elevate Indian culture in total; all that he thought was worth incorporating into Mexican nationalism was their precolonial aesthetic tradition. He encouraged Mexican artists to look to ancient Native sources for inspiration. This would not only distinguish national origin, it would also make Mexican artistic tradition more accessible. Mexican art would no longer be bound by European neoclassical tastes, and the emergence of a unique national art would help to unify Mexico and to solidify a unique national culture.[58] Gamio's renewed indigenismo was responsible for the resurrection of ancient monuments and the creation of profitable tourism and craft industries.[59] This indigenismo was intended to promote economic development in rural Indian communities and plug formally isolated Indians into Mexican nationalism.

While the goal of Gamio's indigenismo may have been to improve the lives of Indian and mestizo peoples, he valorized only the aesthetic component of their culture. Other than that, contemporary Indians were merely to be studied for the purpose of securing their loyalty to the nation. Gamio's objective was ultimately to de-Indianize the citizenry and to modernize the nation. In this sense, Gamio had not moved far from the liberal positivist thought of the nineteenth century. However, his version of indigenismo was useful to the Mexican government because it promoted and incorporated an Indian heritage, celebrated Mexican uniqueness, and fostered new profitable industries (tourism and folk art). It also distracted attention away from the racial and class antagonisms that had lead to the Mexican Revolution.

For both Vasconcelos and Gamio, a woman's contribution to mexicanidad was limited to her offspring. Her social role was reproductive, either biologically or culturally. Gamio credited Indian mothers with sustaining Indian culture in Mexico's large nonwhite population. He reclaimed indigenous artistry, introduced it as a commodity, and used it to enhance Mexican exceptionalism. Vasconcelos focused on the union of Spaniards and Indians to bring forth the birth of mestizos, a hybrid race that ultimately inherited Mexico. Both visions of the future attempt to incorporate Indians into Mexican nationalism and create a stable and loyal citizenry. Yet both men stopped short of demanding full and equal citizenship for Indian peoples. Indians were relegated to symbolic ingredients in mexicanidad. Living Indians were not imagined as active participants in Mexican national life or governance; the main concern was their loyalty. Indians and women were intricate components in Mexico's past, but not necessarily a relevant part of Mexico's future. Gamio characterized Indians as conquered and Indian women as sexually violated; both were obstacles to overcome in the establishment of Mexican nationalism.

Because of Spain's colonial strategy of miscegenation, Mexico's creation story has been consistently portrayed through sexual imagery. In the independence era, the author of *Xicotencatl* characterized the conquest as an immoral sexual encounter to illustrate how continued acceptance of European influence would be detrimental to Mexico's future. Ireneo Paz attempted to reconcile Mexico's past by characterizing the indigenous-Spanish encounter as romantic and beneficial to the creation of the mestizo. And Vasconcelos and Gamio presented the sexual encounter as a practical reality of the conquest, a fact that (for better or worse) defined Mexican uniqueness. For Vasconcelos miscegenation was Spain's deliberate strategy to create a New-World, mixed-race society. For Gamio the sexual conquest began the disintegration of Native Mexico, yet it provided access to Mexico's ancient artistic traditions. By the twentieth century the sexual theme was a proven and powerful paradigm to explain Mexican national origin.

Malinche's sexuality was (and remains) at the center of Mexico's creation myth. Was she a participant in a loving and beneficial union, or was she responsible for the immoral atrocity that crippled Native Mexico's development? Mythic Malinche has been projected through these parallel national narratives for nearly five hundred years. She has been portrayed as the virtuous Indian mother who gave birth to a new race, but she has also been projected as the whore who satisfied her lust and turned her back on Indian people. The work of Vasconcelos and Gamio expressed Mexico's renewed impetus to refine nationalism in the wake of the revolution.

Other nationalist intellectuals also embraced the ideologies of mestizaje and indigenismo. A state-sponsored muralist movement, initiated and endorsed by both Gamio and Vasconcelos, was an especially effective medium for the national objective of building a collective and inclusive nationalism. The government commissioned artists to paint historical murals that illustrated mexicanidad in public buildings, in cities and in the countryside because it was critical that both urban and rural citizens be exposed to a coherent national story. The appeal of murals was two-fold: first, they communicate visually so that illiterate Mexicans could be indoctrinated, and second, murals are a Native art form dating back to the Mesoamerican era.[60]

For our purposes I will focus on the work of three muralists: José Clemente Orozco (1883–1949), Diego Rivera (1886–1957), and a latecomer to the effort, Jorge González Camarena (1908–1980). Their works demonstrate how the Indian was symbolically reclaimed to highlight Mexican distinction. Like Europeans who celebrated ancient Greek, Roman, and Celtic civilizations, Mexicans take pride in the ancient civilizations of the Mayas and Aztecs. The extraordinary remains of these cultures were unearthed and commemorated beginning in the early twentieth century. The intriguing architecture, sculptures, frescos, and artifacts inspired Mexican intellectuals and artists. The Mexican government, moved by the theories of Vasconcelos and Gamio, funded projects to salvage the impressive indigenous past, while it ignored the realities of contemporary Indians. Mexico's precolonial civilizations became a valuable commodity that fostered profitable industries (tourism, arts, and crafts) and legitimized Mexico as an unparalleled cultured nation.

The murals of Orozco, Rivera, and Camarena took inspiration from the cultural traditions and ancient artistic remains that were being unearthed and preserved. All three artists honored Mexico's indigenous past, but they differed dramatically in their depiction of Spanish contributions. Orozco's mural in the National Preparatory School, titled *Cortés and Malinche,* offers a positive portrayal of both the Spaniard and the Indian. Malinche is shown as a beautiful, voluptuous, yet docile Indian woman. She represents the exotic potential of Native Mexico. Cortés is presented as an imposing male figure whose protective arm extends over her; under his (Spanish) protection and guidance, Malinche (Native Mexico) would reach her potential. Orozco portrays the couple as the synthesis of Spanish and Mexican virtue; he offers a visual depiction of mestizaje.

Diego Rivera's murals, some of which decorate the National Palace, offer a different national commentary. His rendition of the conquest reveals contempt for the Spanish legacy in Mexico. He depicts the conquest as an evil event that interfered with the continuation of pristine Indian life. Cortés is portrayed as devilish, and Malinche is characterized as a seductress and a traitor. Camarena, a student of Rivera's, also incorporated indigenismo ideology, but was ambivalent in his commentary on the Spanish. His mural entitled Integration of Latin America decorating a wall at the University of Ceoncepción, Chile, addresses miscegenation in Latin America. Camarena named one section of the mural *La Pareja Original* (*The Original Couple*). The conquistador is an anonymous suit of armor; the Native woman is proud, strong, and beautiful. The two figures step forward together into the future. Camarena borrowed from Vasconcelos's theory of mestizaje in his 1964 mural entitled *Las Razas* (*The Races*). This work is a visual explanation of merging races; they fade together in the creation of a Latin American race, which stands at the forefront. The timeworn ideologies of mestizaje and indigenismo were powerfully illustrated through the Mexican muralist movement (1920–1960s). Both ideologies were used to portray an inclusive national story and define a mexicanidad that would bring worldwide respect to Mexico.

Despite conflicting interpretations of the conquest, there are striking continuities in the representation of Indians over time. Idealizing

José Clemente Orozco, *Cortés and Malinche,* mural at Escuela Nacional Preparatoria, 1926. © 2009 Artists Rights Society (ARS), New York / SOMAAP, Mexico City.

Jorge Gonzalez Camarena, *La Pareja Original* (*The Original Pair*), detail from *Presencia de América Latina* mural in the lobby of the Casa del Arte of the University of Concepción, Chile, 1965.

Indians, cleansing them of what had been perceived as Native savagery at the time of contact, was crucial to their adoption as noble forerunners of modern Mexico. None of the Native practices that appalled colonizing Spaniards (human sacrifice, cannibalism, and sodomy) are depicted. Instead, mythic Indians in art live in pristine environments, build highly cultured societies, and exhibit honorable values. These idealized Indians gave Mexico pride. More objectionable ancient customs and the troubling realities of contemporary Indians were avoided in the development of Mexican nationalism. The intellectual construction of indigenismo consistently celebrated a romanticized Indian contribution to Mexican nationalism.

Another repeating image of Native Mexico is the feminization of the Indian. Native Mexico is often represented in the form of a nude indigenous female. This symbolic Mexican earth mother is nude because she is an extension of nature. She is unclothed and uncivilized; she is voluptuous, desirable, and full of potential. She is accepting of the male gaze to symbolize the acceptance of the Spanish conqueror. Orozco's Cortés and *Malinche* and Rivera's *The Fecund Earth* and *Sleeping Earth* illustrate this docile feminization of Native Mexico.[61] This indigenous earth mother is a complex symbol that has been used to celebrate the beauty of indigenous Mexico and Indian women, yet it has also served to reinforce the subordination of Indian people. This beautiful, open, and accepting female is metaphorically to blame for the Spanish conquest (both sexual and imperial). Like Malinche, the Mexican earth mother is alluring, in need of guidance, vulnerable to foreign domination, and ultimately conquered.

During the first few decades of the century, in the midst of a revolution, a world war, and increasing industrialization, the nostalgic admiration for these pure indigenous societies deflected the realities of a fast-changing world. The work of Gamio and Rivera honored ancient indigenous lifeways that had been corrupted by European interference. Malinche was the whore who had opened Mexico to the malignant intrusion of European culture. The author whose work epitomizes this interpretation of Malinche was the grandson of Ireneo Paz. Octavio Paz did not share his grandfather's regard for Malinche. Instead, he redefined Malinche for the twentieth century. He devoted a chapter to her in his famous book *El Laberinto de la Soledad* (1950).

Diego Rivera, *The Fecund Earth*, detail from mural at Universidad Autónoma Chapingo, 1926. © 2009 Banco de México Diego Rivera Frida Kahlo Museums Trust, Mexico, D.F. / Artists Rights Society (ARS).

Octavio Paz was an internationally received writer, and his interpretation of Mexican nationalism reached a broad worldwide audience. Paz's chapter entitled "The Sons of Malinche" builds on the sexual theme of the conquest and the gender representations painted by Orozco and Rivera.[62] Both Rivera's indigenous approach and Orozco's more Eurocentric perspective present Malinche as a sexual object who is dominated by Spanish men. Octavio describes the conquest as a violation in which women and Indians are victimized. Malinche conveniently represents both. According to Paz, her vulnerability and passivity, demonstrated by her submission to Cortés, present an obstacle to the formation of Mexican national identity.

Paz employs the Spanish verb *"chingar"* to describe the disrespectful sexual union between Cortés and Malinche. Cortés, "el chingado," represents the macho Spanish force that inflicted aggression on Malinche and Native Mexico. Malinche, "La chingada," represents the passive, fallen female and the conquered Indian. He explains,

"The chingon is the macho, the male; he rips open the chingada, the female, who is pure passivity, defenseless against the exterior world."[63] Paz defines manliness as impenetrable, having the capacity to violently impose himself on others. According to his framework, woman has the capacity to be violated. Her vulnerability to penetration and her ultimate submission make her subordinate to the male.

After casually explaining women's ancillary status, Paz assigns a social role to the Mexican female: "Woman transmits or preserves—but does not believe in—the values and energies entrusted to her by her nature or society. In a world made in man's image, woman is only a reflection of masculine will and desire."[64] She is susceptible to being deceived because of the inferior nature of her sex. Malinche, as a woman, cannot believe in Indian values and is willing to trade them for the sexual attention of Cortés. A similar point will be made below: feminist scholars have suggested that she turned away from her Indian heritage because she, as a woman, was exploited by her Native culture. Paz draws a parallel with the biblical Eve by describing Malinche as a negative incarnation of the feminine.[65] His analysis defines a polarized characterization of the Mexican female. He presents Malinche as the Mexican bad woman, presenting her in opposition to the pure maternal image of the Virgin of Guadalupe, who represents the good feminine archetype.

Octavio Paz's explanation presents an uncompromising paradigm for Mexican readers: the rejection of the passive feminine chingada (Malinche/Indian) and the rejection of the violent male chingado (Cortés/Spaniard). The sons of Malinche (the mestizos, the only honorable Mexicans) suffer dishonor and anxiety as a result of their unfortunate heritage. The union of Cortés and Malinche brings together the worst of the female Indian and the worst of the European male. Cortés's sexual domination over Malinche is the nation's origin; together they are the symbolic parents of modern Mexico. Mexicans do not benefit from a positive and productive national creation story. Paz believes the Spanish conquest (which he reduces to a sexual conquest) presents an obstacle to social harmony. This creation story of rape and passivity shames Mexico's founding couple, forcing citizens to deny their national origin. By turning their backs on Malinche/ mother and Cortés/father, Mexicans condemn themselves to isolation and solitude. Like Vasconcelos and Gamio, Paz believed that Mexico could not emerge from a postrevolutionary identity crisis until Mexicans deciphered their complex national heritage. The first step toward national unity was for all Mexicans to reconcile their complicated past.

FEMINIST AND CHICANA REVISIONS

Paz's male-dominant portrayal of Mexico's creation story provided compelling motivation for late-twentieth-century female scholars to reevaluate his gender definitions. It is important to pause and acknowledge consistent feminist interpretations that occasionally interrupted the patriarchal mode of thinking illustrated by Paz. Mexico has a long history of women contributing to the national dialogue, beginning with Sister Juana Inez de la Cruz. She was the seventeenth-century nun, scholar, and poet who chose the convent to pursue her intellectual passion and to offer input into the creation of Mexican nationalism. There were countless Mexicanas who fought for suffrage and *soldaderas* (female soldiers) who fought during the Mexican Revolution.[66] Mexicana painters like Maria Izquierdo and Frida Kahlo exhibited alternative feminine representations, far different from the feminine archetypes depicted by Orozco, Rivera, and Camarena. There have also been female writers (Rosario Castellanos, Elena Poniatowska, Carmen Boullosa, and Angeles Mastretta) who found creative ways to undermine male authority.[67] These feminine voices were typically forced to the periphery, yet they persisted in expressing an alternative perspective on Mexicanidad.

There has been far too little scholarly attention devoted to the feminist movement in Mexico.[68] To be sure, Mexican feminism and American feminism were not always compatible and have been frequently at odds. There is no universal feminism; feminist movements have developed across time and space in response to particular social and cultural circumstances.[69] One commonality of contemporary feminist scholarship across borders is the interjection of a woman-centered consciousness that represents an alternative historical narrative and displaces feminine symbols perpetuated by patriarchal representations womanhood. The Malinche narrative was particularly relevant to late-twentieth-century feminist discussions, and again she represented bipolar extremes. Anglo feminist scholars tended to define her as a female slave oppressed by Indian and Spanish men. Chicana (American women of Mexican heritage) feminist scholars often celebrated Malinche as a strong female activist who threw off the shackles of patriarchy. Patriarchy, however, is a Western gender construction that was institutionalized in New Spain after Malinche's death. She operated according to her own cultural gender ideology, and her actions were motivated by the tumultuous circumstances of her lifetime. Like earlier commentators who used Malinche to profess their particular agendas, feminist scholars also projected Malinche's life through the prism of their own contemporary cultural assessment.

An early focus of feminist scholarship was the reevaluation of national feminine archetypes, including the Virgin of Guadalupe and La Malinche. Initially, Malinche was avoided in Mexican feminist scholarship; less complicated women offered examples of female social activism. Across the border, however, Chicanas appropriated Malinche's symbolism and invested themselves in retelling her history. Early Chicano scholarship often neglected precontact Mesoamerican gender structures that recognized feminine power and influence in indigenous spiritual and social organization because their feminist analyses typically began from the non-Indian, patriarchal gender perspective that they experienced.

By the last quarter of the twentieth century Mexico's cultural traditions (including the racial and gender representations within) migrated across the border. Hundreds of thousands of Mexicans immigrated to the United States during the Mexican Revolution; they were followed by hundreds of thousands more who were lured by jobs during World War I and World War II. Most of these migrants entered the southwestern region of the United States, where they encountered an entrenched population of Hispanics whose families had been there since before the Treaty of Guadalupe Hidalgo. Hispanic Americans initially greeted Mexican immigrants with hostility. Beginning in the 1970s, however, the two groups began to reach out to one another. Mexican American activists (including Hispanics who had always lived in the region and newcomers who came during the twentieth century) formed a Mexican-American heritage that was defined and projected through the Chicano/Chicana Movement.

In the decades following the civil rights movement, the politics of ethnicity gripped the United States in a national discussion on diversity and social justice. Mexican Americans took part in this discussion by making demands for equality and tolerance through the Chicano Movement. Chicanos grounded their twentieth-century cultural identity by claiming descent from Aztec ancestors who originated from the mythical city of Aztlán. They believed the ancestral homeland existed somewhere in the southwestern United States. Establishing a prehistory within the United States strengthened their demands for equal citizenship. They were not outsiders; they were descendants of ancient Native Americans who had migrated to Mexico in the 1200s.

The social antagonisms of the 1970s launched a broader discussion of institutionalized systems of oppression. Gender and sexual orientation became increasingly familiar themes in scholarly research and intellectual debate. Some Chicanas attempted to merge the call for racial equality with their demands for gender equality. They examined Octavio Paz's gendered psychoanalysis of Mexican national identity in relation to the limitations they faced as Mexican American women. These Chicana feminist scholars struggled to negotiate two identities: their Mexican heritage and their feminist academic training. They bristled under a patriarchal Mexican American culture and began rejecting the feminine expectations that Chicano activists celebrated.

According to Chicana feminists, the expectation for a good Mexican American woman was to follow the feminine archetype of the suffering mother. Mexican American women were expected to participate in the movement by supporting and giving birth to male leaders. Chicana feminists were unsatisfied with these gender limitations; they wanted leadership roles and they wanted to participate in defining the movement's agenda.[70] As Chicanas attempted to incorporate gender issues into the movement's demands for a more inclusive and equitable society, they were ridiculed as traitors to their heritage and excommunicated from the movement. Chicanas who focused on gender issues were persecuted for opening themselves to the foreign doctrine of feminism.

Chicanas who accepted Anglo cultural patterns (like feminism) or associated with white men were likened to bad Malinche. Chicano activists and their female supporters accused Chicana feminists of turning against "la raza" for selfish advancement. They were denounced for having been swayed by North American feminist scholars who looked to Latin American gender structures as fertile ground for study. Like Malinche, Chicana feminists were condemned because a foreign ideology corrupted their cultural perspective. The contemptuous adjective *malinchista* was harshly applied to those Chicanas who had been seduced by foreign influences. This pejorative term was an extension of Malinche's negative feminine archetype, and it negatively characterized Mexican American women who consorted with Anglo males or culture. Like Malinche, feminist Chicanas did not reject their Mexicanness, yet they did reject Malinche's negative image as a deformation of themselves. Chicana writers (beginning in the 1970s and continuing through to today) have expropriated Malinche's malleable legend in order to address their contemporary predicament as women of color.

Adelaida Del Castillo's 1974 article, "Malintzin Tenepal: A Preliminary Look into a New Perspective," and Cordelia Candelaria's 1984 essay, "Malinche, Feminist Prototype," are representative of early Chicana feminist revision.[71] Del Castillo's particular contribution is her portrayal of Malinche as a religious activist. Like Bernal Díaz, she stresses the importance of Christianity in Malinche's life. According to Del Castillo, Malinche's actions were motivated by religious faith and an inner drive to end the bloody rituals of Aztec domination. Del Castillo's interpretation does not celebrate the Indian, the Spaniard, or the mestizo. Her story centers on a strong, intelligent, and caring woman who was a force in making history. Candelaria's essay examines Malinche as a cultural symbol. She interprets the sixteenth-century woman as a prototype for Chicana feminists. Candalaria writes of Malinche, "By adapting to the historical circumstances thrust upon her, she defied traditional social expectations of a woman's role."[72] She equates Malinche's personal characteristics (intelligence, initiative, adaptability, and leadership) with the characteristics that she associates with modern Mexican American women who are unfettered by traditional gender restraints. In both Chicana revisions the facts of Malinche's Indian experience, as well as her work as a strategist and diplomat, are irrelevant. For these writers (like many before them) the details of Malinche's life are unimportant.

Yet her symbolic usefulness is central to a contemporary feminist critique of Mexican American culture. While Chicanos tended to vilify Malinche, Chicana feminists celebrated her. For them she was the ultimate example of a strong woman who could step outside the confines of societal norms—albeit twentieth-century societal norms—to become a powerful force in shaping history.

Despite Chicana efforts to dismantle the negative symbolism surrounding mythic Malinche as traitor/whore, the characterization proved difficult to dislodge. In 1982 a statue of Cortés, Malinche, and their son was erected in the town of Coyoacan, where the couple had lived after the conquest. The sculpture was intended to appease the gender debate, to reveal Malinche as a more sympathetic heroine, and to celebrate the mestizo. But students erupted in protest; they rejected the commemoration of Malinche, who to them represented betrayal. The protesters sought to bring attention to the condition of Mexico's living Indians, to resist foreign domination, and to support national sovereignty. Mythic Malinche had abandoned the Indians and Mesoamerican sovereignty. The statue was ultimately removed.

Across the border, Americans were more at ease in their attempt to decipher the complicated legacy of Malinche. In 1991 Sandra Messinger Cypess provided the most extensive study of Malinche's rise to cultural symbol in *La Malinche in Mexican Literature: From History to Myth.* Her work reveals a scholarly feminist perspective, yet Cypess does not use Malinche to reflect her own personal experience as earlier Chicana feminist scholars did. She treats Malinche as a fellow woman who has been confined and explained by patriarchal ideologies.[73] The particulars of Native gender structures are largely neglected, too difficult to incorporate into a feminist argument of female exploitation. Cypess's contribution was her insightful discussion of mythic Malinche through Mexican literature over time. She took the gendered discussion of Malinche out of the realm of Chicana personal identification, and pushed future scholars toward a broader analysis of feminine symbolism.

Malinche left no record to explain her actions, and her silence continues to captivate the imagination of citizens in Mexico and in the United States. Dan Banda's PBS documentary, *Indigenous Always: The Legend of La Malinche and the Conquest of Mexico* (2000), inspired an academic conference on Malinche. The conference brought the foremost authorities on the conquest together in an attempt to draw some conclusions about Malinche. Consensus on Malinche remains an impossible task, yet the conference proved fruitful. It provided analysis for the film (which won several awards and received five Emmy nominations) and produced a book of essays entitled, *Feminism, Nation, and Myth: La Malinche* (2005).[74] The work is unconcerned with Malinche as a woman. The essays instead deal with Malinche as a symbol in relation to social categories of gender and race, with a particular emphasis on national and personal identities. Identity is chosen and strategically crafted; it is the public face we want others to recognize. People and nations draw on specific historical events, often while neglecting others, to legitimize their claims. Most of the essays in *Feminism, Nation, and Myth: La Malinche* explore how mythic Malinche influenced Chicano identity.

Alicia Gaspar de Alba's essay, "Malinche's Revenge," discusses how and why feminism was isolated from Chicano nationalism.[75] She suggests that during the "early chauvinist years" of the movement, women were confined to two roles: helpers who supported male leaders or traitorous malinchistas out for their own interests. According to Gaspar de Alba, these two feminine roles evolved from a heterosexual, patriarchal gender structure that was imposed and institutionalized during the colonial era to foster conformity to male authority. She traces the dichotomous feminine roles through early Chicano works (Armando Rendon's "The Chicano Manifesto," Oscar Zeta Acosta's *Revolt of the Cockroach People*, and Rudolfo Anaya's *Bless Me Ultima*) that celebrate the Chicana who dutifully serves the Chicano. Gaspar de Alba then describes how feminism was defined as a negative foreign influence and not an authentic concern within the Chicano community. Any woman who professed foreign feminist doctrines was counterproductive to Chicano nationalism and was labeled a malinchista.

The isolation of feminist perspective from Chicano nationalism was not limited to the early days. Arturo Rosales, in *Testimonio: A Documentary History of the Mexican Struggle for Civil Rights* (2000), agrees that women in the movement feared being stigmatized as malinchistas and that the movement emphatically kept the two systems of oppression (race and gender) separate.[76] He suggests, however, that the majority of Chicanas were extremely hesitant to upset traditional patriarchal gender roles. Rosales characterizes the feminine voice as a reluctant voice in the Chicano movement because of women's fear of speaking up. According to Rosales, most Chicanas did not want leadership roles.

Fear of being labeled malinchistas certainly did not silence all Chicanas. There were several Chicana feminists calling for gender parity in the movement. Alma Garcia's *Chicana Feminist Thought: The Basic Historical Writings* (1997) brings attention to Chicanas who did not fear "upsetting gender roles," who did speak out, and who fought their classification as malinchistas.[77] Garcia's first examples are early Chicana revisions of Malinche that characterized her as a positive feminine role model, one who could inspire contemporary women to use their voices to bring about change. Garcia highlights Adelaida Del Castillo, Cordelia Candelaria, and the writings of Anna Nieto Gomez. Gomez, like Del Castillo and Candelaria, offers Malinche as an example for Chicana liberation, as someone who broke through gender restraints. Yet Gomez pushes her argument toward tangible gender reform. She was an early advocate calling for an educational reinterpretation of Malinche. Gomez suggests that schoolchildren be introduced to Malinche as a positive force in the creation of the mestizo and a positive symbol in Chicano history.[78]

Garcia's *Chicana Feminist Thought* drew attention to other early Chicana writers who demanded more appreciation for female supporting roles, particularly motherhood, as indispensable to the movement. Yet heterosexual feminism was unsatisfying to some lesbian Chicana feminists who rejected motherhood as the only acceptable contribution to the movement. They insisted that the biological role of mother perpetuated patriarchy within Chicano nationalism. In the last ten years lesbian Chicana writers have been critical of the heterosexual reverence for motherhood. Alicia Gaspar de Alba and Cherríe Moraga have lent their literary talents to a discussion of homosexuality within Chicano culture. Moraga argues in her book *The Last Generation* (1993) that heterosexism was the "cardinal rule" of Chicano culture; it fostered a Chicana's sexual commitment to the Chicano and proved her commitment to the procreation of la raza. Gaspar de Alba is more radical in her claim that Chicanas could only illustrate their commitment to the movement by providing the "three Fs" (feeding, fighting, and fucking the Chicano). Any woman who deviated from this gender norm was a *puta, vendita, jota,* or malinchista. Lesbians were an obvious affront to the female qualities that Chicano nationalism celebrated. They were defined as traitors and expelled from their cultural heritage. Gaspar de Alba, in her essay "Malinche's Revenge," defines Chicana feminism as the resistance to "continued domination of the Father and the rule of the white male penis."[79] She writes of Malinche, "But Chicana feminists and particularly Chicana lesbian feminists have begun to transform the story of Malinche into a mirror of Chicana resistance against female slavery to patriarchy. . . . Malinche also represents affirmation: of a woman's freedom to use her mind, her tongue, and her body in the way that she chooses and to cultivate her intellectual skill for her own survival and empowerment."[80] Gaspar de Alba identifies with Malinche in her description of lesbianism: "To be a woman-loving woman means that men are not the object of desire, and this means that women cannot be controlled by what they are conditioned to desire, i.e., a good man or a heterosexual family. Lesbians show that there is another way that is not dependent on relations with men (as the terms "wife," "mother," "daughter" and "girlfriend" to identify women all suggest), that in fact, women can have autonomous lives without needing to be seen as attachments to men, and thus, become the owners and creators of their own destinies."[81] Feminist and lesbian Chicanas legitimized their personal identity as strong women of Mexican heritage by transforming Malinche's legend to reflect what they wanted others to recognize about themselves. They identified with Malinche as women who had been misrepresented and rejected. Lesbian Chicanas wanted to be—as they wanted Malinche to be—acknowledged for breaking free from societal constraints and for speaking out to bring change and tolerance.

Franco Mondini-Ruiz describes his personal torment and his secret identification with Malinche in his essay "Malinche Makeover: One Gay Latino's Perspective." His poignant humor forces readers to consider the concept of identity (chosen or imposed) and to take an uncomfortable look at issues of race, class, and sexuality in south Texas. He identifies with Malinche, saying he had been a "secret monster" as she was. He was not detectably gay nor was he detectably Mexican. He grew up keeping both parts of himself secret, but was eventually compelled to bare his identity (both his Mexican heritage and his homosexuality) as an adult. He concludes his essay with these comments on Malinche: "I like her, cheap slave girl sandals and all. No, I don't think her eyes look treacherous and I love the red nail polish that matches her teeth. Would you call that Tabasco red? I'm proud of her and she's bilingual too. And her legacy? 'You're soaking in it!'"[82] For nearly five hundred years Malinche's symbolism has proved exceedingly useful to generations of diverse people: male and female, heterosexual and homosexual, people from multiple cultures, from different eras, and from both sides of the border. Mythic Malinche has provided a forum for recurring discussions on conquest, national identity, social harmony, race, and gender. The flexibility of Malinche's narrative has been conducive to national debates, and fundamental to her relevance over time.

Camilla Townsend examines Malinche as a sixteenth-century woman in *Malintzin's Choices: An Indian Woman in the Conquest of Mexico* (2006). Her work presents a courageous Indian slave woman who is caught in the whirlwind of European conquest.[83] Townsend stresses Malinche's resourcefulness, yet gives her little agency in facilitating a new existence in the Valley of Mexico. Townsend's Malinche is reacting to a masculine world that has been thrust upon her; she is surviving racial and gender oppression during the Spanish conquest. Indians, including Malinche, were victims of European colonization not participants in the creation modern Mexico.

My work presents Malinche as a skillful intermediary who intentionally shaped a new reality in the Valley of Mexico. Her actions were dictated by indigenous circumstances, social expectations, gendered responsibilities, and a desire for her own personal well-being. She was given to the conquistadors with an obligation to facilitate interaction with the powerful newcomers. Malinche was an influential evangelist, diplomat, and mediator who advocated for the coexistence of Mesoamericans and Spaniards. Her contemporaries (both Indian and Spanish) recognized her as a woman of influence and consequence.

Mexico experienced a long history of immigration, and Mesoamericans were accustomed to cultural accommodation long before European entrance. Malinche was raised immersed in Mexico's dynamic cultural accumulation. Her actions during the conquest suggest that she saw advantages in the Spanish Christian world. She encouraged other Indians, with remarkable success, to accept a future with Spanish religious and political input. Malinche was like most participants of the conquest; she was driven by complex motivations: social obligation, religious beliefs, and personal ambition, or perhaps a sense of destiny. Spanish invaders had their own agenda. Some conquistadors wanted to enrich themselves, some sought adventure, some were compelled by a divine mission to spread Christianity, and some were motivated by a combination of incentives. The Spanish conquest was a multifaceted and dynamic interaction that both Spaniards and Indians recognized as a moment of transformation. Both sides of the cultural divide strategized to take advantage of new opportunities. My intent is not to judge Spanish colonization, nor to present a nostalgic appreciation for indigenous Mexico. My goal is to understand the initial encounter through the lens of gender and to acknowledge Native and non-Native cultural ingredients in Mexican nationalism.

Forming a collective understanding of national identity is an ongoing project in Mexico, as it is in all nations. Mexicanidad has been sculpted by a long tradition of immigration and cultural diversity, Spanish colonization, Mexican independence, the Revolution, postwar modernity, and periodic debates on social equality. Watershed moments have encouraged national reflection and revisions to nationalist explanations. Over time, shifting gender and racial ideologies have redefined national archetypes and national narratives. Commentators have manipulated race and gender imagery to provide strategic interpretations of the conquest that legitimize a particular social agenda. The Spanish conquest and Malinche's role in it have been repeatedly reworked. Each revision of Mexico's national story is a reflection of contemporary concerns, yet it remains grounded in the cultural collision of the conquest.

CHAPTER SIX

Pocahontas

Pocahontas's public record began in the writings of John Smith. His literary output includes eleven travel-adventure books that detail his globe-trotting heroics. They were published between 1608 and 1612 and were later compiled in *The Generall Historie of Virginia, New England, and the Summer Isles* (1624). Discrepancies in his various accounts haunt his legacy as a historian; later scholars have questioned the validity of his claims.[1] Much like the self-serving account authored by Cortés, Smith distinguishes himself as the pivotal character in an epic tale. Despite his ambivalence regarding the significance of his costar heroine, the Pocahontas legend is rooted in Smith's narrative of his Virginia adventure.

Colonial Period

Pocahontas first encountered Smith in the winter of 1607, after the Englishman was taken captive and ultimately brought before her father, Chief Powhatan. This occasion launched mythic Pocahontas. Smith describes the scene in third person in *The Generall Historie:* "a long consultation was held, but the conclusion was, two great stones were brought before Powhatan: then as many as could layd hand on him, dragged him to them and thereon laid his head, and being ready with their clubs, to beate out his brains, Pocahontas the kings dearest daughter, when no intreaty could prevail, got his head in her armes, and laid her owne upon his to save him from death."[2]

This descriptive sentence links Pocahontas and Smith together in the immortality of myth; America's creation story began in this defining moment when the destinies of Native people and European people collided.

Smith never mentioned the rescue in his initial progress reports from Virginia. He detailed the harrowing scene while compiling his completed works in 1624, after celebrity status had been bestowed on "Princess Pocahontas" during her visit to England in 1616. Smith does, however, briefly mention the incident in a letter he wrote to Queen Anne before Pocahontas's arrival London. His 1616 letter recommends the queen invite Pocahontas to the royal court, something that had already been arranged. The letter describes a gracious, compassionate, and brave Pocahontas. Regarding the rescue, Smith informs the Queen, "at the minute of my execution, she hazarded the beating out of her owne braines to save mine, and not only that, but so prevailed with her father, that I was safely conducted to James towne."[3] Smith's letter circulated among the upper echelon of London society during Pocahontas's visit, before her death, and well before his *Generall Historie* (1624).

There were self-serving reasons behind Smith's 1616 correspondence with the Queen. Earlier in the year he had petitioned the queen's brother for a license to launch an expedition to investigate whale-fishing prospects in New England and to inform the court of publication of his fourth book, *A Description of New England*. The letter may have been an attempt to repay Pocahontas for her gracious treatment toward him in Virginia, to promote his book, to gain favor with the queen, and to secure her support for his next venture. This was the second time a private letter penned by Smith had circulated to ignite enthusiasm for the financially struggling Virginia endeavor.[4]

It is likely that Pocahontas saved Smith in 1607, but it is also likely that Smith failed to understand what had happened to him.[5] *The Generall Historie* implies, on several occasions, that Pocahontas was infatuated with the brave white adventurer and was compelled to save him. Smith's record suffers from ethnocentric biases and must be treated cautiously. Twentieth-century scholars who have accepted Smith's description of events—and not all do—looked for other incentives that pushed Pocahontas to spare his life.

Peter Hulme and Paula Gunn Allen suggest that if Smith's claim was truthful, it is likely that he was ritually adopted. His imminent execution was actually a ritual to recognize his demise as a stranger and his rebirth as a kinsman and an ally.[6] Pocahontas, by saving Smith, became his cultural sponsor who was responsible for acclimating him to the expectations of the Powhatan confederacy. Allen suggests, "Pocahontas became something like the god-mother of this new made Powhatan."[7] This would explain her consistent goodwill toward the English despite frequent hostilities and her captivity in Jamestown. Hulme gives this explanation for the rescue: "Powhatan's decision must have been that the English were too dangerous to be alienated: an alliance should be made, perhaps with a view to absorbing them into the confederacy. . . . At a prearranged signal Pocahontas threw herself upon him and pleaded for his life. Powhatan granted her request."[8]

Subsequent events in Smith's narrative support Hulme's explanation. Smith reports in the *Generall Historie* that, days after the rescue, Chief Powhatan took him to a "great house in the woods," gave him an Algonquian name, made him weroance, and declared he would forever regard him as a son.[9] Hulme clarifies Smith's failure to mention the rescue in his initial progress letters by suggesting that did not understand the significance until years later. Only after Chief Opechancanough (Chief Powhatan's successor) revealed a more hostile alternative to Powhatan's kinship strategy did Smith attempt to explain his Indian initiation. When Smith was wounded and forced to return to England for medical attention in 1609, his departure and rumored death severed the kinship tie, and except for the two years that Pocahontas and Rolfe were married (1614–1616), the peaceful coexistence between the Europeans and Indians steadily deteriorated until Opechancanough's war in the 1620s.

The 1616 conversation between Pocahontas and Smith in London (discussed in chapter 4) offers further validation of the Indian adoption scenario. Smith remembers her ominous words upon their reunion in England: "You did promise Powhatan what was yours should bee his, and he the like to you; you called him father being in his land a stranger and by the same reason so must I doe you."[10] In this passage Pocahontas recognizes the obligations she and Smith shared. Smith admits to her "uncontented" disposition prior to reprimanding him for neglecting his promise to Chief Powhatan. She also recognizes that Smith's Jamestown countrymen were distrustful. Perhaps this was a devastating moment for Pocahontas; a moment in which she realized that the kinship connection that she was responsible for maintaining had been a farce.

Scholarly skepticism emerged during the mid-nineteenth century, during America's sectional ills. Northern scholars discounted the southern hero's claim of rescue, despite corroborating evidence that Pocahontas oversaw his adoption into the Indian confederacy. Cynics refused to consider other incidences of her compassionate disposition. By all accounts, Pocahontas was hospitable when she brought food to starving colonists and gracious during negotiations for the release of prisoners.[11] According to Smith, Pocahontas saved him a second time under the cover of darkness in 1609, at which time she also warned colonist Richard Wiffin of his impending death at the hands of her countrymen.[12] Skeptics have been unconcerned with these demonstrations of Pocahontas's sympathetic posture. It's unlikely that Pocahontas was motivated by spontaneous attraction to Smith's manliness. Rather, her behavior was motivated by an obligation to facilitate cross-cultural understanding and cooperation. When she saved and claimed Smith, she accepted a responsibility to engage the newcomer and indoctrinate him into the standards of the Powhatan Confederacy.

Whether or not Pocahontas actually rescued Smith is less important than the reality of how that event (invented, exaggerated, or misunderstood) pervaded colonial history and early American nationalism. By the early 1800s that perilous scene had come to define the moment of national conception, when the best of Native America and the best of Europe came together. Smith's lovely, virginal Indian benefactor symbolized an open Native landscape that invited European masculine exploration and conquest. His story of Pocahontas and the rescue scene were immortalized in the most accessible early American histories, including those written by William Robertson (1801), Justice John Marshall (1804), James Grahame (1827), and George Bancroft (1834).[13] Smith and Pocahontas's first encounter was rooted in the national consciousness, and his swashbuckling tale went unquestioned for more than two hundred years. Cynicism arose in the second half of the nineteenth century during the sectional tensions of the Civil War era.[14] The attack on Smith's record began as part of an antisouthern campaign to tarnish the Virginia hero and all Virginia aristocrats who claimed descent from the gracious Indian princess.[15]

Smith, like Cortés, had critics in his own time as well. He was young and ambitious, only twenty-six years old when he embarked on his New World adventure. Smith's social betters in Virginia were often annoyed by his brash antics, his violent encounters with Indians, and his disregard for Virginia Company instructions. Smith was a commoner with little education who rose to be president of the Virginia colony in 1608. He was an experienced frontier adventurer, and his savvy often brought tangible benefits to the struggling colony. Prior to his Virginia expedition Smith had participated in Mediterranean trade and piracy, and he had volunteered in European wars against Muslims. These experiences gave him some expertise in dealing with diverse people and taught him a modicum of French, Italian, and probably some Spanish.[16] Smith was a soldier of fortune, trained in the difficulties of frontier communication and cross-cultural understanding. Unlike most of his fellow Jamestown colonists, Smith accepted violence as a necessary frontier strategy. And like Cortés, Smith was forced to defend himself against consistent accusations of impropriety during and after his days of conquest. His various renditions of events in Virginia were strategically crafted to ensure his own prestige and the crown's favor.

William Strachey offers an alternative account of the English settlement in *The Historie of Travell into Virginia Britania*. Strachey's book presents an honest description of what he found when his party finally arrived in Jamestown. Despite colonial reports that exaggerated the colonists' success in Virginia, Strachey found that the colonists were actually starving in a pestilence-ridden town with little hope or optimism. They were terrified of Indians and did not venture beyond the confines of the fort. Strachey describes colonists dismantling their own homes rather than risking a trip into the woods for firewood. As Strachey's group disembarked, colonists were debating whether or not they should abandon Jamestown. Before the dejected settlers fled, however, they met an incoming fleet packed with supplies. If not for this happenstance, Jamestown would have followed Roanoke into oblivion. It is no wonder that the Virginia Company blocked publication of Strachey's book, which highlighted the dire conditions in the New World colony. After Smith's return to England in 1609, rumors had begun to cross the waters on return ships, and it was clear that the Virginia enterprise was in trouble. In London the Virginia Company was forced into court as investors attempted to pull out. Company officials certainly did not want to release Strachey's reports to the public, yet they did begin a campaign to rectify the problems. They immediately sent word to Strachey, instructing him to provide a full and forthright assessment of the colony and its prospects.

Although Strachey corroborates much of Smith's account, he offers a different interpretation of Pocahontas based on the memories of early colonists and his own observations on Indian customs. Whereas Smith portrays Pocahontas as a sensitive, attractive young girl who prevented her people from savagely killing him, Strachey describes her as an uninhibited, energetic prepubescent girl who frequently frolicked naked, performing cartwheels, around the young boys of the colony. According to Strachey's account, she was "a well featured" but "wanton" (that is, mischievous) young girl.[17] And she had an Indian husband, a fact that destroyed the image of Pocahontas as Rolfe's virginal Indian princess bride.[18]

It is not surprising that Smith's portrayal, rather than Strachey's, was appropriately fixed to the mythic Pocahontas. It took 234 years for Strachey's book to be published for popular audiences. His work exhibits a hobbyist's interest in Indian cultures, and his description of Pocahontas is culturally accurate. Algonquian cultural studies (Strachey's as well as later studies) note that prepubescent Powhatan girls did not wear clothing during the warm months, and most were physically fit and athletic. Strachey also indicates that young Algonquian girls wore their hair closely shaven in front and on the sides, leaving the back to hang long.[19] Strachey's realistic portrayal of young Pocahontas (partially bald, running naked in front of English boys, and married to an Indian warrior when she met Rolfe) was hardly acceptable to Euro-American readers who had come to fancy

"Princess Pocahontas"—a beautiful, virginal, and dignified daughter of a noble chief—as their national heroine.

The books offered by Smith and Strachey are not the only primary accounts of Pocahontas. She appears in official colonial documents, particularly in letters penned by Rolfe, Governor Dale, and Strachey's successor, Ralph Hamor. As noted previously, their letters explain Pocahontas's captivity, baptism, and marriage to Rolfe. Their accounts suggest that she instinctively preferred English men and culture. The colonists celebrated Pocahontas's life among them; her consistent aid, her kind and contented demeanor, her religious conversion, and her marriage to Rolfe all demonstrated Native acceptance and legitimized the English conquest.

In addition to distorted colonial accounts, we must also consider Pocahontas's choices within the context of Powhatan culture. Pocahontas did not reject her Indian existence; she was working on behalf of her countrymen. She tried to understand English culture and religion, looking for possible advantages for Powhatan people and in order to facilitate a peaceful coexistence. Primary sources indicate that Pocahontas was intelligent, compassionate, and brave during her interactions with the English. These colonial accounts laid the foundation for mythic Pocahontas.

EARLY NATIONALIST ERA

Early nationalist writers in the United States were intent on assuring readers that their nation had not been built on the exploitation and mistreatment of indigenous people. A more satisfying start for the new nation evolved from an idealized emotional bond between the Indians and the colonists. Pocahontas's generosity and acceptance symbolized that bond. Smith testified that Pocahontas negotiated peaceful resolutions to disputes before violence erupted: she saved Smith on their initial meeting in 1607, she warned Smith and Wiffin of impending danger and advised them to flee her village in 1609, and she routinely took food to starving colonists. It was a small leap to expand her reputation from Smith's gracious protector to an Indian protector for the entire English colony. Pocahontas's intermediary activities were characterized to illustrate how Indians and Europeans willingly came together in North America.

The evolution of the Pocahontas narrative in the eighteenth and nineteenth centuries reflects particular concerns of the nationalist era: the competition among European colonizers, the building of Indian allies, and the question of miscegenation.[20] Despite Governor Dale's attempt to marry another of Powhatan's daughters in 1616, the dominant view among white settlers was that miscegenation was morally wrong and unnatural. Virginia company officials outlawed interracial marriage in 1691, making Pocahontas exceptional and her union with Rolfe an anomaly. However, colonial disapproval certainly did not prevent European men from engaging in sexual relations with Indian women. Undoubtedly there were white men who privately contradicted their public support of antimiscegenation laws.

A few commentators nostalgically theorized about a missed opportunity on the Virginia frontier because of antimiscegenation. Pocahontas's successful union with John Rolfe provided a model that could have been reenacted on a grand scale and perhaps could have mitigated Indian hostility. These writers would not have had to look far to test their hypothesis; miscegenation and intermarriage between Spanish and indigenous peoples had not alleviated racial tensions in New Spain. An early attempt to construct the Pocahontas narrative around the theme of miscegenation was Robert Beverly's *History and Present State of Virginia* (1705). Beverly suggests, "Intermarriage had been indeed the Method proposed very often by the Indians in the Beginning, urging it frequently as a certain Rule, that the English were not their Friends if they refused it. And I can't help but think it wou'd have been happy for that Country, had they embraced this Proposal: For, the Jealousie of the Indians, which I take to be the Cause of most of the Rapines and Murders they committed, wou'd by this Means have been altogether prevented."[21] Beverly relies on the Pocahontas narrative to editorialize on the pressing "Indian question" and imagine an alternative national policy. He wrote, however, in an era of intense imperial rivalry, in which Indian allies were critical.

New England, New France, and New Spain were aggressively pursuing New World expansion, and each pressed Indian groups for their allegiance and their land. Beverly expresses regret over the

English refusal to intermarry, which he suggests could have been an effective strategy for establishing peace and building allies among the Natives. His theory of miscegenation did not diminish Poca-hontas's gracious Indian princess image, yet as Robert Tilton points out, Beverly used the Pocahontas narrative to postulate on diplo-matic and racial policy during a competitive eighteenth-century New World environment.

Tilton exposed the longevity of this miscegenation question when he uncovered an obscure 1803 text by William Wirt, which asks, "It is not probable that this sensible and amiable woman, perceiving the superiority of the Europeans, foreseeing the probability of the subjugation of her countrymen, and anxious as well to soften their destiny as to save the needless effusion of human blood, desired, by her marriage with Mr. Rolf, to hasten the abolition of all distinc-tion between Indians and white men; to bind their interests and affections by the nearest and most endearing ties, and to make them regard themselves as one people, the children of the same great family?"[22] Wirt theorizes that the love shared between Pocahontas and Rolfe put the infant nation on a solid foundation that included Indian acceptance and denied a legacy of racial animosity. Like Vasconcelos's romantic ideal of mestizaje (the celebration of racial mixing in Mexico), Wirt's image of a harmonious union of European and Indian peoples in the United States projects a romantic ideal that obscures racial tensions and alleviates European guilt. Wirt patronizes the image of Pocahontas by describing her as a "sensible and amiable woman." Yet he doubts her capacity to understand what her marriage to Rolfe meant to the creation of a New World.

Like Tilton in the 1990s, Wirt was unable to imagine the possibility that Pocahontas's intermediary work was part of an entrenched sys-tem of Indian kinship diplomacy. She had a Native responsibility to fulfill her diplomatic duty, and she carefully considered the reper-cussions of her actions. If you situate Pocahontas's actions within her Native frame of reference, she worked to assimilate the English into the Powhatan Confederacy and facilitated a new Powhatan reality that included obtaining technology, goods, information, and an alli-ance from the English. Pocahontas tried to manipulate interactions with the English to benefit Tsenacommacah.

Early American nationalist writers, like Creole nationalists in Mexico, cleansed accounts of their colonizing endeavors by high-lighting English efforts to bring enlightenment to indigenous America and by celebrating intelligent noble Indians who were receptive to their efforts. Wirt suggests that Pocahontas immediately appreciated the benefits brought by the "superior" culture. His nationalist per-spective characterizes the marriage of Rolfe and Pocahontas as the symbolic event that merged the destinies of Europeans and Native Americans; together they began a new "great family," a new nation independent from Europe.[23] Colonists in the nationalist era who began to think of themselves as more American than English sculpted the Pocahontas narrative to illustrate how Europeans and Indians began a New World together.

Despite a few early nationalist treatments of Pocahontas, she remained an obscure figure for nearly two hundred years after her death. During most of the eighteenth century colonists were preoc-cupied with fighting off European challengers, capitalizing on New-World economic opportunities, and building a new civilization that eventually broke from the mother country and became the United States. There was little opportunity to pause for national reflection. As the nineteenth century got under way, however, patriotic writers began to scan the nation's earliest beginnings for heroes who could illustrate an appropriate national identity for the United States.

Nineteenth Century

As the century turned, writers began to capitalize on the romantic potential of Smith's dramatic rescue scene. The fact that Pocahontas was about eleven years old at the time was conveniently neglected. Smith had, for his own reasons, portrayed his relationship with Poca-hontas as respectful and platonic. But nearly two hundred years after her encounter with Smith, Pocahontas evolved into a sexualized sym-bol. By the 1800s writers began presenting her as sexually available at the time of her encounter with Smith, on the threshold of femi-nine maturity. She was capable of love, and her openness invited Euro-masculine exploration and penetration. John Davis, author of

Captain John Smith and Princess Pocahontas (1805), was among the first American historians to explicitly focus on Pocahontas's love for Smith as an explanation for national formation.[24] Davis seized the opportunity to condemn the Old World English monarchy and glorify America's uniquely democratic society. The Pocahontas narrative celebrates and unites Indian people and hard-working English commoners like Smith. Together they were a positive force in shaping American destiny, a destiny that was separate from England. A new and better society was planted in the unique environment of Virginia; it was there that the United States was born.

Davis's work ordains Pocahontas as the good Indian princess who saved John Smith, protected the colony, and symbolically nurtured a new nation. His description of events also recognizes a powerful yet merciful Chief Powhatan. By projecting the Indian chief in this way, the author furnishes a positive characterization of Indians. At the dawn of the nineteenth century Indians could be imagined as admirable and appropriate ingredients for the founding of the United States, and for an emerging American mythology. Writers who followed Davis's model throughout the 1820s, 1830s, and 1840s offered a sympathetic depiction of noble Indians. This genre of nostalgic writers (including Cooper, Thoreau, Longfellow, and Whitman) provided a counterweight to the fading, yet still prevalent, notion of Indians as savages. This romantic nationalism emerged after the American Revolution succeeded in throwing off the shackles of the mother country, after disease and the War of 1812 decimated Indian tribes in the East. The literary shift came when the threat of Indian resistance had abated, at least for the moment. Like the celebration of ancient Indians in Mexico through the ideology of indigenismo, nationalists in the United States expropriated strategic elements of an indigenous past to enrich a uniquely American national identity.

By mid-century, writers selected heroic figures from the colonial past that could symbolize national sentiments. The rigid social hierarchy of Europe and the arbitrary rule of a monarchy had been cast off, and a democratic future had taken root in the United States. The history of Jamestown symbolized this achievement in North America. John Smith was not an aristocrat but rather a hardworking colonist who was bold enough to take charge in the New World. He was unwilling to tolerate the incompetence of his superiors, and he appreciated the power and dignity of the Indians. Smith's mythic character became a template for an American national character: a rugged individualist who was undaunted by social constraints and adversity. He tamed the wilderness, dealt fairly with noble Indians, and severely punished savage Indians. Smith was mythologized as an individual who paved the way for a new civilization—a civilization that the Old World of Europe should envy. Together, a mythologized Smith (rugged and bold) and a mythologized Pocahontas (beautiful and gracious) forged a cross-cultural relationship that provided a perfect foundation for a new and improved nation. They were ideal early Americans. This nineteenth-century canonization of Pocahontas and Smith also elevated historic Virginia to a level that could rival Puritan New England.

Pocahontas became the feminine counterpart to Smith's strong, independent character. She also disagreed with her countrymen's behavior. She restrained their savage acts and tamed the frontier by mitigating violence and hardship. Virginia was a productive environment for the exceptional Englishman (the best of Europe) and the noble Indian woman (the best of the indigenous world) to form a new American family. This nationalist sentiment is exemplified in Henry Howe's painting *Virginia* (1852). Howe presents Smith's rescue scene as the foundation on which Virginia and America were built. Pocahontas is symbolically featured holding a defeated savage Indian under her foot. An engraving by Alonzo Chappel entitled *Pocahontas Saving the Life of Capt. John Smith* (1886) also illustrates the mythic proportions of Smith's rescue. Pocahontas is not presented as a partially bald, naked eleven-year-old, but as a lovely and caring young beauty with long flowing hair. A halo of light crowns Pocahontas as proof of her superior character. A fierce Indian stands ready to deliver a deadly blow to a helpless yet brave Smith, while a stately and contemplative Chief Powhatan presides over the iconic moment. These pictorials reveal the romantic power of the nation's creation story and the central role of Smith and Pocahontas.

Smith's account of his rescue in the arms of a tender Pocahontas was eventually questioned. The only firsthand account of the event was Smith's, and his reliability as a historian came under scrutiny

Alonzo Chappel, *Pocahontas Saving the Life of Captain John Smith*, engraving, 1861.

in the latter half of the 1800s. Henry Adams, a historian/journalist, was particularly harsh in his criticism of Smith. Adams portrays Smith, not as a hero, but as a braggart and a liar. Adams launched a full-scale attack on Smith in an 1867 article that describes Smith as an incompetent official, an unreliable historian, and an egomaniac.[25] Adams focuses on Smith's omission of the rescue scene in his early progress letters from Virginia. He suggests that such a terrifying and important event would not have been left out, and that Smith must have concocted the scene for self-aggrandizement after Pocahontas's subsequent fame and death. There was certainly reason to doubt Smith; according to his accounts, Indian women routinely came to his rescue, a fact that makes his story seem rather dubious. In 1624 he acknowledged this strange coincidence in a preface to his tale of Pocahontas, "the kings dearest daughter" who saved him from certain death, in the *Generall Historie*.

Scholars have argued the validity of Smith's rescue for generations. In 1992 historian Leo Lemay devoted an entire book to the controversy. In his study, *Did Pocahontas Save Captain John Smith?* Lemay suggests that Adams had his own reasons for recasting Smith as a despicable southerner in the late 1860s.[26] Lemay researched personal letters penned by Adams that reveal his intentions behind the inflammatory revision. During these years of lingering sectional ills, Adams's objective was to enrage southern politicians who claimed to be proud descendants of Captain Smith and who challenged his great-grandfather John Adams and his grandfather John Quincy Adams.[27] Adams condemned Smith for exaggerating Indian women's attraction to him and highlighted Smith's discrepancies in the various editions of his exploits. The doubt that Adams cast over Smith's claim proved permanent in academia, yet it had little impact on popular culture.

In 1992 Lemay attempted to put the question to rest by dissecting Adams's critique of Smith's documentation. First Lemay reasons that Smith could not have mentioned any connection with Pocahontas, particularly any romantic relationship, at a time when he was under suspicion for ignoring colonial instructions, for his violent interactions with the Indians, and for attempting to make himself King of Virginia.[28] Lemay dismisses Smith's many inconsistencies by suggesting that discrepancies are a fact of life. Ultimately, Lemay reminds readers that Smith's first letters were written from the field without time to edit or reflect. Smith's goal at the time of those early reports was to highlight his good rapport with the Indians, eliminate questions regarding his behavior, and encourage continued financial support from England.[29] By the 1624 publication of the *Generall Historie of Virginia,* Smith had had time to reflect and was free to give more complete details. Lemay ends his work personally convinced that Pocahontas saved Smith, yet readers are invited to draw their own conclusions.

Pocahontas was not the primary interest of Lemay or Adams; their arguments pertain to Smith's character. Lemay focuses on male historians Smith and Adams. Adams focuses on Smith and does not directly criticize Pocahontas. Her heroine status remained intact, having been confirmed by her marriage to Rolfe and her visit to London in 1616. She did not need Smith's testimony for validation of her feminine virtue. Her prestige as mother of the nation was unaffected by the controversy surrounding Smith. She was, however, politicized during the contentious debate over slavery in the antebellum years.

Some abolitionists invoked Pocahontas as the protector of an endangered captive and as a symbol for the possible coexistence of two races. Robert Tilton uncovered a pamphlet entitled *Pocahontas: A Proclamation* (1820) in which the author, William Hillhouse, Esq., takes on the persona of Pocahontas to provide a ridiculous justification for slavery in order to convince readers that there is no justification.[30] Emily Clemens Pearson uses Pocahontas's name for a character in her abolitionist novel *Cousin Franck's Household* (1852). By the second half of the nineteenth-century the Pocahontas narrative was so ingrained in the American consciousness that authenticity was no longer relevant. Her name, with no explanation, personified what it meant to be an exemplary American female, a woman who was compassionate toward others. She had become a recognizable symbol that illustrated feminine virtue and could be utilized for commentary on the national issue of racial harmony.

The characterization of the Smith-Pocahontas narrative was influenced by a young nation's quest to define itself. Cultural disseminators created the image of a nation that was built by individuals who, like our heroes, were bold enough to challenge the status quo and progressive enough to envision an alternative. The legend of Smith and Pocahontas demonstrates that the United States need not be divided by race; their mythologized example illustrates how diverse people came together to build a better future. In reality, of course, life was not better for the Powhatan people. This myth was not unmitigated truth, but it was a historical force intended to legitimize America's origin and identity. National heroes and heroines were chosen to illustrate appropriate images to outsiders and to provide an example of appropriate behavior for citizens.

No clear lines separate eras of interpretation. Once a particular perspective is introduced, it remains in the cultural reservoir available to later writers. Each of the interpretative themes (Smith and Strachey's colonial justification for conquest in the 1600s, the celebration of American nationalism at the turn of the nineteenth century, and the encouragement of racial harmony in the second half of the 1800s) reemerged in the twentieth century. By the middle of the twentieth century growing questions regarding cultural diversity and gender equality required that alterations be made to mythic Pocahontas. Thus scholars again redirected their academic inquiry, this time questioning the historical representation of women and minorities. The Pocahontas narrative was reconsidered to address contemporary emerging debates on nationalism, imperialism, race, and gender.

Twentieth Century

In 1953 Bradford Smith produced an autobiography of Captain Smith entitled *Captain John Smith: His Life and Legend*.[31] The author devotes considerable attention to answering Adams's skepticism, which at that time had tarnished Smith's legend for nearly one hundred years. The author assures readers that Smith did not fabricate his adventures; rather, he wrote in a Shakespearian age that evoked excessive passion and drama. Bradford Smith admits that the captain's description of Pocahontas fits a pattern of feminine portrayal found in many of Smith's writings. Bradford Smith accepts that Pocahontas, like many of the young Native women John Smith mentions, was of high birth, was overcome by her attraction to him, and saved him from certain death. There is a hint toward romantic entanglement, but as an honorable hero, Captain Smith consistently managed to deflect the young woman's attention. Pocahontas is not a significant figure in Captain Smith's self-serving account of Virginia, nor is she important in Bradford Smith's explanation in 1953. Instead, in both works her presence confirms the captain's heroics. Pocahontas's attraction to Smith assures readers that this special Englishman was wanted and protected in the New World: Captain Smith had a young, beautiful female benefactor who appreciated his European greatness. Bradford Smith wrote in an age of national confidence as post-war America enjoyed its new status as global superpower and an era of conservative gender values.

Bradford Smith's feminine characterization of Pocahontas resonated with American citizens who felt both exhausted and validated by victory in World War II. Americans in the 1950s were eager for a return to normalcy. When the war ended, women were encouraged to leave the labor pool, return to their homes, and resume the traditional female responsibility of providing loving care for their families. Women laborers had been intended as a temporary solution for a worker shortage during World War II, not a permanent strategy for American productivity. The preferred feminine ideal encouraged women to stay home, raise families, and consume an impressive abundance of American consumer goods; men were supposed to be the sole economic providers for the household. The postwar feminine ideal also had little to do with reality, since the number of working women continued to rise throughout the 1950s.[32] In this era of celebrated feminization and material consumption, the national ethos encouraged women to strive for feminine perfection: women should be attractive, sexy, and committed to others. Bradford Smith remade the Pocahontas myth in order to display these idealized womanly traits in 1953. His Pocahontas was nurturing, loving, and beautiful.

In 1956 Cassell & Co. in London commissioned a statue by David McFall to commemorate Pocahontas. England and the United States enjoyed a particularly cozy relationship after Word War II because the United States had come to aid Europeans in their hour of need, just as Pocahontas had in the 1600s. The statue presents a beautifully naked Pocahontas. The imagery of a naked Indian woman, in need

of clothing and civilization, was still a powerful symbol that justified colonization. This 1950s artistic interpretation depicts Pocahontas
as an Indian approximation of Rosie the Riveter. She is young, physically capable, and focused, yet she is also demure and sexy. She is
not voluptuous and leisurely (as Diego Rivera's Indian earth goddess
is). She is not saintly; she has no halo over her head (as in Alonzo
Chappel's 1886 engraving). Pocahontas is dignified and contemplative in this 1956 rendition. This mythic Pocahontas epitomizes a
mid-century idealized American woman. She is young, strong, pensive,
and beautiful. By honoring Pocahontas according to America's mid-
century ideal woman, England acknowledged that America had
again come to their rescue. Just as Pocahontas saved the English
colony in the 1600s, America's Rosie the Riveter intervened during
World War II to save the vulnerable English by manufacturing military products that overcame the enemy.

In 1962 Philip Young examined Pocahontas's role as national
mother in his article "The Mother of Us All: Pocahontas Reconsidered."[33] Young traces the evolution of the Pocahontas tale from Smith's
boastful beginnings, through its romantic tendencies, to the debunking of Smith's hero status. According to Young, the validity of the
Pocahontas narrative is unimportant. What matters is the usefulness
of her story and the way it makes Americans feel. The testimony of
Captain Smith and the interpretation of early secondary writers (like
Beverly, Wirt, and Davis) reassure readers that Indians welcomed
Euro-Americans. Pocahontas was compelled to help Europeans settle
in Virginia, and she preferred to live among them. Young suggests
that Pocahontas's real-life actions were blended with strategic imagery
to support a cherished foundational myth: noble Indians, like Pocahontas, embraced the newcomers. Young argues that mythic Pocahontas alleviated American guilt over the nation's treatment toward
Indian peoples. She accepted Euro-Americans and was treated well
by them. This implies that if only all Indians had been as reasonable
and gracious, perhaps the destruction of Indian life may have been
avoided; what befell the "savage Indian" was unfortunate and self-
inflicted. This was a prevalent message in the 1960s. Hopefully
emerging third-world nations would not make the same mistake,
and they, too, would choose the superior civilization. Pocahontas

David McFall, *La Belle Sauvage* (*The Beautiful Savage*), statue, 1956. Courtesy of the estate of David McFall.

exemplified a brave, intelligent, and welcoming Native who ulti-mately made the right choice.

In 1976 Frances Mossiker compiled an extensive analysis of Poca-hontas, in life and in legend. Uninterested in the Powhatan cultural perspective, she relies on English colonial accounts of Powhatan people to describe Pocahontas. Her presentation of Pocahontas's role in the establishment of Jamestown is certainly influenced by the romantic imagery that had seeped into the national conscious-ness. She accentuates her exotic beauty; Mossiker's Pocahontas (like Davis's Pocahontas in 1805 and Bradford Smith's in 1953) is irre-sistibly sexy. She writes that Pocahontas "could only be categorized as one of the biblically proscribed strange wives of the people of the land, dark and sultry, voluptuous, forbidden, but perennially tempting to the fair Anglo-Saxon newcomer."[34] A 1970s discussion on race and interracial sex is evident in Mossiker's work. The author highlights the young Indian princess's physical characteristics and her selfless acts of kindness that benefited Anglos; she was a perfect Indian woman.

Mossiker accepts the notion that Pocahontas turned against her own people, suggesting that she preferred to live within Anglo culture: "she was imbued with a profound yearning, an irresistible impulse to make the great leap forward, to plunge ahead—centuries, perhaps a millennia—ahead of her own people in their measured ascent to that rung of the cultural ladder."[35] Mossiker implies that romantic attraction led Pocahontas to risk her own life when she protected Smith (and Richard Wiffin) from Indian attack. She compares Pocahontas to Malinche by saying, "a traitor to her race, the red race's Uncle Tom? (If so, not the first: that had been Cortez's Malinche—both Indian women infatuated, enamored perhaps of whites, both dazzled by white skin, both subject to an overpowering physical attraction, to the lure of the exotic, both in a total surrender to 'Wayfaring gods.')."[36] Mossiker, writing during the sexual revolution of the 1970s, seems fascinated by temptations of the flesh and interracial sex on the frontier. She describes early English settlers as relics of an aristocratic society that needed to be expelled from America: "Smith could neither jolly nor coerce those indolent, insolent, improvident English gentlemen into honest labor—into labor of any kind. They were untrained, undisciplined; many were ne'er-do-wells—or worse."[37] Mossiker celebrates Indians and Americans, both of whom cleansed themselves of backward customs and built a new biracial civilization, although Americans occupied the highest "rung of the cultural ladder." Like Cortés and Malinche who had come together to forge modern Mexico, Smith and Pocahontas began a new American nation. Mossiker describes Smith and Pocahontas as the best of their cultures; both rejected unpleasant cultural antecedents within their own cultures to create a new and improved civilization.

Mossiker's analysis presents several obscure treatments of the Pocahontas legend, including literary and theatrical. The author successfully illustrates how various cultural explanations of Pocahontas were rooted in the colonial experience and how her representation was manifested in a logical progression through the nineteenth century. Ultimately, Mossiker's *Pocahontas: The Life and the Legend* fueled the myth of a beautiful Indian princess who loved, welcomed, and chose Anglo men and their superior culture. Her idealized and sexy feminine portrayal of Pocahontas may well have been an irritant to an emerging group of feminist scholars in the 1970s who began to dismantle male-centered histories and reevaluate female representation in the historical narrative.

FEMINIST REVISIONS OF THE 1970S AND 1980S

Rayna Green's 1976 article, "The Pocahontas Perplex: The Image of Indian Women in American Culture," interprets the Pocahontas legend as an unfortunate model for the unrealistic characterization of Indian women throughout American history.[38] Green, a Cherokee feminist scholar, explains how the positive portrayal of Pocahontas contrasts with the portrayal of her negatively viewed "squaw" sisters. Europeans adopted the noble Pocahontas as an iconic representation of an earth goddess who was beautiful, young, and full-bodied. She signified the opulence and peril of a virgin land. According to the mythology, Pocahontas and the indigenous landscape were open to European civilization and ultimately reached their full potential. Just as Pocahontas became a Christian and the wife of an Englishman, the indigenous landscape was tamed and made productive in a market economy. Other Indian women were defined as overworked and degraded "squaws"; their harsh existence justified the need to displace and dismantle uncivilized Native societies. According to Green, the dichotomous (goddess/squaw) image is damaging to Indian women who cannot live up to the fantasies of Pocahontas.

Green's complaint is valid, yet the dichotomous historical representation of Indian women is not unique. White western women were often described as whores who entertained frontier men or as gentle tamers who brought civilization (families, churches, and schools) to the New World. Frontiersmen were likewise characterized either as rugged individuals who blazed a trail for civilization or as uncouth "squaw men" who were corrupted by the wilderness. And Indian men were portrayed either as noble savages or as hostile enemies. These good/bad categories were consistent cultural shortcuts that illustrated appropriate and inappropriate behavior for a national audience.

Green's 1980 article, "Native American Women: A Review Essay," pleads with scholars to end their "fixation on Pocahontas and puberty rites."[39] She challenges feminist scholars to shift the historical focus to address the needs of Native American women. She writes, "Feminists have long insisted that women have the right to personal definition, to an individual agenda. It is now time for feminist scholars to ask Native American women—indeed, all groups of women they study—what their agendas are and how feminist scholars might lend themselves to the task."[40] According to Green, academics should further culturally specific feminist agendas. Her contribution to women's history was a much-needed Native American female perspective, and she encouraged feminist scholars to recognize the diversity of experiences among women. Green insisted that other Indian women, not just Pocahontas, were also relevant.

Feminist scholars occasionally encountered resistance from Indian women who avoided enlistment in their feminist agenda. Many Indian women were ambivalent toward the suggestion of a common gender struggle and occasionally resented the paternalism of academia. As feminist scholars turned to the lives of Indian women as fertile ground for study, their analyses frequently neglected the details of Indian cultures, and their discourse rarely included input from Indian women. Too often, minority women's stories were gathered and characterized to support an academic gender debate that seemed alien to the cultural perspective of the feminine subjects under study.

Ideological differences separated academic feminists, who were typically white, middle-class, college-educated women, from the Indian women they studied. While Indian cultures are incredibly diverse, many Native women did not define gender in terms of the powerful and the powerless. They were less likely to view gender as an exploitive social structure.[41] Many Indian women described men's and women's roles to be complementary, each valued and necessary to the survival of the community.[42] Native women recognized outlets for social authority within their communities, but outsiders consistently failed to acknowledge Indian women's social influence. The feminist agenda (defined by white, middle-class, college-educated women) did not resonate among many American Indian women, who tended to define oppression in terms of race. Amy Trice (a Kootenai leader in the 1970s) and Wilma Mankiller (a Cherokee leader in the 1980s and 1990s) were active leaders in their communities and beyond; they did not fit into a feminist narrative of women's universal oppression.

By the 1990s Rayna Green dedicated scholarly attention to exposing real Indian women, their social responsibilities, and their positions of authority within Indian communities. In 1992 Green wrote a book geared toward young adults entitled *Women in American Indian Society*, in which she again deconstructs the unrealistic imagery of Indian women.[43] She highlights the traditional and contemporary influence exerted by Indian women across Native American societies, but her complaint against Pocahontas does not waver. For Green, Pocahontas does not illustrate female power and authority in Powhatan culture; rather, Pocahontas has been an impediment to understanding real Indian women. Green does not consider Pocahontas as a living, breathing Indian woman who impacted the course of Powhatan history. Instead, she describes Pocahontas as a stereotyped Indian princess, designed as a "protector and hostess" for Europeans. She explains how other Indian women came to be defined as squaws; squaw was "the Algonquian word for a married or mature woman that later became a demeaning term for all Indian women, Algonquian or not."[44] She writes, "When Indian women appear in literature or in movies, their role is often demeaning and negative. They are neither accurately portrayed nor given adequate historical representation."[45]

In the late 1990s, Ramona Ford addressed another central problem women's historians faced when dealing with American Indian women. Her article "Native Women: Changing Statuses, Changing Interpretations" (1997) suggests that interpretations of Indian women have been hindered by a lack of familiarity with cultural variety among indigenous peoples.[46] Feminist scholars often talked of Indian women as a homogenous group whose experiences might be correlative to the experiences of non-Indian women. By providing examples of cultural difference, Ford makes the point that Indian concepts of gender are far more complex than white feminist scholars imagined. According to Ford, any analysis based on Euro-American observations in primary records is misguided from the onset. She challenges today's gender historians to provide specific Native American cultural context as the only means to provide an accurate and meaningful understanding of Native gender roles.

Pocahontas's life was shrouded in myths that were established and perpetuated by European male confusion and fantasy at the point of contact. Feminist analysis of Indian women was often misguided, based on those men's erroneous descriptions and a foreign doctrine of patriarchy. Sherrole Benton's 1995 article "Pocahontas as Traitor: For One Child, the Story of Pocahontas Inspired Pride and Anger" describes the effect of the Pocahontas story on a contemporary young Indian woman who struggled to understand Pocahontas.[47] Benton asks, Was Pocahontas a traitor who sold out her people and Native culture to live in the Anglo world, or was she a neglected and angry daughter with few choices? Benton does not answer the question, but her two alternatives are interesting. Either way, Benton's Pocahontas endured race and gender oppression. Benton uses the legend of Pocahontas (with no focus on the circumstances of her life) to address current social issues regarding cultural respect, race, and gender in the 1990s.

Anthropologist Helen Rountree restored focus on a male-centered rendition of Virginia history. She has spent a large part of her career researching the Algonquian Indians of the Tidewater region. She has presented her findings in a number of books, several of which will be considered here. Rountree is not Native American, a point she makes clear in the introduction of *Pocahontas, Powhatan, Opechanca-nough: Three Indian Lives Changed by Jamestown* (2005). Her knowledge of Algonquian peoples has been scientifically gathered through anthropological analysis. Her extensive work on Powhatan culture and society has added to our understanding Algonquian peoples.

Rountree focuses on the parts of Powhatan culture and society that can be explained and proven through tangible records; she rarely broaches the more nebulous aspects of the Native world such as spiritual or religious understanding. Her first work, *The Powhatan Indians of Virginia: Their Traditional Culture* (1989), describes a "prescientific people who looked to the supernatural as the cause of a very wide variety of phenomena and the means for controlling them."[48] She does not attempt to understand or explain the supernatural force. This book does, however, include a chapter entitled "Medicine and Religion," which lists rituals, ceremonies, temples, funeral customs, cures, and medicinal herbs that the English documented. Rountree's work does not address a Powhatan spiritual worldview, yet it provides an explanation of the social structures that organized the Powhatan world: family, politics, and the diplomatic organization of Tsenacommacah.

Rountree's second work, *Pocahontas's People: The Powhatan Indians of Virginia Through Four Centuries* (1990), is a chronology that begins in precontact Virginia, moves through the Powhatans' dealings with the outsiders, and ends with the Indians' tenacious survival. Although Pocahontas's name graces the title of this work, she is not the focus. *Pocahontas's People* describes the interaction between Indians and colonists as men's domain, carried on by Smith, Powhatan, Opechancanough (Powhatan's brother and the leader after Powhatan's death), and other weroances. Pocahontas, as a female child, was insignificant to the cross-cultural relationship. Rountree debunks America's national myth by comparing Smith's record to her anthropological evidence of Powhatan people and reveals how severely Smith misinterpreted his experiences. Rountree is skeptical of Pocahontas; the telling of her story relies on Smith's misunderstood observations. Rountree does not trust Smith's account and disregards Pocahontas as too obscured by mythical fantasy to be taken seriously.

Rountree's later work *Pocahontas, Powhatan, Opechancanough: Three Indians' Lives Changed by Jamestown* (2005) illustrates her estimation of Pocahontas. She writes, "It is highly unlikely that Pocahontas was even inside the building, either while Powhatan feasted John Smith or later when the two sat and tried to converse through the language barrier. What transpired after the meal between Pocahontas's father and the prisoner was no business of hers, nor could she have expected to be told any of it until later, when the meeting was over. So Pocahontas was probably nowhere near her father and his guest when the 'rescue' is supposed to have happened."[49] She further suggests, "The 'rescue' is part of a sequence of events that would be farcical if so many people did not take it seriously as 'Virginia history.'"[50] Rountree discounts Smith's testimony that there were young women present during the ceremony that decided his fate and his claim that Pocahontas saved him from death. She dismisses other scholars' explanations of the rescue as well: Tilton's suggestion that Powhatan may have been testing Smith's courage, or Hulme, Barbour, and

Allen's interpretation that it may have been some kind of adoption ritual. Rountree remains steadfast that these explanations do not correspond to the procedures of Woodland Indians, according to her expertise.[51]

Rountree tells readers that Pocahontas's heroine status was created well after her lifetime. According to Rountree, the colonists and the Powhatans cared little about her. In actuality Pocahontas's life was insignificant to the real-life drama swirling around her father and uncle; they were the ones who decided the Powhatan response to invaders, not an eleven-year-old girl. Rountree rejects Smith's rescue claim and is unconcerned with evidence of Pocahontas's intermediary work that was recorded by Smith, Strachey, Hamor, and Rolfe. She is also uninterested in Pocahontas's adult life, her marriage to Rolfe, and her trip to England. Rountree provides an impressive amount of anthropological information on how Powhatan Indians lived, yet she dismisses Pocahontas's role as a cultural intermediary, Powhatan gender ideology, and the Powhatan spiritual frame of reference.

For that type of investigation one can turn to Paula Gunn Allen's *Pocahontas: Medicine Woman, Spy, Entrepreneur, Diplomat* (2003). Allen was a Laguna Pueblo Indian scholar with a particular interest in Indian women's social responsibilities and influence. Her most famous work, *The Sacred Hoop: Recovering the Feminine in American Indian Traditions* (1986), offers a comparison of how Indian and non-Indian people define gender and gendered responsibilities. *The Sacred Hoop* acknowledges women's outlets for social authority across Indian cultures. Allen's work on Pocahontas recognizes Powhatan women's (including Pocahontas's) considerable social authority and responsibility.[52] She describes Pocahontas as a priestess, interpreter, diplomat, spy, wife, and agricultural expert and as a dignitary representing both the colonists and the Powhatans while in London. By contrast, Rountree describes Powhatan women (and particularly young Pocahontas) as inconsequential to international matters and tribal concerns. Unlike Rountree's insignificant and powerless Pocahontas, Allen's Pocahontas was relevant, skilled, and influential.

Allen tells her tale from a mystical worldview. She begins with the Powhatan creation story of Sky Woman's descent to Turtle Island

and the formation of their world.[53] She then describes Smith's rescue scene as the realization of a Powhatan religious prophecy that had been initiated by an astrological event, interpreted by Powhatan priests, and celebrated with a feast of Nikomis.[54] Allen accepts the Powhatan prophecy that foretold the third coming of outsiders and the ultimate rebirth of Tsenacommacah. Smith's rescue was part of the Nikomis celebration and signified that the Indians were prepared to enter their new existence. Allen suggests that the Powhatans interpreted Pocahontas as a Beloved Woman in the tradition of Sky Woman, and she would escort the changes coming to their world.[55] Pocahontas was identified as exceptional from an early age, chosen at the age of six or seven to begin training for the spiritual role of a Beloved Woman.[56] She had a unique gift enabling her to listen on a level that others were incapable of. This was the Pocahontas that Disney depicted in the 1995, in which she was seen listening to the wind and communicating with Grandmother Willow. Allen's Pocahontas had extraordinary insight into the forces of nature, the mystical world, and human interaction. She could access and process information from multiple worlds. This gave Pocahontas a broad understanding. She, as well as the Powhatan people, respected the spiritual guidance that her honed talents offered. Even though Pocahontas was merely eleven when she saved Smith, her people acknowledged her as a trained Beloved Woman who was capable of this important assessment and the decision to adopt Smith as part of Tsenacommacah.[57]

Allen enters the Powhatan mystical world to explain, not prove, the qualifications that led Chief Powhatan and Pocahontas to become leaders during this time of great transition. Both rose to positions of authority because of their unusual attributes, gifts from their creator. Both were believed to have possessed the power of the *Powa*, a paranormal ability to connect to the spiritual world and compel others.[58] Chief Powhatan and Pocahontas were trained in the "Dream Vision discipline"; they were recognized as experts in deciphering the correct course to take.[59] Proving the validity of Powhatan beliefs is unimportant to Allen. Like all spiritual beliefs they were true because people believed them to be. Allen tells her story of Pocahontas with a commitment to penetrating and respecting a Powhatan worldview,

with a particular sensitivity to the mystical world and a determination to reveal female authority. She utilizes extensive anthropological and ethnographical research on Powhatan people.[60] However,
because Allen addresses the more nebulous aspects of the Powhatan
spiritual world on which tangible evidence is lacking, academics
have been quick to marginalize her work. As a Native scholar, she
was perhaps more accepting of undocumented evidence of the
spiritual world.

Allen's particular contribution is her gender analysis (in both
The Sacred Hoop and *Pocahontas*), in which she demonstrates the
inaccuracies of Anglocentric explanations of the feminine in Indian
societies. Her work suggests that Native women had powerful roles
of consequence and that they exerted social authority, regardless of
Europeans' unwillingness to understand or document it. We know
from the journals and letters of European adventurers (throughout
the Americas) that Indian women were regularly involved in cross-
cultural interaction, yet their participation was mentioned only briefly
and was often downplayed in favor of celebrating white male heroics.
Allen considers Indian women's actions within their specific cultural and spiritual frame of reference. Her book puts Pocahontas at
the center of the cultural collision to consider an Indian woman's
perspective and how she would have participated at the moment of
contact. This shift in perspective provides Indian context and makes
Pocahontas's actions more logical.

Camilla Townsend, author of *Pocahontas and the Powhatan Dilemma*
(2004), is skeptical of Pocahontas's relevance.[61] Like Rountree, she
denies that Pocahontas saved John Smith. Townsend dismisses primary records left by Smith, Strachey, Rolfe, and Hamor; she considers them unreliable and unusable. She prefers to "piece together"
evidence from contemporary academic scholarship.[62] Unlike Rountree's work, Pocahontas is the focus of Townsend's study. Townsend
describes a powerless young girl who was treacherously taken captive
by white male conquerors. She had few choices as an indigenous
female caught in a masculine whirlwind. In Townsend's words, "My
book represents the first effort to piece together every shred of what
we know with surety, listening carefully for hints of what the Powhatans and Pocahontas seemed to be saying about themselves, proceeding

cautiously, taking nothing that tends to be repeated for granted."[63]
The preference for evidence gained through modern scholarly analysis often tends to disqualify eyewitness accounts because of their
cultural bias (particularly primary evidence that doesn't fit contemporary arguments). There has also been a scholarly tendency to
downplay or ignore Indian explanations due to a lack of tangible
evidence. But Indian perspective (past and present) is critical; it gives
Indian cultural context to early European observations.

All history is influenced by cultural and contemporary biases.
Today's historians must examine early European observations of
Indian lifeways with caution, but it is imprudent to throw them out
as unusable. These sources need to be considered within the circumstances of their time and place. Indian worldviews must also be
included in the history of initial contact; ethnology and oral tradition
provide valuable evidence. Early European observations become
applicable to Native experience only when Native cultural information is integrated. Allen's attempt to depict Pocahontas as a significant and powerful Indian woman within an indigenous society
that recognized female authority is characterized by Townsend as
a fascinating and charming alternative to real history.[64] Conflicting
portrayals of Pocahontas, including those offered by Rountree, Allen,
and Townsend, tell us as much about the currents of historical debates
over gender, ethnicity, and Native American voice as they do about
Pocahontas's life in the 1600s.

Pocahontas Redesigned for a Contemporary Mass Audience

In 1995 Disney redesigned the Pocahontas narrative for a modem
mass audience. Disney executives hoped that *Pocahontas* would bring
huge profits, similar to *Aladdin* (1992) and *The Lion King* (1994). But
they also had a second goal in mind. They wanted to address rising
criticism of Disney's racial stereotyping. Because of this, the studio
had to be sensitive in their portrayal of Native Americans. Film-
makers traveled to Tidewater Virginia to hire Indian consultants and
performers in order to ensure Indian voice and cultural sensitivity.

However, Indian consultants and actors claimed they were alienated from the project after they objected to the Disney portrayal. They accused the studio of paying them off and insisted that the studio had no interest in giving an accurate version of Powhatan history.[65]

Disney certainly exploited aspects of the Pocahontas legend that would resonate with viewers and meet the audience's expectations of a Disney product. According to codirector Mike Gabriel, Disney intended to update the story by focusing on the theme of "two separate clashing worlds trying to understand each other."[66] The story also provided a coming-of-age story of a spunky female heroine. Scriptwriters chose certain episodes from Pocahontas's life and invented others to construct a narrative that highlighted contemporary values: an appreciation for nature, the significance of spiritualism, and the coexistence of diverse races.

Like earlier mythmakers, Disney had to negotiate some difficult realities to make its story work. The most important change was that Pocahontas had to be matured to an appropriate age. In addition, to exonerate Indians and Americans of any blame for frontier violence, greedy British colonists are the villains. Kocoum is not Pocahontas's Indian husband, but her fiancé who is killed by an Englishman. This fictitious event provokes the hostility that leads to Smith's capture and the famous rescue scene. It also makes Pocahontas available to find love among the white men. The film ends with Pocahontas's choice to remain with her people and follow her path as a peacemaker. The film suppresses the more unsettling realities: her tender age of eleven at first contact, her captivity, her conversion to Christianity, her marriages to Kocoum and Rolfe, and her untimely death in England.

The Powhatan Renape Nation was irritated by Disney's portrayal of Pocahontas and Powhatan people. In his response to the film, Chief Roy Crazy Horse points out the departures from reality and complains, "Of all of Powhatan's children, only Pocahontas is known, primarily because she became the hero of Euro-Americans as a 'good Indian,' one who saved the life of a white man. Not only is the 'good Indian/bad Indian theme' inevitably given new life by Disney, but history, as recorded by the English themselves, is badly falsified in the name of entertainment."[67] Representatives of the Walt Disney

Company insist that they never intended to produce a documentary, but to use the legend as a jumping-off point.[68] The film company
may have failed in its effort to present a satisfying multicultural perspective, yet they were incredibly successful in their primary goal.
Pocahontas generated more than one billion dollars in the first year.[69]

The historical narrative *Love and Hate in Jamestown: John Smith,
Pocahontas, and the Heart of a New Nation* (2003) by David Price comes
closer to portraying a multicultural perspective. It is a well-researched
popular history that the *New York Times* chose as a notable book of
2003. It is also a book that offers a healthy dose of American patriotism, in which Smith and Pocahontas are presented as America's
first national heroes. Price describes the English settlers as greedy,
incompetent, and completely ill-prepared to meet the challenges they
faced in Virginia. He focuses on the 105 British adventure capitalists
who go looking for gold and a trade route to the Orient, yet find
disappointment, desperation, starvation, disease, and hostile Natives.
These upper-crust English settlers are depicted as buffoons, except
for the extraordinary commoner John Smith. He manages to fight
his countrymen and the Indians while he single-handedly saves the
British settlement. His complete disdain for class distinction and
hierarchy infuriates his English superiors. He is, after all, a lowly sort.
Unlike his wealthy companions, Smith is undaunted by challenge and
hard work. Smith is also unique because he has traversed Eurasia
prior to the Virginia expedition; he is enlightened and experienced
in dealing with diverse cultures. Price highlights Smith's ability to
deal with the Indians as people according to their individual character. Sometimes that requires kindness and accommodation, other times
it requires a strong arm. Price develops Smith as the perfect American
hero. He is different and better than the greedy and incompetent Englishmen who are afraid of manual work and afraid of the Indians.

Price seems to have taken a clue from Smith in his interpretation
of Indians. Price presents a contemplative and powerful Powhatan
and a generous and merciful Pocahontas who saves Smith's life twice.
Her actions seem to puzzle Price. He explains her deeds by suggesting that she holds a unique fascination with Smith and the Englishmen. He writes, "In electing to stay with the English, she had several
evident motives. One was her longtime affinity for the English, going

back to December 1607 when she first laid eyes on John Smith and her subsequent girlhood visits to converse with Smith and to play with the boys of the fort. Another was her attraction to Christianity, which had struck a resonant chord in her; she proved an eager student of the English faith."[70] Price describes a great love that overtakes Rolfe, whom he describes as a "handsome," "gentle[,] and devout" family man whose wife and child tragically died en route to Virginia. Rolfe is drawn to Pocahontas who possesses "exceptional vitality, intelligence, and good looks," with "light brown skin, her dark eyes, and long hair running down her back."[71] Price's Pocahontas is an Indian princess with modern sensibilities. While Pocahontas is celebrated for her nonconformist attitude toward the English, the author presents other Indians as justified in their hostile response to the lazy and demanding Englishmen.

Love and Hate in Jamestown is a tale of survival in which the weak (the wealthy Englishmen) perish. The colony's hardships do not relent until England begins sending settlers (hardworking families and future Americans) to populate Jamestown instead of slothful elites. Price offers an updated, patriotic narrative of national origin. Americans have evolved from a dysfunctional elitist and hierarchical society that could not survive in the New World; only those who are brave enough and who work hard enough (Indians and English commoners) are able to forge a new nation together.

Terrence Malick attempts to capture the emotional drama of the cultural collision in Virginia for a mass audience with his film *The New World* (2006). Yet it proved too slow-paced to hold viewers' interest and drew scant critical or popular attention. There is little dialogue, and the story is told by a whispering narrator to give the illusion of inner thoughts. It is a visually stunning film that takes place in a primeval Eden, but it is unconcerned with pesky realities. Once again, Pocahontas has to be aged up for her encounter with the handsome newcomer. Smith is a tender seducer who is moved by Pocahontas's exotic beauty. She is presented as an earth goddess and forest naïf. Smith juggles his fondness for Pocahontas with his job in Virginia and painfully warns her not to trust him. Pocahontas is cast as a trusting, playful, proud, and soulful young woman involved a complicated romance. The lovers are caught between their obligation to their communities and their feelings for each other.

Malick portrays the Powhatans as dignified and ferocious warriors who are justified in a violent defense of their way of life. Chief Powhatan is thoughtful and cautious when he releases Smith from the grips of death. The chief spares Smith so that he and Pocahontas can learn each other's language, and so that she can discover the invaders' intentions. The English, except for Smith, are characterized as gluttonous, petty, and backstabbing colonists. They are the real villains of the story. Smith, Pocahontas, and the Powhatan Indians are the admirable heroes of Malick's mythic tale.

Price and Malick both worked on their nationalist projects in an atmosphere of intense patriotism after the United States suffered the terrorist attacks of September 11, 2001. These two works celebrate a unique and superior American character. They remind readers that Americans have faced adversity and hardship in the past; proud Indians and Europeans came together and overcame their differences to create a better world. This uplifting message resonated with anxious audiences at the dawn of the twenty-first century.

The legend of Pocahontas, like the legend of Malinche, has undergone continuous revision to address contemporary debates. In this process Pocahontas has often been reduced to a symbolic caricature. Cultural and generational biases have sculpted her legend, and the problem has been made worse by limited Native cultural information. The legends of Malinche and Pocahontas have each been shaped by generational national moods, yet there are glaring differences between the two. Although Pocahontas's image remains virtuous, Malinche's does not. Europeans portrayed both Malinche and Pocahontas as having been betrayed by their own people. Malinche was sold to Mayan merchants, who traded her to a Tabascan cacique, who ultimately turned her over to Cortés, and Pocahontas was led into English custody by the weroance of her husband's village. Both women were intimately connected to European invaders, yet Cortés characterized Malinche as a slave whereas the English never presented their Indian savior as a slave. More importantly, Pocahontas was married to the father of her mixed-race son. Malinche, however, can be portrayed as a fallen woman; she had a child by Cortés out of wedlock, and the Black Legend insinuated that she had been raped. Pocahontas's perceived dignity and virtue remain intact. The age difference between Smith and Pocahontas works to the benefit of her legend because Smith, and most of the mythmakers who followed, kept their relationship platonic. The type of conquest in Virginia also influenced Pocahontas's more positive image. It was not an immediate full-scale war for dominance led by conquistadors, but rather a slow set of manipulative maneuvers carried out by both sides. Pocahontas did not stain her image with the blood of Indian people as Malinche had. These factors protected Pocahontas's admirable feminine characterization.

CHAPTER SEVEN

SACAGAWEA

Legends benefit from controversy; discrepancies beg further explanation and keep interest alive. As with the legend of Malinche, persistent historical disputes have antagonized Sacagawea's legend. Compared to the emotionally charged issues that haunted the Mexican woman, questions regarding Sacagawea seem mundane in comparison. Commentators in Mexico have argued about whether or not Malinche was a whore/traitor who was seduced by conquistadors and turned on the Indian people. There is no evidence to suggest that Sacagawea slept with the Euro-American invaders, nor were the invaders a conquering force. Therefore, she was not accused of having slept with the enemy. Unlike Malinche, Sacagawea was a married mother with a child. Although her feminine maternal qualities were emphasized, her sexuality was not a focal point in the creation of her legend.

Sacagawea was not portrayed as a traitor during the early stages of American nationalism. Nationalist mythmakers in the United States did not characterize their forefathers as brutal foreign conquerors (as Mexicans had portrayed the Spanish). Rather, American filibusters were mythologized as bold men who had a divine destiny to civilize the land. Sacagawea had not participated in a violent conquest as Malinche had, nor was she part of a dominant force that was eventually expelled. The United States never relinquished its claim to the North American West as Spain had been forced to abandon Mexico. It is significant to Sacagawea's legend that the Lewis and Clark exploratory expedition was not a fighting force intent on military victory (that would come later). Sacagawea's legend was less susceptible to an indictment of being a whore/traitor, yet other less salacious questions arose.

The controversies that occupied historians in Sacagawea's case were the spelling and pronunciation of her name, as well as the time and location of her death. Sacagawea was known by many aliases. In addition to generic epithets such as squaw, wife of Charbonneau, and Indian woman, she was known among the Hidatsas as Sakaka-wea, meaning "Bird Woman," and the Shoshones called her Sacaja-wea, meaning "Boat Launcher."[1] Some Indians (and historians) believed her to be Wadze-wipe ("Lost Woman") among the Comanches, and Porivo among reservation Shoshones. Native American naming practices have made it difficult to track Indian women through time and space. It is likely that Sacagawea's name changed every time she entered a new cultural environment. Yet writers have spent a great deal of energy debating how to address this Indian woman.

The confusion surrounding Sacagawea's death motivated researchers who wanted to solve the mystery of where and when she died. There is written evidence that she died in 1812 at Fort Manuel in South Dakota. The woman who died there was not identified by name, but as the wife of Charbonneau who accompanied Lewis and Clark. This lack of precision in the primary record leaves enough doubt to conclude that the woman who died in 1812 was not Saca-gawea. In the 1920s historian Grace Hebard and Charles Eastman, an investigator working for the Office of Indian Affairs, presented an alternative theory of Sacagawea's death. They suggest that the author of the 1812 record was confused by Charbonneau's habit of taking multiple Indians wives. According to Hebard and Eastman, the woman who died near Fort Manuel was another of Charbonneau's wives. They claim that Sacagawea died an old woman in 1884 on the Wind River Reservation in Wyoming, where she was known as Porivo. This woman spoke French, mothered mixed-race sons, advocated the white man's way, had a presidential medal among her effects, and mentioned to reservation officials that she had seen "the great water" in the company of Americans. However, Porivo never spoke of the Lewis and Clark expedition to anyone at Wind River. After she died, Hebard and Eastman reconstructed her life and came to believe that she was Sacagawea. Porivo's personal characteristics provided the only evidence. Certainty remains elusive.

Opinions regarding Sacagawea's name and her place of death are essentially a dispute over historical ownership.[2] American nationalists call her Sacagawea, the Lemhi Shoshones claim her as Sacajawea, reservation Shoshones recall her as Porivo, the Hidatsas remember her as Sakakawea, and the Comanches suggest that she was Wadzewipe (a lost woman they adopted). Four Indian groups claim Sacagawea as part of their unique history. Idaho, Montana, South Dakota, and Wyoming celebrate her as a marketable aspect of their state heritage. Claiming Sacagawea, in whatever form, gives each group distinction. As we will see shortly, each perspective tells a different tale.

Although the questions regarding her name and her death are debated, other writers suggest that the heroine has been overrated. The original expedition journals, which together contain more than a million words, rarely mention Sacagawea. The captains clearly kept her in the background. Participants in the masculine mission consistently categorized her as "other"; she was Indian, she was young, and she was a female. Lewis and Clark recorded Sacagawea's usefulness, yet they interpreted her as part of the untamed world that would ultimately be replaced by civilization. Regardless of her efforts to advance American entrance into the West, expedition journals reveal that the men of the corps considered her a "savage," not necessarily a potential member of their civilized society. Over the course of the journey Lewis and Clark came to appreciate her work ethic, her knowledge, her generosity, and her calm demeanor. They did not interpret these characteristics as indicative of Indian women in general, but as attributes unique to Sacagawea. It is interesting that the only Indian woman Lewis and Clark knew intimately, they admired. Other Indian women are consistently described as unfortunate wretches who were degraded by barbaric societies. Lewis and Clark did not expect to appreciate a young Indian woman.

Throughout most of the nineteenth century Sacagawea was not portrayed as a hero of the expedition. That role was reserved for the Euro-American men who charted unknown territory (at least, territory that was unknown to them). Sacagawea, however, did have a pivotal role. Like Malinche and Pocahontas, she, too, became a symbol for Indian acceptance. She is portrayed as an open and accepting indigenous female. She was the feminine noble savage who understood and appreciated the superiority of the coming order. The men of the expedition describe her as knowledgeable, reliable, and compassionate. They were impressed by her resourcefulness and her approach to humanity. Other Native women mentioned in the journals are described as miserably exploited, overworked, unattractive, and lacking in dignity and virtue.[3] Lewis criticizes Indian men for exploiting women's labor and sexuality.[4] Sacagawea, on the other hand, is described as the wife of a Frenchman and a young mother; she was helpful to the foreigners but never overworked. She was separated from other Indian women and imagined as an admirable and sympathetic Native woman, an appropriate feminine complement to the masculine heroics of the expedition.

Both captains acknowledge her consistent efforts to obtain food, as well as her expertise on topography, routes, and abandoned Indian camps. When the corps finally encountered the elusive Shoshone people, Sacagawea proved a valuable intermediary and translator.[5] She negotiated with them and ensured the delivery of Shoshone horses to the expedition. The captains' recognition of Sacagawea's skills and service to their cause laid the foundation for later American writers to celebrate their own gracious Indian princess. The distinction between Sacagawea (the nurturing married mother) and other unfortunate Indian women (degraded and overworked) provides a historical foundation that has fueled her legend.

The realities of Sacagawea's indigenous life were obscured by the culturally biased descriptions of Euro-American explorers and were later ignored by nationalist literature devoted to maintaining the myth of Manifest Destiny. Nineteenth-century nationalism conditioned citizens to accept westward expansion as part of the nation's divine mission to extend its democratic system over the continent. The goal was not to extend freedom and democracy to the Natives who already occupied the landscape, but to extend the boundary for U.S. citizens. In the days of Lewis and Clark, and throughout most of the 1800s, the majority of Euro-Americans did not imagine Indian people as potential American citizens.[6] Rather, Indians were obstacles in a land of untapped potential. In 1804 Indian men were simplistically portrayed as either good or bad: they were potential allies and trading partners, or they were hostile and dangerous. Most Indian women were seen as squaws degraded by savage societies. A select few were imagined as Indian princesses in the mold of Pocahontas. The few journal entries regarding Sacagawea assure secondary writers that she fit into the more elite category of Indian women.

Early sculptors of the Sacagawea legend used the journal entries to define her as an exceptional Indian woman who was worthy of attention because of her devotion to America's western heroes. In this first phase of legend building during the late nineteenth century, Sacagawea emerged as the symbolic feminine character in America's epic frontier story. She epitomized the best of her gender and race; she nurtured American expansion and American heroes as they conquered the wilderness. Early secondary works, like Elliott Coues's four-volume publication of expedition journals (1892), rationalize her choice to aid Lewis and Clark by suggesting that she sought to attach herself to the superior culture. Coues, and those who followed his example, describes how Sacagawea was drawn to the American heroes and believed in their alternative way of life. The journals condemn the treatment of Indian women in Native societies, and this helps explain Sacagawea's willingness to aid America's civilizing mission.

Sacagawea's story evolved over the course of the twentieth century as contemporary social questions forced a reexamination of America's frontier narrative. By the turn of the twentieth century American attitudes toward Indian people had changed. Indians were no longer obstacles to expansion, but they had not yet assimilated into American society, nor had they vanished. Helen Hunt Jackson's influential book *A Century of Dishonor* (1881) forced Americans to consider how Indians had been treated during America's triumphant march across the continent. As the century turned, government officials, the United States Army, and eastern reformers pondered the Indian question: how to incorporate Indian people into the national culture and relieve the administrative burden of the reservation system. Indian policy was a disturbing failure; reservations were physically, spiritually, and culturally unhealthy places. The Dawes Act (1887) also failed; it had not created independent family farmers, but further shrunk

Indian claims to western land. Captain Richard Henry Pratt's strategy to save Indian children through an American education was
another a devastating disappointment. Carlisle Indian Industrial
School closed in 1918 after thirty-nine years of the grand experiment
to "kill the Indian to save the man." Many other Indian boarding
schools (there were twenty-six that used Carlisle as a model) also
closed during the early decades of the new century. As the twentieth
century opened, Indian policy was a glaring national problem.

Social reformer John Collier formed the American Indian Defense
Association in the 1920s. Collier, who later became commissioner
of Indian affairs (1933–1945), pushed Indian policy in a new direction, seeking civil rights for Indian people, promoting Indian self-
government on reservations, and demanding the recognition and
encouragement of Indian traditions and cultures. Reform-minded
Americans, like Helen Hunt Jackson and Collier, suggested that Indians
had been misunderstood, misrepresented, and ultimately trampled
by the country's enthusiastic expansion across the continent. The 1890
census report declared the frontier closed. There was no longer a
clear line separating civilization and wilderness; the continent had
been won. The characterization of savage Indians dissipated along
with the frontier. Indians had been segregated on reservations as
wards of the state, living under disastrous assimilationist polices,
although many defiantly clung to elements of their traditional cultures.
Indians were left behind as the American future looked increasingly industrial, urban, and complex.

The industrial age brought nostalgia for America's perceived loss
of a simpler life—a time when the environment was clean, before
money and greed corrupted men and depleted a pristine landscape.
Collier began idealizing Native cultures as an alternative to the fast-
paced and filthy urban environment of the industrial age. The Sacagawea legend benefited from the more sympathetic appreciation
for Indian cultures, particularly as the expedition's centennial celebrations got underway. Her legend also benefitted from changing
attitudes toward the role of women in American society as the new
century opened.

In the decades after the Civil War, Americans were forced into a
national discourse on race and gender equality. Americans painfully

decided that the national government was responsible for ensuring a modicum of racial equality and unfettered political participation. Women were a significant force in the abolitionist movement and the debates on race and suffrage that followed the war. By the late 1800s there existed an influential population of college-educated white women (like Jackson) who were devoted to social issues. They moved into reform, establishing mutual aid societies and settlement houses, developing progressive solutions to social problems, and making demands on public officials. During the Progressive Era (1880s–1920s) female activists celebrated women's capacity for public service and demanded a voice in the political process.

As upper-middle-class white women expanded their public roles, Sacagawea's story took on a new relevance. She was reimagined to illustrate female commitment and service to the nation. Mythic Sacagawea was applicable to feminist demands, including their demand for national female suffrage. Eva Emery Dye and Grace Raymond Hebard, two women who began their professional careers during the Progressive Era, transformed Sacagawea into a grand American heroine. Their interpretation of Sacagawea offered a feminine prototype for twentieth-century American women to follow. Dye's 1902 book, *The Conquest*, and Hebard's 1907 article, "Pilot of First White Men to Cross the American Continent," introduced a feminine perspective to the nation's past. They tell the story of American expansion through the eyes of a woman. Hebard expands the breadth of the narrative further by looking to Native sources, which were irrelevant to earlier writers. Dye and Hebard highlight Sacagawea's feminine involvement in the development of the United States, although they do not deviate from the main theme of America's triumphant march toward national greatness. They do not concern themselves with the legacies of America's triumph in the West, nor with contemporary Indian conditions on the reservation. Dye and Hebard's mythic Sacagawea remains estranged from her Native culture.

Despite the Civil War, constitutional amendments, and generations of contentious debate, true freedom and equality remained elusive in twentieth-century America. Increasingly, scholars and commentators recognized that various groups experienced events of the past differently. By the second half of the century scholarly analysis began to focus on the experiences of subaltern groups, including women and Native people. Lingering race and gender inequality culminated in a second push for civil rights from the 1950s through the 1970s and a second feminist movement during the 1970s and 1980s. Historians and social critics began raising new questions and reexamining history to find the answers.

Late-twentieth-century scholars debunked the masculine, Anglocentric, celebrationist tone that dominated history of the American West. Patricia Limerick's book *The Legacy of Conquest* (1987) represents this more skeptical analysis. She writes in her introduction, "Historians will see the 1980s as a watershed decade. In countless ways, events in the 1980s suggest a need to reevaluate Western history."[7] Limerick's work (along with others) dismantled American frontier mythology. *The Legacy of Conquest* argues that America's westward expansion was not an inevitable victory that extended democracy over a vacant land. Her history focuses on the consequences of America's westward expansion, particularly for those who stood in America's path. Limerick's study makes no specific reference to Sacagawea, yet her spirit of critical inquiry has influenced Sacagawea's myth.

The legend of Sacagawea (like the legends of Malinche and Pocahontas) has ample ambiguity and flexibility, allowing commentators to grapple with difficult social issues. Over time Sacagawea's story has been used as a forum for discussion of Manifest Destiny, suffrage for women, taboos against miscegenation, racial justice, modern feminism, and the inclusion of Indian voices in the telling of western history. The remainder of this chapter will explore how generations of writers have reinvented the legend of Sacagawea to accommodate contemporary social questions.

Early Nationalist Era

The Lewis and Clark journals offer significant evidence of Sacagawea's skills and cooperation, although they do not describe her as indispensable to the success of their mission. One can only imagine the predicament of the expedition had Sacagawea not provided nourishment, guidance through the mountainous terrain, or inter-mediary services among the Shoshones who ultimately supplied horses for the corps. Journal descriptions of Sacagawea offer clues to Euro-American expectations in the West. The men of the expedition viewed their work in conjunction with the nation's mission to civilize the continent. They consistently characterize Indians according to estab-lished stereotypes found in colonial captivity narratives. These early accounts tantalized readers and eventually merged into an American literary genre that solidified ethnocentric explanations of frontier encounters and defined Indians as savages.[8] This stylized interpre-tation of Indian people was productive in the colonial era, and con-tinued to be useful during the era of expansion. Captivity narratives projected Indian savagery as an obstruction to national greatness and legitimized Indian removal and elimination.

In addition to captivity narratives, nineteenth-century preachers popularized the image of Indian savagery in religious sermons designed to encourage missionary work in the West. Captivity narra-tives, missionary literature, colonial histories, and Indian pictorials painted by George Catlin (1796–1872) disseminated skewed inter-pretations of Indian people and established a national consensus on Indian savagery. The journals of Lewis and Clark reinforced the prevailing rhetoric on Indians and seemingly offered historical evi-dence to support it. Their characterization of Sacagawea must be viewed within the context of their American cultural perspective.

In 1814 Nicholas Biddle and Paul Allen edited and published the journals of Lewis and Clark in one abridged narrative with a very long title: *History of the Expedition under the Command of Captains Lewis and Clark to the Sources of the Missouri, thence across the Rocky Mountains and down the Columbia River to the Pacific Ocean. Performed during the Years 1804–5–6. By Order of the Government of the United States.* The two-volume work came to be known as the "Biddle edi-tion." It maintained the attitudes of the original journals and reflected the cultural milieu that celebrated American expansion, including categorizing Indians as savages, but it reached only a moderate reader-ship. This edition does not characterize Sacagawea as a heroine, although it does note much of the work she contributed. Biddle con-sulted with Clark, who filled in gaps with the benefit of hindsight.

It was at this point that Clark went back and finally named his female helper. He attempted to spell Sacagawea phonetically to the best of his ability, offering several different spellings.

Sacagawea's story lay dormant, buried in the original journals that Biddle stored in the archives of the American Philosophical Society of Philadelphia. She was resurrected in 1892 by Elliott Coues. He published a four-volume work that condensed various expedition journals (Lewis, Clark, Ordway, and Gass) into a single, coherent narrative.[9] Coues uses footnotes to elaborate on the entries regarding Sacagawea. In a character comparison of Charbonneau and Sacagawea he writes in a footnote that Charbonneau was "a poor specimen, consisting, chiefly, of a tongue to wag in a mouth to fill. . . . He would have been a minus function still in comparison with his wife Sacajawea, the wonderful 'Bird-woman,' who contributed a full man's share to the success of the Expedition, besides taking care of the her baby."[10] He elaborates on Sacagawea in several other footnotes. Referring to Clark's July 14 entry regarding Sacagawea's recommendation of the Bozeman Pass, Coues adds, "He very sensibly followed the advice of that remarkable little woman, who never failed to rise to the occasion, even when it was mountains high."[11] Coues's side comments elevate Sacagawea to legendary status and present her as an appropriate female to adorn America's story of Manifest Destiny. She was the nurturing Indian mother who recognized the benefits of a superior civilization and was compelled to plant that civilization in her Native wilderness.

By the 1890s, when Coues was writing, the savage imagery had begun to dissipate, along with the threat of Indian resistance. Sacagawea was purified, no longer considered a member of a savage race (as she had been in the original journals). At the opening of the twentieth century Sacagawea emerged as a strong, competent woman who actively participated in America's future. Coues was likely influenced by the expanding social role of American women during the Progressive Era. Yet Coues's Sacagawea still illustrated Indian acceptance of American democracy. She symbolically adopted America's Manifest Destiny and legitimized American roots in the western landscape.

Eva Emery Dye consulted the original journals and the Coues edition to compile *The Conquest: The True Story of Lewis and Clark* in 1903. Dye bases her work on historical evidence but it is a novel that

invents characters, dialogue, and inner thoughts. She, too, celebrates the rightfulness of Manifest Destiny and Sacagawea's role in
it. Her description of Sacagawea fulfills the familiar image of the
Indian princess. Dye sets Sacagawea apart from other Native women
by adopting the distinctions made by Lewis and Clark. Dye makes
Sacagawea an exception to her race and gender by describing her
as the "the handsome young Sacajawea," which contrasts with the
description of a "leathery old dame of the Minnetarees."[12] Dye's
Sacagawea is special, beautiful, wise, and drawn to white men who
recognize her feminine attributes.

Dye establishes the superiority of Euro-Americans in a fictional
conversation between Sacagawea and one of her childhood friends
during the emotional reunion with her people. The friend is described
as happy for Sacagawea and the life that has befallen her: "the
wonderful fortune that had come to Sacajawea, the wife of a white
man."[13] At the point in the narrative where it is discovered that
Chief Cameahwait is Sacagawea's brother, Dye affixes her with the
Indian princess image by proclaiming, "Sacajawea, too, a princess,
come home now to her mountain kingdom."[14] Like Spanish and
English writers who over-emphasized the indigenous royalty of
Malinche and Pocahontas, Dye capitalizes on the opportunity to
assure American readers that their ancestors were also adopted and
protected by an Indian princess.

Dye's historical novel legitimizes Sacagawea as a worthy American heroine. Her treatment of Charbonneau is similar to Coues's.
She describes him as a despicable "squaw-man" who is inept and
cowardly in his duties. According to Dye, Charbonneau chose to
accept a savage culture and is therefore cast aside as retrograde.
Sacagawea, on the other hand, is elevated by her association with
white men. She was married to the Frenchman, yet she was drawn
to the Euro-American heroes and their civilized culture. Whereas
Charbonneau was uncouth and violent toward Sacagawea, Lewis and
Clark were kind toward her. From Dye's perspective, Sacagawea
benefitted from her relationship with Lewis and Clark, and they benefitted from their relationship with the beautiful Indian princess.

Sacagawea helped Lewis and Clark traverse the landscape, plant-
ing the seeds of interaction so the Native world could benefit from
an American future. Dye showcases Sacagawea as a guide and as a

leader of men. The author gives the Indian woman an indispensable role in American expansion to demonstrate the potential of American women. Although Dye's Sacagawea worked in a man's world, she never lost her "true womanhood," and the author takes every opportunity to ensure readers that Sacagawea was a doting mother. Dye's message was important to early-twentieth-century readers who were concerned about the increasing number of women who were working outside the home and demanding more participation in the public arena. Dye stresses notions of domesticity and women's moral superiority in her description of Sacagawea: "The firelight flickered on Sacagawea's hair, as she sat making moccasins, crooning a song . . . with baby Touissant toddling around her. . . . The modest Shoshone princess never dreamed how the presence of her child and herself gave a touch of domesticity to that Oregon winter."[15] Her role as a pathbreaker through the wilderness did not come at the expense of her womanhood.

A Boost to the Suffrage Movement in the Twentieth Century

Dye affixed Sacagawea with the mythic image of an Indian princess, reinforced the concept of Manifest Destiny, and even helped promote women's suffrage by portraying Sacagawea as an example for all American women. Sacagawea's life provided a template for contemporary women who were also venturing into the unknown. Dye's Sacagawea overcame the restraints of her Native culture, created her own destiny, and helped lay the foundation for a better future. Women suffragists in the West quickly adopted Dye's version of Sacagawea.

In 1905 the Women's Club of Portland organized the Sacagawea Statue Association. Their goal was to commission a Sacagawea statue to commemorate the centennial anniversary of the expedition and showcase women's potential. The bronze statue, designed and executed by Alice Cooper, was funded by contributions from Federated Women's Clubs across the country. When Dye spoke at the dedication of the statue, she referred to Sacagawea as a "forerunner of civilization, great leader of men."[16] The Federated Women's Club of Eastern North Dakota began a statewide campaign to erect its own statue to honor Sacagawea. This bronze work, completed by Leonard Crunelle in 1910, enshrines a beautiful and noble Sacagawea carrying baby Baptiste on her back. The North Dakota women's group created and circulated a promotional brochure that celebrated Sacagawea's contribution to America and exhibited an extraordinary degree of literary license. These feminist efforts to sanctify Sacagawea were a Euro-American crusade to honor the woman, not the Indian. North Dakota's Indians, by then segregated on reservations, were irrelevant to Sacagawea's celebrity. Indian people—their conditions on the reservation, their citizenship, and their suffrage rights—were of no concern to the white feminist movement of the early 1900s.

Grace Hebard (1861–1936), the next major contributor in the procession of Sacagawea boosters, was a professor of political economy, a librarian at the University of Wyoming, and an active participant in the women's suffrage movement.[17] She was not a trained historian, yet she wrote several historical texts on the West. Her books displayed a glorification of the western pioneer and a desire to correct the omission of women in western history.[18] Her 1933 book was considered the most extensive work on Sacagawea and became the foremost popular authority. It was the most widely accessible work on the topic, available in libraries around the world. Hebard built on the image of Sacagawea provided by Coues and Dye, and broadened the scope of interest to include Sacagawea's life after the expedition. Hebard was unique in her inclusion of Native sources. She sought input from Shoshone and Comanche Indians, including testimonies from reservation Indians whom she believed were descendants of Sacagawea.

Hebard's research on Sacagawea first gained attention in 1907 after she published an article in the *Journal of American History* entitled "Pilot of the First White Men to Cross the American Continent: Identification of the Indian Girl Who Led the Lewis and Clark Expedition over the Rocky Mountains in their Unparalleled Journey into the Mysteries of the Western World in Recognition of Sacajawea as the Woman Who Guided the Explorers in the New Golden Empire." Hebard presents Sacagawea as the guide of the expedition and an

Alice Cooper, *Sacajawea and Jean Baptiste*, statue, 1905.

Leonard Crunelle, *Sacajawea*, statue, 1910. Photo by Hans Andersen.

indispensable member of the group. Hebard also suggests that Saca-gawea lived a long life after her journey with Lewis and Clark and that her tracks were obscured by Charbonneau's habit of taking multiple Indian wives. Her thesis is contrary to the prevailing interpretation of the time, that Sacagawea died shortly after the expedition. As mentioned above, her death was recorded in the journals of trader/trappers working the Missouri River between 1811 and 1813.[19] Like the men of the expedition, these frontiersmen also failed to specifically name Sacagawea. Henry Brackenridge, offers the most detail by referring to the woman who died as the wife of Charbonneau who accompanied Lewis and Clark. As Brackenridge's trapping party departed St. Louis in 1811, he described this young Indian woman as sickly, yet "a good creature of mild and gentle disposition." The fact that Charbonneau had several Indian wives left the possibility that the sickly woman, who later died when the party reached Fort Manuel, may have been someone else.

Hebard dedicated nearly three decades to proving that Sacagawea was not the young wife who died in 1812 but rather a wise old leader among her people at the Wind River Reservation in Wyoming. In 1933 Hebard published her findings in *Sacagawea: A Guide and Interpreter of the Lewis and Clark Expedition, with an Account of the Travels of Toussaint Charbonneau, and of Jean Baptiste, the Expedition Papoose.* Hebard based her theory on the oral testimonies of Euro-American agents, missionaries, and traders living and working among the Shoshones at Wind River. Her principal informant was Dr. John Roberts, an Episcopalian missionary who buried the elderly Shoshone woman in 1884. Indians and agents at the reservation described the dead woman as dignified, beautiful, influential, and respected by whites and Indians.[20] The old woman, who went by the name Porivo, had two sons named Baptiste and Bazil. One of them was half French and spoke Shoshone, English, and French. Several Indians testified that Porivo and her sons were present when the Shoshones signed the 1868 treaty establishing the Wind River Reservation, and that Porivo spoke in favor of whites. Euro-American witnesses told Hebard that Porivo was of superior genetic makeup and more closely akin to American women. From these facts, Hebard extrapolated a theory refuting the written evidence that Sacagawea had died in her early twenties near Fort Manuel, North Dakota.

Scholars questioned Hebard's hypothesis for two reasons. First, Brackenridge's record specifically states that the wife with Charbonneau on the 1812 Missouri expedition had accompanied Lewis and Clark. Second, the old woman who died at Wind River was not believed to be Sacagawea until Hebard suggested it. Hebard deflected the

Rev. John Roberts at the burial place
of Porivo, believed to be Sacagawea,
at the Wind River Reservation.
Courtesy James Willard Schultz
Collection, Montana State University
Libraries, no. 421.

skepticism by taking every measure to authenticate her oral sources.
She conducted all interviews with official interpreters and transcri-
bers and had all Indian witnesses stamp their interviews with a
fingerprint. Hebard demanded that her sources (white reservation
administrators and reservations Indians) be respected.

Hebard's Sacagawea (Porivo) lived a long and meaningful life
among her people, and she continued to aid Euro-Americans in
winning Indian acceptance. According to Hebard, when Sacagawea
left her young son with Clark in St. Louis to be educated, she also
left Charbonneau. Hebard describes him as a terrible and violent
husband. Sacagawea left her abusive French husband in St. Louis,
headed west on her own, and eventually took refuge among the
Comanches, whose language she quickly mastered.[21] Comanche informants called this woman Wadze-wipe (lost woman). They described

her to Hebard and suggested she possessed characteristics similar to Hebard's subject.[22] Wadze-wipe lived among the Comanches for twenty-seven years, married, and gave birth to five children, although only two survived. When her Comanche husband died, Wadze-wipe began her long journey back to the land of her childhood. She finally returned to the Shoshones (by then living near Fort Washakie, Wyoming) as an old and experienced woman. Hebard traces Sacagawea's trip to her homeland through John Frémont's journal. He, too, mentions an anonymous helpful Indian woman.

Hebard presents Frémont's journal entry for July 1848 in which he writes, "A French engage at Lupton's fort in Colorado had been shot in the back on July 4th and died during our absence to the Arkansas. The wife of the murdered man, an Indian woman of the Snake nation, desirous, like Naomi of old, to return to her people, requested and obtained permission to travel with my party to the neighborhood of Bear river, where she expected to meet with some of their villages. Happier than the Jewish widow, she carried with her two children, pretty little half-breeds, who added much to the liveliness of the camp."[23] Hebard was willing to accept this anonymous woman as Sacagawea despite being skeptical of the Indian woman Brackenridge describes and despite his clarification that she had traveled with Lewis and Clark. Frémont describes the Shoshone woman's effort to dig roots for the nourishment of his party, and this convinced Hebard that she was most likely Sacagawea.

In 1920, after Hebard's 1907 article but before the publication of her book, the Missouri Historical Society found another journal and published it under the title *Journal of a Fur Trading Expedition on the Upper Missouri, 1812–1813*.[24] The journal was kept by John Luttig, a Philadelphia businessman who journeyed to the West and became the clerk at Fort Manuel. In a daily log that he kept, recording the chaotic events leading up to the War of 1812, he mentions Charbonneau several times. On December 20, 1812, he writes, "This evening the wife of Charbonneau, a Snake squaw, died of a putrid fever. She was a good and the best woman in the fort, aged about 25 years." This is the second account of a Shoshone wife with Charbonneau, yet neither account (Brackenridge nor Luttig) calls her by name. Hebard argues that the woman Luttig and Brackenridge describe was Otter

Woman, another of Charbonneau's wives. According to Hebard, both men were confused, and it was Otter Woman who died in 1812 at Fort Manuel. Porivo was the real Sacagawea, and she died in 1884. Without offering evidence, Hebard insists that Charbonneau must have taken both Shoshone wives with him to St. Louis. No one mentions the Frenchmen having two wives with him in St. Louis. Clark specifically invited Sacagawea to St. Louis in a letter to Charbonneau after the expedition. And Brackenridge's journal says that Charbonneau had his wife with him, not wives. Brackenridge does not name her, but he clarifies that Charbonneau and this wife had accompanied Lewis and Clark.

Hebard's interpretation set off an intense controversy over the time and place of Sacagawea's death. Hebard remained emphatic that Sacagawea continued a long life of service after the expedition. Reservation officials and Indian witnesses told Hebard that Porivo encouraged the Shoshones to accept the 1868 treaty, to take up agriculture, and to adopt the white man's way. Hebard writes, "Sacajawea proved of the greatest value to the whites through her influence with her own people. She was able to understand the white man's point of view and to present it to the Indians." Hebard traces various Indian women through scraps of evidence in the historical record (Sacagawea, Wadze-wipe, Frémont's companion, and Porivo), synchronizes Indian oral tradition, and develops a feasible hypothesis: Sacagawea returned to her people where she continued in service to America.

Hebard's theory offers a more satisfying end to the life of America's national heroine. Her theory also gives Wyoming (Hebard's home state) historical ownership in Sacagawea's legend. However, historians in Hebard's era were quick to challenge her research. She was not a trained historian, she was an outspoken suffragist, and she ventured into uncharted territory when she offered Indian oral tradition as a legitimate historical source. Conservative scholars considered Hebard a feminist renegade who was operating on the edge of acceptable scholarship.

However, Hebard's attempt to include the Native American perspective was admirable. She was ahead of her time; scholars today consider Native perspectives essential in the telling of western history.

The problem is that Porivo was not known to have accompanied Lewis and Clark prior to Hebard's arrival; she never spoke of the famed expedition to anyone during her many years on the reservation. Scholars then and now have concluded that Hebard used questionable evidence and that her testimonies were coaxed.

More evidence of Sacagawea's early death surfaced in 1955 when Clark's personal papers were organized for posterity. Among his writings was a ledger (in use 1825–1828) that offers more confirmation that Sacagawea died in 1812.[25] The ledger lists the expedition's members and what became of them. Next to Sacagawea's name is one word: dead. Even written records can be misleading, however. Clark's ledger also declares Patrick Gass dead when, in fact, he had moved back East where he lived to be an old man. But the case of Gass was different from Sacagawea: whereas Gass severed all ties when he left the West, there was a fondness between Clark and the Charbonneau family. They had shared a tent together for nineteen months, and their friendship and correspondence continued after the expedition. Clark took responsibility for raising and educating the couple's young son, whom he affectionately called "my boy Pomp." Clark, as legal guardian of the boy, likely knew of Sacagawea's fate. The records on Indian women are hazy, but one thing is absolute: Sacagawea, Wadze-wipe, Porivo, and Frémont's unnamed pleasant and helpful acquaintance were all real women who negotiated diverse cultures on the frontier.

When Hebard claimed all of these women as Sacagawea, she distorted their lives and experiences. Who were these women and what were their stories? They (Sacagawea, Porivo, Wadze-wipe, Frémont's companion, and the woman that Breckenridge and Luttig described) were rarely identified by name, but they were respected by diverse people on the frontier. These women were mobile and transnational; they successfully interacted with various people on an ethnically diverse frontier. They were all described as admirable and helpful by Anglo journals and Indian oral tradition. They were not drudges, not victims, and not princesses; they were real Indian women who delicately negotiated a changing social and cultural environment.

Hebard conflated several Indian women and presented one idealized Sacagawea who fit America's appetite for an Indian princess who advocated for white civilization and illustrated a competent American female. There was enough ambiguity, coincidence, and similarity to make Hebard's argument plausible. Her work was immensely popular with mainstream audiences, yet scholars discredited her findings. Her work nonetheless revived Sacagawea's legend and intensified historical investigation into her life and death.

In 1924 the commissioner of Indian affairs sent Charles Eastman to Indian country to resolve the issue. His instructions were to locate the final burial place of the American heroine. Eastman was a Dakota Sioux who had been educated at Carlisle Indian School. Many considered him a success of assimilationist policy. He had attended Dartmouth College, was a noted author and trained physician, married a white woman, and became a government official who investigated conditions on reservations. Eastman devoted much of his adult life to Indian issues. His investigation among the Shoshones (who had, by then, worked with Hebard for nearly two decades and ultimately gave Eastman the same information) substantiated Hebard's rendition of Sacagawea's life. Eastman concluded that Sacagawea's final resting place was at Fort Washakie, Wyoming; she was indeed the old woman, Porivo, who had died there in 1884.[26] His report assured his superiors that the Indian informants were respectable, adding that many were educated Christians.

With regard to Brackenridge and Luttig's evidence of Sacagawea's sickness and death, Eastman agreed with Hebard that Charbonneau must have taken both Shoshone wives to St. Louis and that it was Otter Woman who died in 1812. Eastman explained that the old woman who died at Wind River had not been recognized as Sacagawea, but was known as the mother of two mixed-blood sons, Bazil and Baptiste who died 1886 and 1885, respectively. Eastman suggested that Porivo's silence about her grand adventure with Lewis and Clark was likely attributed to her modesty.[27] He further suggested that an Indian mother would never have left her baby in the care of strangers, like Sacagawea was supposed to have done when she left baby Baptiste in St. Louis.[28] Eastman wrote that his experience with Indian mothers convinced him that Sacagawea most likely stayed in St. Louis to oversee the child's transition, while Charbonneau and Otter Woman accompanied the Missouri expedition in 1812.

With Hebard's work confirmed by Eastman in 1925, scholars backed away from Sacagawea as a topic of study, avoiding the sensitive issue regarding the legitimacy of Indian oral tradition. In September 1928 John E. Rees of Salmon, Idaho, allegedly wrote an obscure letter to the commissioner of Indian affairs, Charles H. Burke. Rees lived among the Lemhi Shoshones from 1877 until his death in 1928, not long after he penned the letter. The Lemhi County Historical Society in Salmon, Idaho, uncovered two slightly varying drafts of Rees's letter among his personal effects. The official correspondence could not be authenticated through the Bureau of Indian Affairs. The historical society, using both renditions, published a reconstruction of the letter in 1970.

The Historical Society's rendition of Rees's letter is titled "Madame Charbonneau: The Indian Woman Who Accompanied the Lewis and Clark Expedition 1804–1806, How She Received Her Indian Name and What Became of Her."[29] The letter reveals an intimate awareness of Lemhi people and offers some clarification on Sacagawea. According to Rees, over the course of his long interaction with the Shoshones he sat for countless hours listening to their stories (that is, their history). He clarifies how the Lemhis were named the "Snake Indians." Rees suggests that other Indians knew the Lemhis as the "Grass Lodge People" due to their unique dwellings constructed of woven grass; white men had misinterpreted the Indian sign, an index finger moving in a serpentine motion to indicate the process of weaving grass. He also explains why Sacagawea sucked her fingers as she approached her people when the expedition entered the territory of her childhood: "The primitive Indian was a wild man and like any other wild animal always guarded against surprise. It is only in the bosom of its own people that the Indian child would go to sleep in that relaxed and contented attitude which is displayed by the child sucking its fingers."[30]

Rees explains the various renditions of Sacagawea's name, the different spellings and meanings, and the Indian stories of Porivo and Wadze-wipe. He discusses her wanderings and her eventual return to the Lemhi. He ends his letter by saying, "I would say that the evidence produced by Dr. Hebard is not only competent, relevant and material, but it is also conclusive in its scope and is well summed up by the doctor when she says, 'These three men, Irwin, Patten and Roberts, must, through the important positions they occupied, be classed as intelligent, accurate, trustworthy and capable of arriving at results without jumping at a hasty conclusion, of which an ordinary traveler might be accused.' They all three lived among these Shoshones for years, working with them in the endeavor for their betterment spiritually, mentally and domestically."[31] Rees had also lived and worked among the Lemhis; he had grown intimately connected with them and eventually earned access to their oral tradition. He explains, "If the work of missionaries among the Indians and the knowledge gained from them is to have no weight, then American history is shorn of its greatest asset, for all our knowledge concerning the aborigine was first acquired by the Jesuit or zealous religious missionary who usually preceded permanent civilization."[32] Both Rees and Hebard legitimized Shoshone oral tradition by stressing that Indian oral history was told to trustworthy non-Indian people who dedicated their lives to the betterment of Indian people.

The Native testimonies given to Hebard, Eastman, and Rees did not eliminate all doubts regarding Sacagawea's life. Yet those Indian accounts did prove that Native women were active on a multiethnic international frontier. Indian women were influential and respected during critical social discussions such as negotiating treaties or establishing relationships with outsiders. Unlike previous historians, Hebard, Eastman, and Rees considered Indian people within the context of Indian culture. Yet they interpreted this previously untapped historical evidence within their own cultural framework that accepted American westward expansion as divinely inspired and an inevitable success. Their work characterized Native Americans as an important ingredient in national history, not merely as a savage obstacle.

While Hebard, Eastman, and Rees introduced Indians as an admirable part of national identity, they each had personal goals in mind. Hebard was intent on revealing a capable and influential female American heroine during the push for suffrage. Eastman wanted to assure government officials in Washington that Indian people led dignified lives, cared for their children, and had respectable cultural traditions. Rees wanted recognition for early western white men who were the first to live among the Indians as missionaries, reservation officials, and traders. Armchair scholars, who researched the archives without ever knowing a Shoshone, could not know them as he did. Rees considered himself an authority on Shoshone people. By publishing Rees's letter in the 1970s, the Lemhi Shoshones wanted recognition and acceptance of their oral tradition as a legitimate historical account of initial contact. All parties had a particular and personal stake in their theory of Sacagawea.

Part of the controversy over Sacagawea was fueled by historical ownership. In an era of a burgeoning tourism industry in the early 1900s, North Dakota, Wyoming, Idaho, and Montana all claimed the American heroine as part of their state history. The investigation into Sacagawea's death was initiated when state governments in Wyoming and North Dakota appropriated funds for a statue to commemorate her on the centennial of the Lewis and Clark expedition. In 1907 Montana erected a monument at Three Forks in memory of this famous Indian woman who had led the Americans through their state.[33] Three Native American nations claimed her: the Shoshones, the Hidatsas, and the Comanches. Although the controversy died down, it was never fully settled. State histories and Native oral traditions ultimately learned to share the legend of Sacagawea.

Sacagawea's Detractors

Despite Sacagawea's romantic attraction as an Indian princess, her heroine status began to tarnish by mid-century when revisionist scholars reexamined the journals and discovered that the journals did not actually say that much about her. After Coues, Dye, and Hebard built this flesh-and-blood woman into a national icon, several scholars returned to the primary sources to interrogate the legitimacy of Sacagawea's grandiose saga. C. S. Kingston's article "Sacajawea as Guide: The Evolution of a Legend" (1944) illustrates this emerging group of detractors. He blatantly accuses writers like Hebard of adding romantic embellishments. Kingston disputes Sacagawea's role as a guide but does not address her role as an interpreter or intermediary. Regarding Clark's description of Sacagawea as a "pilot" through the mountains, he writes that it "is to be understood more as an expression of good natured and generous congratulation than a sober assertion of unadorned fact." Kingston is less vicious than some detractors; he treats Sacagawea gently and rates her as a useful but not an indispensable member of the corps. Kingston objects to the premise that an Indian girl led the captains where no man (at least no white man) had ventured before.

Other detractors were more aggressive in debunking Sacagawea's myth. Ronald W. Taber's article "Sacajawea and the Suffragettes: An Interpretation of Myth" (1967), suggests that Sacagawea's legend was strategically crafted to legitimize feminist demands during the women's suffrage movement. Richard L. Neuberger's article "Was Sacajawea Guide for Lewis and Clark? Explorer's Journal Indicates Tale Only a Myth" (1951) and John C. Hunt's article "A Reason for Statues and Plaques in Her Honor" (1969) consider Sacagawea as merely an object of romantic fantasy. Kingston, Tabor, Neuberger, and Hunt reject the mythic Sacagawea put forth by Coues, Dye, Hebard, and even Clark. Sacagawea's detractors suggest that Clark was just being nice. Coues romanticized the nation's frontier myth by adding an Indian princess. Dye and Hebard used Sacagawea's narrative to legitimize a contemporary feminist agenda. Detractors were intent on revealing and discrediting the biased perspectives and the questionable historical evidence presented by earlier writers.

Ultimately, Kingston, Taber, Neuberger, and Hunt attempted to restore full credit to Captains Lewis and Clark. These two American male leaders were responsible for opening the West, not an Indian girl. Detractors had no interest in Sacagawea as a historical topic. Her Native experience, social obligation, and expertise as a cultural intermediary were irrelevant to the mission carried out by Lewis and Clark. Detractors were certain that a young Indian girl should not be credited (even partially) with the success of the mission. They defused the controversies surrounding Sacagawea by suggesting that she was not very historically relevant anyway.

Writer and historian Bernard De Voto illustrates the skepticism and confusion surrounding Sacagawea when he describes her contribution in his elegant 1952 work entitled *The Course of Empire*:

And Sacajawea had long since proved her value. She was always busy,
digging edible roots they were familiar with and finding strange ones,
tailoring buckskins, making moccasins, explaining novelties, cool and
swift in emergencies. . . . She is remarkable, this girl who may have
been no more than seventeen in 1805, and of whom no word is directly
reported since she could speak only Shoshone and Minnetraree. She is
better known than any other Indian woman and she has unusual resourcefulness, staunchness, and loyalty, a warmth that can be felt through the
rugged prose of men writing with their minds on a stern job, and a gaiety
that is childlike and yet not the childishness we have associated with
primitives. All diarists liked her, Lewis gave her detached admiration, Clark delighted in her, and she has charmed the imagination of
readers ever since Nicholas Biddle wrote his book. In so much that
she has become a popular heroine and something of a myth, a Shoshone Deirdre created out of desire. And from Bismarck to the sea many
antiquaries and most trail makers have believed that Lewis, Clark and
their command were privileged to assist in the Sacajawea Expedition,
which is not quite true.[34]

De Voto seems to appreciate her work ethic, yet his sarcasm draws
attention to his opinion that she was overrated, even by Clark, whom
De Voto implies was smitten with Sacagawea. Despite the skepticism of De Voto and others, the cynical backlash was short-lived,
and Sacagawea would again capture the romantic fancy of writers and
their audiences. As with the sentimental narratives of Malinche and
Pocahontas, people have been drawn to Sacagawea's tender tale of
hospitality and acceptance. Creative writers successfully sculpted
the ambiguities within their legends to profess personal convictions,
whether patriotic, political, racial, or gender oriented.

Sacagawea in Romance Novels

In the aftermath of World War II, when victory in Europe instilled
pride in America and race was becoming an increasingly prevalent
issue in American society, novelists offered a new motive for Sacagawea's devotion to the expedition. They employed the entrenched

Indian princess model to demonstrate how a young, beautiful, noble, Sacagawea fell in love with the bold Captain Clark. Clark's temperament was open and outgoing, while Lewis was reserved and withdrawn. She was drawn to Clark because of his strength, wisdom, kindness, and civilized culture. Romance novelists reveled in Sacagawea's relationship with Clark, who represented the best of American masculinity. Her affection toward Clark was plausible because his journal entries and letters seem to suggest a genuine respect and fondness for the young woman. There is no explicit evidence that Sacagawea was intimately involved with anyone other than her husband along the journey. But that certainly does not eliminate the possibility that there was physical or emotional intimacy between Clark and Sacagawea. The captains would never have recorded such an indiscretion. Novelists were therefore forced to read between the lines of the journal entries, looking for emotional clues.

According to romance writers, the considerate treatment Lewis and Clark showed to Sacagawea stimulated her affection. She was not accustomed to such fair treatment in her savage world, so she bore the burden of an unattainable love. Her marriage to Charbonneau and American social taboos regarding miscegenation prevented a union with Clark. Her respectability in the white man's world required demure restraint. Clark's emotional connection to Sacagawea was also inhibited because his complete focus was devoted to his patriotic duty.

The original journals, as well as secondary works, consistently depict Indian women as degraded. Romance writers used these observations to suggest that once Sacagawea received feminine respectability within an American social setting, she committed herself to the American men and their cause. The journals' depiction of Charbonneau as a French "squaw-man," only slightly better than his Indian counterpart, also fueled the romantic narrative of a love denied. The journals make several references to Charbonneau's inadequacy as a husband and protector of his Indian bride. For instance, Clark had been compelled to reprimand him for striking Sacagawea. Building on modest evidence in the primary record, romance writers characterized Clark as the best man Sacagawea had ever known, her perfect man, but a man she could not have.

Like Pocahontas's love for Smith, Sacagawea's love for Clark remained platonic. Their emotional and physical restraint enhanced their status as heroes. Writers of this romantic genre employed Coues's and Dye's characterizations of Charbonneau to legitimize Sacagawea's vulnerability and provide a negative comparison for Clark. Dye describes a hierarchy for the men in Sacagawea's life indicating that Charbonneau had "been kind to the captive Indian girl, and her heart clung to the easy-going Frenchman as her best friend. The worst white man was better than an Indian Husband."[35] In 1907 Dye saw no romance between Sacagawea and Clark. A love affair between them would have complicated her patriotic tale of a strong, independent woman and a captain dedicated to his mission.

By mid-century more records surfaced, particularly personal letters written by Clark that reveal his fondness for the Charbonneau family. Despite no proof of lust or romance, his warmth and admiration ignited the imagination of writers. Della Gould Emmons's *Sacajawea of the Shoshones* (1943) and Will Henry's *The Gates of the Mountains* (1963) exemplify this romantic theme. Donald Culrass Peattie describes the relationship between Sacagawea and Clark in his book *Forward the Nation* (1942): "Her braids he loved, for the way they fell straight down from her head, sloped in pride over her bosom, and swung free with every stroke of her paddle. He took secret pleasure in her sturdy figure going ahead of him."[36] Peattie was clearly infatuated with the idea of an exotic natural beauty in the wilderness, and he could not imagine that the men of the expedition failed to notice. These works celebrate Sacagawea as America's Indian princess and celebrate Clark as the American frontier hero who opened the territory to American greatness. Romance writers consistently left the love unsatisfied and unresolved, suggesting a metaphor for the complex race reality that the twentieth-century nation endured.[37]

Della Gould Emmons's romance novel was the basis for a Paramount movie entitled *Far Horizons* that appeared in 1955. The forbidden love between Sacagawea (Donna Reed) and Clark (Charlton Heston) is a central theme in this Hollywood version of America's epic tale. Clark and Sacagawea are portrayed as a lovesick couple that heroically conquers the wilds of nature together. The obstacle of Charbonneau (Alan Reed) is removed after the inadequate Frenchman is sent home midway through the journey. Yet the lovers are still prevented from acting on their feelings because of an uncompromising social stigma. When Clark informs Lewis that he intends to marry the Indian beauty, he is threatened with a court-martial. The movie ends (as Emmon's novel ends) when a crushed but dignified Sacagawea meets Clark's second choice, Julia (Barbara Hale), in Washington. The unrealized interracial romance provides a framework for considering social questions of race and miscegenation. The audience is left to ponder what might have been.

Authors of these romantic portrayals often swore to their historical authenticity, yet they are pure fantasy. They add to a cultural consensus on the opening of the West and to the legend of Sacagawea as the noble Indian princess. Mainstream audiences devoured these tales of forbidden passion. Some sober-minded historians rejected such literary license, while others (like De Voto) gave into the temptation and read between the lines of Clark's journal. The unfortunate truth is we can never know the inner thoughts of Sacagawea. Did she love Clark? We have no records from her. Clark left countless pages of journal entries, letters, and remembrances, yet we cannot say for certain whether or not he loved Sacagawea.

Toward a Balanced Interpretation

In 1971 Harold Howard published *Sacajawea,* a nonfiction biography intent on debunking Sacagawea's legend, which had run amok since the work of Coues, Dye, and Hebard. Howard was not an academic; he was a newspaperman and entrepreneur in South Dakota. In his preface Howard states his goal: to reconcile early-twentieth-century attempts to glorify Sacagawea's role in Manifest Destiny with mid-century attempts to minimize her contributions, and thus find Sacagawea's rightful place in history. Widely praised by academia, his work remained largely unknown in the popular genre. Howard sifts fact from fantasy and offers his explanation of the relationship between Sacagawea and Clark: "As for the often repeated suggestion that Sacajawea had a romantic attachment for Captain Clark, it is indeed possible that she did. No doubt he was a much more attractive man than Charbonneau. But Lewis and Clark had to maintain a certain posture before their men. They were emissaries of the President and were under the constant observation of their men."[38] Howard concedes that Sacagawea may have been in love with Clark, but he refuses to imagine that the captain could have felt the same. He suggests that military decorum would have prevented Clark from being sidetracked by a woman.

Howard's work tries to find balance. He rejects the early-twentieth-century portrayals offered by Dye and Hebard as feminist propaganda. He also dismisses mid-century detractors (like Kingston, Taber, Neuberger, and Hunt) who minimized her contributions. He writes, "This book, the product of many years spent in research and in sifting fact from romance, represents an effort at an unbiased appraisal of Sacajawea and her achievement." He largely succeeds in his attempt, but his claim of a complete unbiased account is questionable.

Howard recognizes Sacagawea's contributions: her skill at providing food, her ability to embody a sign of peace, her communication skills, her knowledge of the landscape, her recommendation of the Bozeman Pass, and her overall endurance and warmth. However, in a chapter entitled "Sacajawea—What Was She Like?" he writes, "During that time she served the United States faithfully and without pay, although it is doubtful that she comprehended the significance of the expedition."[39] Why did Howard think she was incapable of understanding the significance of the mission? Sacagawea had spent more than twenty months with the white men. By 1806—after two hundred years of European incursions—most North American Indians, including Sacagawea, were preparing for a new future. As an intermediary Sacagawea was exposed, more intimately than most Indians, to the newcomers and was likely aware of their intentions in her homeland. It is entirely possible that she was trying to gain an advantage for herself, her family, and her people. Sacagawea's decision to give her son to Clark suggests that she envisioned a new future and wanted her child to have a secure place in that future.

Howard shows his cultural bias again when he states, "It was the pinnacle of many Indian girls' ambitions to marry a fur trader."[40] The Native American role of female culture broker was a respected career for young Indian women, yet facilitating communication and understanding on a multinational frontier was demanding and dangerous work that required extensive travel. Successful intermediaries were skilled and vital to both sides of the cultural divide. Howard's implication that Indian girls dreamt of being rescued from the harshness of their Native culture by European traders belittles their work as intermediaries. It is unrealistic to portray all Indian women as vulnerable, naïve, and incapable of foresight. Malinche, Pocahontas, and Sacagawea all lived in dynamic multinational environments during eras of profound transformation. Their Native experiences provided feminine skills that helped them negotiate frontier encounters. They were not caught in a whirlwind of masculine heroic adventure; these women had an eye to the future, they had responsibilities, and they were deliberate in their work.

In 1976 E. G. Chuinard wrote "The Actual Role of the Bird Woman: Purposeful Member of the Corps or 'Casual Tag Along'?" This article is perhaps the best answer to the Sacagawea detractors of the 1940s and 1950s. Chuinard examines the journal entries that pertain specifically to Sacagawea's role in the expedition. He accepts the captains at their written word and concludes that Sacagawea was indeed an interpreter, guide, and "contact agent." Like Howard, Chuinard neglects any Native cultural information that might explain why Sacagawea provided these services. On this point, the reader is left to the conclusions provided by earlier writers: that Sacagawea was enamored with the American heroes and their culture.

The theme of romance proved too titillating to discard. A late romance novel by Anna Lee Waldo entitled *Sacajawea* (1979) revives the love story and reiterates Sacagawea's role in Manifest Destiny. Waldo updated the story to address the feminist movement of the 1970s. Although her book received unanimously negative reviews from historians, it was on the *New York Times* bestseller list for more than eight months and sold more than one million copies in less than four years. Waldo's Sacagawea possesses the familiar characteristics of an Indian princess. She is a young and intelligent rare beauty with creamy brown skin. She is unfulfilled by an unhappy marriage to Charbonneau and is drawn to Clark, who recognizes her Native beauty. Their passions are described through countless pages of heart-throbbing adventure, yet the physical aspect of their love is never realized. Once again, social taboos tragically prevent the lovers from fulfilling their desires. Clark and Sacagawea (unlike Cortés and Malinche) do not give into temptation, and retain their altruistic reputations.

Waldo recalls the image of the strong, independent woman initiated by Dye and Hebard during the suffrage movement seventy years earlier. This image allows her to participate in the contemporary 1970s debate on women's roles. Waldo uses Sacagawea as an example of a woman who rises above her constraints and takes control of her life. Despite forceful male attempts to dominate the diminutive and economically dependent heroine, Waldo's Sacagawea prevails due to her inner feminine strength. As a model for modern feminism, Sacagawea offers the promise that women can break free from their dependency and eventually triumph.

Like earlier romance writers, Waldo combines historical fact and fantasy to entertain readers, while reassuring them of America's promise. Readers are coaxed into accepting the validity of Manifest Destiny, while they are encouraged to reconsider social standards of gender and race. This is a productive strategy for authors who question prevailing social mores; a commitment to American nationalism legitimizes the author's suggestion for national improvement. Waldo celebrates America's Manifest Destiny while forcing the reader to acknowledge the strength and potential of women. If Sacagawea could rise above her exploitive treatment in Native society and her abusive French husband, then contemporary American women were capable of taking control over their lives and could be contributing members of twentieth-century society. Waldo reconstructs Sacagawea as a prototype for American women to follow and for American men to accept, if not appreciate. Waldo denies her main characters the fulfillment of their love, forcing readers to ponder the missed opportunity of an interracial marriage. What good could have come had this grand hero and heroine been allowed to marry? Would their union have been a more constructive beginning for race relations in the western United States and prevented a legacy of resentment?

As the century progressed, scholars and social critics increasingly expressed doubts regarding America's westward experience. By the

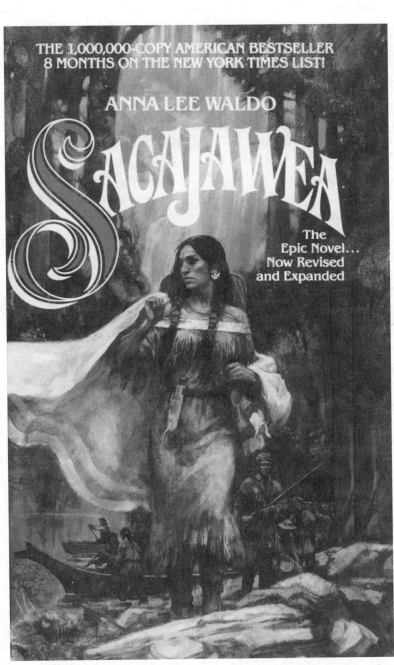

Cover of Anna Lee Waldo's novel *Sacajawea*, 1979. © 1978 by Anna Lee Waldo. Reprinted by permission of HarperCollins Publishers.

closing decades of the twentieth century a new generation of historians (calling themselves "new western historians") interrogated the
American myth of "taming" the West. They refused to accept Manifest Destiny as an adequate explanation for American expansion and
suggested that the accepted ideology merely justified America's
landgrab in the West. They disputed the legitimacy of traditional
frontier history, or what they described as the white man's adventure story. The Sacagawea legend was again debunked during this
era of cynicism. She was described as an object of male fantasy, an
invented Native beauty, an Indian princess who was infatuated with
the American heroes. Some new western historians rejected the premise that Sacagawea illustrated Indian acceptance. They insisted that
she had no choice. She was a victim enslaved by the men around
her. New western historians illustrated the illusions and the limitations of grounding western history in the fallacy of America's divine
mission to expand democracy.

National and international events during the 1970s generated difficult social questions about race, conquest, and cultural imperialism.
During that tumultuous decade Americans had come to distrust
the generation in charge, and rising skepticism permeated national
discourse (historical, political, and cultural). The civil rights movement of the sixties descended into race wars in cities across America.
Government officials lied to citizens about realities in Vietnam. American citizens increasingly questioned the "credibility gap" between
what officials said and the unpleasant truth. President Nixon and
Vice President Agnew were both forced to resign after their illegal
activities were discovered. In a social atmosphere racked by generational distrust and rebellion, "old western historians" were accused
of misrepresenting (or glossing over the injustice of) American westward expansion. Younger historians and a broad section of American
citizens lost faith in what they had always been told. By the end of
the decade traditional frontier myths failed to resonate with a large
segment of the population.

By the 1980s America's frontier story was being reevaluated through
the lenses of race, class, and gender. The new historical perspective
offered great value as stories of nonwhite people came into focus.
The history of the West was traditionally told as a triumphant tale

from a white male perspective. All others (nonwhite people and women) were mentioned only as symbolic complements that supported the grand national narrative. New western historians put the other at the center; how did women and nonwhite people experience westward expansion? The first impulse was to define them as victims. The history of the West was recast as a story of conquest with opposing sides: the victors and the vanquished. The old western characterization of the continent as an open and untapped wilderness in which Indians were a vanishing race was no longer convincing on the eve of the twenty-first century. Living Indians contradicted the frontier myth; they had not vanished and many were demanding political and cultural recognition. Toward the end of the century, the vanquished were seeking acknowledgement and retribution.

Festering Native American issues (land seizures, the denial of hunting and fishing rights, tribal recognition, and self-determination on reservations) were complicated by arbitrary and often-shifting federal policies. Indigenous peoples were increasingly petitioning the courts for justice. Indians of the upper Great Lakes banded together in a push for civil rights through the Red Power movement, aggressive pan-Indian activism. In the 1970s and 1980s Indians launched a series of protests including "fish-ins" in the Northwest; the takeover of the Bureau of Indian Affairs headquarters in Washington, D.C., and Alcatraz Island in San Francisco; the "Trail of Broken Treaties" march to the capital; and the occupation of Wounded Knee on Pine Ridge reservation in South Dakota. Despite the rhetoric of frontier myth, Indians had not disappeared. Contemporary Indians joined the national debate and intensified the discussion of conquest and racism toward indigenous populations at home and abroad. As the twentieth century came to a close, mythic representations of Indian people exploded. If Indians had been misrepresented in the national narrative, what was their story and who are they today?

The dichotomous characterization of Indian women was challenged. Was Sacagawea really a princess and all other Indian women unfortunate wretches? In a 1980 article entitled "Boat Pusher or Bird Woman? Sacagawea or Sacajawea?" Blanche Schroer extends the descriptions of Sacagawea—her personal qualities and contributions—to all Shoshone women. She concludes her article by saying, "Strangely,

however, the Shoshone woman's helpfulness during the great journey lay not in the fact that it was unique but because it was typical.
The kindly nature and staying qualities inherent in her were integral to most young Indian women of her time and place. By honoring her, we honor her race—particularly the Shoshonis—and this
is fitting."[41] Schroer dismantles the myth of the Indian princess/
degraded squaw and portrays all Shoshone women as kind and
helpful. She provides no cultural information to substantiate her claim,
idealizes all Shoshone women, and deemphasizes Sacagawea's work
in establishing a cooperative multicultural frontier.

The skilled job of a female culture broker was not likely suited to
all Shoshone women, just as the rigors of frontier life were not suited
to all Anglo men. Intermediary work required specific skills and
personality traits. Successful intermediaries were gifted in communication as well as intelligent, tolerant, and more traveled than most
members of their community. Primary records indicate that there
were a significant number of Indian women who provided this
delicate work during initial contact; yet most of them received little
recognition in the historical record. Sacagawea was a particularly
adept cultural intermediary.

The only other Native woman mentioned by name in the Lewis
and Clark journals is a Nez Perce woman, Watkuweis. She was a
mobile frontier woman who had been taken north as a captive where
she was traded to a white man and then ultimately made her way
back to the Nez Perces. By the time she met the Corps of Discovery,
she, too, was an experienced multicultural frontier woman. Yet we
know almost nothing about her. In September 1805 Clark briefly
acknowledged her for convincing the men in her party to aid the
expedition. Clark literally erased her from history as he prepared
the final published account of the journey.[42] Like the scant records
of so many other Indian women (including Porivo, Wadze-wipe, and
Frémont's Native female companion), Watkuweis's faint tracks indicate the regularity of women's intricate participation in cross-cultural
interaction on the frontier. Native female cultural intermediaries
were moving around, learning a broad section of land, and master-
ing a variety of languages and interpersonal skills in a culturally
diverse environment. These women negotiated relentless change

in a complex network of people, all working to advance their own particular goals.

Sacagawea, Watkuweis, Porivo, and Frémont's companion were real Indian women, yet they are difficult to track because of a white male perspective that considered them peripheral to their heroic adventures. There are many brief accounts of Indian women's cross-cultural activities during early frontier contact. These snippets are like mysterious Polaroid snapshots found in the attic; no one wrote a caption, leaving the subject without context. History failed to tell the story of indigenous female cultural intermediaries. Instead we are left with culturally biased and gender-biased fantasies of Indian women. As the twentieth century came to a close, new western historians—some of them Indian women themselves—wanted to introduce a more realistic image of Native American women.

Rayna Green (Cherokee) launched an attack against the Sacagawea legend in her 1980 article, "Native American Women: A Review Essay." As discussed in the last chapter, Green blamed the legends of Malinche, Pocahontas, and Sacagawea for their damaging influence on the perception of Native women. Reacting to the mythical image of the Native American princess, Green writes, "They have captured hearts and minds, but as studies of other women had demonstrated, the level and substance of most passion for them has been selective, stereotyped and damaging." She complains, "Debates over Pocahontas, Sacagawea and Tekakwitha historically remained the historian's preoccupation, while a procession of significant tribal leaders passed by unnoticed or with a bare nod."[43] A dozen years later Green celebrated Indian women leaders in her book *Women in American Indian Society* (1992). She is relentless in her attack on the mythic Indian princess stereotype and brought recognition to Indian women's continuous vision and leadership in Native communities.

Green's complaint regarding the stereotypical treatment of Indian women was not unique to Native American women.[44] Moreover, the construction of Sacagawea's legend is strikingly similar to Euro-American frontier heroes from Kit Carson to Buffalo Bill and Billy the Kid. Cultures select and celebrate only a few individuals as legends and frequently credit them for the exploits committed by others, as was the case with Sacagawea.[45] The ambiguity surrounding legendary figures, regardless of race or gender, is essential; flexibility keeps a legendary figure relevant and useable over time. Each generation manipulates the legend to suit contemporary needs, and repetition solidifies culturally significant information.

Green denied legitimacy to legendary Indian women. She was uninterested in (and irritated by) Malinche, Pocahontas, and Sacagawea because their national notoriety had been destructive to other Indian women. Green contributed a fresh focus on other Indian women and demanded that scholars look to Native American people and their cultures to explain the vital role of women. Had Green applied her method of research to the real Malinche, Pocahontas, and Sacagawea, these heroines would have supported her conclusion. Indian women have a long tradition of public service in their Native communities, particularly in matters of national consequence.

Late in the twentieth century American Indian women were speaking for themselves in historical discourse. Paula Gunn Allen's most famous works (*Sacred Hoop* and *Pocahontas*) have already been discussed, but she also mused on Sacagawea's life and legend. She takes on the persona of Sacagawea in a poem entitled "The One Who Skins Cats." She incorporates Shoshone oral tradition, expedition journals, history, and pop culture to interrogate mythic Sacagawea. Allen, speaking as Sacagawea, nonchalantly talks to the audience with a sense of detachment as she unravels the legend and accepts it as a separate entity from reality. Ultimately, the poem is about competing meanings. Allen's Sacagawea accepts multiple identities and defines herself as a "wanderer, whose tracks were washed away in certain places." She is a chief, a mother, and a wife. She is enslaved and beaten. She is one who knows and one who weeps. She goes where she pleases. She is posthumously defined in many different ways. Allen gives voice to Sacagawea so that she can finally define herself. The last line of the poem suggests how Sacagawea might have come to terms with the ambiguity of her legend: "It's not easy skinning cats when you're a dead woman."[46]

Jeanne Eder, a Shoshone historian, took on the persona of Sacagawea in a one-woman show that was filmed by the North Idaho College "Popcorn Forum" in 1996. The short film is part of a series entitled, *Journey through Time: Conversations with the World's Great*

Women and Men. Eder, as Sacagawea, defines her life and role in history within Native cultural context. She explains how and why she was taken captive by the Hidatsas. She says she was treated well by them and became part of that tribe. She describes how and why the Hidatsas sold her to Charbonneau, and the many gifts that were exchanged between the Frenchman and her Hidatsa family. Eder, as Sacagawea, devotes considerable attention to clarifying women's roles in Native societies by informing the audience, "Indian women held great power" and "contributed many things to the life of their people."[47] Women could be great warriors or peace advocates. Like other Indian women, Sacagawea appreciated the tradition of multiple wives because the workload was shared. She also suggests that multiple wives produced more children in an era of declining Indian men. Eder explains that oral tradition foretold the coming of Lewis and Clark. Sacagawea was not to blame for leading the whites to the Shoshones; they were already coming. With a wry tone Eder's Sacagawea closes by saying, "They always show me pointing: I was not guiding them, I was telling them to go over there."

Like Allen, Eder embraced Shoshone oral tradition that insisted Sacagawea eventually returned to her people as a leader; she lived a long life and was buried on the Indian reservation in Wyoming. At the conclusion of the first-person narrative, Eder removes her wig to distinguish herself from the Indian woman of the past. Eder then assures the audience that Indians not only survived, they were united: "We have all become friends (Hidatsa, Shoshone, Comanche and Nez Perce), we have a connection." They shared the experience of frontier interaction with whites through Sacagawea's involvement.

Native American women (like Green, Allen, and Eder) offered culturally relevant information on the role of Indian women. They redefined Indian women not as symbolic princesses or degraded squaws but as important contributing participants in the history of their people and in the history of the United States. The twentieth-century interpretation of Indian people also benefited from the call to respect diversity among Indian nations. Indigenous people were no longer presented as a monolithic race of Indians. Indians of all nations have occasionally come together in demand of civil rights, as evident by the Red Power movement and the American Indian

Women's Advocacy Organization, yet they have simultaneously demanded respect for the cultural characteristics that distinguish each group. Sacagawea moved through several tribes, in life and in myth, and those tribes share her legend.

The Journey of Sacagawea, a documentary made for PBS Home Video in 2003, also celebrates Indian cultural diversity. This narration of Sacagawea's life illustrates a multicultural and multitribal point of view. Indian leaders and historians from the Hidatsas, Shoshones, Comanches, and Nez Perces offer stories from their respective oral traditions explaining Sacagawea's wanderings and experiences among their people. The Shoshone informant is Rose Anne Abrahamson, a seventh-generation descendant of Cameahwait (Sacagawea's brother). She explains how Sacagawea's Northern Shoshone culture sustained her throughout her life: "Our teachings saw her through and saw her home."[48] The Hidatsa informant describes Sacagawea's abduction by Hidatsa warriors and insists that she was never a slave: "She was taken in by a large family and she was loved." Sacagawea was traded to Charbonneau for the economic benefit of all parties and the bride price signified her value to both sides. The Nez Perce informant describes their tribe's interaction with Lewis, Clark, and Sacagawea as respectful and hospitable. Each group reveals how Sacagawea touched their tribe's history, although none of the pesky discrepancies are broached.

In 2000 a copy of an oil painting by Bonnie Butterfield (Cherokee/Mohawk) accompanied an article she wrote entitled "Sacagawea Native American Legend: Why Did She Turn Her Back on Her Own People?" This pairing demonstrates the complexity of Native interpretations regarding Sacagawea. Butterfield's painting presents a tormented Sacagawea, whose face appears worn with apprehension and guilt. She is haunted by other Native women who are left in the background. The article condemns the treatment that Native American women, including Sacagawea, received in both the Indian and non-Indian worlds. Butterfield substantiates her feminist perspective using Lewis and Clark journal entries on the Indian mistreatment of women. She provides no Native cultural context for women's roles and relies solely on the impressions of nineteenth-century white men. Butterfield uses the Sacagawea narrative to illustrate universal female

Bonnie Butterfield, *Sacagawea,* painting, 2000. Courtesy of the artist.

oppression that extends beyond any one culture. She closes her article by saying, "Sacagawea's female status and her ethnic identity in the early 1800s kept her in the background of both white and tribal society. Only after the Expedition's incredible value became popularly, and politically well accepted, did Sacagawea's personal courage, sacrifices and contributions to the opening of the West gain the recognition they deserve."[49] Butterfield concludes that Sacagawea turned her back on Indian people because her own society had oppressed her as a woman. Americans also took advantage of her social position and her work. Butterfield's Sacagawea is wracked with guilt and should be forgiven because she is a slave to both cultures.

Sacagawea's story has been called upon to celebrate American expansion and Indian acceptance. Her legend has periodically been used as a forum to reconsider issues of race, miscegenation, and gender. Discussion of her sexuality was avoided until mid-twentieth-century romance writers began to fantasize about a love that could have crossed racial boundaries. She has represented the strength of American women, she has been used to illustrate universal feminine oppression, she has been rejected as a male fantasy, and she has personified the ideal Shoshone woman. She symbolizes the potential and hospitality of the Native environment and celebrates the contributions of Indian people to American nationalism. There may be a grain of truth in these explanations of Sacagawea, yet each particular focus reveals more about the authors and the times in which they were writing than they do about Sacagawea and the time in which she lived. Sacagawea's legacy is due, in part, to the ambiguities and adaptability of her story. But this is true of all western heroes, regardless of their race and gender.

Over the past four decades intellectual and scholarly critics have focused on how myths have been constructed and maintained and for what reasons. The result of this contentious scholarship is a composite historical record made up of conflicting elements and a national identity tormented by self-doubt. Heroes have been debunked, and the notion of a noble American mission to extend the boundaries of democracy has been reworked to reveal expansionist policies based on insensitive self-interest. New western historians characterize westward expansion as opportunistic, if not sinister, and an example of America's willful social injustice. The legacy of the frontier experience (or the "legacy of conquest" as Patricia Limerick calls it) complicates the telling of America's foundational myth of Manifest Destiny.

The twentieth century opened with scholarly and popular acceptance of Frederick Jackson Turner's famous 1893 frontier thesis, "The Significance of the Frontier in American History." Turner suggests that Americans perfected democratic institutions as the nation continually re-created itself on its move westward. That frontier experience determined American exceptionalism. In the closing decades of the century, new western historians refocused historical inquiry. They no longer presented expansion as an American triumph of Manifest Destiny. They broadened the story to include the experience of nonwhites, those who occupied the continent prior to American dominance. New western historians offer an uncompromising parallel narrative of conquest. History is no longer a mechanism for national consensus and social instruction; it has become a forum for more critical national reflection.

The Making of Sacagawea: A Euro-American Legend by Donna Kessler (1996) illustrates how Sacagawea's legend can be used to address this new focus. Kessler is particularly interested in how Americans have defined "otherness" through time. Kessler is unconcerned with Sacagawea as an Indian woman during frontier contact. Her book is not about Sacagawea; it is about how Euro-Americans defined her as other. Kessler demonstrates how writers have blended historical fact and strategic literary invention to weave a story that supports specific social commentary. Institutionalized national myths have occasionally been challenged by generational inquiry, and social categories and expectations have been reevaluated over time. The story of Sacagawea (like the stories of Malinche and Pocahontas) was applicable to the recurring national dialogue on race, gender, and national origin.

America attempted to find some consensus regarding the significance of Lewis and Clark's Indian benefactor in 1999 with the release of the Sacagawea coin. U.S. Mint officials had to negotiate some difficult questions: Was Sacagawea an American heroine worthy of adorning U.S. currency? Was she indispensable to the expedition or a feminine victim caught in a whirlwind of masculine heroics? Did she graciously open the door to Euro-American conquest, or did she commit treason against indigenous America? If she were celebrated, would that overshadow the reality of living Indian people? Could she be all of these things, and if so, what should she look like, and how should the coin be marketed? As the century came to a close, public officials attempted to decipher Sacagawea's significance to American nationalism.

In an effort to please as many Sacagawea enthusiasts as possible, the Mint devised the most inclusive coin selection process ever conducted. After consulting with Shoshone people, twenty-three artists were invited to submit designs. The winner was chosen by public vote on a mint website.[50] On May 4, 1999, in an extravagant unveiling at the White House, First Lady Hillary Clinton unveiled the chosen design by Glenna Goodacre. Important Native and non-Native dignitaries were in attendance to celebrate Sacagawea and to attempt to explain her legacy. Mrs. Clinton took the opportunity to honor all

The Sacagawea one-dollar coin

Native American women, past and present. She opened her comments by saying, "As we honor and remember the life and contributions of Sacagawea, we pay tribute as well to other Native American women who have carried on her role as path makers and breakers."[51] She also took an opportunity to acknowledge her husband's commitment to Native American issues by outlining programs that had been initiated by the Clinton administration.

At the same event Interior Assistant Secretary for Indian Affairs Kevin Gover (Pawnee) referred to Sacagawea as the "ultimate working mother." According to Gover she should be honored because she displayed the finest qualities of Native people, both yesterday and today. He said, "This coin is an excellent way to commemorate a remarkable woman and honor all Native Americans."[52] He expressed relief that the predominant image of Native Americans, which had been relegated to football helmets and baseball caps, was being replaced with the image of Sacagawea. Gover suggested that the coin would be a more appropriate representation of Indian people for future generations. His comment seemed optimistic. There has never been a successful one-dollar coin in the United States, and Sacagawea's has upheld this tradition.

The flexibility of Sacagawea's legend proved useful again at the dawn of the twenty-first century. On this occasion her image served to acknowledge and appreciate Indian women, Indian people, Indian policy, and working mothers. The introduction of the Sacagawea coin was not a celebration of the nineteenth-century woman; it was a celebration of the nation and its people in the twenty-first century. The legend of Sacagawea (like the legends of Malinche and Poca-hontas) has been used as a historical mirror to reflect a particular national image. The 1999 portrayal of Sacagawea reflected a tolerant and diverse nation, a nation in which Indian and non-Indian people worked together, and a nation of fine women and fine mothers. The Sacagawea coin illustrates the best of American character; she was strong enough to break from convention, brave enough to envision something better, and she carried the next generation forward.

We do not know what Sacagawea looked like, but her legend insists that she was beautiful. The artist who designed the coin said she wanted to show the beauty of a young Sacagawea looking back, as if beckoning to the rest of the expedition. Goodacre's Sacagawea is engaging as she looks over her shoulder. She is depicted as a nurturing mother, carrying baby Baptiste on her back. The Santa Fe artist chose a stunning twenty-three-year-old Shoshone woman as a model for Sacagawea's image on the coin. Contemporary main-stream America made its choice; we fancy a beautiful and nurturing Sacagawea, a woman that Native and non-Native people can cele-brate. Late-twentieth-century Americans saw no advantage in cloud-ing national perception with harsh realities or pesky inconsistencies. The introduction of the Sacagawea coin afforded contemporary Americans an opportunity to honor women, Indians, and a multi-cultural heritage.

CONCLUSION

A pattern emerges when you trace the mythic evolution of Malinche, Pocahontas, and Sacagawea. Each of their legends began in the tales told by the white men of conquest. These national heroes in the making mentioned the women merely as background figures for their courageous deeds. European invaders described them according to their own cultural definitions of the feminine and in reference to their goals in the New World. Malinche, Pocahontas, and Sacagawea were therefore presented as one-dimensional feminine characters to illustrate Indian acceptance and to justify European expansion. They were described as indigenous feminine helpmates who wanted the foreigners to succeed in their homeland.

Shirley Park Lowry has suggested that myths about women have routinely supported their lack of power in Western civilization.[1] According to Lowry, it was Christianity that defined women as help-mates for men. The foundation for this feminine stereotype is the Judeo-Christian creation story, in which man was made first in God's image. Woman was created as an afterthought, from a spare part of the man's body, to be his helper. Cortés, Smith, Lewis, and Clark understood and presented Malinche, Pocahontas, and Sacagawea as feminine helpers according to this Christian ideal. The men's prog-ress reports, journals, and remembrances celebrate white male exploits and their commitment to national development. Because of this Malinche, Pocahontas, and Sacagawea played the only feminine role Europeans understood: helpmate for man. They also conveniently represented uncivilized Indian societies that were in desperate need of Christian uplifting. These early records evolved into institution-alized explanations of national origin and social hierarchy.

European expansion into the New World was characterized at the time as a grand and glorious mission to benefit mankind. The Spaniards were extending Catholicism, saving souls, and putting an end to pagan worship and barbarous traditions. The English intro-duced Anglican Christianity, but more importantly, they brought economic development to an untamed world. And the Euro-American mission was to extend a democratic regime across the continent. All three nations characterized colonization as a noble pursuit in order to perfect humanity. The exploitation of New World resources was interpreted as a reward for their efforts.

The nationalist works of Ralph Waldo Emerson, Henry David Thoreau, and Henry James express a prevalent nineteenth-century rationalization for exploration and empire: a botched civilization in Europe motivated God to provide a New World, giving mankind another chance.[2] They portrayed the land as practically vacant and rich in natural resources. Those who went to develop a new Chris-tian paradise were characterized as a special breed with a special energy, self-reliant men who went forth with pure hearts. And God protected those who took up his special mission. He guided them and inspired them in the creation of new institutions; a purified society in the New World would serve as the moral guide for all others.[3] This myth of expansion legitimized an international com-petition to build empires across the sea. To the pride of their coun-tries, European male adventurers entered the perceived wilderness to establish new and improved societies. In this way the European primary accounts considered here all celebrate a moral mission in the New World.[4]

Early historical literature, compiled from Europeans' accounts of frontier encounters, has produced what historian David Weber charac-terizes as "lying histories."[5] These instructional stories explain colo-nial social hierarchy and justify European inheritance rights to the indigenous landscape. Malinche, Pocahontas, and Sacagawea emerge as gracious Indian princesses of noble birth who were drawn to European men and European cultures. They were unique to their race and became appropriate Native mothers for the imposed new culture. Smith's *The Generall Historie of Virginia, New England, and the Summer Isles* (written nearly two decades after his experiences in Virginia), Diaz's *The Discovery and Conquest of Mexico: 1517–1521* (which also had the benefit of hindsight), and Elliot Coues's abridged edition of the Lewis and Clark journals, entitled *History of the Expedition under the Command of Lewis and Clark,* illustrate this treatment of the women. These works celebrate the romance of an epic quest and the creation of new regimes. They are Eurocentric, masculine tales that describe an inevitable victory ordained by divine favor.

These fables evolved into national creation stories that launched national heroes and presented Malinche, Pocahontas, and Sacagawea as metaphors in an explanation of European dominance. The young, noble, and beautiful Indian women adopted and embraced the Euro-invaders. The women conveniently represent the feminine and the Indian components in emerging national narratives. As women, they were nurturing feminine admirers who helped European men. As Indians, they were portrayed as exceptional because they had the innate wisdom to adopt the newcomers and their superior culture. Malinche, Pocahontas, and Sacagawea demonstrated Indian potential, and it was unfortunate that other Indians failed to recognize European superiority.

When colonial communities in Mexico and the United States began to formulate nationalist perspectives independent of their mother countries, the legends of Malinche, Pocahontas, and Sacagawea were redrawn. They were no longer interpreted as noble exceptions to their race, but as part of admirable indigenous societies. Old World Europeans had often considered far-flung colonial societies inferior because of their isolation from the centers of Western culture. Colonists in the United States and Mexico offset this devalued status by creating unique and honorable American identities. Colonials in both nations began to expropriate Indian cultures for their own patriotic uses, at the same time elevating their representations of indigenous peoples. Nationalists no longer portrayed Indians as childlike creatures in need of guidance. Instead, Indians were described as dignified people who contributed to an evolving national identity, an identity that was unique to the New World paradise.

The noble savage appeared as an integral symbol during the nationalist eras in both Mexico and the United States as disgruntled colonists pushed for independence by forging an ideological bond with a distinguished indigenous past. Thus Creoles in Mexico began to advertise an Aztec Empire that rivaled ancient Old World societies in Rome and Greece; indigenous Mexicans were reimagined as impressive peoples with societies that were rich in culture, history, art, and architecture; and colonials in North America reinterpreted its Indian past as one in which noble savages lived in a pristine environment that was unspoiled by the excesses of European civilization. This virgin land had the power to redeem civilized men. Early nationalists in North America celebrated the nonaristocratic foundations of Native societies, portraying them as infant democracies.[6] English colonists imagined the New World as a garden of innovation where republican precepts could flourish; it was a perfect home for Enlightenment ideals. The indigenous world provided nationalists in Mexico and the United States with an opportunity for self-discovery and national distinction.

Nationalists in Mexico and the United States located their origins in an idealized Indian past, a prehistory that was completely independent of Europe. The infant nations adopted long Native histories as part of their own national story in an attempt to bind Indians and non-Indians together in a new national identity. Native cultural elements were idealized and celebrated as valuable ingredients in a new national culture. Early nationalist representations of the frontier period also explained how cumbersome Old World traditions could be modified and improved in the New World. The nationalists believed an independent country held the promise of perfecting the marred social institutions of Europe, particularly the arbitrary rule of a monarchy and a rigid social hierarchy. Their works glorified select elements of European and Native cultures, while denying unpleasant antecedents in both, to create a distinct cultural hybrid that forged a unique and unified nationalism. In this way Malinche, Pocahontas, and Sacagawea were mythologized as Native mothers who nurtured and softened this cultural syncretism. European settlers in the Americas described their chosen homeland as an environment brimming with potential that was being harnessed through their efforts.

The imagined cultural union between Europeans and Indians made the legacy of racial animosity difficult to explain, however. The United States and Mexico were both based on Enlightenment principles regarding the natural rights of man, but simultaneously denied Indian rights. This contradiction proved troublesome over time. Each nation devised and maintained frontier myths to address the complex racial legacies of its frontier past. For instance, a persistent myth in the United States explained how the pull of a supposedly vacant continent developed a national character of rugged individualism. This rationalization denied Indian rights to the land. Mexico could not make such a claim, as the large indigenous populations in Mexico forced Spain into commandeering huge cultural and administrative urban centers. Spain therefore layered its culture and religion over the already-existing elaborate indigenous cities and facilitated the process with miscegenation. The strategy in North America, on the other hand, was to dislodge, remove, and segregate Native peoples. Miscegenation was neither an official policy nor an acceptable solution to English or Euro-American settlers; they did not envision Indians as potential members of the new social structure, so they portrayed them as a disintegrating component of the indigenous landscape.[7] Mexican Indians were too numerous and could not be physically or ideologically phased out, so the Spanish adopted an imperial strategy of miscegenation, which sexualized the creation myth of Mexico and the legend of Malinche.

Race and gender came to be contentious issues in all three women's mythologies. The creative forces of Mexican nationalism invented a flexible Malinche/Cortés paradigm to postulate on issues of race and gender. On one side they are portrayed as social deviants who indulged in their own sexual gratification: Malinche was a Native whore whose lust for Cortés led her countrymen into destruction, and thus she has been objectified as a conquered female Indian and Cotés as a sexual conqueror. This portrayal of a Spanish rapist and a Native whore who sold out her people gave Mexico a twofold racial identity to reject. The violent Spanish father and the sexual Indian mother were renounced while the innocent by-product of their union, the mestizo, inherited and redeemed Mexico. Racial animosity was a complicated legacy of the Spanish conquest and the unfortunate result of Malinche's moral weakness (or gender weakness, according to Octavio Paz) and the brutality of Spanish conquistadors. An alternative national narrative explains a romantic love between Malinche and Cortés, a love that transcended racial boundaries and merged the best of two worlds. This portrayal celebrates racial mixing in Mexico and presents Malinche as the ultimate mother of modern mestizo Mexico. These two representations of national origin give Malinche a bipolar identity: she was a traitor/whore who brought devastation to Native Mexico, and she was the loving mother of a new race. Both creation myths spare the mestizo from blame. Just as the United States was able to deny its Indian reality with the myth of a vacant continent, Mexico was able to devise mythical explanations to deflect the reality of racial hostility.

A unique blend of Spanish and Native religious elements sculpted the gender ideology expressed in the Malinche narrative.[8] Two indomitable feminine powers are represented in her legend: the power to create and the power to destroy. Both creation myths (the birth of the mestizo and destruction of Native Mexico) encode social expectations. In Malinche's legend Mexicans not only find an explanation of gender and racial categories but also see an illustration of appropriate and inappropriate behavior. Over time those national definitions have been reexamined and periodically contested.

The legends of Pocahontas and Sacagawea are also applicable to discussions of race and gender, albeit in a different manner. Unlike Malinche, Pocahontas and Sacagawea were never considered whores, and their sexuality was not a major theme in the foundational narrative of the United States. Although they have not been portrayed as sexual objects, they were depicted as desirable females. And the extreme feminine powers that Malinche embodied in Mexico (creation and destruction) were not assigned to Pocahontas or Sacagawea. Racial demographics and religious particulars explain much of this difference. Because the North American landscape was characterized as vacant, Pocahontas and Sacagawea were less likely to be blamed for the fall of Native North America. Instead, they were immersed in America's tale of taming a virgin wilderness. Therefore as symbols, they did not need to engage a large Native or mixed-blood constituency. Pocahontas and Sacagawea were thus effectively isolated from their Native cultures to an extent that Malinche could not be. There was little incentive to synchronize Indian and non-Indian ideologies in United States. As representations of the feminine gender, Pocahontas and Sacagawea were characterized according to the gender standards of European culture; they were defined as the Native equivalent of the "good Victorian lady." According to this standard, they illustrated positive female attributes as they nurtured European men and the seeds of European civilization. They did not have the power to create or destroy, only to nurture.

Despite these differences, there is a striking similarity in how Mexico and the United States explain their national origins. Creation myths in both countries portray the birth of their nations through heterosexual love that gave Europeans paternity rights in the Americas. This love trope demonstrates how loving Indian princesses welcomed European men and adopted their alien civilizations. This foundational fiction was questioned almost immediately, however, beginning with the push for independence when European benevolence was recharacterized as European domination. Nationalist sentiments then began to portray European traditions and social hierarchies as exploitive and as a hindrance to national development. Over time European conquerors have been scrutinized, particularly the Spaniards and the Englishmen who were redrawn as European villains. Mestizos and Euro-Americans—those who remained—fared better. Cortés could be identified as a morally deficient and brutal rapist, and Smith as an egomaniac who repeatedly claimed that Indian women fell in love with him, but Lewis and Clark did not suffer the same level of skepticism because the United States was never forced to abandon its claim in America.

Cynicism has arisen periodically during moments of national crisis when national identity was being reevaluated (during the push for independence, epochs of internal strife, or struggles associated with modernity). Like earthquakes that relieve internal stress, national creation myths occasionally fracture to alleviate deep social tensions. At times of social unrest, the legends of all three women have experienced periods of interrogation. During Mexico's revolt for independence (1810–1821) and again during the Revolution (1910–1920), Malinche was rejected and excommunicated because of her association with the Spaniards. She became a biblical Eve character who was responsible for the fall of Native Mexico. Fifty years later Chicana feminists, who themselves were labeled malinchistas, attempted to remake Malinche to address their gender critique in the 1970s. The legend of Pocahontas was likewise debunked during the sectional ills of the 1860s. Virginia's national hero, John Smith, was accused of concocting the famous rescue scene for self-aggrandizement, thereby denying Pocahontas's contribution to the creation of America. In a similar manner, mid-twentieth-century historians and commentators debunked earlier suffragist interpretations of Sacagawea. Sacagawea detractors insisted she was an Indian woman with no particular merit, whose presence was not essential to the success of Lewis and Clark. These phases of skepticism were a response to contemporary social antagonisms and a backlash against earlier celebrationist histories. Cynicism flourished during epochs of social discontent when national identity and national standards of race and gender were being readjusted.

During the 1980s and 1990s the legitimacy of their legends was again questioned. Some second-wave feminists suggested that Malinche, Pocahontas, and Sacagawea were nothing more than male fantasies of beautiful and adoring Native women decorating masculine adventure stories. Other feminist scholars used their historical narratives to illustrate the universal exploitation of women, presenting them as feminine slaves exploited by Indian and non-Indian men. All three women have been described as women who were exceedingly vulnerable to the sexual interests of the men around them. I do not deny the possibility that Malinche, Pocahontas, and Sacagawea may have experienced unwanted sexual encounters. But I am suggesting that these women viewed their sexuality in vastly different ways from our own modern sensibilities, and their significance to frontier contact went well beyond their sexual activities. The legends of all three women have been extraordinarily useful to generational debates on race and gender. Scholars and commentators have relentlessly manipulated their legends to support contemporary social agendas: to legitimize or condemn conquest, to evaluate social categories of race or gender, and to redefine national identity.

The construction of nationalism is an ongoing project; it changes over time according to contemporary social tensions. Successive generations have reinterpreted national origin in order to maintain or transform national sentiments. National creation myths were invented within a European masculine domain of exploration and frontier conquest, but ongoing manipulation of these stories has not been the exclusive prerogative of male elites. Instead, competing narratives have emerged from diverse social factions. Disgruntled nationalists constructed a frontier myth to build unity during the independence movement. Creoles and mestizos transformed the myth to proclaim their innocence and explain their claim to Mexico. Native American scholars, feminist and Chicana scholars, and gay and lesbian scholars have also reimagined national creation myths for personal reflection and relevance during the twentieth century. Alternative renditions have periodically interrupted, if not debunked, prevailing social explanations. Through this long process Malinche, Pocahontas, and Sacagawea have become ingrained in the national consciousness and entrenched in a system of political mythology, yet their lives as Indian female intermediaries have largely been irrelevant.

After hundreds of years Malinche, Pocahontas and Sacagawea are still relevant figures in Mexico and the United States. Their stories have never been confined to the realm of history; rather they exist in the nebulous and eternal world of symbolism and myth. Examination of Malinche, Pocahontas, and Sacagawea illustrate the intersection of race and gender during the moment of frontier contact and in the continuing development of national mythology. We need these women. They are the symbolic mothers of the Americas; they are mothers we love and mothers we fight with. They can be credited and blamed for who we have become.

NOTES

INTRODUCTION

1. Cabeza de Vaca made this observation during an eight-year overland trek across the southern part of North America from the Gulf Coast of Florida to New Spain in Mexico City. See Cabeza de Vaca, *Adventures in the Unknown Interior of America*, trans. Cyclone Covey (Albuquerque: University of New Mexico Press, 1998), 112.

2. Discussion of the discrepancies and confusion surrounding Sacagawea's death is taken up in chapter 4 and again in chapter 7.

3. Robert Grumet, "Sunksquaws, Shamans and Tradeswomen: Middle Atlantic Coastal Algonkian Women during the 17th and 18th Centuries," in *Women and Colonization: Anthropological Perspectives*, ed. Mona Etienne and Eleanore Leacock (New York: Praeger, 1980), 49. Grumet points to several primary sources that indicate Native women's ability to inherit the office of chief and influence the outcome of Native councils. Paula Gunn Allen discusses this point in *The Sacred Hoop: Recovering the Feminine in American Indian Traditions* (Boston: Beacon, 1986), 35–36.

4. Historians have debated the spelling, pronunciation, and translation of these women's names, yet Indian naming practices were complicated. There are several names associated with each woman, indicating that their names changed according to various stages in their lives (childhood, entry into a clan or other group). For this reason, I chose to use the names that most readers recognize. More detailed discussion of the Indian women's names occurs throughout this book.

5. For an explanation of nationalist ideologies of race and gender and how those ideologies cooperated with one another to justify white male supremacy, see Rebecca Blevins Faery, *Cartographies of Desire: Captivity, Race, and Sex in the Shaping of an American Nation* (Norman: University of Oklahoma Press, 1999), 9; Jane Tompkins, "Indians: Textualism, Morality, and the Problem of History," in *"Race," Writing and Difference*, ed. Henry Louis Gates, Jr., (Chicago: University of Chicago Press, 1986), 59–77; Jane Tompkins, *Sensational Designs: The Cultural Work of American Fiction, 1790–1860* (New York: Oxford University Press, 1985), xvii.

6. Tompkins, *Sensational Designs*, xi–xii.

7. Richard Slotkin, *Gunfighter Nation: The Myth of the Frontier in Twentieth-Century America* (New York: Harper Collins, 1992), 655.

8. Kent Ladd Steckmesser makes a similar point in his study of male frontier heroes. See *The Western Hero in History and Legend* (Norman: University of Oklahoma Press, 1997), viii.

9. Richard White, *The Middle Ground: Indians, Empires, and Republics in the Great Lakes Region, 1650–1815* (Cambridge: Cambridge University Press, 1991).

10. Lillian Ackerman has contributed a particularly impressive analysis of Native gender systems on the Columbia Plateau. See Ackerman, *A Necessary Balance: Gender and Power among Indians of the Columbia Plateau* (Norman: University of Oklahoma Press, 2003).

11. William Hart, "Black 'Go-Betweens' and the Mutability of Race, Status, and Identity on New York's Pre-Revolutionary Frontier," in *Contact Points: American Frontiers from the Mohawk to the Mississippi, 1750–1830,* ed. Andrew R. L. Cayton and Fredrika J. Teute (Chapel Hill: University of North Carolina Press, 1998), 88–112.

CHAPTER 1

1. For basic archaeological information on the city of Teotihuacan and the people who lived there, see Rene Millon, "The Place Where Time Began: An Archaeologists Interpretation of What Happened in Teotihuacan History," in *Teotihuacan: Art from the City of the Gods,* ed. Kathleen Berrin and Esther Pasztory (New York: Thames and Hudson, 1993), 16–43.

2. For a brief history of Teotihuacan's rise and fall, see Alan Knight, *Mexico: From the Beginning to the Spanish Conquest* (Cambridge: Cambridge University Press, 2002), 52–54, 104–107; Miguel León-Portilla, *The Broken Spears: The Aztec Account of the Conquest of Mexico* (Boston: Beacon, 1962), x–xiii; and Richard Townsend, *The Aztecs* (New York: Thames and Hudson, 1992), 46.

3. The original name has not yet been deciphered from the ancient hieroglyph system. See Townsend, *The Aztecs,* 37.

4. This explanation of Mexican prehistory is based on the following sources: León-Portilla, *The Broken Spears*; Townsend, *The Aztecs*; Diego Durán, *The History of the Indies of New Spain,* trans. Doris Heyden (Norman: University of Oklahoma Press, 1994); Francis F. Berdan and Patricia Rieff Anawalt, *Codex Mendoza,* vol. 4 (Berkeley: University of California Press, 1992); Knight, *Mexico.*

5. León-Portilla, *The Broken Spears,* xx, and Townsend, *The Aztecs,* 61.

6. See Knight, *Mexico,* 119–31.

7. There will be more discussion on Quetzalcoatl, in relation to his prophesized return in 1519, in the next chapter. For more on Quetzalcoatl as a central deity among the Toltecs, see Townsend, *The Aztecs,* 46; León-Portilla, *The Broken Spears,* xii; and Knight, *Mexico,* 123, 130. For a more complete history of Tula, see Richard Diehl's *Tula: The Toltec Capital of Ancient Mexico* (1983).

8. There are many accounts of the foundation of Tenochtitlán. See León-Portilla, *The Broken Spears*, xiv, and Townsend, *The Aztecs*, 76–78. For a Nahuatl historical source, see the *Codex Chimalpahin* or Fray Bernardino de Sahagún, *Florentine Codex*, trans. Arthur J. O. Anderson and Charles E. Dibble (Salt Lake City: School of American Research and University of Utah, 1982). For a description of Tenochtitlán and Mexica social organization, see Caroline Dodds Pennock, *Bonds of Blood: Gender, Lifecycle, and Sacrifice in Aztec Culture* (New York: Palgrave Macmillan, 2008), 55–58, and James Lockhart, *We People Here: Nahuatl Accounts of the Conquest of Mexico* (Eugene, Ore.: Wipf and Stock, 2004), 24–26. See also Knight, *Mexico*, 143–63.

9. Townsend, *The Aztecs*, 209–10.

10. Durán, *The History of the Indies of New Spain*, 213–14. Townsend addresses the story of Aztlán in *The Aztecs*, 55–56.

11. This rendition of the Aztec rise to greatness is described in León-Portilla, *The Broken Spears*, xxi. See also Townsend, *The Aztecs*, 54–110. Knight gives a powerful description of Aztec state building in the Valley of Mexico in *Mexico*, 132–63; Knight specifically addresses Tlacael's ideological reformation on p. 146.

12. León-Portilla, *The Broken Spears*, xxi. Caroline Dodds Pennock discusses Huitzilopochtli in relation to war and sacrifice in *Bonds of Blood*, 14–16, 21, 161, 169. Townsend traces the legend of Huitzilopochtli to the migration of the Mexicas into the Valley of Mexico prior to being deified in Townsend, *The Aztecs*, 57–63.

13. See Fray Diego Durán, *Book of the Gods and Rites and the Ancient Calendar*, trans. Fernando Horcasitas and Doris Heyden (Norman: University of Oklahoma Press, 1971), 90–95.

14. As Bernal Díaz moved throughout the Valley of Mexico, he recorded his ever-present fear of being sacrificed; for an example, see Díaz, *Conquest of New Spain*, trans. J. M. Chen (New York: Penguin, 1963), 236–37.

15. Jerome Offner, *Law and Politics in Aztec Texcoco* (Cambridge: Cambridge University Press, 1988), 88–95.

16. Frances F. Berdan et al., *Aztec Imperial Strategies* (Washington, D.C.: Dumbarton Oaks, 1996).

17. See Townsend, *The Aztecs*, 67–69; Knight, *Mexico*, 144–46.

18. See Knight, *Mexico*, 166–67.

19. Ibid., 173. See also Berdan et al., *Aztec Imperial Strategies*.

20. See Townsend, *The Aztecs*, 94–96.

21. Ibid., 97–100.

22. It is important to bear in mind that several important factors led to the Spanish victory, despite their inferior numbers, including Spanish technological advantages in war making, Native religious particulars (which will be discussed shortly), and intense cultural disruption as a result of relentless European disease. Malinche has often been both credited and blamed for indigenous defeat, yet most contemporary scholars have identified her as a victim and slave of the Spaniards. Malinche's role as translator is considered by linguist Anna Lanyon in *Malinche's Conquest* (St.

Leonards, N.S.W.: Allen and Unwin, 1999). For Lanyon's reference to Malinche's explanation of Aztec tribute collectors, see p. 80, and for Malinche's role in Spaniards' alliance with Tlaxcalans, see p. 100. Díaz mentions Malinche's role as a diplomat in *The Conquest of New Spain*. See p. 135 for her participation in the area of "Socochitna," p. 147 for description of her negotiating in the area of Tlaxcala, and p. 247 for her negotiation with Moctezuma in Tenochtitlan.

23. This characterization of the Aztec empire is discussed in Brian Fagan, "If Columbus Had Not Called," *History Today* 42 (1992): 30–36.

24. Bernal Díaz del Castillo was a lowly foot soldier in Cortés's army. His work is the best Spanish primary source on the conquest of Mexico. His story, although written almost thirty years after the conquest, offers a complex narrative of the cultural collision in Mexico. He attempts to explain Indian perspectives and motivations. He acknowledges the violence of the frontier, although he firmly believed in his divine mission to bring Christianity to Natives. He does not present himself as a hero but as a humble eyewitness, and it is from Díaz that we learn the most about Malinche. See Bernal Díaz del Castillo, *The Discovery and Conquest of Mexico: 1517–1521*, trans. A. P. Maudslay (London: Percy Lund, Humphries, 1933). There are many editions of his book. In addition to the Maudslay edition, I consulted two others: the 1963 Cohen translation cited above (Díaz, *The Conquest of New Spain*) and a Spanish edition entitled *Historia Verdadera de la Conquista de la Nueva España: Por Bernal Díaz Del Castilla, Uno de sus Conquistadores* (Mexico City: Ediciones Mexicanas S. A., 1950). Díaz introduces Malinche as a main character in the events of the conquest. Much of Díaz's information on Malinche was corroborated by other conquistadors as well as their children and grandchildren. See Andres de Tapia and Francisco de Aguilar, *The Conquistadors: First-Person Accounts of the Conquest of Mexico*, ed. and trans. Patricia de Fuentes (New York: Orion, 1963), 24, 138, 141.

25. Díaz, *The Conquest of New Spain*, 82.

26. For an explanation of Aztec education system, see Townsend, *The Aztecs*, 158–64. For an example of Native women's obligations and rights in early Mexico, see Sahagún, *Florentine Codex*, 10:1–57; S. D. McCafferty and G. D. McCafferty, "Powerful Women and the Myth of Male Dominance in Aztec Society," *Archaeological Review from Cambridge* 7 (1988): 45–59; and L. M. Burkhart, "Gender in Nahuatl Text of the Early Colonial Period: Native Tradition and the Dialogue with Christianity," in *Gender in Pre-Hispanic America*, ed. C. F. Klein (Washington, D.C.: Dumbarton Oaks, 2001).

27. For a discussion of women in Mexica society, including inheritance rights, see Susan Kellogg, "The Woman's Room: Some Aspects of Gender Relations in Tenochtitlán in the Late Pre-Hispanic Period," *Ethnohistory* 42, no. 4 (1995): 563–71.

28. This description of Malinche's early life can be found in Díaz, *The Conquest of New Spain*, 82–85.

29. Ibid., 82.

30. The Yucatan's chief exports were cotton and other cloths, salt, honey, beeswax, and slaves. For more on Aztec economy and production, see R. Hassig, *Trade,*

Tribute and Transportation: The Sixteenth-Century Political Economy of the Valley of Mexico (Norman: University of Oklahoma Press, 1985).

31. See Frances Karttunen, "Rethinking Malinche," in *Indian Women of Early Mexico*, ed. Susan Schroeder, Stephanie Wood, and Robert Haskett (Norman: University of Oklahoma Press, 1997), 301.

32. For explanation of the informants Sahagún used, see Sahagún, *Florentine Codex*, 1:9–23.

33. For Sahagún's various definitions of the feminine, see ibid., 10:2–3.

34. For Sahagún's definition of a "procuress," see ibid., 10:57.

35. This quote is taken from Fray Bautista, *Huehuetlatolli*, which is excerpted in Arthur J. O. Anderson, "Aztec Wives," in Schroeder, Wood, and Haskett, *Indian Women of Early Mexico*, 76.

36. Louise Burkhart, "Mexica Women on the Home Front" in Schroeder, Wood, and Haskett, *Indian Women of Early Mexico*, 25–54.

37. Ibid., 25. For an interesting portrait of goddesses in precolonial Mesoamerica, see Durán, *Book of the Gods and Rites*, 210–52. For an expanded discussion of the power of the feminine in precolonial cultures, see McCafferty and McCafferty, "Powerful Women and the Myth of Male Dominance in Aztec Society," 45–59; Pennock, *Bonds of Blood*; and Irene Silverplatt, *Moon, Sun, and Witches: Gender Ideologies and Class in Inca and Colonial Peru* (Princeton: Princeton University Press, 1987).

38. *Codex Mendoza* was commissioned by the Viceroy of New Spain, Antonio Mendoza, and it, too, was compiled within a generation after the conquest.

39. Alonso de Zorita, *Life and Labor in Ancient Mexico: The Brief and Summary Relation of the Lord of New Spain*, ed. and trans. Benjamin Keen (New Brunswick: Rutgers University Press, 1963), 136–37.

40. Ibid., 147–48.

41. This quote is taken from Bautista, *Huehuetlatolli*, which is excerpted in Anderson, "Aztec Wives," 60

42. Ibid.

43. Ibid., 62.

44. For an explanation of precontact Algonquian lifeways, see William Strachey, *Historie of Travell Into Virginia Britania, 1612*, ed. Louis B. Wright and Virginia Freund (London: Hakluyt, 1953), 53–56; Helen Rountree, *The Powhatan Indians of Virginia: Their Traditional Culture* (Norman: University of Oklahoma Press, 1989); Helen Rountree, *Pocahontas's People: The Powhatan Indians of Virginia through Four Centuries* (Norman: University of Oklahoma Press, 1990); Helen Rountree and Randolph Turner III, *Before and After Jamestown: Virginia's Powhatans and their Predecessors* (Gainesville: University Press of Florida, 2002).

45. Strachey, *Historie of Travell*, 79–81.

46. Appropriate terminology to describe Powhatan political organization has been a point of scholarly contention. Non-Natives have described Tsenacommacah as an empire, a confederacy, and a monarchy. It has proved problematic to categorize Native institutions according to non-Native ideologies and social structures. See

scholarly squabbles and attempts to label the Powhatan political and diplomatic structures in Frederic W. Gleach, *Powhatan's World and Colonial Virginia: A Conflict of Cultures* (Lincoln: University of Nebraska Press, 1997), 22–24; Rountree, *The Powhatan Indians of Virginia*, 140–44.

47. Unlike Nahuatl, the Powhatan language was not recorded by early Europeans and was nearly extinct by 1800. Smith and Strachey preserved a few Native words in their accounts, but understanding the language is problematic. This description of Chief Powhatan as the chief dreamer, the keeper of many spirits, and the leader in tune with what would please the gods has been accepted by several historians including Margaret Holmes Williamson, *Powhatan Lords of Life and Death* (Lincoln: University of Nebraska Press, 2003), 206; Camilla Townsend, *Pocahontas and the Powhatan Dilemma* (New York: Hill and Wang, 2004), 21; and Paula Gunn Allen, *Pocahontas: Medicine Woman, Spy, Entrepreneur and Diplomat* (San Francisco: Harper, 2003), 65.

48. Because much of the Powhatan language has been lost, the best translation for Manito is "the spirit" or "spirits." See Williamson, *Powhatan Lords of Life and Death*, 176, and Allen, *Pocahontas*, 210–11.

49. For description of intertribal alliances and political structure within Tsenacommacah, see Rountree, *Pocahontas's People*, 10–11; Gleach, *Powhatan's World*, 26–35; and Williamson, *Powhatan Lords of Life and Death*, 47–72.

50. For more on the power of the chief and how Powhatan people regarded him, see Strachey, *Historie of Travell*, 59–60, 63–69; John Smith, *The Complete Works of Captain John Smith 1580–1631*, ed. Philip Barbour (Chapel Hill: University of North Carolina Press, 1986), 2:127; Williamson, *Powhatan Lords of Life and Death*, 205–206; and Allen, *Pocahontas*, 21–22.

51. Strachey, *Historie of Travell*, 104–105. Helen Rountree dismisses Strachey's account of the prophecy by suggesting, "he may not have known what he was talking about." See Rountree, *The Powhatan Indians of Virginia*, 120n69. The scholarly skepticism over Native explanations for European entrance in the New World is routine. The Nahua prophecy of Quetzalcoatl's return that was recorded by Bernal Díaz has also been dismissed by contemporary scholars of Mesoamerica. The circumstances of Nahua prophecy will be taken up chapter 2.

52. Strachey, *Historie of Travell*, 61. For more on marriages and polygamy, see Rountree, *Powhatan Indians of Virginia*, 90–93; and Williamson, *Powhatan Lords of Life and Death*, 67–72, 162–64.

53. Smith, *The Complete Works*, 1:174, and Strachey, *Historie of Travell*, 61.

54. This translation is according to Chief Roy Crazy Horse of the Powhatan Renape Nation at the reservation visitor center in New Jersey. He prepared a visitor center flier, "The Pocahontas Myth" (Rankokus, N.J.: Powhatan Renape Nation), 1995, to provide a Powhatan version of Pocahontas's life (also available at www.powhatan.org). Paula Gunn Allen translates Pocahontas to mean "playful, mischievousness, trickster and intelligent" in *Pocahontas*, 32. For an explanation of all four of her names

(Pocahontas, Matoaka, Amonute, and Rebecca), see Townsend, *Pocahontas and the Powhatan Dilemma*, 13–14.

55. Strachey, *Historie of Travell*, 62.

56. Ibid., 84.

57. For an explanation of marriage, sex roles, and family life in Powhatan culture, see Rountree, *Powhatan Indians of Virginia*, 89–99, and Williamson, *Powhatan Lords of Life and Death*, 214–17.

58. See Williamson, *Powhatan Lords of Life and Death*, 64–71, for more on political alliances by marriage.

59. In late Tudor and early Stuart England, the state defined wives and children as the property of men. Husbands were positioned ahead of wives in the social hierarchy and as heads of the estate. The reality of settlers' lives in the Americas deviated from this gender structure. Marriages were seen more as partnerships, although not equal partnerships—men were still the authority, yet colonial women took on more economic responsibilities. There were more female-headed families in colonial Jamestown due to widowhood, and these surviving women took charge of the family's estate. For an interesting treatment of English immigrants in eastern North America and their attitudes toward marriage and family, see James Horn, *Adapting to a New World* (North Carolina: University of North Carolina Press, 1994), 204–34.

60. See Smith, *The Complete Works*, 1:162; Strachey, *Historie of Travell*, 114–15; and Rountree, *Powhatan Indians of Virginia*, 88–89.

61. The famous rescue scene that Smith retold will be discussed in depth in the following chapter, but for another example of Pocahontas serving in a diplomatic capacity, see Smith, *The Complete Works*, 1:93. See also Williamson, *Powhatan Lords of Life and Death*, 215–16. Allen depicts much of Pocahontas's interactions among the English as diplomatic service in *Pocahontas*.

62. Rountree provides an interesting analysis of manliness in chap. 4 of *Powhatan Indians of Virginia*, 79–87. According to her anthropological study, men were under considerable pressure to perform their duties with success, particularly hunting and extracting vengeance.

63. Rose Anne Abrahamson, a Lemhi Shoshone woman and seventh-generation descendent of Sacagawea's brother, in oral interview with the author, April 15, 1998.

64. According to Lewis and Clark's journals, Charbonneau used the Hidatsa rendition of Sacagawea's name to introduce her to Lewis and Clark. All of the journal entries considered in this work have been taken from Gary Moulton, ed., *The Journals of the Lewis and Clark Expedition*, by Meriwether Lewis and William Clark, 13 vols. (Lincoln: University of Nebraska Press, 1983). The two American captains usually refer to her as "squaw," "Indian woman," or "Janey" for convenience. Because Sacagawea has been the most used version of her name, it is the version I use in this study. An in-depth explanation of her name is provided by Irving Anderson, "Sacajawea, Sacagawea, Sakakawea?" *South Dakota History*, 8 (1978): 303–11; Bob

Saindon, "Sacajawea: Boat-Launcher, the Origin and Meaning of A Name . . . Maybe," *We Proceeded On* (August 1988): 5–10; John E. Rees, *Madame Charbonneau the Indian Woman Who Accompanied the Lewis and Clark Expedition 1804–1806, How She Received Her Indian Name and What Became of Her* (Salmon, Idaho: Lemhi County Historical Society, 1970).

65. The Shoshone claim is particularly relevant to a contemporary political dispute over federal tribal recognition and compensation for illegal land seizure. For an explanation of Shoshone identity, prehistory, and contemporary issues, see John W. Mann, *Sacajawea's People: The Lemhi Shoshone and the Salmon River Country* (Lincoln: University of Nebraska Press, 2004); Steven Crum, *The Road on Which We Came: A History of the Western Shoshone* (Salt Lake City: University of Utah Press, 1994).

66. There are several variations of Shoshone creation stories; this one can be found in Mann, *Sacagawea's People*, 7–8.

67. See Crum, *The Road on Which We Came*, 1.

68. For an interesting examination of the plains as a highly diverse and intermixed region, see Theodore Binnema, *Common and Contested Ground: A Human and Environmental History of the Northwestern Plains* (Norman: Oklahoma Press, 2001).

69. Access to horses was largely determined by the group's proximity to Indian tribes within the Spanish trade networks. Environmental factors determined the group's level of success in raising horses. See Binnema, *Common and Contested Ground*, 140–41.

70. For an interesting treatment on how European traders interacted and traded with Natives, see Arthur Ray, *Indians in the Fur Trade: Their Roles as Trapper, Hunter, and Middlemen in the Land Southwest of Hudson Bay 1660–1870* (Toronto: University of Toronto Press, 1998).

71. See Virginia Bergman Peters, *Women of the Earth Lodges: Tribal Life on the Plains* (Norman: University of Oklahoma Press, 1995), 143–57, for an examination of the plains trade network and women's roles in particular.

72. See ibid.,155–57, and Katherine M. Weist, "Beasts of Burden and Menial Slaves," in *The Hidden Half: Studies of Plains Indian Women*, ed. Patricia Albers and Beatrice Medicine (Washington, D.C.: University Press of America, 1983), 43.

73. See Alan Kline, "The Political Economy of Gender: A 19th Century Plains Indian Case Study," in Albers and Medicine, *The Hidden Half*, 143–73. Joseph Jablow argued in the 1950s that this trade introduced dramatic changes in patterns of authority among the Cheyennes. See Jablow, *The Cheyenne in Plains Indian Trade Relations 1795–1840* (New York: J. J. Augustin, 1950).

74. For a discussion of gender concerning female tasks among Plains Indians, see Weist, "Beasts of Burden and Menial Slaves," 29–52, and Janet Spector, "Male/Female Task Differentiation among the Hidatsa: Toward the Development of an Archeological Approach to the Study of Gender," in Albers and Medicine, *The Hidden Half*, 77–99. Both of these essays illustrate the work conducted by Plains Indian women and how their "manly" work (production of food and construction of village dwellings) was misinterpreted by Euro-centered ethnographers during the early

reservation period. According to these early ethnographers who were sent out to record Indian lifeways, the arduous work conducted by Plains women did not reveal their independence or strength; rather, it classified them as oppressed and enslaved by "slothful" Indian men. For an interesting excursion into the European cultural bias that shaped this beast-of-burden perspective of Indian women, see Alice Kehoe, "The Shackles of Tradition," in Albers and Medicine, *The Hidden Half*, 53–73. Kehoe analyzes how Eurocentric, middle-class-educated ethnographers were constrained by their gender notions of a good Victorian woman. These record keepers contrasted overworked industrious Indian women with the model of a good Victorian woman in European "civilized society": she was a decoration that adorned her husband's accomplishments, her work was unnecessary, she was incapable of strenuous labor, and dependent on her husband (see pp. 56–57). According to this upper-middle-class gender expectation of leisured women, workingwomen (especially hard-working Indian women) were low-class women. Kehoe also recognizes the fact that the early ethnographers overwhelmingly preferred to interview Indian men, and that by 1900 Indian women had grown "accustomed to being put down by Euro-American men" and avoided discussions with the outsiders (see p. 54). A gender analysis of the female cultural intermediary will be taken up in chapter 4 of this work, and the mythology of Indian women's oppressive workload will be taken up in chapter 5.

75. There are some fascinating fur trapper journals that provide scattered observations on Plains Indian women and the heavy work they shouldered. See Henry Marie Brackenridge, "Views of Louisiana: Together with a Journal of a Voyage up the Missouri in 1811," in *Early Western Travels, 1748–1846*, ed. Reuben Gold Thwaites, vol. 6 (Chicago: Quadrangle, 1962); John Bradbury, *Travels in the Interior of America in the Years 1809, 1810, 1811* (Lincoln: University of Nebraska Press, 1986). See also Moulton, ed., *Journals*. Further discussion of non-Indian firsthand accounts of Plains Indian women will be discussed in the next chapter and again during the discussion of myth in chapter 5.

76. See Moulton, ed., *Journals*, 5:120

77. For an interesting discussion of masculine honor and shame in the taking of captives, see James Brooks, *Captives and Cousins: Slavery, Kinship, and Community in the Southwest Borderlands* (Chapel Hill: University of North Carolina Press, 2002), 22–27.

78. For explanations of Hidatsa culture and lifeways, see Alfred W. Bowers, *Hidatsa Social and Ceremonial Organization* (Washington, D.C.: U.S. Government Printing Office, 1965). For special attention to women's duties, see Jeffery Hanson, introduction to *Buffalo Bird Woman's Garden: Agriculture of the Hidatsa Indians*, by Gilbert Wilson (St. Paul: Minnesota Historical Society Press, 1987), and Binnema, *Common and Contested Ground*.

79. See George Will and George Hyde, *Corn among the Indians of the Upper Missouri* (Lincoln: University of Nebraska Press, 1964), and Peters, *Women of the Earth Lodges*, 108–24.

80. Peters, *Women of the Earth Lodges,* 146.

81. Bowers, *Hidatsa Social and Ceremonial Organization,* 199–207. For another example of female power and participation in religious ceremonies on the Northwest Plains, see Alice Kehoe, "Blackfoot Persons," in *Women and Power in Native North America,* ed. Laura F. Kline and Lillian Ackerman (Norman: University of Oklahoma Press, 1995), 113–25.

82. Bowers, *Hidatsa Social and Ceremonial Organization,* 199–207; Peters *Women of the Earth Lodges,* 79.

83. This characterization of young women's approach to men and community was originally given to Dr. Melvin Gilmore during a 1926 oral interview with an Arikara midwife informant. Gilmore's study resulted in an article entitled "Notes on Gynecology and Obstetrics of the Arikara Tribe of Indians," *Papers of the Michigan Academy of Science, Arts and Letters* 14 (1931): 71–81. The passage is reprinted in Peters, *Women of the Earth Lodges,* 75.

84. See Weist, "Beasts of Burden and Menial Slaves," 29–46. The next chapter will discuss and provide examples of Euro-invaders' descriptions of Indian women.

85. See Peters, *Women of the Earth Lodges,* 153.

CHAPTER 2

1. For a description of Aguilar's experience, see Díaz, *The Conquest of New Spain,* 59–61. Aguilar spoke Mayan and was a link in the chain of communication. Malinche translated Nahuatl into Mayan, and Aguilar translated Mayan into Spanish; the system reversed as the conversation progressed. Díaz acknowledges the skillful manner in which Aguilar and Malinche communicated the Spanish message to Native peoples.

2. This description is based on Díaz, *The Conquest of New Spain,* 69.

3. Ibid., 75.

4. Ibid., 77.

5. Díaz comments on this custom several times; for an example, see *The Conquest of New Spain,* 175. See also Townsend, *The Aztecs,* 65.

6. Díaz, *The Conquest of New Spain,* 82.

7. Hernán Cortés, *Letters from Mexico,* trans. Anthony Pagden (New Haven, Yale University Press, 1968), 376.

8. See Cortés, *Letters From Mexico,* 73.

9. Díaz, *The Conquest of New Spain,* 196–97.

10. Ibid., 214.

11. Ibid., 215.

12. Ibid., 247.

13. Cortés, *Letters from Mexico,* 246.

14. For a discussion of the Spaniards' technological advantage, see Camilla Townsend, "Burying the White Gods: New Perspectives on the Conquest of Mexico,"

American Historical Review 108, no. 3 (2002): 658–87. Townsend highlights the Spaniards' material advantage to disprove an indigenous explanation for Spanish victory from the postconquest era that suggested Mexicans interpreted Cortés as the return of Quetzalcoatl.

15. Alfonso Caso originally pointed out the Aztec succession of the ages in his work *The Aztecs: People of the Sun,* trans. Lowell Dunham (Norman: Oklahoma Press, 1958). León-Portilla discusses the cyclical nature of the Aztec belief system in his introduction to *The Broken Spears,* as does Charles E. Dibble in *The Conquest through Aztec Eyes* (Salt Lake City: University of Utah Press, 1978). Richard Townsend addresses this rise and fall of civilizations in "The Aztec Symbolic World," chap. 7 in *The Aztecs,* 122–28. See Pennock, *Bonds of Blood,* 28–29, for a gender interpretation of creation cycles.

16. Durán, *History of the Indies of New Spain,* 445; Townsend, *The Aztecs,* 119–20.

17. Susan Gillespie, *The Aztec Kings: The Construction of Rulership in Mexica History* (Tucson: University of Arizona Press, 1989), 173–207.

18. See Durán, *History of the Indies of New Spain,* 497–98; Townsend, *The Aztecs,* 123–25; Dibble, *The Conquest through Aztec Eyes,* 15–17. Sahagún makes similar references to this in book twelve of the *Florentine Codex,* particularly in chaps. 2, 3, and 16. On several occasions in *The Conquest of New Spain* (220, 223) Díaz recorded how the Spanish were often referred to as the gods who had been destined to return to the Valley of Mexico.

19. See Lockhart, *We People Here,* 20–21; Townsend, *The Aztecs,* 116.

20. It must be remembered that Díaz wrote many years after the conquest, after the prophecy of Quetzalcoatl's return was a widely accepted and an often-repeated explanation for indigenous defeat. See Díaz, *The Conquest of New Spain,* 220.

21. Townsend, *The Aztecs,* 22–25.

22. See introduction to Lockhart, *We People Here,* 1–46.

23. See Jerald T. Milanich, *Laboring in the Fields of the Lord: Spanish Missions and Southeast Indians* (Gainesville: University of Florida Press, 2006), 98–99. European interlopers routinely captured, or otherwise acquired, male and female adolescents who could learn a new language quickly, while retaining their own, and thus could become useful as interpreters. As noted previously, Sahuagún's young male informants helped the friar penetrate and record Mesoamerican social structures in the 1530s. Being a cultural intermediary was rigorous work that required tremendous physical and intellectual stamina. Don Luis, Sahagún's interpreters, Malinche, Pocahontas, and Sacagawea were all young indigenous cultural intermediaries and interpreters who worked to bridge the gap between people of the New World and people of the Old World.

24. For an explanation of Don Luis and the punitive force sent to avenge the deaths of the Spanish missionaries, see Rountree and Turner, *Before and After Jamestown,* 50–51.

25. Strachey, *Historie of Travell,* 104–105.

26. Smith's description is taken from Smith, *The Generall Historie of Virginia, New England, and the Summer Isles,* which was reprinted in two texts: Edward Arber,

ed., *Travels and Works of John Smith: President of Virginia and Admiral of New England 1580–1631* (Edinburgh: John Grant, 1910), 2:400, and Philip Barbour, ed., *The Complete Works of Captain John Smith 1580–1631*, (Chapel Hill: University of North Carolina Press, 1986), 2:127, both of which were consulted for this study.

27. According the ethnographic research presented in Allen's book *Pocahontas*, some of the distinguished women were Beloved Women, including Pocahontas. Beloved Women are discussed at length in chapter 3 of this book. See Allen, *Pocahontas*, 111–12.

28. For a description of the Nikomis ceremony and its significance, see ibid., 42–54.

29. Rountree and Turner, *Before and After Jamestown*, 34.

30. This was a reality made clear throughout Smith's account. See Smith, *The Complete Works*, vols. 1 and 2. This point has been reinforced by later sources as well. See Rountree, *Pocahontas's People*, 29, and Rountree and Turner, *Before and After Jamestown*, 127.

31. See Smith, *Travels and Works*, 1:154.

32. Ibid., 155; Mossiker, *Pocahontas*, 118.

33. Smith, *Travels and Works*, 1:106.

34. Ibid., 1:106–107.

35. Ibid., 1:121–25.

36. Ibid., 1:127.

37. Ibid., 1:130–39.

38. Ibid., 2:455.

39. Ibid., 2:456–57

40. Philip Barbour, *Pocahontas and Her World* (Boston: Houghton Mifflin, 1970), 53.

41. Smith, *Travels and Works*, 2:460.

42. Ibid., 1:165.

43. For a complete history of Argall's endeavors in North America, see William T. Vollmann, *Argall: Seven Dreams, a Book of North American Landscapes* (New York: Viking, 2001).

44. Smith, *Travels and Works*, 2:510–12.

45. For accounts of Pocahontas's capture, see Vollmann, *Argall*, 401; Smith, *Travels and Works*, 2:511–12; Smith, *The Complete Works*, 2:243–44.

46. Strachey, *Historie of Travell*, 77–79.

47. For details on the construction of Powhatan homes and how English observers described them, see Rountree, *The Powhatan Indians of Virginia*, 61–62.

48. A map of tribal territories in the plains and mountains was created for the Hudson's Bay Company by a Siksika chief known as Old Swan. A copy of his map was sent west with Lewis and Clark.

49. See James Rhonda, *Lewis and Clark Among the Indians* (Lincoln: University of Nebraska Press, 1984), 28–30.

50. See Moulton, ed., *Journals*, 3:111–12.

51. See Rhonda, *Lewis and Clark*, 43.

52. More explanation on Indian women's work, and how non-Natives represented it will be provided shortly. For an example of this kind of description, see

Annie Heloise Abel, ed., *Tabeau's Narrative of Loisel's Expedition to the Upper Missouri*, (Norman: University of Oklahoma Press, 1939), 148–49. See also Moulton, ed., *Journals*, 5:120–21; Weist, "Beasts of Burden and Menial Slaves," 29–52.

53. For Lewis and Clark's extended commentary on the Arikara, see chapter 7 in Moulton, ed., *Journals*, 3:111–203. For an explanation of the expedition's goals among the Arikara, see Rhonda, *Lewis and Clark*, 42–66.

54. See Rhonda, *Lewis and Clark*, 67–112.

55. Charbonneau pops up in several primary records left by fur traders, and he, too, had several aliases. He is usually referred to as Charbono or Shabona in the expedition journals. He did *not* receive the admiration of his American contemporaries, nor of American writers. They often describe him as a once-civilized Frenchman who was degraded by his wilderness experience, reduced to a "squawman" because of his habit of taking Indian wives.

56. For more on interracial marriages in the fur trade, see Jennifer Brown, *Strangers in Blood: Fur Trade Company Families in Indian Country* (Norman: University of Oklahoma Press, 1980), and Sylvia Van Kirk, *Many Tender Ties: Women in Fur-trade Society, 1670–1870* (Norman: University of Oklahoma Press, 1983).

57. Moulton, ed., *Journals*, 5:106.

58. Ibid., 3:228.

59. Ibid., 3:312.

60. Ibid., 3:313.

61. Ibid., 4:11.

62. Ibid., 4:299.

63. Ibid., 4:416.

64. Ibid., 5:8–9.

65. Ibid., 5:59.

66. Ibid., 5:106.

67. John E. Rees of Salmon Idaho ran a trading post among reservation Shoshones as the nineteenth century came to a close. In his office several drafts of a letter he sent to the Bureau of Indian Affairs in the early 1920s describe various customs of the Shoshones and their interpretation of Sacagawea. According to a reconstruction of his lost letter (the official letter was never found within the Bureau of Indian Affairs, but it was recomposed from various drafts found in his office), the sucking of one's fingers indicated a childlike contentment that can only be enjoyed in the bosom of one's own people. See Rees, *Madame Charbonneau*, 11.

68. Moulton, ed., *Journals*, 5:165.

CHAPTER 3

1. Díaz, *The Conquest of New Spain*, 220. Fray Sahagún offers a translation of Moctezuma's speech to Cortés, which can be found in Sahagún, "The Conquest of Mexico," in *Florentine Codex*, 12:42.

2. Durán, *History of the Indies of New Spain*, 212–22. For this mythical tale of the search for Aztlán, including the feud between Huitzilopochtli, Malinalxochitl, and Copil, see Townsend, *The Aztecs*, 55–60.

3. See Townsend, *The Aztec*, 23–32.

4. See Lanyon, *Malinche's Conquest*, 185.

5. See Lockhart, *We People Here*, 20; Townsend, *The Aztecs*, 115–16.

6. Lanyon, *Malinche's Conquest*, 184.

7. The sexual conquest is not mentioned in primary accounts written by Cortés or Díaz. This accusation came later with the advent of the "Black Legend," the tendency of other Europeans who were critical of Spain's imperial ambitions in the New World to question the morality of the Spaniards. See Charles Gibson, ed., *The Black Legend: Anti-Spanish Attitudes in the Old World and the New* (New York: Alfred A Knopf, 1971). The vast population of mixed-blood people in Spanish America was evidence of Spain's sexual conquest. For an explanation of the complications of sex during the conquest, see Antonia I. Castaneda, "Sexual Violence in the Politics and Policies of Conquest: Amerindian Women and the Spanish Conquest of Alta California," in Adela de la Tone and Beatriz M. Pesquera, eds., *Building with Our Hands: New Directions in Chicana Scholarship* (1993); James Brooks, "'This Evil Extends Especially to the Feminine Sex': Captivity and Identity in New Mexico, 1700–1846," in Jameson and Armitage, *Writing the Range*, (1997); Albert Hurtado, *Intimate Frontiers: Sex, Gender, and Culture in Old California* (1999); Luis Martin, *Daughters of the Conquistadors: Women of the Viceroyalty of Peru* (1989); Joane Nagel, *Race, Ethnicity, and Sexuality: Intimate Intersections, Forbidden Frontiers* (2003).

8. Díaz, *The Conquest of New Spain*, 247.

9. Ibid., 172.

10. Ibid., 176.

11. Ibid., 153.

12. Ibid., 86.

13. The various groups within the Powhatan Confederacy had several other creation myths. The most frequently recorded can be found in Rountree, *Powhatan Indians of Virginia*, 138. The creation myth that Allen describes can be seen in her work *Pocahontas*, 43–46. For an Ojibwa explanation of Pocahontas as a trained Beloved Woman, see "Pocahontas," *Native American Netroots*, last modified January 13, 2010, http://nativeamericannetroots.net/diary/342.

14. For an explanation of the world renewal ceremony that Smith was a part of or the feast of Nikomis, see Allen, *Pocahontas*, 34–36, 42–43.

15. Ibid., 18–19.

16. Ibid., 30–34.

17. Smith, *The Generall Historie*, in *The Complete Works* 2:150.

18. This was the Pocahontas that Disney depicted in the 1995 blockbuster, in which she was seen listening to the wind and communicating with "Grandmother Willow."

19. Allen, *Pocahontas*, 39.

20. Smith, *Travels and Works*, 2:401.

21. See Smith, *The Generall Historie,* in *The Complete Works,* 2:156–57; Mossiker, *Pocahontas,* 62; J. A. Lemay, *Did Pocahontas Save Captain John Smith?* (Athens: The University of Georgia Press, 1992), 102; and Rountree, *Pocahontas's People,* 34–37.

22. Smith, *Travels and Works,* 1:106–107.

23. Ibid., 2:455.

24. See Ibid., 2:511–12; Smith *The Complete Works,* 2:243–44; and Vollmann, *Argall,* 401.

25. Ralph Hamor was the official secretary of Jamestown from 1611 to 1614. He was charged with sending reports to London officials. After his return to London, he reorganized his reports for publication in 1615. Smith reprinted some of Hamor's reports in his *Generall Historie,* which was published in 1624. For Hamor's explanation of Pocahontas's capture and the negotiations for her release, see his *A True Discourse of the Present Estate of Virginia* (New York, Da Capo, 1971), 4–7. For an explanation of the negotiations between Argall and Powhatan and her life as a captive, see Barbour, *Pocahontas and Her World,* 108–11.

26. See Hamor, *A True Discourse,* 40. Hamor also includes a letter Rolfe wrote to Governor Dale (pp. 61–68) expressing his emotional connection to Pocahontas that clarifies Pocahontas's contentment among the English. Smith comments on her eagerness among the English, using Hamor's words in his *Generall Historie,* in *The Complete Works,* 2:250–51. Hamor's rendition of her life as a captive suggests her willingness to be among the foreigners. See also Mossiker, *Pocahontas,* 157–69.

27. Smith, *Generall Historie,* in *The Complete Works,* 2:245–47.

28. Crazy Horse, "The Pocahontas Myth."

29. This engraving was completed by Dutch artist Simon Van de Passe. It is the only known authentic likeness of Pocahontas.

30. For a brief history of Powhatan-English relations after the death of Pocahontas and Chief Powhatan, see Chief Roy Crazy Horse, *A Brief History of the Powhatan Renape Nation,* Renape, (N.J.: Powhatan Renape Nation, 1999); Helen Rountree, *Pocahontas, Powhatan, Opechancanough: Three Indian Lives Changed by Jamestown* (Charlotte: University of Virginia Press, 2005).

31. For a complex explanation of the war's instigation, see Margaret Connell-Szasz, *Indian Education in the American Colonies 1607–1783* (Albuquerque: University of New Mexico Press, 1988).

32. To learn more about Powhatan descendants today, see Sandra F. Waugaman and Danielle Moretti-Langholtz, *We're Still Here: Contemporary Virginia Indians Tell Their Stories* (Richmond: Palari, 2001).

33. Moulton, ed., *Journals,* 5:8–9.

34. E. G. Chuinard, "The Actual Role of the Bird Woman: Purposeful Member of the Corps or 'Casual Tag Along'?" *Montana: The Magazine of Western History* 26, (1976): 18–29.

35. Moulton, ed., *Journals,* 3:228.

36. Ibid., 4:10.

37. Ibid., 5:106.

38. Ibid., 5:109.
39. Ibid., 5:120.
40. Ibid., 5:268.
41. Ibid., 5:306.
42. Ibid., 4:216.
43. Ibid., 4:403.
44. Ibid., 4:15
45. Ibid., 4:89.
46. Ibid., 4:128.
47. Ibid., 4:416.
48. Ibid., 5:59.
49. Ibid., 8:182.

CHAPTER 4

1. Karttunen, *Between Worlds*, 22.
2. Díaz, *The Conquest of New Spain*, 80.
3. Ibid., 82.
4. Ibid., 121.
5. Ibid., 121–22.
6. Ibid., 122.
7. Ibid., 138.
8. Ibid., 147.
9. Ibid., 178.
10. Ibid., 82.
11. Ibid., 153
12. See Lanyon, *Malinche's Conquest*, 142.
13. Martín would return to New Spain where he would get entangled in a brief independence movement that would have placed his younger half brother (also named Martín) in control of Mexico. He was forced into exile in 1568.
14. For an account of the various court proceedings after Malinche's death, see Lanyon, *Malinche's Conquest*, 154–73, 205–19.
15. Ibid., 161–63.
16. See Townsend, *Pocahontas and the Powhatan Dilemma*, 41. For another work that discusses Smith's fascination with Cortés, see John Hart, *Representing the New World: The English and the French Uses of the Example of Spain* (New York: Palgrave, 2001), 214
17. Smith, *The Generall Historie*, in *The Complete Works*, 2:41–42.While there have been those who question the validity of these various feminine rescues, is it unfathomable that Smith ran across a few women (of diverse cultures) in his hour of need who were inclined to take pity on a struggling creature? Smith clearly assumed it

was because of his masculine English charm, but the fact that Smith ran into a few sympathetic individuals does not seem unrealistic.

18. Ibid., 1:274.

19. Ibid., 1:274.

20. Ibid., 2:182–83.

21. Strachey, *The Historie of Travell,* 72.

22. Ibid., 112–13.

23. Ibid., 62.

24. Firsthand accounts and contemporary anthropological studies confirm that a potential husband had to win over his potential wife with presents of food and prove himself a good provider. In his *Map of Virginia* Smith observes that young Powhatan women had freedom of choice in marriage and looked for men who proved to be good hunters and warriors. Strachey, who plagiarized Smith's work, also mentions women's choice in marriage partners. For more on marriage customs, see Rountree, *The Powhatan Indians of Virginia,* 90. For an extended discussion of Pocahontas's attraction to Kocoum, see Mossiker, *Pocahontas,* 147–49.

25. This quote is from the letter Rolfe sent to Governor Dale. It was reprinted in Hamor, *A True Discourse,* 61–68. Frances Mossiker included a copy of Rolfe's letter in her *Pocahontas,* 346.

26. Mossiker, *Pocahontas,* 348.

27. Smith, *The Generall Historie,* in *The Complete Works,* 2:251.

28. Mossiker, *Pocahontas,* 198.

29. Hamor, *A True Discourse,* 40.

30. Ibid., 42.

31. Smith, *The Generall Historie,* in *The Complete Works,* 2:249.

32. The English officially gave up on kinship diplomacy when they declared miscegenation illegal in 1691. By that point, indigenous populations had been ravaged by European diseases, and Indian dispossession became the routine.

33. Smith, *The Generall Historie,* in *The Complete Works,* 2:260–61.

34. Ibid., 2:261.

35. Strachey, *The Historie of Travell,* 81.

36. See Smith's *Map of Virginia* in *The Complete Works,* 162, and Strachey, *The Historie of Travell,* 85.

37. The engraving by Simon Van de Passe remains the only tangible evidence of her physical characteristics: she had high cheekbones, almond-shaped eyes, and a cleft chin. She told the young painter, as she sat for him, that she was in her twenty-first year. Van de Passe was also in his twenties.

38. Moulton, ed., *Journals,* 3:291.

39. For details on Hidatsa childbirth, see Bowers, *Hidatsa Social and Ceremonial Organization,* 128 or Peters, *Women of the Earth Lodges,* 65.

40. Moulton, ed., *Journals,* 4:10.

41. Ibid., 4:299.

42. Ibid., 4:152.

43. Ibid., 4:171.

44. Ibid., 4:325.

45. Ibid., 5:93.

46. Rose Anne Abramson, oral interview with the author, March 15, 1998.

47. Moulton, ed., *Journals*, 8:225.

48. Elliott Coues, ed., *The History of the Expedition under the Command of Lewis and Clark Expedition: To the Sources of the Missouri River, thence across the Rocky Mountains and down the Columbia River to the Pacific Ocean, Performed during the Years of 1804–05–06, by Order of the Government of the United States* (New York: Francis P. Harper, 1893), 4:1184.

49. Moulton, ed., *Journals*, 8:305.

50. Brackenridge, "Journal of a Voyage up the Missouri River in 1811," in Thwaites, ed., *Early Western Travels, 1748–1896*, 19–166

51. John C. Luttig, *Journal of a Fur Trading Expedition on the Upper Missouri, 1812–1813* (St. Louis: Missouri Historical Society, 1920), 106.

52. "Putrid fever" was a term usually associated with an infection after childbirth. Luttig's journal, however, does not mention Sacagawea being pregnant (nor recently giving birth) as the party arrived at Fort Manuel in 1812. The fur trapping expedition from St. Louis would have traveled for weeks together on a relatively small craft; surely the Charbonneau family and the fur trappers would have been acquainted with one another well enough that such information would have been shared.

53. Grace Raymond Hebard, *Sacajawea: A Guide and Interpreter of the Lewis and Clark Expedition, with an Account of the Travels of Toussaint Charbonneau, and of Jean Baptiste, the Expedition Papoose* (Glendale, Cal.: Arthur H. Clark, 1933). Hebard first presented her hypothesis that Sacagawea had eventually returned to the Shoshone people and lived a long and influential life among them in "Pilot of the First White Men to Cross the American Continent," *The Journal of American History* 1 (1907): 467–84. Wadze-wipe and Porivo were real women that Hebard's Indian informants remembered when Hebard was conducting her research from 1907 to 1933. How and why Hebard came to believe these women were Sacagawea will be taken up shortly.

54. Moulton, ed., *Journals*, 5:120–21.

55. Ibid., 5:120–21.

56. Ibid., 8:167.

57. Interestingly, Malinche was described as both.

58. Moulton, ed., *Journals*, 5:120–21.

59. Ibid., 5:165.

60. For lively scholarly discussions of the relationship between gender and power in Native societies, see Allen, *Sacred Hoop*; Klein and Ackerman, *Women and Power in Native North America*; and Theda Perdue, *Sifters: Native American Women's Lives* (Oxford: Oxford University Press, 2001).

61. For an explanation of American middle- and upper-class ideologies of the female in the first half of the 1800s, see Barbara Welter, "The Cult of True Womanhood,"

in *Our American Sisters: Women in American Life and Thought*, ed. Jean E. Friedman and William G. Shade (Boston: Allyn and Bacon, 1973). The ideology that Welter describes is certainly race and class specific, yet it certainly pertained to Lewis and Clark's gender expectations.

62. Rose Anne Abrahamson, oral interview with the author, April 15, 1998. She did not consider Shoshone women oppressed, and described the roles of men and women as "bi-turnal."

63. For an explanation of the power of women's sexuality (transferring one man's power to another through ceremonial intercourse), see Weist, "Beast of Burden," 44–45. For an explanation of the power of women's sexuality in kinship ties, see Susan Sleeper-Smith, *Indian Women and French Men: Rethinking Cultural Encounter in the Western Great Lakes* (Amherst: University of Massachusetts Press, 2001), 63–64; Brown, *Strangers in Blood*, 59–61; and Van Kirk, *Many Tender Ties*, 159–60, 164–65.

CHAPTER 5

1. Speech scrolls are a classic Maya tradition that appeared in the ancient ruins of Xochicalco (A.D. 600–900) and are evident in Fray Bernardino de Sahagún's ethnographic Aztec pictorials (1550s) and continued to appear throughout the colonial era. Speech scrolls can be read in terms of Nahuatl language as metaphors to reference discourse on rulership. Sahagún, *Florentine Codex*, 12:55. See Townsend, *The Aztecs*, 40.

2. This is a main point in Lockhart, *We People Here*. There is an impressive and growing body of scholarly literature that illustrates Indian reconstruction of Spanish religion and culture in the colonial era including Lockhart, *We People Here*; Eleanor Wake, *Framing the Sacred: The Indian Churches of Early Colonial Mexico* (Norman: University of Oklahoma Press, 2010); and Stephanie Wood, *Transcending Conquest: Nahua Views of Spanish Colonial Mexico* (Norman: University of Oklahoma Press, 2003).

3. Many preconquest indigenous texts were either burned by the Spaniards or hidden by indigenous priests so well that some have only recently been recovered. There has been a recent effort to uncover and study these codices; the most extensive analyses can be found in Lockhart, *We People Here*, and Wood, *Transcending Conquest*. I have chosen the most prominent of these indigenous texts, *Lienso de Tlaxcala* and the *Florentine Codex*. For scholarly debates on these indigenous sources see Inga Clendinnen, *Aztecs: An Interpretation* (1991). There is a recent collection of essays from the Guggenheim Museum that discusses these Native sources entitled *The Aztec Empire* (2004).

4. Sahagún, *Florentine Codex*. For more information on the life of Sahagún, see L. N. D. Olwer, *Fray Bernardino de Sahagún (1499–1590)* (1987).

5. For a discussion of *Lienso de Tlaxcala*, and other pictorial representations of Malinche, see Maria Herrera-Sobek, "In Search of La Malinche: Pictorial Representations of a Mytho-Historical Figure," in *Feminism, Nation, and Myth: La Malinche*,

ed. Rolando Romero and Amanda Nolacea Harris (Houston: Arte Publico, 2005), 112–33, and Gordon Brotherston, *Painted Books from Mexico* (London; British Museum, 1996).

6. Bartolomé de las Casas was a sixteenth-century historian, a social reformer, a Dominican friar, and the first resident Bishop of Chiapas (a post he held for only a short time after trying to abolish the *encomienda* system). He returned to Spain and became Protector of the Indians, an administrative post charged with the well-being of Native populations. Las Casas passionately criticized Spain's treatment of the Indians. On the other side of Las Casas's argument was the opinion of John Major, a scholastic philosopher, who insisted that the Indians were barbarous and were therefore classified as slaves by nature. Major's position was taken up by Juan Gines de Sepulveda in the famous debates at Valladolid in 1550. While Las Casas passionately defended the Indians, Sepulveda defended the conquistadors by suggesting that Indians were unfit and in need of correction, and that civilized men had to lead them out of darkness. These questions regarding Spain's dominion in the Americas were ongoing during the physical and the spiritual conquest in Mexico, and these national doubts certainly shaped Cortés's representation of events. See D. A. Brading, *The First America: The Spanish Monarchy, Creole Patriots and the Liberal State 1492–1867* (Cambridge: Cambridge University Press, 1991), 75–101.

7. Cortés, *Letters from Mexico*, 376.

8. Díaz, *The Conquest of New Spain*, 196–97.

9. The following discussion on Díaz can be found in the introduction to Díaz, *The Conquest of New Spain*, 7–8.

10. Ibid., 82.

11. Ibid., 153.

12. Ibid., 176.

13. Ibid., 86.

14. For Sahagún's various definitions of the feminine, see Sahagún, *Florentine Codex*, 10:2–3.

15. For his definition of a "procuress," see ibid., 10:57.

16. David Brading, *The Origins of Mexican Nationalism* (Cambridge: Cambridge University Press, 1983), 14–19. The conflict between the descendants of the conquistadors and the newly arrived Spaniards is also discussed in Brading, *The First America*, 4, 76, 79–101, 298, 301.

17. Brading, *The First America*, 272–75.

18. This point is considered in Jacques Lafaye, *Quetzalcóatl and Guadalupe: The Formation of Mexican National Consciousness 1531–1813* (Chicago: The University of Chicago Press 1976): 7–9. Brading also takes up this point of Creoles' unfitness for colonial administration in *The First America*, 293–300.

19. Lafaye, *Quetzalcóatl and Guadalupe*, 65–67

20. Brading, *The First America*, 273–84

21. The Creoles were influenced by the success of Las Casas's humanist interpretation of indigenous peoples and the histories of ancient Mexico presented by Fernando de Alva Ixtlilxochitl. See ibid., 273–75. Creoles presented ancient Mexicans as admirable peoples who lived in civilized, moral societies and who built grand cities. Two of the more famous contributors to this genre were Sister Juana Inés de la Cruz and the 1794 sermon of Dominican Fray Servando Teresa de Mier. Both La Cruz and Mier were early Mexican patriots. For a concise discussion of La Cruz in relation to Mexican nationalism, see Lafay, *Quetzalcóatl and Guadalupe,* 68–76. For a discussion of Mier's sermon, see Brading, *The First America,* 583–87.

22. Brading, *Origins of Mexican Nationalism,* 11.

23. For more information on the Virgin of Guadalupe, see Lafaye, *Quetzalcóatl and Guadalupe;* Brading, *First America,* 343–61; Brading, *Mexican Phoenix Our Lady of Guadalupe: Image and Tradition Across Five Centuries* (Cambridge: Cambridge University Press, 2001); and Linda Hall, *Mary, Mother and Warrior: The Virgin in Spain and the Americas* (Austin: University of Texas Press, 2004).

24. While the apparition of the Virgin of Guadalupe at Tepeyac inspired local devotion, it was not until 1622 that a chapel was dedicated to her at the sacred site, and it was only in 1648 that a written record of the apparition was published by Father Miguel Sanchez. By this time Creole clerics had been using the symbol to attract Indians to the church. During the great plague of 1737 popular devotion mounted to new heights. In 1746 delegates from all the dioceses of New Spain met to acclaim Our Lady of Guadalupe as their universal patron. See Brading, *Mexican Phoenix,* and Brading, *The First America,* 343–61. The Virgin of Guadalupe certainly meant different things to the different peoples of Mexico. To friars she was a mask so that Indians could worship their traditional pagan goddess. To Creoles and Jesuits she was an intercessor who could reach Indians and help in their conversion, and she legitimized Mexico as an autonomous Christian land. To Indians, depending on local beliefs and conditions, she was the protector to be called on during epidemics and disasters; she was their available and approachable divine link to God and Catholicism. But during the push for independence she was the rallying cry that inspired Mexicans (Creoles, Mestizos, and Indians) to rise up against the King of Spain and his Spanish representatives in New Spain, the Gachupines. The partisan conflict between the Creole clergy (who viewed Mexico as the land chosen by the Virgin herself) and friars from Spain (who saw New Spain as a missionary spiritual conquest) aided the push for Mexican independence. After the Bourbon Reforms and the expulsion of the Jesuits in the 1770s, the Mexicans revolted and rallied under the banner of the Virgin of Guadalupe. See Hall, *Mary Mother and Warrior,* and Lafaye, *Quetzalcóatl and Guadalupe,* 99–136.

25. Hall, *Mary, Mother and Warrior,* 266–67

26. Mexico had transformed Christianity to suit Native understanding. See William Taylor, "The Virgin of Guadalupe in New Spain: An Inquiry into the Social History of Marian Devotion," in *American Ethnologist* 14 (February 1987): 9–33; Lafaye, *Quetzalcóatl and Guadalupe,* 6–7; Hall, *Mary, Mother and Warrior,* 186–91.

27. Brading, *The First America*, 292–301

28. Hall, *Mary, Mother and Warrior*, 187

29. This was a point made early on in the 1570s by Diego Durán, a Dominican who had been brought to Mexico as a child, but who came to identify himself with Mexico. Durán suggested that Mexico's Indians descended from the ten lost tribes of Israel and that the Toltecs at Tula had been evangelized to by a Christian apostle, probably St. Thomas. Durán authored several books on indigenous spiritualism, including *Book of the Gods and Rites of the Ancient Calendar*. Durán stressed the similarity between indigenous religious rituals and Christian practices in order to reveal a Native moral code that would offset their image as demonic barbarians who worshiped pagan gods. See Brading, *First America*, 283–84.

30. Mier was expelled from Mexico for such blasphemy in 1775, the year following his sermon. He fled to Italy where he continued to call for Mexican patriotism and international acceptance of an autonomous Mexican nation based on an autonomous Catholic premise. See Brading, *First America*, 583–90.

31. Guillermo Castillo-Feliu, trans., *Xicotencatl: An Anonymous Historical Novel about the Events Leading up to the Conquest of the Aztec Empire* (Austin: University of Texas Press, 1999).

32. For an extended feminist analysis of *Xicotencatl*, see Sandra Messinger Cypess, *La Malinche in Mexican Literature: From History to Myth* (Austin: University of Texas Press, 1991), 43–56.

33. Octavio Paz, *Labyrinth of Solitude: The Other Mexico, and Other Essays*, trans. Lysander Kemp, (New York: Grove, 1985). Paz's gender analysis is addressed in more depth later in this chapter.

34. This void allowed other nations to condemn Spanish imperial ambitions and fueled the Black Legend, which highlighted Spanish atrocities committed against the Native peoples of Mexico.

35. William Prescott, *History of the Conquest of Mexico, with a Preliminary View of the Ancient Mexican Civilization, and the Life of the Conqueror Hernando Cortés*, 3 vols. (Philadelphia: David McKay Publisher, 1843), 1:401

36. Prescott's characterization of Malinche as an Indian protector influenced portrayals of Pocahontas and Sacagawea. Writers often adopted the same phrases to describe America's Indian heroines.

37. For an interesting discussion of the legend of La Llorona, and how that legend came to be tangled with the legend of Malinche, see Luis Leal, "The Malinche-Llorona Dichotomy: The Evolution of Myth," in Romero and Harris, *Feminism, Nation, and Myth: La Malinche*, 134.

38. Hammon Innes, *The Conquistadors* (New York: Random House, 1970), 128. Innes's descriptions of Malinche are strikingly consistent with the Indian princess portrayals of Pocahontas and Sacagawea, whose actions were motivated by love for the foreigners.

39. For an interesting discussion of the "erotics of politics" and nationalist romance novels as "foundational fictions," see Doris Sommer, *Foundational Fictions: The National Romance of Latin America* (Berkeley: University of California Press, 1991).

40. These small, local communities were called "pequenas patrias" by Manuel Gamio in his famous work *Forjando Patria*, (Mexico: Editorial Porrua, A. A., 1916). Gamio will be discussed shortly.

41. Creole nationalists in the independence era attempted to distance themselves from the atrocities committed by conquistadors and from the tyrannical Spanish colonial regime. Their strategy to build consensus was to celebrate the Indian as a partner in the creation of a new Christian paradise.

42. As a child Vasconcelos lived in the United States as the son of a customs collector. This experience instilled a deep-seated contempt for that country. After being forced into exile in 1910, he returned to the United States, where he developed his theory of discontented North Americans; he saw them as a materialistic and racially segregated society. He returned to Mexico in 1919 and became the first rector of the National University, and later the Minister of Education, until he resigned in 1924. His most important legacy is a public school system that extended into the small rural villages that had been isolated from Mexican nationalism. After an unsuccessful attempt at the presidency, Vasconcelos again went into exile, where he published his famous work, *The Cosmic Race*, trans. Didier T. Joen (Los Angeles: Centro de Publicaciones, Department of Chicano Studies, 1979).

43. Vasconcelos, *Aspects of Mexican Civilization: Lectures on the Harris Foundation* (Chicago: University of Chicago Press, 1926), 85.

44. For a discussion of eugenics in Latin America see Nancy Leys Stepan, *The Hour of Eugenics: Race, Gender, and Nation in Latin America* (Ithaca: Cornell University Press, 1991).

45. Vasconcelos used the United States as his comparison model; he lived in the United States at various times in his life and was sensitive to racial discrimination there.

46. This was one aspect of his argument that did not sit well with fellow Mexicans, as many were dissatisfied with social and racial injustices in Mexico.

47. Vasconcelos, *The Cosmic Race*.

48. Vasconcelos, *Aspects of Civilization*, 103–104.

49. Ibid., 92.

50. Ibid., 92.

51. Ibid., 81.

52. Gamio's greatest professional accomplishment was a reconstruction of the ancient city Teotihuacan; its magnitude evoked comparison with the ancient pyramids of Egypt and thus could legitimize Mexico's national glory.

53. Gamio was trained under the influence of the anthropologist Franz Boas. Gamio delighted in characterizing precolonial groups as civilizations to illustrate Boas's theory that civilizations were natural intellectual manifestations of any human group, including ancient Mexicans. Boas's theory of cultural relativism allowed Gamio to discredit the theory of genetic determinism argued by European social Darwinists. For an explanation of Boas's influence on Gamio's anthropological work, see Brading, "Manuel Gamio and Official Indigenismo in Mexico," *Bulletin of Latin American Research* 7, no. 1 (1988): 75–89.

54. Ibid., 75–76.

55. Ibid., 76.

56. This point resonates in most of Gamio's writings; it is particularly pervasive in *Mexican Folkways*, a Mexican magazine from the 1920s that he wrote for and edited. See his editorial "The Utilitarian Aspect of Folklore," in *Mexican Folkways* (June/July 1925): 7.

57. Gamio, "The Indian Basis of Mexican Civilization," in *Aspects of Mexican Civilization*, 105–88. This particular quote is on p. 110.

58. Brading, "Manuel Gamio and Official Indigenismo," 80.

59. Gamio led a campaign to revive traditional Mexican artisan industries in textiles, ceramics, lacquer, metal works, and porcelain. Like the restored ancient monuments that had fostered a tourism industry, the Native crafts industry met immediate success. He promoted the establishment of the Department of Fine Arts, funded by the state.

60. Vasconcelos, as the minister of education, initiated a literacy campaign and a nationalist campaign through schools, libraries, and fine arts. Gamio expanded these efforts into rural Indian communities. Much of their efforts were discussed and celebrated in the pages of the 1920s magazine *Mexican Folkways*.

61. It is interesting to compare these male-created representations of the Mexican earth mother with female artistic representations: Maria Izquierdo's (1902–1955) painting *Earth Pain* and Frida Kahlo's (1907–1954) painting *My Nurse and I* show agonized earth mothers. The work of Izquierdo and Kahlo was marginalized by art critics.

62. He offers no chapter on the daughters of Malinche.

63. Paz, *The Labyrinth of Solitude*, 77.

64. Ibid., 35.

65. Paz's analysis reflects a historical conception of original sin. For Mexico, Paz implies, the repercussions of that sin are felt deeper and are more genuine than for other Christians.

66. These feminine soldiers were mythologized as a feminine archetype; see Maria Herrera-Sobek, *The Mexican Corrido: A Feminist Analysis* (Bloomington: Indiana University Press, 1990), 84–90.

67. For an interesting gender analysis of Mexicana literature, see Jean Franco, *Plotting Women: Gender and Representation in Mexico* (New York: Columbia University Press, 1989).

68. For interesting treatments of Mexican feminism, see Franco, *Plotting Women*; Herrera-Sobek, *The Mexican Corrido*; Anna Marie Sandoval, *Toward a Latina Feminism of the Americas: Repression and Resistance in Chicana and Mexicana Literature*; Jocelyn Olcott, et al, *Sex in Revolution: Gender, Politics, and Power in Modern Mexico*. There are also several excellent works on the feminist perspective of Sister Juana de la Cruz, who was often recognized as the first feminist writer in the Americas.

69. For a comparison of Mexican and U.S. feminism, see Sandoval, *Toward a Latina Feminism of the Americas*.

70. Similar gender animosity fractured other Civil Rights groups of the era. In the late 1960s Casey Hayden and Mary King wrote an anonymous position paper to the leaders of SNCC (Student Non-violent Coordinating Committee) encouraging them to tackle gender oppression as part of their agenda, intensifying the racial tensions within the organization.

71. Adelaida R. Del Castillo, "Malintzin Tenepal: A Preliminary Look into a New Perspective," in *Essays on La Mujer*, ed. Rosaura Sanchez and Rosa Martinez Cruz (Los Angeles: Chicano Studies Center, 1977), 124–49; Cordelia Candelaria, "La Malinche, Feminist Prototype," *Frontiers* 5, no. 2 (1980): 1–6.

72. Candelaria, "La Malinche, Feminist Prototype," 6.

73. See Cypess, *La Malinche in Mexican Literature*. Franco, *Plotting Women* can also be categorized in this genre of feminist scholarship. While she does not specifically analyze Malinche, Franco does reveal a long tradition of female dissenting voices that managed to sporadically interrupt the male-dominated discourse on institutional knowledge. Franco and Cypess take the feminist perspective out of the realm of personal experience and into the sphere of public consciousness and institutional knowledge.

74. See Romero and Harris, *Feminism, Nation, and Myth*.

75. Alicia Gaspar De Alba, "Malinche's Revenge," in ibid., 44–57.

76. For an explanation of Chicanas' role in the movement, see Arturo Rosales, *Testimonio: A Documentary History of the Mexican American Struggle for Civil Rights* (Houston: Arte Publico, 2000), 391–93.

77. See Alma M. Garcia, *Chicana Feminist Thought: The Basic Historical Writings*. (New York: Routledge, 1997).

78. Her educational plan demands that Malinche be given a new historical interpretation as a positive symbol for the mestizo and that a history of Chicanas be recognized. See Anna Nieto Gomez, "The Chicana—Perspectives for Education," in Garcia, *Chicana Feminist Thought: The Basic Historical Writings*, 130–31.

79. Gaspar De Alba, "Malinche's Revenge," 50.

80. Ibid., 55.

81. Ibid., 53.

82. Franco Mondini-Ruiz, "Malinche Makeover: One Gay Latino's Perspective," in Romero and Harris, *Feminism, Nation, and Myth*, 157.

83. Camilla Townsend, *Malintzin's Choices: An Indian Woman in the Conquest of Mexico* (Albuquerque: University of New Mexico Press, 2006).

Chapter 6

1. An entire book is devoted to unraveling the controversy surrounding Smith's reliability as a historian and the authenticity of his accounts. See Lemay, *Did Pocahontas Save Captain John Smith?* Lemay's work will be discussed later in this chapter.

2. Smith, *The Complete Works*, 2:151.

3. See a copy of the letter in Smith, *The Generall Historie*, in *The Complete Works*, 2:258–59.

4. *True Relation* was originally written by Smith as a private letter to a friend back in England before it was edited and published without his knowledge. It was the fist account of the Jamestown colony's first year to appear in London. See Philip Barbour's introduction to *The Complete Works*, 1:1.

5. See Lemay, *Did Pocahontas Save Captain John Smith?*; Peter Hulme, *Colonial Encounters: Europe and the Native Caribbean 1492–1797* (London: Routledge, 1992); and Allen, *Pocahontas*.

6. Hulme, *Colonial Encounters*, 148.

7. Allen, *Pocahontas*, 50.

8. Hulme, *Colonial Encounters*, 150.

9. Smith, *The Generall Historie*, in *The Complete Works* 2:151.

10. Ibid., 261.

11. Pocahontas's compassion is evident throughout Smith's work and the work of William Strachey, who conducted interviews with Jamestown's first settlers for his book *The Historie of Travell into Virginia Britania*. For an example of her negotiation for the release of prisoners, see Smith, *The Complete Works*, 1:220.

12. Smith, *The Complete Works*, 2:203.

13. The works mentioned here are discussed in Kevin Hayes, *Captain John Smith: A Reference Guide* (Boston: G. K. Hall, 1991).

14. A discussion of the skepticism regarding Smith's rescue narrative will be taken up later in this chapter. See Lemay, *Did Pocahontas Save Captain John Smith?* Powhatans who were present at Smith's adoption ceremony did not record the event in the white man's world. Paula Gunn Allen, however, attempted to trace Powhatan oral tradition to recreate a Powhatan interpretation of the event in her book *Pocahontas*. An explanation of Allen's Native interpretation will be offered shortly.

15. Lemay, *Did Pocahontas Save Captain John Smith?*, 4.

16. Smith, *The Complete Works*, 1:xix.

17. Strachey, *The Historie of Travell*, 72.

18. Ibid., 62.

19. Ibid., 114.

20. For an explanation of the Pocahontas narrative in the eighteen and nineteenth centuries, see Robert S. Tilton, *Pocahontas: The Evolution of an American Narrative* (Cambridge: Cambridge University Press, 1994).

21. Ibid., 16.

22. Ibid., 37. The title of William Wirt's book is *Letters of the British Spy*; it was first published in Richmond in 1803. Subsequent editions were in 1832 by J. and J. Harper and in 1855 by Harper and Brothers.

23. Ibid., 34–57. Tilton's point is not entirely original, but rather one that Frances Mossiker hints at in her 1976 work *Pocahontas*, 171, 179–80, 188–92. Mossiker's work will be discussed in the following pages.

24. For analysis of the romantic genre, including Davis, see Tilton, *Pocahontas,* 32–33.

25. See Henry Adams, "Captain John Smith," *North American Review* 104 (1867): 1–30; revised and republished as Henry Adams, "Captain John Smith," in *Historical Essays* (New York: Charles Scriber's Sons, 1891), 42–79.

26. Lemay, *Did Pocahontas Save Captain John Smith?*

27. Ibid., 4.

28. Ibid., 26.

29. Ibid., 24–25.

30. For an expanded explanation of Pocahontas's treatment during America's sectional ills, including Hillhouse, see Tilton, *Pocahontas,* 145–75.

31. Bradford Smith, *Captain John Smith: His Life and Legend* (Philadelphia: Lippincott, 1953).

32. To consider how this feminine ideal was compromised in real life, see Joanne Meyerowitz, *Not June Cleaver: Women and Gender in Postwar America, 1945–1960* (Philadelphia: Temple University Press, 1994).

33. Philip Young, "The Mother of Us All: Pocahontas Reconsidered," *Kenyon Review* 24 (Summer 1962): 391–441.

34. Mossiker, *Pocahontas,* 176–77.

35. Ibid., 123.

36. Ibid., 127.

37. Ibid., 127.

38. Rayna Green, "The Pocahontas Perplex: The Image of Indian Women in American Culture," *Massachusetts Review* 16 (Autumn 1976): 698–714.

39. Rayna Green, "Native American Women: A Review Essay," *Signs: A Journal of Women in Culture and Society* 6 (1980): 248–67.

40. Ibid., 267.

41. The feminist perspective suggesting that all women share a common context of struggle continues to be a problematic. Some Indian women feel empowered by the domestic sphere and recognize ample avenues of female authority in their traditional cultures. This is a point taken up in Devon Mihesuah, "Commonality of Difference: American Indian Women and History," in *Natives and Academics: Researching and Writing about American Indians,* ed. Devon Mihesuah (Lincoln: University of Nebraska Press, 1998), 40–54.

42. For an explanation of gender construction in Native North America, see Kline and Ackerman, *Women and Power in Native North America;* Allen, *The Sacred Hoop;* Ackerman, *A Necessary Balance;* Patricia Crown, ed., *Women and Men in the Prehispanic Southwest: Labor, Power, and Prestige* (2001); Louise Lamphere, Pamela L. Geller, and Miranda K. Stockett, *Feminist Anthropology: Past Present and Future* (2006).

43. See Rayna Green, *Women in American Indian Society* (New York: Chelsea House, 1992).

44. Ibid., 14.

45. Ibid., 16.

46. Ramona Ford, "Native American Women: Changing Statuses, Changing Interpretations," in *Writing the Range: Race, Class, and Culture in the Women's West*, ed. Elizabeth Jameson and Susan Armitage (Norman: University of Oklahoma Press, 1997), 42–68.

47. Sherrole Benton, "Pocahontas as a Traitor," *Tribal College* 6 (Spring 1995): 34–35.

48. Rountree, *Powhatan Indians of Virginia*, 126.

49. Rountree, *Pocahontas, Powhatan, Opechancanough*, 78.

50. Ibid., 78.

51. Ibid., 80.

52. Allen, *Pocahontas*, 51.

53. Ibid., 43–46.

54. For an explanation of the Feast of Nikomis, or the world renewal ceremony that Smith was a part of, see ibid., 34–36, 42–43.

55. Ibid., 18–19.

56. Ibid., 30–34.

57. Ibid., 39.

58. Ibid., 335.

59. For an explanation of Pocahontas's training see ibid., 21, 95–97; for her role as a Beloved Woman, see 31–32, 50; for an explanation of Chief Powhatan's role as "Chief Dreamer," see 65, 75.

60. Allen benefited from the lifetime of anthropological research of Helen Rountree, as well as Gleach, *Powhatan's World and Colonial Virginia*.

61. See Townsend, *Pocahontas and the Powhatan Dilemma*.

62. See Ibid., 52–54, for discussion of the rescue, and 25–27 and 74–75 for commentary on Smith and Strachey as sources of information.

63. This is a claim that many works, on all three female intermediaries, make. Ibid., 213.

64. Ibid., 213.

65. There are mixed reviews from Powhatan people working on the film. Two of the consultants regretted their involvement. See Gary Edgerton, "Redesigning Pocahontas," *Journal of Popular Film and Television* 24 (1996): 90–97; Crazy Horse, "The Pocahontas Myth."

66. Edgerton, "Redesigning Pocahontas," 91.

67. Crazy Horse, "The Pocahontas Myth."

68. Edgerton, "Redesigning Pocahontas," 93.

69. Ibid., 92. Like all successful Disney movies, Pocahontas has a sequel.

70. David Price, *Love and Hate in Jamestown: John Smith, Pocahontas, and the Heart of the Nation* (New York: Alfred Knopf, 2003), 154.

71. Price, *Love and Hate*, 155.

Chapter 7

1. There are many sources for the translation of Sakakawea, Sacagawea, and Sacajawea, yet there is little consensus. See Saindon, "Sacajawea: Boat-Launcher: The Origin and Meaning of a name . . . Maybe." Also see Rees, *Madame Charbonneau*.

2. This type of discrepancy in Indian history lends to a contentious debate over who is the authority on Indian people and which sources are to be considered most accurate. Tangible primary records are not infallible, historical analysis can be faulty, and oral tradition is difficult to trace and prove. For a discussion of this debate, see Vine Deloria, Jr., "Comfortable Fictions and the Struggle for Turf: An Essay Review of the Invented Indian: Cultural Fictions and Government Policies," in *Natives and Academics: Researching and Writing about American Indians,* ed. Devon Mihesuah (Lincoln: University of Nebraska Press, 1998), 65–83.

3. Moulton, ed., *Journals,* 5:120–21

4. Ibid., 5:120–21

5. Ibid., 8:167.

6. There were American officials who believed that Indians would eventually assimilate and intermarry among citizens of the United States; this was a possibility that President Jefferson entertained. Yet Indians did not obtain official citizenship until 1924.

7. Patricia Limerick, *The Legacy of Conquest: The Unbroken Past of the American West* (New York: W. W. Norton, 1987), 31–32.

8. Lucille Van Keuren argues that the personal writings of early colonists describe a variety of Indian lifeways, yet only certain traits capture the fascination of readers. Over time fixed patterns of Indian characterizations have served the purpose of Manifest Destiny. See Van Keuren, *American Indian Responses and Reactions to the Colonists as Recorded in Seventeenth- and Eighteenth-Century American Literature* (Ann Arbor, Mich.: University Microfilms International, 1981). For an analysis of captivity narratives, see Richard VanDerBeets, *The Indian Captivity Narrative: An American Genre* (New York: University Press of America, 1984).

9. The title of the original (1892) four-volume edition was *History of the Expedition under the Command of Lewis and Clark, To the Sources of the Missouri River, thence across the Rocky Mountains and down the Columbia River to the Pacific Ocean, Performed during the Years 1804–5–6. by Order of the Government of the United States. A New Edition, Faithfully Reprinted from the Only Authorized Edition of 1814, with Copious Critical Commentary, Prepared upon Examination of Unpublished Official Archives and Many Other Sources of Information, including a Diligent Study of Original Manuscript Journals and Field Notebooks of the Explorers, together with a New Biographical and Bibliographical Introduction, New Maps and Other Illustrations and a Complete Index.* It is understandable that the 1965 edition was re-titled; see Coues, *History of the Expedition.*

10. Coues, *History of the Expedition,* 1:190.

11. Ibid., 3:132.

12. Eva Emery Dye, *The Conquest: The True Story of Lewis and Clark* (Chicago: A. C. McClurg, 1902), 188.

13. Ibid., 227.

14. Ibid., 228.

15. Ibid., 245.

16. Blanch Schroer, "Boat-Pusher or Bird Woman? Sacagawea or Sacajawea?" *Annals of Wyoming* 52 (Spring 1980): 46–54.

17. Wyoming was a territory when it granted women's suffrage in 1870, well before most states. The nation did not guarantee universal women's suffrage until 1920.

18. Other works by Hebard include *The History and Government of Wyoming* (1904), *Pathbreakers from River to Ocean* (1911), *The Bozeman Trail* (1922), *Washakie* (1930) and the 1933 work on Sacagawea considered here, *Sacagawea*.

19. The three men who recorded Sacagawea's presence with Charbonneau (or at least an Indian wife) as he worked the Missouri River in 1811, 1812, and 1813 were Henry Brackenridge, John Bradbury, and John Luttig.

20. Hebard emphasizes the authenticity of her evidence by describing how interviews were conducted at the reservation and then offering the transcripts in the appendix of her 1933 book. For testimonies of Indian agents, missionaries, and teachers among the Shoshones see Hebard, *Sacagawea*, 223–42, 243–60.

21. Ibid., 154.

22. Ibid., 155.

23. Ibid., 157.

24. Luttig, *Journal of a Fur Trading Expedition*, 106.

25. Clark's notebook and other personal papers are now kept at the Newberry Library in Chicago.

26. Eastman, *Burial Place of Sacajawea*, 8.

27. Ibid., 6.

28. Working for the Bureau of Indian Affairs, Eastman witnessed Indian mothers painfully giving up their children to boarding schools; he states that Sacagawea would not have given her baby to whites "at such a tender age." Ibid., 4.

29. See Rees, *Madame Charbonneau*.

30. Ibid., 11.

31. Ibid., 26.

32. Ibid., 26–27.

33. Hebard, "Pilot of First White Men to Cross the American Continent," 467.

34. Bernard De Voto, *The Course of Empire* (Cambridge: Riverside, 1952), 478. This winner of the National Book Award was part of his trilogy on westward expansion. The other two were *The Year of Decision: 1846* (1942) and *Across the Wide Missouri* (1947), the latter of which won the Pulitzer Prize and the Bancroft Award.

35. Dye, *The Conquest*, 197.

36. Donald Culross Peattie, *Forward the Nation* (New York: G. P. Putnam's Sons, 1942), 148.

37. For an extensive explanation of romantic portrayals of Sacagawea and Clark, see Arlen K. Large, "The Clark-Sacagawea Affair: A Literary Evolution," *We Proceed On: The Official Publication of the Lewis and Clark Trail Heritage Foundation Inc.* (August 1988): 14–18, and Donna Kessler, *The Making of Sacagawea: A Euro-American Legend* (Tuscaloosa: University of Alabama Press, 1996), 102–37.

38. Harold P. Howard, *Sacajawea* (Norman: University of Oklahoma Press, 1971), 153.

39. Ibid., 147.

40. Ibid., 151.

41. Schroer, "Boat-Pusher or Bird Woman?," 46–54.

42. Virginia Scharff, *Twenty Thousand Roads: Women, Movement and the West* (Berkeley: University of California Press, 2003), 20.

43. Green, "Native American Women," 250.

44. Stereotyping in history is a problem that has been analyzed by many scholars. Other sources to consult are Green, "The Pocahontas Perplex"; Susan Armitage, "Through Women's Eyes: A New Review of the West," in *The Women's West*, ed. Elizabeth Jameson and Susan Armitage (Norman: University of Oklahoma Press, 1987), 9–18; Corlann Gee Bush, "The Way We Weren't: Images of Women and Men in Cowboy Art," in Jameson and Armitage, *The Women's West*, 19–34; Patricia Albers and William James, "Illusion and Illumination: Visual Images of American Indian Women in the West," in Jameson and Armitage, *The Women's West*, 35–50.

45. For an interesting study specifically on the male western hero in myth and history, see Steckmesser, *The Western Hero*.

46. Paula Gunn Allen, "One Who Skins Cats," *Sinister Wisdom* 22 (1983): 12–17.

47. Jeanne Eder, perf., "Sacagawea," *Journey through Time: Conversations with the World's Great Women and Men* (North Idaho College: Coeur d' Alene, Popcorn Forum, 1996), DVD.

48. *The Journey of Sacagawea* (Idaho Films Inc. and Idaho Public Television, Boise, PBS Home Video, 2003), DVD.

49. Bonnie Butterfield, "Sacagawea: Native American Legend: Why Did She Turn Her Back on Her Own People?" This article was found in 2000, at *www.aeocities.com/ ColleaePark/Ha11/9626fNative Americans.html*. It has since been removed, but a similar argument can be found at www.bonniebutterfield.com/NativeAmericans.html.

50. According to Scott Sandlin's article, "History Lesson on a Coin," *The Albuquerque Journal* (February 8, 2000), the Mint's unparalleled public outreach campaign to select a winning design was matched by the Treasury's decision to get the coin in circulation quickly by issuing $100 million of them to Wal-Mart. The discount retail giant received them on January 30, 2000, and ran out immediately.

51. Transcript of the May 4, 1999, Whitehouse unveiling of the Sacagawea one-dollar coin, *www.smalldollars.com/dollar/unveil.html*.

52. Ibid.

CONCLUSION

1. Lowry's explanation of women in myth can be found in Shirley Park Lowry, *Familiar Mysteries: The Truth in Myth* (New York: Oxford University Press, 1982), 7–8. Lowry also discusses countermyths that arose to contest existing social definitions; she uses black people's countermyth of the Muslim holy city of Mecca and women's biological explanation of the Y male and X female chromosomes (that men's Y

chromosome is a deformed female chromosome), 6–11. The practice of contesting traditional explanations and presenting alternatives to existing social definitions has been prevalent in the myths surrounding Malinche, Pocahontas, and Sacagawea.

2. The development and maintenance of this myth in the United States is taken up by R. W. B. Lewis in *The American Adam: Innocence, Tragedy, and Tradition in the Nineteenth Century* (Chicago: University of Chicago Press, 1955). Lewis traces the myth through the writings of Emerson, Thoreau, and Henry James.

3. Renditions of this myth are also discussed by Henry Nash Smith in *The Virgin Land: The American West as Symbol and Myth* (Cambridge: Harvard University Press, 1950).

4. Vine Deloria, Jr., (a Yankton Sioux scholar/activist) suggests that the missionary zeal that followed initial encounters was motivated by a European belief that Jesus would not return until his disciples carried his Christian message to all peoples of the world. See Vine Deloria, Jr., *God Is Red: A Native View of Religion* (Golden, Colo.: Fulcrum, 1972).

5. Weber is specifically referring to Spanish colonial histories.

6. Thomas Jefferson and Benjamin Franklin discuss how America and its Indians provided an ideal setting for commerce and republican ideals in *Remarks Concerning the Savages of North America*. For an explanation of the United States as virgin land, see Smith, *The Virgin Land*.

7. Thomas Jefferson entertained the idea of incorporating Indian people, as well as a few others, as citizens, but for the most part Americans preferred to think of Indian peoples as part of a vanishing race. See Brian Dippie, *The Vanishing American: White Attitudes and U.S. Indian Policy* (Lawrence: University Press of Kansas, 1982).

8. There has been fascinating research on religious synchronization in Mexico. The example that has received significant scholarly attention is the Virgin of Guadalupe, Mexico's patron saint who was modeled on the Virgin Mary. See Hall, *Mary, Mother and Warrior*; Brading, *Mexican Phoenix*; Lafaye, *Quetzalcóatl and Guadalupe*; and Taylor, "The Virgin of Guadalupe in New Spain."

Bibliography

Malinche

Adams, Richard E. W. *Prehistoric MesoAmerica*. Norman: University of Oklahoma Press, 1931.

Alberu de Villava, Helena. *Malintzin y el Señor Malinche*. Mexico: Edamex, 1995.

Anderson, Arthur J. O. "Aztec Wives." In Schroeder, Wood, and Haskett, *Indian Women of Early Mexico*, 76.

Banda, Dan. *Indigenous Always: The Legend of La Malinche and the Conquest of Mexico.* PBS, 2000. DVD.

Berdan, Frances F., Richard E. Blanton, Elizabeth H. Boone, Mary G. Hodge, Michael E. Smith, and Emily Umberger. *Aztec Imperial Strategies*. Washington, D.C.: Dumbarton Oaks, 1996.

Berdan, Francis F., and Patricia Rieff Anawalt. *Codex Mendoza*. 4 vols. Berkeley: University of California Press, 1992.

Brading, David. *The First America: The Spanish Monarchy, Creole Patriots, and the Liberal State, 1492–1867*. Cambridge: Cambridge University Press, 1991.

———. "Manuel Gamio and Official Indigenizmo in Mexico." *Bulletin of Latin American Research* 7, no. 1 (1988): 75–89.

———. *Mexican Phoenix: Our Lady of Guadalupe: Image and Tradition across Five Centuries*. Cambridge: Cambridge University Press, 2001.

———. *The Origins of Mexican Nationalism*. Cambridge: Cambridge University Press, 1983.

Brandt, Jane Lewis. *La Chingada*. New York: McGraw-Hill, 1979.

Broda, Johanna, David Carrasco, and Eduardo Matos. *The Great Temple of Tenochtitlan: Center and Periphery in the Aztec World*. Berkeley: University of California Press, 1987.

Burkhart, Louise. "Mexica Women on the Home Front." In Schroeder, Wood, and Haskett, *Indian Women of Early Mexico*, 25–54.

Cabeza de Vaca, Álvar Nuñez. *Adventures in the Unknown Interior of America.* Translated by Cyclone Covey. Albuquerque: University of New Mexico Press, 1998.

Candelaria, Cordelia. "La Malinche, Feminist Prototype." *Frontiers* 5, no. 2 (1980): 1–6.

Carrasco, David. *Aztec Ceremonial Landscapes.* Colorado: University Press of Colorado, 1991.

Castillo-Feliu, Guillermo, trans. *Xicotencatl: An Anonymous Historical Novel about the Events Leading up to the Conquest of the Aztec Empire.* Austin: University of Texas Press, 1999.

Cortés, Hernán. *Letters from Mexico.* New Haven: Yale University Press, 1986.

Cypess, Sandra Messinger. *La Malinche in Mexican Literature: From History to Myth.* Austin: University of Texas Press, 1991.

Del Castillo, Adelaida R. "Malintzin Tenepal: A Preliminary Look into a New Perspective." In *Essays on La Mujer,* edited by Rosaura Sanchez and Rosa Martinez Cruz, 124–42. Los Angeles: Chicano Studies Center Publications, 1977.

Díaz del Castillo, Bernal. *The Conquest of New Spain.* Translated by J. M. Cohen. New York: Penguin, 1963.

———. *The Discovery and Conquest of Mexico: 1517–1521.* Translated by A. P. Maudslay. London: Percy Lund, Humphries, 1933.

Dibble, Charles. *The Conquest Through Aztec Eyes.* Salt Lake City: University of Utah Press, 1978.

Durán, Diego. *Book of the Gods and Rites and the Ancient Calendar.* Translated by Fernando Horcasitas and Doris Heyden. Norman: University of Oklahoma Press, 1971.

———. *History of the Indies of New Spain.* Translated by Doris Heyden. Norman: Oklahoma Press, 1994.

Fagan, Brian. "If Columbus Had Not Called." *History Today* 42 (1992): 30–36.

Figueroa Torres, Jesus. *Doña Marina: Una India Ejemplar.* Mexico: Costa-Arnie, 1975.

Florescano, Enrique. *Memory, Myth, and Time in Mexico: From the Aztec to Independence.* Translated by Albert G. Bork and Kathryn Bork. Austin: University of Texas Press, 1994.

Franco, Jean. "The Nation as Imagined Community." In *Dangerous Liaisons: Gender, Nation, and Postcolonial Perspectives,* edited by Anne McClintock, Aamir Mufti, and Ella Shohat, 130–37. Minneapolis: University of Minnesota Press, 1997.

———. *Plotting Women: Gender and Representation in Mexico.* New York: Columbia University Press, 1989.

Gamio, Manuel. *Forjando Patria.* Mexico: Editorial Porrua, A. A., 1982.

———. "The Utilitarian Aspect of Folklore." *Mexican Folkways* (June/July 1925): 7–25.

Garcia, Alma. *Chicana Feminist Thought: The Basic Historical Writings.* New York: Routledge, 1997.

Gillespie, Susan. *The Aztec Kings: The Construction of Rulership in Mexica History.* Tucson: University of Arizona Press, 1989.

Glantz, Margo. *La Malinche Sus Padres y Sus Hijos.* Mexico: Facultad de Filosofia y Letras, Universidad Nacional Autonoma de Mexico, 1994.

Gómara, Francisco Lopez de. *Cortés: The Life of the Conqueror by His Secretary.* Translated by Lesley Byrd Simpson. Los Angeles: University of California Press, 1964.

Gomez de Orozco, Frederico. *Doña Marina, la Dama de la Conquista.* Mexico: Ediciones Xochitl, 1942.

Hall, Linda. *Mary, Mother and Warrior: The Virgin in Spain and the Americas.* Austin: University of Texas Press, 2004.

Herrera-Sobek, Maria. "In Search of La Malinche: Pictorial Representations of a Mytho-Historical Figure." In Romero and Harris, *Feminism, Nation, and Myth: La Malinche*, 112–33.

———. *The Mexican Corrido: A Feminist Analysis.* Bloomington: Indian University Press, 1993.

Herrin, Ricardo. *Doña Marina, la Malinche.* Mexico, D.F.: Planeta Mexicana, 1993.

Houstin-Davila, Daniel. *Malinche's Children.* Jackson: University of Mississippi Press, 2003.

Innes, Hammond. *The Conquistadors.* New York: Random House, 1970.

Karttunen, Frances. "Rethinking Malinche." In Schroeder, Wood, and Hasket, *Indian Women of Early Mexico,* 291–312.

———. "To the Valley of Mexico: Dona Marina, 'La Malinche' (1500–1527)." In Karttunen, *Between Worlds: Interpreters, Guides and Survivors,* 291–312.

Kellog, Susan. "The Woman's Room: Some Aspects of Gender Relations in Tenochtitlan in Late Pre-Hispanic Period." *Ethnohistory* 42, no. 4 (1995): 563–76.

Knight, Alan. *Mexico: From the Beginning to the Spanish Conquest.* Cambridge: Cambridge University Press, 2002.

Krueger, Hilde. *Malinche, or Farwell to Myths.* New York: Storm, 1948.

Lafaye, Jacques. *Quetzalcoatl and Guadalupe: The Formation of Mexican National Consciousness 1531–1813.* Translated by Benjamin Keen. Chicago: University of Chicago Press, 1974.

Lanyon, Anna. *Malinche's Conquest.* St. Leonards, N.S.W.: Allen and Unwin, 1999.

Leal, Luis. "The Malinche-Llorona Dichotomy: The Evolution of Myth." In Romero and Harris, *Feminism, Nation, and Myth: La Malinche*, 134–38.

León-Portilla, Miguel. *The Broken Spears.* Boston: Beacon Press, 1962.

Lockhart, James. *The Nahuas: After the Conquest: A Social and Cultural History of the Indians of Central Mexico, Sixteenth through Eighteenth Centuries.* Stanford: Stanford University Press, 1992.

———. *We People Here: Nahuatl Accounts of the Conquest of Mexico.* Eugene: Wipf and Stock, 1993.

Long, Haniel. *Malinche: Doña Mariana.* Santa Fe: Rydal, 1939.

Marshall, Edison. *Cortez and Marina: A Novel about the Conquest of Mexico.* Garden City, N.Y.: Doubleday, 1963.

Meza, Otilia. *Malinalli Tenepal, la Gran Calumniada.* Mexico, D.F.: Edamex, 1985.

Milanich, Jerald T. *Laboring in the Fields of the Lord: Spanish Missions and Southeast Indians.* Gainesville: University of Florida Press, 2006.

Millon, Rene. "The Place Where Time Began: An Archaeologists Interpretation of What Happened in Teotihuacan History." In *Teotihuacan: Art from the City of the Gods*, edited by Kathleen Berrin and Esther Pasztory, 16–43. New York: Thames and Hudson, 1993.

Mondini-Ruiz, Franco. "Malinche Makeover: One Gay Latino's Perspective." In Romero and Harris, *Feminism, Nation, and Myth*, 157.

Nunez Becerra, Femanda. *La Malinche: De la Historia al Mito*. Mexico, D.F.: Instituto Nacional de Antropologia y Historia, 1996.

Offner, Jerome. *Law and Politics in Aztec Texcoco*. Cambridge: Cambridge University Press, 1988.

Paz, Ireneo. *Amor y Suplicio*. Mexico: J. Rivera, 1873.

———. *Doña Marina*. Mexico: Impr. y Litographia de Paz, 1883.

Paz, Octavio. *The Labyrinth of Solitude: The Other Mexico City and Other Essays*. Translated by Lysander Kemp. New York: Grove, 1985.

Pennock, Caroline Dodds. *Bonds of Blood: Gender, Lifecycle, and Sacrifice in Aztec Culture*. New York: Palgrave Macmillan, 2008.

Prescott, William. *History of the Conquest of Mexico, with a Preliminary View of the Ancient Mexican Civilization, and the Life of the Conqueror Hernando Cortés*. 3 vols. Philadelphia: David McKay Publisher, 1843.

Ramos, Samuel. *Profile of Man and Culture in Mexico*. Translated by Peter G. Earle. Austin: University of Texas, 1962.

Romero, Rolando, and Amanda Nolacea Harris, eds. *Feminism, Nation, and Myth: La Malinche*. Houston: Arte Publico, 2005.

Ruiz, Felipe Gonzalez. *Doña Marina: La India que Amo a Hernan Cortés*. Madrid: Ediciones Morata, 1944.

Sahagún, Fray Bernardino. *Florentine Codex: General History of the Things of New Spain*. Translated by Arthur J. O. Anderson and Charles E. Dibble. Salt Lake City: University of Utah Press, 1982.

Sandoval, Anna Marie. *Toward a Latina Feminism of the Americas: Repression and Resistance in Chicana and Mexican Literature*. Austin: University of Texas Press, 2008.

Schroeder, Susan, Stephanie Wood, and Robert Haskett, ed. *Indian Women of Early Mexico*. Norman: University of Oklahoma Press, 1997.

Taylor, William. "The Virgin of Guadalupe in New Spain: An Inquiry into the Social History of Marian Devotion." *American Ethnologist* 14 (February 1987): 9–33.

Townsend, Camilla. *Malintzin's Choices: An Indian Woman in the Conquest of Mexico*. Albuquerque: University of New Mexico Press, 2006.

Townsend, Richard. *The Aztecs*. London: Thames and Hudson, 2009.

Vaillant, George C. *Aztecs of Mexico: Origin, Rise, and Fall of the Aztec Nation*. Garden City, N.Y.: Doubleday, 1947.

Vasconcelos, José. *Aspect of Civilization: Lectures on the Harris Foundation*. Chicago: University of Chicago Press, 1926.

———. *The Cosmic Race*. Translated by Didier Tjoen. Los Angeles: Centro de Publicaciones, Department of Chicano Studies, 1926.

Wood, Stephanie. *Transcending Conquest: Nahua Views of Spanish Colonial Mexico*. Norman: University of Oklahoma Press, 2003.

Zorita, Alonso de. *Life and Labor in Ancient Mexico: The Brief and Summary Relation of the Lord of New Spain.* Edited and translated by Benjamin Keen. New Brunswick: Rutgers University Press, 1963.

POCAHONTAS

Abrams, Ann Uhry. *The Pilgrims and Pocahontas: Rival Myths of American Origin.* Boulder: Westview, 1999.

Adams, Henry. "Captain John Smith." In *Historical Essays,* 42–79. New York: Charles Scriber's Sons, 1891.

Allen, Paula Gunn. *Pocahontas: Medicine Woman, Spy, Entrepreneur and Diplomat.* San Francisco: Harper, 2003.

Barbour, Philip. *Pocahontas and Her World.* Boston: Houghton Mifflin, 1969.

Benton, Sherrole. "Pocahontas as a Traitor." *Tribal College* 6 (Spring 1995): 34–35.

Connell-Szasz, Margaret. *Indian Education in the American Colonies, 1607–1783.* Albuquerque: University of New Mexico Press, 1988.

Crazy Horse, Chief Roy. "A Brief History of the Powhatan Renape Nation." Rankokus, N.J.: Powhatan Renape Nation, 1999.

———. "The Pocahontas Myth." Rankokus, N.J.: Powhatan Renape Nation, 1995.

Custalo, Linwood, and Angela Daniel. *The True Story of Pocahontas: The Other Side of History.* Golden: Fulcrum, 2007.

D'Aulaire, Ingrid. *Pocahontas.* Garden City, N.Y.: Doubleday, 1946.

Dorsey, Ella Loraine. *Pocahontas.* Washington, D.C.: Howard, 1906.

Early, P. H. *By-ways of Virginia History: A Jamestown Memorial, Embracing a Sketch of Pocahontas.* Richmond: Everett Waddey, 1907.

Edgerton, Gary. "Redesigning Pocahontas." *Journal of Popular Film and Television* 24 (Summer 1992): 90–98.

Eggleston, Edward. *Pocahontas: Including an Account of the Early Settlement of Virginia and of the Adventures of Captain John Smith.* New York: Dodd, Mead, 1879.

Fleming, E. McClung. "Symbols of the United States: From Indian Queen to Uncle Sam." In *Frontiers of American Culture,* edited by Ray B. Brown, Richard H. Crowder, Virgill Lokke, and William T. Stafford, 1–19. Lafayette, Ind.: Purdue Research Foundation, 1968.

Gleach, Frederic W. *Powhatan's World and Colonial Virginia: A Conflict of Cultures.* Lincoln: University of Nebraska Press, 1997.

Green, Rayna. "The Pocahontas Perplex: The Image of Indian Women in American Culture." *Massachusetts Review* 16 (Autumn 1976): 698–714.

———. *That's What She Said: Contemporary Poetry and Fiction by Native American Women.* Bloomington: Indiana University Press, 1984.

Grumet, Robert. "Sunksquaws, Shamans and Tradeswomen: Middle Atlantic Coastal Algonquian Women during the 17th and 18th Centuries." In *Women and Colonization: Anthropological Perspectives,* edited by Mona Etienne and Eleanore Leacock, 46–55. New York: Praeger, 1980.

Hamor, Ralphe. *A True Discourse of the Present Estate of Virginia: London 1613.* New York: Da Capo, 1971.

Harris, Aurand. *Pocahontas: A Play in Two Acts for Children's Theatre, Based on the Historic Records Written about the Indian Princess Pocahontas.* Anchorage: Children's Theatre, 1961.

Hart, William. "Black 'Go-Betweens' and the Mutability of Race, Status, and Identity on New York's Pre-Revolutionary Frontier." In *Contact Points: American Frontiers from the Mohawk to the Mississippi, 1750–1830,* edited by Andrew R. L. Cayton and Fredrika J. Teute, 88–113. Chapel Hill: University of North Carolina Press, 1998.

Hayes, Kevin. *Captain John Smith: A Reference Guide.* Boston: G. K. Hall, 1991.

Horn, James. *Adapting to a New World.* Williamsburg: University of North Carolina Press, 1994.

Kupperman, Karen Ordahl. *Indians and English: Facing Off in Early America.* Ithaca: Cornell University Press, 2000.

Lemay, Leo. *Did Pocahontas Save Captain John Smith?* Athens: University of Georgia Press, 1992.

Mossiker, Frances. *Pocahontas.* New York: Alfred A. Knopf, 1976.

Price, David. *Love and Hate in Jamestown: John Smith, Pocahontas, and the Heart of a Nation.* New York: Alfred A. Knopf, 2003.

Quarles, Marguerite Stuart. *Pocahontas: Bright Stream between Two Hills.* Richmond: The Association of the Preservation of Virginia Antiquities, 1939.

Rebello, Stephen. *The Art of Pocahontas.* New York: Topan, 1995.

Reddish, Jennifer Gray. "Pocahontas." *Tribal College* 6 (Spring 1995): 22–33.

Rountree, Helen C. *Pocahontas, Powhatan, Opechancanough: Three Indian Lives Changed by Jamestown.* Charlotte: University of Virginia Press, 2005.

———. *Pocahontas's People: The Powhatan Indians of Virginia through Four Centuries.* Norman: University of Oklahoma Press, 1990.

———. *The Powhatan Indians of Virginia: Their Traditional Culture.* Norman: University of Oklahoma Press, 1989.

Rountree, Helen C., and Randolph Turner, III. *Before and After Jamestown: Virginia's Powhatans and their Predecessors.* Gainesville: University Press of Florida, 2002.

Smith, Bradford. *Captain John Smith: His Life and Legend.* Philadelphia: J. B. Lippincott, 1953.

Smith, John. *The Complete Works of Captain John Smith.* Edited by Philip Barbour. 3 vols. Chapel Hill: University of North Carolina Press, 1986.

———. *Travels and Works of Captain John Smith: President of Virginia and Admiral of New England 1580–1631.* Edited by Edward Arber. 2 vols. Edinburgh: John Grant, 1910.

Strachey, William. *The Historie of Travell into Virginia Britania 1612.* Edited by Louis B. Wright and Virginia Freund. London: Hakluyt, 1953.

Tilton, Robert S. *Pocahontas: The Evolution of an American Narrative.* Cambridge: Cambridge University Press, 1994.

Townsend, Camilla. *Pocahontas and the Powhatan Dilemma*. New York: Hill and Wang, 2004.

Vollmann, William T. *Argall: Seven Dreams, a Book of North American Landscapes*. New York: Viking, 2001.

Wertenbaker, Thomas. *The Shaping of Colonial Virginia*. New York: Russell and Russell, 1958.

Williamson, Margaret Holmes. *Powhatan Lords of Life and Death: Command and Consent in Seventeenth Century Virginia*. Lincoln: University of Nebraska Press, 2003.

Woodward, Grace Steele. *Pocahontas*. Norman: University of Oklahoma Press, 1969.

Young, Philip. "The Mother of Us All: Pocahontas Reconsidered." *Kenyon Review* 24 (Summer 1962): 391–441.

SACAGAWEA

Ackerman, Lillian. *A Necessary Balance: Gender and Power among Indians of the Columbia Plateau*. Norman: University of Oklahoma Press, 2003.

Albers, Patricia and Beatrice Medicine, eds. *The Hidden Half: Studies of Plains Indian Women*. Washington, D.C.: University Press of America, 1983.

Anderson, Irving W. "Probing the Riddle of the Bird Woman." *Montana: The Magazine of Western History* 23 (1973): 2–17.

———. "Sacajawea, Sacagawea, Sakakawea?" *South Dakota History* 8 (1978): 303–11.

Binnema, Theodore. *Common and Contested Ground: A Human and Environment History of the Northwestern Plains*. Norman: University of Oklahoma Press, 2001.

Bowers, Alfred. *Hidatsa Social and Ceremonial Organization*. Washington, D.C.: U.S. Government Printing Office, 1965.

Brackenridge, Henry Marie. "Views of Louisiana: Together with a Journal of a Voyage up the Missouri in1811." In vol. 6 of *Early Western Travels, 1748–1846*, edited by Reuben Gold Thwaites, 19–166. Chicago: Quadrangle, 1962.

Brown, Jennifer. *Strangers in Blood: Fur Trade Company Families in Indian Country*. Norman: University of Oklahoma Press, 1980.

Bruchac, Joseph. *Sacajawea*. New York: Scholastic, 2001.

Chuinard, E. G. "The Actual Role of the Bird Woman: Purposeful Member of the Corps or 'Casual Tag Along'?" *Montana: The Magazine of Western History* 26 (1976):18–29.

Churchill, Clair Warner. *South of the Sunset: An Interpretation of Sacagawea, the Indian Girl that Accompanied Lewis and Clark*. New York: R. R. Wilson, 1936.

Coues, Elliott. *History of the Expedition under the Command of Lewis and Clark: To the Sources of the Missouri River, thence across the Rocky Mountains and down the Columbia River to the Pacific Ocean, Performed during the Years of 1804–05–06, by Order of the Government of the United States*. 4 vols. New York: Dover, 1965.

Crum, Steven. *The Road on Which We Came: A History of the Western Shoshone*. Salt Lake City: University of Utah Press, 1994.

Defenbach, Byron. *Red Heroines of the West.* Caldwell, Idaho: Caxton, 1935.

De Voto, Bernard. *The Course of Empire.* Cambridge: Riverside, 1962.

Dye, Eva Emery. *The Conquest: The True Story of Lewis and Clark.* Chicago: A. C. McClurg, 1902.

Eastman, Charles. *Burial Place of Sacajawea: Letter from Chas. Eastman, Inspector and Investigator, to the Commissioner of Indian Affairs.* March 2, 1925. Washington D.C.: University of Idaho, Special Collections.

Farnsworth, Frances Joyce. *Winged Moccasins: The Story of Sacajawea.* New York: J. Messner, 1954.

Hebard, Grace Raymond. "Pilot of the First White Men to Cross the American Continent." *The Journal of American History* 1 (1907): 467–84.

———. *Sacajawea: A Guide and Interpreter of the Lewis and Clark Expedition, with an Account of the Travels of Toussaint Charbonneau, and of Jean Baptiste, the Expedition Papoose.* Glendale: Arthur H. Clark, 1933.

Howard, Harold P. *Sacajawea.* Norman: University of Oklahoma Press, 1971.

Jackson, Donald, ed. *Letters of the Lewis and Clark Expedition with Related Documents 1783–1854.* Champaign: University of Illinois Press, 1962.

Kessler, Donna J. *The Making of Sacagawea: A Euro-American Legend.* Tuscaloosa: University of Alabama Press, 1996.

Kingston, C. S. "Sacajawea as Guide: The Evaluation of a Legend." *The Pacific Northwest Quarterly* 35 (January 1944): 3–18.

Kline, Alan. "The Political Economy of Gender: A 19th Century Plains Indian Case Study." In Albers and Medicine, *The Hidden Half,* 143–73.

Luttig, John C. *Journal of a Fur Trading Expedition on the Upper Missouri, 1812–1813.* St. Louis: Missouri Historical Society, 1920.

Mann, John W. *Sacagawea's People: The Lemhi Shoshones and the Salmon River Country.* Lincoln: University of Nebraska Press, 2002.

Moore, Bob. "The Mythic Lewis and Clark: Their Story Helps Define Us as a Nation and Connect Us to Cultures around the World." *We Proceed On: Official Publication of the Lewis and Clark Trail Heritage Foundation* 26 (February 2000): 35–56.

Moulton, Gary, ed. *The Journals of the Lewis and Clark Expedition.* By Meriwether Lewis and William Clark. 13 vols. Lincoln: University of Nebraska Press, 1983.

O'Dell, Scott. *Daughters of the Country: The Women of Fur Traders and Mountain Men.* New York: Harcourt, Brace, 1986.

Peattie, Donald Culross. *Forward the Nation.* New York: Editions of the Armed Services, 1942.

Peters, Virginia Bergman. *Women of the Earth Lodges: Tribal Life on the Plains.* Norman: University of Oklahoma Press, 1995.

Rees, John E. *Madame Charbonneau the Indian Woman Who Accompanied the Lewis and Clark Expedition 1804–1806, How She Received Her Indian Name and What Became of Her.* Salmon, Idaho: Lemhi County Historical Society, 1970.

Reid, Russell. *Sakakawea: The Bird Woman.* Bismarck: State Historical Society of North Dakota, 1986.

Rhonda, James P. *Lewis and Clark among the Indians*. Lincoln: University of Nebraska Press, 1988.

Roland, Della. *The Story of Sacajawea, Guide to Lewis and Clark*. New York: Dell, 1989.

Ross, Nancy Wilson. *Heroine in Buckskin*. Pleasantville, N.Y.: Reader's Digest, 1944.

Saindon, Bob. "Sacajawea: Boat-Launcher, the Origin and Meaning of A Name . . . Maybe." *We Proceeded On* (August 1988): 5–10.

Scharff, Virginia. *Twenty Thousand Roads: Women, Movement, and the West*. Los Angeles: University of California Press, 2003.

Schroer, Blanche. "Boat-pusher or Bird Woman? Sacagawea or Sacajawea?" *Annals of Wyoming* 52 (Spring 1980): 46–54.

Schultz, James Willard. *Bird Woman (Sacajawea) the Guide of Lewis and Clark: Her Own Story Now First Given to the World*. Boston: Houghton Mifflin, 1918.

Trenbolm, Virginia Cole, and Maurine Carley. *The Shoshonis: Sentinels of the Rockies*. Norman: University of Oklahoma Press, 1964.

Waldo, Anna Lee. *Sacajawea*. New York: Avon, 1984.

Weist, Katherine M. "Beasts of Burden and Menial Slaves." In Albers and Medicine, *The Hidden Half*, 29–52.

Wilson, Gilbert L. *Buffalo Bird Woman's Garden*. St. Paul: Minnesota Historical Society Press, 1987.

Wolfam, Anna. *Sacajawea the Indian Princess: The Indian Girl Who Piloted the Lewis and Clark Expedition across the Rocky Mountains: A Play in Three Acts*. Kansas City: Burton, 1918.

General Works

Allen, Paula Gunn. *The Sacred Hoop: Recovering the Feminine in American Indian Traditions*. Boston: Beacon, 1986.

Barr, Juliana. *Peace Came in the Form of a Woman: Indians and Spaniards in the Texas Borderland*. Chapel Hill: University of North Carolina Press, 2007.

Berger, Peter, and Thomas Luckmann. *The Social Construction of Reality: A Treatise in the Sociology of Knowledge*. New York: Doubleday, 1966.

Brooks, James. *Captives and Cousins: Slavery, Kinship, and Community in the Southwest Borderlands*. Chapel Hill: University of North Carolina Press, 2002.

Connell-Szasz, Margaret. *Between Indian and White Worlds: The Culture Broker*. Norman: University of Oklahoma Press, 1994.

Cooper, Fredrick, and Ann Laura Stoler. *Tensions of Empire: Colonial Cultures in a Bourgeois World*. Los Angeles: University of California Press, 1997.

Cronon, William, George Miles, and Jay Gitlan. *Under an Open Sky: Rethinking America's Past*. New York: W. W. Norton, 1992.

Deloria, Vine, Jr. *Custer Died for Your Sins: An Indian Manifesto*. Norman: University of Oklahoma Press, 1988.

———. *God Is Red: A Native View of Religion*. Golden, Colo.: Fulcrum, 1972.

————. *Red Earth, White Lies: Native Americans and the Myth of Scientific Fact.* Golden, Colo.: Fulcrum, 1997.

Dippie, Brian. *The Vanishing American: White Attitudes and U.S. Indian Policy.* Lawrence: University Press of Kansas, 1982.

Doty, William. *Mythography: The Study of Myths and Rituals.* Tuscaloosa: University of Alabama Press, 2000.

Faery, Rebecca Blevins. *Cartographies of Desire: Captivity, Race, and Sex in the Shaping of an American Nation.* Norman: University of Oklahoma Press, 1999.

Ford, Ramona. "Native American Women: Changing Statuses, Changing Interpretations." In Jameson and Armitage, *Writing the Range: Race, Class, and Culture in the Women's West,* 42–68. Norman: University of Oklahoma Press. 1997.

Green, Rayna. "Native American Women: Review Essay." *Signs: A Journal of Women in Culture and Society* 6 (1980): 248–67.

Hagedon, Nancy. "A Friend to Go between Them: The Interpreter as Culture Broker during Anglo-Iroquois Councils, 1740–70." *Ethnohistory* 35, no.1 (Winter 1988): 60–80.

Hennessy, Alistair. *The Frontier in Latin American History.* Albuquerque: University of New Mexico Press, 1978.

Hulme, Peter. *Colonial Encounters: Europe and the Native Caribbean 1492–1797.* London: Routledge, 1992.

Hurtado, Albert. *Intimate Frontiers: Sex, Gender, and Culture in Old California.* Albuquerque: University of New Mexico Press, 1999.

Jameson, Elizabeth, and Susan Armitage, eds. *The Women's West.* Norman: University of Oklahoma Press, 1987.

Kandiyoti, Deniz. "Identity and Its Discontents: Women and the Nation." *Millennium Journal of International Studies* 20, no. 3 (1991): 431.

Karttunen, Frances, ed. *Between Worlds: Interpreters, Guides, and Survivors.* New Brunswick: Rutgers University Press, 1994.

Kidwell, Clara Sue. "Indian Women as Cultural Intermediaries." *Ethnohistory* 39 (Spring 1992): 97–107.

Klein, Laura, and Lillian Ackerman. *Women and Power in Native North America.* Norman: University of Oklahoma Press, 1995.

Lowry, Shirley Park. *Familiar Mysteries: The Truth in Myth.* New York: Oxford University Press, 1982.

McClintock, Anne. *Imperial Leather: Race, Gender, and Sexuality in the Colonial Contest.* New York: Routledge, 1995.

————. "No Longer in a Future Heaven: Gender, Race, and Nationalism." In *Dangerous Liaisons: Gender, Nation, and Postcolonial Perspectives,* edited by Anne McClintock, Aamir Mufti, and Ella Shohat, 89–112. Minneapolis and London: University of Minnesota Press, 1997.

Midgley, Mary. *Indigenous American Women: Decolonization, Empowerment, Activism.* Lincoln: University of Nebraska Press, 2003.

————. *The Myths We Live By.* London: Routledge, 2003.

Nugent, Walter. "New World Frontiers: Comparisons and Agendas." In *Where Cultures Meet: Frontiers in Latin American History*, edited by David Weber and Jane Rausch, 72–85. Wilmington: Scholarly Resources, 1994.

O'Gorman, Edmundo. *The Invention of America: An Inquiry into the Historical Nature of the New World and the Meaning of its History*. Bloomington: Indiana University Press, 1961.

Pagden, Anthony. *Europeans' Encounters with the New World*. New Haven: Yale University Press, 1993.

Perdue, Theda. *Sifters: Native American Women's Lives*. New York: Oxford University Press, 2001.

Pratt, Mary Louise. "Women Literature and National Brotherhood." In *Women Culture and Politics in Latin America*, Seminar on Feminism and Culture in Latin America, 48–73. Berkeley: University of California Press, 1990.

Pryke, Sam. "Nationalism and Sexuality: What are the Issues?" *Nations and Nationalism* 4, no. 4 (October 1998): 529–46.

Scheckel, Susan. *The Insistence of the Indian: Race and Nationalism in Nineteenth-Century American Culture*. Princeton: Princeton University Press, 1998.

Sheehan, Bernard. "Indian-White Relations in Early America: A Review Essay." *The William and Mary Quarterly* 26, no. 2 (April 1969): 267–86.

Shoemaker, Nancy. *Negotiators of Change: Historical Perspectives on Native American Women*. New York: Routledge, 1995.

Sleeper-Smith, Susan. *Indian Women and French Men: Rethinking Cultural Encounter in the Western Great Lakes*. Amherst: University of Massachusetts Press, 2001.

Slotkin, Richard. *Gunfighter Nation: The Myth of the Frontier in Twentieth-Century America*. New York: Harper Collins, 1992.

Smith, Henry Nash. *Virgin Land: The American West as Symbol and Myth*. Cambridge: Harvard University Press, 1950.

Sommer, Doris. *Foundational Fictions: The National Romances of Latin America*. Berkeley: University of California Press, 1991.

Spector, Janet. *What This Awl Means: Feminist Archeology at a Wahpeton Dakota Village*. St. Paul: Minnesota Historical Press, 1993.

Steckmesser, Kent Ladd. *The Western Hero in History and Legend*. Norman: University of Oklahoma Press, 1997.

Sunquist, Asebrit. *Pocahontas and Company: The Fictional American Indian Women in Nineteenth-Century Literature: A Study of Method*. Atlantic Highlands, N.J.: Humanities Press International, 1987.

Tompkins, Jane. "Indians: Textualism, Morality, and the Problem of History." In *"Race," Writing, and Difference*, edited by Henry Louis Gates, Jr., 59–77. Chicago: University of Chicago Press, 1986.

———. *Sensational Designs: The Cultural Work of American Fiction, 1790–1860*. New York: Oxford University Press, 1985.

Tuhiwiai Smith, Linda. *Decolonizing Methodologies: Research and Indigenous Peoples*. London: University of Otago Press, 1999.

Valdes, Maria Elena. *The Shattered Mirror: Representations of Women in Mexican Literature.* Austin: University of Texas Press, 1998.

Van Kirk, Sylvia. *Many Tender Ties: Women in Fur-Trade Society, 1670–1870.* Norman: University of Oklahoma Press, 1980.

Weber, David, and Jane Rausch, eds. *Where Cultures Meet: Frontiers in Latin American History.* Wilmington, Del.: Scholarly Resources, 1994.

Welch, Deborah. "American Indian Women: Reaching beyond the Myth." In *New Directions in American History,* edited by Colin G. Calloway, 34–44. Norman: University of Oklahoma Press, 1987.

Wolf, Eric. *Europe and the People without History.* Los Angeles: University of California Press, 1997.

Zavala, Silbio. "The Frontiers in Hispanic America." In Weber and Rausch, *Where Cultures Meet: Frontiers in Latin American History,* 42–50.

INDEX

References to illustrations appear in italic type.